Mothering

Ideology, Experience, and Agency

PERSPECTIVES ON GENDER

Mothering

Ideology, Experience, and Agency

Edited by

Evelyn Nakano Glenn, Grace Chang,
and Linda Rennie Forcey

ROUTLEDGE
New York • London

Published in 1994 by
Routledge
29 West 35 Street
New York, NY 10001

Published in Great Britain by
Routledge
11 New Fetter Lane
London EC4P 4EE

Printed in the United States of America on acid free paper.

Library of Congress Cataloging-in-Publication Data
Mothering : ideology, experience & agency / edited by Evelyn Nakano
Glenn, Grace Chang and Linda Rennie Forcey.
      p.   cm.—(Perspectives on gender)
   Includes bibliographical references and index.
   ISBN 0-415-90775-6. — ISBN 0-415-90776-4 (pbk.)
      1. Motherhood. 2. Feminist theory. I. Glenn, Evelyn Nakano.
   II. Chang, Grace. III. Forcey, Linda Rennie. IV. Title: Mothering,
   ideology, experience and agency. V. Series: Perspectives on gender
   (New York, N.Y.)
   HQ759.M883 1994
   306.874'3—dc20   93-5497
                                                               CIP

British Library Cataloguing-in-Publication Data also available.

CONTENTS

PREFACE

This volume originated in a conference, "Contested Terrains: Constructions of Mothering," at the State University of New York (SUNY) at Binghamton. The conference was organized by Evelyn Nakano Glenn, Elsa Barkley Brown, and Linda Rennie Forcey. Its purpose was to bring together an interdisciplinary group of scholars "to provide a variety of perspectives on mothering as a socially constructed set of activities and relationships involved in nurturing and caring for people." We wanted to focus on two themes: the existence of historical, cultural, class, and ethnic variation in mothering, and the existence of conflict and struggle over competing conceptions and conditions under which mothering is carried out. About half of the articles in this volume are drawn from papers from the conference. The other contributions were solicited to cover areas and issues that we felt were crucial.

The conference was made possible by funding from a grant from the statewide SUNY "Conversations in the Discipline" program. Supplemental funding was provided by the Women's Studies Program, the Vice Provost for Graduate Studies and Research, the Dean of Harper College and School of Arts and Sciences, and the SUNY Binghamton Foundation. The Sojourner Center provided clerical and graduate student assistance. We are grateful to these sources.

We wish to thank our colleagues and students at Binghamton for their participation and support. We wish especially to acknowledge the contributions of the following: Elsa Barkley Brown, our co-organizer, for drawing in several key participants and for taking on numerous responsibilities, including hospitality, during the conference; Janet Caplan, the graduate research assistant for the Sojourner Center, for preliminary research, correspondence, and contact work; Deborah Hertz, then Acting

Director of Women's Studies and the Sojourner Center, for enthusiastic support and for generously providing facilities and staff assistance; and Gladys Jimenez, Patricia Washington, Jane Collins, and Catherine Lutz for chairing or providing commentary at sessions.

Chapter 1

SOCIAL CONSTRUCTIONS OF MOTHERING: A THEMATIC OVERVIEW

Evelyn Nakano Glenn

> Ordaining a woman as a priest is as impossible as me having a baby . . .
> it's not going to change.
>> Auxiliary Bishop Austin Vaughan of New York,
>> quoted at a meeting of Catholic bishops on role
>> of women in the Church.[1]

Abortion rights; the ethics of reproductive technology; children's right to "divorce" parents; the establishment of maternity and family leave policy; requiring workfare for welfare recipients; women's entry into the priesthood: some of the most heated social and political debates taking place in late–twentieth–century America turn out to revolve around disputed meanings of mothering and motherhood in contemporary society. These disputed meanings lead to different orientations toward such fundamental questions as: Is mothering women's primary and sole mission and chief source of satisfaction, or one of many roles and sources of satisfaction? Is women's fate tied to their biological role in reproduction, or is biology only a minor factor? How much significance should we place on pregnancy and childbirth as putting women in a unique position that justifies special treatment?

Opposing orientations to these questions lie at the heart of the national debate over abortion. Kristin Luker's interviews with activists in the right–to–life and pro–choice movements revealed that these women's positions on abortion were rooted not just in their differing beliefs about the embryo—as unique individual or as fetus—but in their divergent definitions of motherhood. The pro–life position grew out of a conviction that women were bound by their biological roles, and that motherhood should be women's sole mission and source of gratification. In contrast, pro-choice women's position grew out of a conviction that women were not or should not be subject to the dictates of biological reproduction, and that motherhood was one of many roles, "a burden when defined as the only role."[2]

In a similar vein, contending ideas about the significance of motherhood in delimiting women's place in society are central to debates over whether institutions should be required to make special accommodations for women because of their unique responsibility for bearing and caring for children. Feminist lawyers took opposing sides in a case brought by an employer challenging a California law requiring employers to provide pregnancy and maternity leave. Lawyers at Equal Rights Advocates, pioneers in the fight against sex discrimination, filed a brief in the Supreme Court supporting special treatment for women, saying it was valid to recognize "the real differences in the procreative roles of men and women." The sex discrimination and reproductive rights staff at the American Civil Liberties Union filed a brief on the other side, opposing special treatment for women, arguing in part that pregnancy should be treated as one of a number of temporary disabilities warranting accommodation by employers.[3] This position reflected the belief that codifying "difference" would work against women, since historically, women's capacity for bearing children has been the rationale for excluding them from public roles and high–paying jobs.[4]

Another case of controversy over the issue of special policy for mothers was sparked by an article in the *Harvard Business Review* proposing that employers establish a so–called "mommy track," a separate, slower, career track for women who "want to participate actively in raising their children." The author, Felice Schwartz, claimed her proposal would expand opportunities for women by allowing them to combine mothering and careers. Her conception at least avoided lumping all women together as mothers or potential mothers by distinguishing between "mothers" and other (presumably career-oriented) women. Still, most feminists felt that legitimating special treatment of women labeled "mommies" served to regularize women's secondary status in the labor market. Moderate observers pointed out that the proposal simply recognized the reality that women still carry the primary responsibility for parenting.[5]

As these examples show, mothering is contested terrain in the 1990s. In fact, it has always been contested terrain. However, a particular definition of mothering has so dominated popular media representations, academic discourse, and political and legal doctrine that the existence of alternative beliefs and practices among racial, ethnic, and sexual minority communities as well as non–middle–class segments of society has gone unnoticed. As Third World women, women of color, lesbians, and work-ing–class women began to challenge dominant European and American conceptions of womanhood, and to insist that differences among women were as important as commonalities, they have brought alternative con-structions of mothering into the spotlight. The existence of such historical and social variation confirms that mothering, like other relationships and institutions, is socially constructed, not biologically inscribed.

As a working definition, I propose looking at mothering as a historically and culturally variable relationship "in which one individual nurtures and cares for another."[6] Mothering occurs within specific social contexts that vary in terms of material and cultural resources and constraints. How mothering is conceived, organized, and carried out is not simply determined by these conditions, however. Mothering is constructed through men's and women's actions within specific historical circum-stances. Thus agency is central to an understanding of mothering as a social, rather than biological, construct.

The notion of mothering developed here is closely linked to the notion of gender that has emerged in feminist theorizing in the humanities and social sciences. Gender is used to refer to socially constructed relation-ships and practices organized around perceived differences between the sexes. Using gender as a central analytic concept, feminist scholars have documented the ways relations of gender are played out in structural and institutional domains, such as the economy, family, and political and legal systems, as well as in social interaction and identity.[7] Their studies have challenged notions of womanhood and manhood as inherent qual-ities linked to biological sex by showing that relationships between men and women, and definitions of womanhood and manhood, are contin-ually constituted, reproduced, changed, and contested.[8]

Mothering and gender are closely intertwined: each is a constitutive element of the other. As R. W. Connell notes, social relations of gender are fundamentally "organized in terms of, or in relation to, the repro-ductive division of people into male and female."[9] Perhaps because the gendered allocation of mothering appears to flow inevitably from the division based on reproductive function, mothering—more than any other aspect of gender—has been subject to essentialist interpretation: seen as natural, universal, and unchanging. Indeed, for most of the twentieth century an idealized model of motherhood, derived from the situation of the white, American, middle class, has been projected as universal. In this model, responsibility for mothering rests almost exclusively on one woman (the biological mother), for whom it constitutes the primary if not sole mission during the child's formative years. The corollary view of children is that they require constant care and attention from one caretaker (the biological mother).

This collection of articles documents the existence of diverse, often submerged, constructions of mothering that have coexisted alongside this dominant model. I wish to stress that these constructions, like constructions of gender to which they are integral, take form not just in the realm of ideas and beliefs, but importantly in social interactions, identities, and social institutions. The emphasis of this volume is on variations within nineteenth– and twentieth–century U.S. cultures. Focusing on this narrow range within the global context allows a relatively fine–grained picture of the tense, contested, and dialectical relationship between dominant and alternative constructions. The authors bring a variety of disciplinary perspectives to bear: sociology, anthropology, history, literature, political science, and ethnic studies. The materials and approaches are diverse, but taken together the articles highlight several recurrent themes that arise from feminist analysis of mothering.

To set the larger context for these papers, I will organize my discussion around five themes or issues. I will describe each issue, review some of the feminist literature addressing it, and discuss how particular articles in this collection contribute to its explication. The questions that underlie this essay and the collection as a whole are: How does looking at mothering as a socially constructed, historically specific relationship redirect our attention to new issues? How does this approach change the ways we think about women and about caring?

CHALLENGING UNIVERSALISM: DIVERSITY IN MOTHERING

In order to free women from the inevitability of current mothering arrangements, feminists have had to challenge theories that tie women's position to biological imperatives. Feminist writers have attempted to develop theories that locate the origins of the seemingly universal pattern of women mothering in social, rather than biological, sources. The most influential of these writers is Nancy Chodorow. Chodorow uses psychoanalytic object relations theory to develop a compelling account of how the pattern of female mothering is transmitted by the very experience of being mothered by women. She argues that an orientation toward nurturance and care becomes part of women's personality because the process of identity formation in girls takes place through continuous attachment to and identification with the mother. In contrast, boys develop a sense of self as independent and distinct from others because they must construct a male identity by a process of separation from and contrast with the mother.[10] Also influential in theorizing about motherhood without resorting to natural or biological explanations is Sarah Ruddick's attempt to account for mothers' concern for nurturing and protecting children. She does so in two ways; by attempting to show that mothers' nurturance involves higher philosophical thought (as opposed to instinct), and by arguing that their focus on protecting and preserving life, fostering growth, and molding an acceptable person grows out of "doing mothering"—that is, maternal practice. The implication is that anyone who engages in mothering would develop these same concerns.[11]

Both theorists have been attacked for universalizing from a narrow social and class base of experiences—presumably their own. I don't want to engage in what has become an overblown debate, even though the issue is important.[12] What is interesting for the purposes of this volume is the following irony: both Chodorow and Ruddick decry the negative outcomes of saddling mothers with primary responsibility for mothering (for example, boys becoming sexist in the process of distancing themselves from what is feminine), and they catalogue major benefits of men and others sharing in mothering (for example, men becoming more concerned with preserving life.) Yet the message that many readers seem to take away is that the arrangement of "biological mother as sole and exclusive caretaker" is universal, and that the issues that all mothers face are identical. The problem for those attuned to the concerns of non-dominant groups is that the analyses do not sufficiently "decenter" the dominant model. In trying to build a general or "universal" theory, the authors' focus remains centered on a single, normative pattern, with variation relegated to the margins.

What may be needed to emphasize the social base of mothering is attending to the variation rather than searching for the universal, and to shift what has been on the margins to the center. Women scholars of color have mounted the most serious challenges to universalistic theory. They have documented the different historical experiences of communities of color, and therefore the differing cultural contexts and material conditions under which mothering has been carried out. Because of varying historical experiences, these communities have constructed mothering in ways that diverge from the dominant model

Bonnie Thornton Dill has argued that historically African–American, Latina, and Asian–American women were excluded from the dominant cult of domesticity. Because they were incorporated into the United States largely to take advantage of their labor, there was little interest in preserving family life or encouraging the cultural and economic development of people of color; people of color were treated as individual units of labor, rather than as members of family units.[13] My own study of the labor histories of African–American women in the South, Mexican–American women in the Southwest, and Japanese–American women in California and Hawaii revealed that these women's value as cheap labor—especially as domestic workers in white households or in lower–level service work in institutional settings—usually took precedence over their value as mothers. Thus they were not expected or allowed to be full-time mothers; nor did their circumstances allow them even to harbor the illusion of a protected private haven. Women had to move back and forth constantly between "public" and "private" labor, since economic provision for the family was an expected part of mothering. In turn, responsibility for mothering often had to be shared with other family members or other women in the community. Mothering or caring was not seen as exclusively women's work, and the boundaries of domestic cooperation were more expansive than that encompassed in the notion of the private household.[14]

Shared mothering has been characteristic of African–American communities since slavery. This tradition continues in many contemporary African–American communities.[15] Carol Stack's and Linda Burton's ethnographic study of low–income multigenerational African–American families across the United States between 1968 and 1990 ("Kinscripts: Reflections on Family, Generation, and Culture") reveals that caring for kin is shared among male and female adults, elders, and children. Caring is reciprocal, so that members may be recruited (kinscripted) to take care of other kin who cared for them earlier; for example grandchildren are expected to migrate to take care of grandparents who raised them. Further, the timing of personal transitions is "scripted" by agendas negotiated collectively by all kin. For example, young, adolescent females may be encouraged to bear children and seek employment while their mothers are young enough to keep up with the physical demands of "mothering" grandchildren. Stack and Burton argue that African–American families have historically experienced issues that mainstream families have only recently become attentive to, such as combining work and family roles, single parenthood, and extended family relationships; therefore the kinscripts model is useful for studying many family forms existing in American society today.

Centering on the experiences of African–American women and other women of color can lead to new ways of looking at mothering, and can raise questions and issues different from those centering on dominant–culture women. In her chapter, "Shifting the Center: Race, Class, and Feminist Theorizing about Motherhood," Patricia Hill Collins notes that much feminist theorizing about motherhood has failed to recognize diversity in mothering, and has projected white, middle–class women's concerns as universal. She points out two problematic assumptions based on white, middle–class experience: first, that mothers and their children enjoy a degree of economic security, and second, that women have the luxury of seeing themselves as individuals in search of personal autonomy, instead of as members of communities struggling for survival. According to Collins, these assumptions have led white feminists to be concerned primarily about such issues as the effects of maternal isolation on mother–child relationships, all–powerful mothers as conduits for gender oppression, and the possibilities of an idealized motherhood freed from patriarchy. Collins proposes that focusing on the experiences of women of color reveals very different concerns: the importance of working for the physical survival of children and community; the dialectics of power and powerlessness in structuring mothering patterns; and the significance of self-definition in constructing individual and collective racial identity. Collins thus highlights the importance of race and class in differentiating women's mothering experience.

In my own research on the racial division of labor among women, I explore the ways race and class hierarchy creates interdependence as well as difference between white, middle-class mothers and working-class ethnic mothers.[16] The idea that the labor market is simultaneously segmented by race and gender, with different jobs being assigned to white men, white women, men of color, and women of color, is familiar. The idea that domestic labor, including mothering or caring work, is "women's work" is also familiar. What may be less familiar is the idea that mothering is not just gendered, but also racialized. The concept of mothering as universally women's work disguises the fact that it is further subdivided, so that different aspects of caring labor are assigned to different groups of women. Historically, more privileged women have been able to slough off the more physical and taxing parts of the work onto other women—white, working-class women and women of color. Instances range from wet-nursing and infant and child care to care of the elderly and infirm. Often the women who perform these services are mothers themselves; yet they are forced to neglect their own children and families to take care of other women's children or elderly parents. The racial division of mothering labor simultaneously buttresses gender and race privilege: it permits white, middle-class women to enjoy the benefits and status of being mothers, and elevates them to the position of "mother-managers."[17] It also releases them for outside careers if they desire them. Because they gain these privileges, white, middle-class women have less impetus to challenge an arrangement that ultimately oppresses them. Middle-class men can keep the illusion (or reality?) of the home as a private haven, while enjoying the services of their wives or their wives' substitutes in maintaining that haven. Thus, the notion of mothering as women's responsibility is left unchallenged.

The race and class division of mothering labor has been evident since at least the late nineteenth century. Generally those women who have done mothering and other domestic labor for other women have done so because they lacked other choices. Until the civil rights movement, color bars in employment restricted the options of African-American women. Continuing the pattern from slave times, domestic service, including infant and child care, was the most common form of employment for Black women, not only in the south, but also in the urban North. In the Southwest, Mexican–American and Native American women were the domestic servant class for Anglos. In Hawaii and northern California, Chinese and Japanese men and women were concentrated in domestic service in the pre–World War II era. The breakdown of color barriers— not complete, but nonetheless considerable—has enabled native–born African–Americans, Latinos and Asian–Americans to move out of domestic service. Since the 1970s, the ranks of nannies and "baby–sitters" have been filled by immigrants from the Caribbean and Latin America. These women lack options because they do not speak English or do not have legal status. In some cities, such as Los Angeles, middle–class women who would not formerly have been able to afford household help have the services of full–time "housekeeper baby–sitters" for less than minimum wage.

The historic division of mothering labor not only continues in the present day, it has expanded in new directions, with technological, demographic, and economic changes. In one direction, the advance of reproductive technology has extended the domain of race and class division of women's mothering work to include actual physical reproduction. Embryos created by *in vitro* fertilization can be transplanted into another woman's womb, and thus a surrogate can bear a child to whom she has no genetic connection. That a woman of color can now bear a "white" baby for a "white" couple breaks the last barrier to women of color doing all reproductive labor for white women, and greatly expands the possibilities for exploiting poor women's lack of economic options.[18]

In another direction, medical and nutritional advances have greatly extended life span and increased the elderly population in the United States, thereby expanding the number of people dependent on "mothering" care. Although the care of the dependent elderly is still largely being done by daughters, wives, and sisters, as an extension of their domestic responsibilities, a large share of it has been transferred to paid caregivers—home health care attendants in private homes, and nursing aides and assistants in nursing homes. These workers perform both physical caretaking—bathing, feeding, and toileting—and emotional labor— soothing, reassuring, and providing the only daily social contact many elderly residents of nursing homes have. The vast majority of the elderly requiring care are white women, while the caregivers are disproportionately women of color, African–American and immigrants from the Caribbean, Latin America, and the Philippines. The reasons are not hard to understand: In addition to being arduous, aide work is among the lowest paid forms of labor—even lower than child care workers.[19]

Sau–ling C. Wong's "Diverted Motherhood: Representations of the Caregiver of Color in the Age of Multiculturalism," examines the images of the caretaker of color in novels, autobiographies, and films of the 1980s and 1990s. These works typically represent a woman of color who has to put her own mothering—pregnancy or child rearing—on hold in order to nurture the white employer's family. A related image is the figure of the desexualized man of color who, as servant or healer, steers his white employer out of crises by performing mothering functions. While mainstream critics have tended to focus on the heartwarming aspects of the relationship between whites and their caregivers, Wong's analysis reveals the parasitic nature of the relationship. The subtext of frustrated motherhood points to a larger dynamic in American society in which the vibrancy of the cultures of people of color is diverted and appropriated to shore up a dominant culture in decline.

IDEOLOGY AND THE CONSTRUCTION OF MOTHERING

Feminist analysis of mothering must also contend with the ideologies that have shaped our culture's thinking about motherhood. These ideologies serve as lenses that filter and, to varying degrees, distort our experience and understanding. An ideology is the conceptual system by which a group makes sense of and thinks about the world. It is a collective rather than individual product. Groups develop ideologies which are distillations of experience, and, because their experiences differ, so do their ideologies.[20] However, ideologies do not have equal sway. A dominant ideology represents the view of a dominant group; it attempts to justify this domination over other groups, often by making the existing order seem inevitable. Thus, by depicting motherhood as natural, a patriarchal ideology of mothering locks women into biological reproduction, and denies them identities and selfhood outside mothering.

Writing in the 1970s, Ann Oakley described the contemporary myth of motherhood as resting on three beliefs: "that all women need to be mothers, that all mothers need their children and that all children need their mothers."[21] Each of these beliefs is made plausible by the social and cultural conditioning that impel women to become mothers. Further, the beliefs are buttressed by "science." In the 1920s and 1930s, psychoanalytic theory posited that "normal" women desire a child, and that those who reject motherhood are rejecting femininity. In the 1960s, child development researchers "discovered" maternal bonding.[22] The concept was used to argue that the infant needed a single caretaking figure, preferably the biological mother, to develop a healthy sense of self and an ability to relate to others. Oakley reviews evidence to show that each of these beliefs is false, and concludes that they must serve some oppressive purpose. Two detrimental results of these beliefs are that women who might otherwise not have children do so, and that women who would be happier sharing child care responsibilities nonetheless make motherhood an all-absorbing job in order not to appear abnormal or selfish.

Feminist writers who disagreed about the desirability of biological motherhood nonetheless agreed that the ideology that encapsulates women in motherhood is damaging to women and children. Shulamith Firestone, who described pregnancy and childbirth as profoundly unpleasant experiences, saw the desire for children less as a natural liking for children than a displacement of ego-extension needs. The ideology of motherhood justified women's homebound existence and kept them outside the centers of real power.[23] Adrienne Rich, in contrast, argued that the experience of motherhood was—at least potentially—a powerful emotional experience that put women in touch with their bodies and their children. Yet she too saw the ideology that prescribed mothering as women's one and only job to be one of the main ways men have succeeded in turning mothering into alienated and alienating labor. The ideology prevents mothers from developing woman-centered desires and goals, and denies them interests and activities outside the family. The ideology imposes expectations—for instance, twenty-four-hour devotion—that generate anger, frustration, and resentment. These negative feelings sometimes lead to behavior that is less than "maternal."[24]

In her essay in this volume, "An Angle of Seeing: Motherhood in Buchi Emecheta's *The Joys of Motherhood* and Alice Walker's *Meridian"* Barbara Christian probes the destruction wrought on women by ideologies of all-encompassing mothering. Emecheta and Walker examine the disjunction between prevailing ideologies of motherhood and the actual experiences of mothering at particular historical moments, as liberation movements are emerging in Nigeria and in the Southern United States. Both African and African-American cultures prescribe motherhood as women's central and primary mission, and their only means of gaining status (but not power). Christian argues that when women are reduced to the function of mother, they are rendered so selfless that they are no longer capable of cherishing life. Thus, Christian laments, the unique "angle of seeing" provided by motherhood is lost to women and ultimately to their communities. Without valuing their own lives they can no longer contribute toward struggles for freedom.

Ideology is a powerful tool for keeping people in their place, in part because it is so flexible. For example, Ann Oakley notes that the rationale for medical control of the birth process has shifted, so that the blatant language of male domination and female inferiority has given way to a softer language of "monitoring" the birth process. Yet the implication is still that the woman bearing the child cannot be trusted to make rational decisions or accurately report her symptoms.[25] Feminist analysis needs to examine the relationship between economic, political, and social changes, and changes in mothering ideology. Do particular shifts in language and imagery represent major transformations in thought, or simply reconstitution of the same ideas in new guises?

In the United States, middle–class women have made great advances in achieving civil and political rights, including control of their own fertility, thus asserting their right not to be mothers except by choice. By becoming increasingly visible as actors in a variety of arenas outside the family, they also have challenged the monolithic identification of women with motherhood. The most dramatic change has been the movement of mothers of all social classes into the work force. Since at least the early 1980s, the majority of women with young children have been gainfully employed. Although women's identities as mothers may still be primary, they are no longer the only ones. As women affirm their personhood outside the boundaries of home and motherhood, we find new twists and turns in ideology, and new ways to reassert the doctrine that a mother's interests must be subordinated to the child's.

In her essay, "Look Who's Talking, Indeed: Fetal Images in Recent North American Visual Culture," Ann Kaplan examines a particularly interesting new ideological turn in the proliferation of images of the fetus in commercial media. Kaplan finds several different groups of images, all of which represent the fetus as an already human, white, and gender unspecified—but presumed male—subject. In some depictions, as in Lennart Nilsson's enormously enlarged and color–enhanced photographs of the fetus floating in a disembodied environment, the mother is literally rendered invisible. In other cases, as in the antiabortion film, *The Silent Scream,* and the popular film, *Look Who's Talking,* the fetus displaces the mother as the subject. This "interpellation" of the fetus as "subject"— a separate being with interests that at times conflict with those of the woman—reverses the usual assumption of a fusion between mother and infant. Why the sudden proliferation of such images? Kaplan suggests that this interpellation has come at a time when women have won new freedoms, and when there has been a "reorientation of consciousness (at least in America) . . . that at least puts women near the male center point." Fetal interpellation constructs another subject—the fetus—to challenge female centrality.

Kaplan's analysis also reveals another reason why ideology is so powerful: it can accommodate complex and often contradictory elements. Motherhood ideology certainly encompasses multiple contradictions. Mothers are romanticized as life–giving, self–sacrificing, and forgiving, and demonized as smothering, overly involved, and destructive. They are seen as all–powerful—holding the fate of their children and ultimately the future of society in their hands—and as powerless—subordinated to the dictates of nature, instinct, and social forces beyond their ken. Feminist theorizing, according to Nancy Chodorow and Susan Contratto, has been constrained by these same contradictions. They note the spate of writing by feminists about their experiences as daughters which associates mothers with destruction and aggressiveness.[26] These writers seem to yearn for a perfect mother, while blaming their own mothers for being less that perfect. Their accounts reflect a belief in the all–powerful mother and the isolated mother–child dyad that is surprisingly similar to that held by conservatives, who enjoin women to devote themselves exclusively to mothering. Both versions deny mothers agency and personhood. Chodorow and Contratto trace the belief in the all–powerful and perfect or perfectible mother to infantile psychodynamic process stemming from the early, exclusive, mother–child dyad. This is certainly one part of the picture, but to explain the complex and often contradictory elements of motherhood ideology, we need to broaden our field of vision beyond the family.

Barbara Katz Rothman's essay, "Beyond Mothers and Fathers: Ideology in a Patriarchal Society," reminds us that ideologies of mothering exist not in isolation, but as part of complex ideologies that buttress male dominance (patriarchy), the economic system of exploitation (capitalism), and the privileging of mind over body (technology). Rothman exposes the ways that these three ideologies shape the experience of motherhood in American society. Patriarchal ideology emphasizes the seed as the basis for parental—or, more to the point, paternity—claims. Initially the concept of seed was invoked to privilege the biological father, but later was extended to biological mothers as givers of egg. In legal rulings, relationships based on seed are given precedence over relationships established through nurturance and commitment. Capitalist ideology recognizes women's ownership of their own bodies, but not their rights or power as mothers. Instead women are subject to attempts to control their behavior during pregnancy, on the grounds that their bodies may "house" babies which "belong" to other people (as in gestational surrogacy) or in which the state claims an interest. Finally, the ideology of technology produces a mind–body dualism which leads to the view of pregnant women as unskilled workers, machines, or containers for genetic material. Thus women's bodies may be used to provide the menial physical labor of bearing and raising children, while moral authority and control over children's lives are still conferred on men (or women) who perform none of this labor.

Each of these ideologies discounts the actual labor involved in mothering and in developing relationships of caring. To see mothering work and relationships of caring as central requires getting outside these ideologies. Feminist analysis needs to examine the reciprocal relationship between motherhood ideology and other prevailing ideologies, and to consider how conceptions of mothering help maintain ideologies that justify race, class, and gender hierarchy.

DECOMPOSING MOTHERING: FUSIONS AND DICHOTOMIES

How do we break mothering free of ideological encapsulation? Such an effort involves deconstruction at two levels. First we need to decompose mothering into constituent elements that are fused within the master definition of mother. Woman is conflated with mother, and together appears as an undifferentiated and unchanging monolith. (In contrast, men appear in all of their historical specificity in a variety of roles and contexts.) Actor and activity are similarly conflated when only women or birth–mothers are recognized as nurturers and caregivers. This fusion excuses others from responsibility, denies recognition to those, including men, who also provide nurturance and care, and assumes nurturance flows in only one direction. Thus, women's need to be mothered is ignored. Another form of fusion involves treating mother and child as a single entity with unitary interests. This fusion denies personhood and agency to both. In fact, mothers' interests and children's interests may conflict, and mothers may be forced to choose between them. Examples such as the widespread practice of bourgeois women in Europe farming their children out to rural wet nurses in order to be sexually available to their husbands suggest that women sometimes choose against children's interests to further those of husbands, fathers, and other men with whom they have a relationship.[27] Decomposing mothering would broaden our field of vision to encompass the variety of actors who mother, the multiple identities/roles of women who mother, and the separate personhood and agency of mothers and children.

At a broader level, we need to recognize the way dominant constructions of mothering have been shaped by the Western philosophical tradition, which rests on binary oppositions. The fixed oppositions conceal the extent to which things that appear oppositional are in fact interdependent—that is, derive their meaning from the contrast. Moreover the interdependence is hierarchical, with one term accorded primacy or dominance over the other, which is represented as weaker or derivative.

Mothering in Western culture has been defined in terms of binary oppositions between male–female, mind–body, nature–culture, reason–emotion, public–private, and labor–love. Mothering has been assigned to the subordinate poles of these oppositions: thus it is viewed as flowing from "natural" female attributes, located only in the private sphere of family and involving strong emotional attachment and altruistic motives. Critical analysis of mothering requires deconstructing these oppositions. Deconstruction involves a two–step process, the reversal and displacement of binary oppositions. According to Joan Scott, "This double process reveals the interdependence of seemingly dichotomous terms and their meanings relative to a particular history. It shows them to be not natural but constructed oppositions, constructed for particular purposes in particular contexts."[28]

Feminist historians have uncovered the historical specificity of the construction of mothering as women's primary and exclusive identity, the encapsulation of women and children in the nuclear household, and the emphasis on mothering as emotional care. These ideas evolved among the white bourgeoisie in western Europe and North America in the latter part of the eighteenth century. With the rise of industrialization, manufacturing gradually shifted out of the household and into capitalist industry. The transfer left the household as the unit of responsibility for "reproduction"—the activities and relationships involved in maintaining people on a daily basis and intergenerationally. The ideological split between publicly organized production and privately organized consumption and reproduction was given concrete form in a doctrine of separate spheres. A natural division of labor was posited, with men ruling the "public" sphere of economy and polity, while women and children inherited the shrunken "private" sphere of the household.

The period also saw the rise of social childhood. Childhood came to be seen as a special and valued period of life, and children were depicted as innocent beings in need of prolonged protection and care. This new conception of childhood required a complementary conception of motherhood as a serious responsibility, one that required total and exclusive devotion. Women were deemed naturally suited for dedication to child care because of their innate qualities of self–sacrifice, moral purity and narrowness of intellect.[29] These interdependent constructions suggest that notions of motherhood and childhood must be tackled simultaneously. Feminist theorizing about motherhood requires questioning idealized notions of infancy and developing conceptions of childhood that recognize the agency and separate interests of mothers and children.

The extent to which women and families accepted the dominant binary oppositions cannot be verified. What is clear is that the oppositions, if they were valid at all, applied only to a very limited subgroup within a narrow time period, namely the European and American bourgeoisie of the nineteenth and twentieth centuries. For the majority of working–class families and women—native whites, immigrants, African–Americans and other racial ethnic minorities, the separation between private and public spheres, between love and labor, and between full–time motherhood for women and full–time employment for men, even if desired, could not be maintained. Men's employment in these families was often discontinuous, and rarely provided a "family wage." Women had to combine income earning in and out of the home with child care and domestic labor. The period when children were completely dependent was brief. By the age of seven or so, many were earning their keep doing child care or domestic tasks, taking on odd jobs, and helping parents with home labor. By their early teens, they contributed to family income by leaving school and working full–time.[30] Within comparable income levels, women in different ethnic groups adopted varying strategies for combining mothering, income earning, and child labor; thus, for example, Italian women preferred to remain at home and send children out to work, while African–American women went out to work themselves and kept children in school.[31]

Several contributions in this collection illustrate the ways in which women construct their own mothering in ways that are both constrained by and transcend the constructed oppositions of public–private, labor–love, male–female. Eileen Boris's article, "Mothers Are Not Workers: Homework Regulation and the Construction of Motherhood, 1948–1953," demonstrates how the ideal of full–time, homebound motherhood, and the illusion of the private sphere retained their hold on white, working–class women engaged in homework, even when their actual circumstances contradicted the ideology. In the debate on regulating clerical homework, all parties invoked this ideal to assert their position, whether defending or opposing regulation. Social reformers saw home labor as importing exploitative relations into the home, indeed as "violating domesticity," by transforming homes into sweatshops and using child labor. Homework employers and contractors, on the other hand, claimed that homeworkers enjoyed the comforts of working in their own homes, "assured of privacy, and with freedom to work in such spare time as is available." Only the Congress of American Women (an organization in the Communist Party orbit) challenged the false dichotomy between mother and worker, arguing that homework conditions—unregulated wages and working standards, and the absence of child care—were inimical to the interests of homeworking women as workers and mothers.

In the 1990s the majority of mothers were employed outside the home, thus seeming to invalidate the idea of exclusive mothering. Yet employed women remained responsible for arranging alternate care, and in many cases they tried to replace their own care with "mother–like care," that is, in a private household provided by a woman like themselves. Margaret K. Nelson's study, "Family Day–care Providers: Dilemmas of Daily Practice," reveals the contradictions in that arrangement. Family day–care providers are motivated to do this work by the desire to preserve the ideal of at–home mothering for both the children they care for and their own children. Paradoxically, by providing the service, they enable other women to redefine mothering to incorporate paid work and substitute care. They are therefore providing a service in which they don't believe. By bringing other people's children into their homes, they are often forced to pay less attention to their own children, and thus compromise their own standards of good mothering.

An ideology that places mothering exclusively in the private, emotional realm creates conflicts for mothers who have to work outside the home. In "Working at Motherhood: Chicana and Mexican Immigrant Mothers and Employment," Denise A. Segura reports making a surprising discovery when she interviewed Mexicana and Chicana employed mothers. Contrary to the expectation that the more "traditional" Mexicanas would experience greater conflict between work and motherhood than more "modern" Chicanas, she found the latter reporting greater conflict. Segura found that Mexicanas think of providing economically for their children as intrinsic to mothering, while Chicanas have internalized white, middle–class, U.S. ideology that categorizes employment as oppositional to mothering. These findings should not be taken to mean that the problems employed mothers experienced existed only in their minds, but to indicate that alternative constructions of motherhood exist within U.S. society that do not locate mothering and employment within the same oppositional framework as "mainstream" culture.

All of these examples suggest that we need ways of conceptualizing mothering that transcend the constructed oppositions of public–private and labor–love, and the relegation of mothering to the subordinate pole of each of these dichotomies. Mothering is not an exclusive activity of biological mothers. Mothers have identities and activities outside and often in conjunction with mothering. At the same time, the variety of actors engaged in mothering needs to be recognized. The public–private opposition, in particular, needs to be deconstructed. Mothering takes place not only in the "private" sphere, but also outside the household and family, and at the boundaries of private and public. Mothering often requires mediating private and public (for example, coordinating family and school schedules; negotiating services from a variety of agencies and institutions; and taking part in political organizing to gain resources needed to nurture children and others). Finally, mothering in the "private" sphere is crucially affected by what goes on in the "public" sphere of the political economy. The labor–love dichotomy is closely linked to the public–private opposition. When mothering is set up in opposition to economics and politics, it is seen as originating from love or altruism, and thus as needing no reward. This reinforces the conception that mothers should be endlessly self–sacrificing. Seeing mothering as not just labor and not just love, but encompassing both, is thus a necessary step in releasing women from encapsulation within all–consuming motherhood.

THE POLITICS OF MOTHERING: THE DIALECTICS OF STRUGGLE AND AGENCY

Because mothering is often romanticized as a labor of love, issues of power are often deemed irrelevant or made invisible. Yet, as some of the preceding discussion shows, mothering takes place in social contexts that include unequal power relations between men and women, between dominant and subordinate racial groups, between colonized and colonizer. Thus mothering cannot escape being an arena of political struggle.

Feminist writers have been concerned primarily with patriarchal control over mothering. By patriarchal control they refer not just to individual husbands and fathers controlling their wives' and daughters' reproduction, but also male–dominated institutions controlling women as a group. Adrienne Rich and Ann Oakley have focused on how male-dominated medicine "annexed" the role of birth attendant—a traditional area of female power—by establishing a monopoly over health care and suppressing midwives and other healers. By discrediting women's own traditional knowledge, medicine rendered them dependent on male experts. Physicians set up procedures to force women into a passive position so that they could be "worked on" by the physician. Rich points out, for example, that obstetricians replaced the squatting or sitting position for women in labor with the lithotomy position, in which the woman lies prone on her back. This position makes birth more difficult and dangerous by countering the helpful effects of gravity, and by reducing oxygen flow to the fetus; delivery then requires more assistance. Forced passivity and dependence, according to Rich, resulted in women being alienated from their bodies and their labor. Patriarchal control also extended to infant and child care. Mothers' traditional wisdom, passed down from older, experienced mothers, was discredited as useless superstition or possibly harmful nonsense by "scientific experts," who churned out huge volumes of advice to mothers.[32]

In this volume we focus on other dimensions of power and inequality. Mothers of all races and classes have been subjected to patriarchal control, but they have experienced that control differently. Poor women, especially women of color, have been subjected to particularly invasive forms of control. Thus, while middle–class women have had to struggle for the right to limit pregnancy through birth control and abortion, poor women, especially women of color, have contended with assaults on their rights to have babies at all. For example, Black, Native American, and Latina women have been disproportionately sterilized, often without their consent or with consent coerced by the threat of withheld medication, loss of jobs, or other dire consequences.[33] The sterilization of women of color has resulted from racism generally, and has been a stated goal of some anti–immigrant, antiminority movements. The eugenics movement of the early twentieth century argued of the dangers of uncontrolled "breeding" by the "unfit," a code word for racial and ethnic minority women. Margaret Sanger, the pioneer fighter for legalized contraception, sought support for birth control by linking it to reducing birth rates among the mentally and socially defective. Thus, in a kind of devil's pact, she was willing to trade away the rights of immigrant women and women of color to have children to gain the rights of middle–class women to limit their fertility.[34]

Mothers of all classes have not simply acquiesced to oppression, but have struggled to gain resources needed to nurture and preserve life. They have also asserted the validity of their own knowledge and skill in the face of messages that they were inadequate mothers. For this reason, it is important to look at the other side of the coin, focusing not just on the way women are oppressed as mothers, but on the way they act to assert their own standards of mothering and to attain the resources necessary to sustain their children's lives. Minna Caulfield dealt with this dialectic of oppression and resistance in her classic article, "Family and Cultures of Resistance," which examined the role of women in situations of colonial and racial domination.[35] Because it is a source of alternative values and is a competitor for authority and loyalty, and most importantly because it is the place where children are socialized to know their place in society, the family is a central locus for resistance to imperial control. The family therefore becomes a target for colonizer attempts to break down resistance, for example, by breaking down communal systems of land ownership or the authority of elders over younger members of the family. The colonizer's attempts to undercut or disrupt traditional institutions, however, motivate the colonized to defend and recreate their ways of life. The everyday activities of mothers in maintaining tradition and in keeping kin ties alive can be seen as resistance.

The assaults on family systems of people of color in the United States have taken several forms. From the mid–nineteenth century until the 1950s, Asian immigrant male laborers were prevented from forming nuclear households by laws and practices that barred entry to women. Mexican families in the Southwest were often broken up by men being forced to migrate to remote laboring camps alone in search of work. Under slavery, bondsmen and bondswomen were individual chattel; marriage, reproduction, and household arrangements were all manipulated by slave owners to maximize their economic return. Thus mothering under slavery in the United States constitutes the most extreme case for exploring contestation and struggle over the meaning and practice of mothering.

In "Mothering Under Slavery in the Antebellum South," Stephanie Shaw explores the dialectics of oppression and resistance and the differing constructions of mothering held by slave masters and slave mothers. Motherhood brought out a basic contradiction in the slave master's economic interests. On the one hand, he had an interest in extracting as much labor as possible, even from potential mothers and pregnant women; on the other hand, he had an interest in breeding healthy slaves, who were valuable commodities. The latter interest might be served by lightening pregnant and nursing mothers' work loads or providing larger

and better rations. The treatment of slave mothers also revealed a contradiction in slaveowner's ideology about slaves. The justification of slavery rested on the conception of slaves as completely dependent on white
beneficence for their survival. Yet because they wanted to maximize their
profits, slave owners did not provide adequately, and relied on slaves to
be self–sufficient. Slave mothers employed considerable ingenuity to attain necessities for themselves and their children. In doing so, they fur-
thered their owners' interests, but they simultaneously refuted the slave
owner's conception of them as completely dependent.

When slavery was abolished, so too was direct personal control of Black
women's biological reproduction and mothering labor. Yet, within the
market relations of twentieth–century capitalism, a parallel conflict exists
between twin needs of the capitalist economy for the labor of women of
color as mother/reproducers and as low–wage workers in the labor market. Personal direct control has been displaced, to some extent by the
"impersonal" control of the welfare state. Mimi Abramovitz examines
the historical role of the state in mediating conflicting economic demands
by subsidizing some women to remain home to reproduce and nurture
valuable future workers, while channeling others into traditional "female," low–wage work outside the home. The state has achieved this
objective through practices and policies that define mothers as "fit" and
"deserving" if they conform to dominant cultural norms: that is, are
married, full–time mothers. Those who don't fit the model are denied
support and thus forced to seek low–wage work. The model turns out to
be racially constructed. An example is the use of employable–mother
rules mandating that mothers were ineligible for Aid to Families with
Dependent Children (AFDC) when work was "available." These rules
were a response to employer demands for seasonal labor for field hands,
and middle–class housewives' complaints about the shortage of domestic
help. The rules were selectively applied to Black mothers, who were
viewed as employable because of prevailing assumptions that Black mothers had always worked in the past and were not handicapped by child
care concerns, since grandmothers were always available to provide such
care.[36]

Grace Chang explores a contemporary manifestation of the use of government policies and practices to coerce some groups of mothers into
the secondary labor force in her article, "Undocumented Latinas: The
New Employable Mother." The Immigration and Naturalization Service
(INS) has implemented immigration law so that undocumented women
whose children have received public benefits are deemed ineligible for
legal residency. In effect, undocumented mothers are forced to chose
between legal status for themselves or critical services and assistance for
their children. The practice seems to stem from public views that undocumented Latinas are undesirable "breeders," and "drains" on public

resources. Yet the practice itself locks them into poverty, and ensures that they remain in the secondary labor market. Thus the state succeeds in extracting low–wage labor from these women while minimizing its own costs and responsibility for the welfare of their children, many of whom are U.S. citizens. Ironically, these women are not recognized as mothers worthy of support; yet many provide mothering and other re-productive labor for other people's families.

These case studies point out that mothering is differentially constructed for women of different races, ethnicities, and classes, and that the con-structions are linked: the construction of some groups of mothers as full–time, stay–at–home, and worthy rests on the construction of other groups of mothers as employable and unworthy of public support. The divergent constructions also follow from the different values placed on children of different races and classes. White, middle–class children have the highest value, and are deemed worthy of full–time, stay–at–home mothers to nurture them to their full potential.

In "Race and 'Value': Black and White Illegitimate Babies, 1945–1965," Rickie Solinger links the differential values placed on Black and white infants to contrasting conceptions of white and Black unmarried mothers. She finds that in the years after World War II, the conception of the white unmarried mother shifted from someone who was morally tainted, to someone who was psychologically troubled, but redeemable. The high value of white babies in the adoption market made it possible for their mothers to resume their lives without the burden or stain of unwed motherhood. In contrast, Black single women continued to be viewed as culturally and biologically flawed, doing what came naturally to them out of unrestrained sexuality and love of babies. While Black children had no economic value for society, their mothers were stig-matized as acting out of economic motives—having babies to get welfare. Solinger shows that, against these dominant cultural constructions, Black women constructed their own identities as mothers in accordance with a strong African–American moral code. Black women rarely gave up children for adoption because they believed in maternal responsibility and the respect one earned as a mother.

Historically, class hierarchy has also generated conflict and struggle over the conditions of mothering and definitions of appropriate moth-ering. Reformers, often middle–class women, have attempted to mold immigrants and working–class "inferiors" to fit the middle–class models of family and womanhood. During the early twentieth century in the United States, the effort to "Americanize" immigrants and minorities focused especially on women, because of their central role in socializing future generations. In the Southwest, for example, reform efforts directed toward Mexican girls and women focused on instilling domestic skills and virtues they supposedly lacked, such as preparing healthful (i.e. non–

Mexican) foods, personal hygiene, and hard work. Only by such training would Mexican women be prepared to conduct orderly, virtuous home lives when they became mothers, and to instill the same virtues into the next generation. Not so incidentally, well–trained Mexican girls would help alleviate the servant problem by being available as a pool of cheap servants for Anglo households.[37]

In late nineteenth– and early twentieth–century England, officials and social reformers, concerned about the perceived drop in the quality of the population, strove to "educate" working class women to better health and safety standards, often without offering them the means to achieve those standards. Education officials sought to keep working–class children in school longer, but mothers resisted, insisting they needed their children's wages. At stake was a working–class mother's right to define what was in the family's best interest. Susan Tananbaum's study, "Biology and Community: The Duality of Jewish Mothering in East London, 1880–1939," reveals class contestation within one ethnic community. Women reformers of established, middle–class Jewry saw their role in helping to "anglicize" newer, working–class Jewish immigrants as an extension of mothering work. The motivations behind their efforts were both altruistic—extending their mothering responsibilities to working–class children—and self–interested—warding off anti–Semitism by helping the newer immigrants blend in. Yet here, too, were conflicting class ideals and interests. The reformers sought to expand young women's occupational choices by offering training beyond the needle trades, while mothers saw their daughters' employment as temporary, and therefore felt it was not worth investing in training time or foregoing the income of immediate work. Their resistance may have been an assertion of an oppositional stance—a struggle to retain traditional constructions of motherhood and womanhood in the face of pressures to anglicize.

The struggle against dominant constructions of mothering also involves heterosexual privilege. Lesbian mothers have to construct their identities as mothers in the face of cultural denial of their existence. Ellen Lewin's study, "Negotiating Lesbian Motherhood: The Dialectics of Resistance and Accommodation," based on interviews with lesbian mothers, reveals that by demanding the right to be mothers, these women challenged the cultural opposition between "mother" and "lesbian." This opposition grows out of a more basic opposition between sexuality and motherhood. In prevailing public perceptions, lesbianism represents women seeking pleasure for themselves, in contrast to motherhood, which represents the feminine qualities of altruism and selflessness. Yet the ongoing management of being a lesbian mother often requires that they separate these two statuses, thus reinscribing the opposition they seek to subvert. Lewin concludes that "subversion of gender expectations is hypothetical at best in the lives of many lesbian mothers, at the same time that knowledge of their existence can only be imagined by the wider public as a rebellion of the most fundamental sort".

MOTHERING AND THE DIFFERENCE-EQUALITY KNOT

Feminist thinking about mothering is not all of a piece: there remain fundamental divides. Some feminists have seen women's role in biological reproduction as the original source of women's subordination. Shulamith Firestone argued that it led to the first division of labor, which was the basis for excluding women from all but domestic concerns.[38] Sherry Ortner argued that women's direct bodily involvement in procreation led to the universal association of women with nature, which was always deemed inferior to culture, men's domain. Taking a slightly different tack, Michelle Rosaldo posited that women's childbearing and lactation restricted their mobility and led to their being assigned responsibility for domestic tasks. Conversely, men's relative freedom from child care and domestic labor freed them to participate in larger-scale organizations that transcended the household. In these formulations, liberation for women would have come only when women were freed from having to be mothers, or released from primary responsibility for mothering. In contrast, other feminist writers have sought to reclaim motherhood for women, seeing it as a source of special power, creativity, and insight. Mary O'Brien acknowledged that motherhood has been a "bitter trap" for women, but argued that in many societies, including patrilineal ones, women gained status when they produced heirs; that they occupied an emotionally central position because of their role in maintaining kin connections; and that in some matrilineal societies, such as the Iroquois, mothers (matrons) collectively exerted considerable political power, including the right to appoint and depose chiefs.[39] In Adrienne Rich's view it is precisely this maternal power that men attempted to limit when they wrested control over motherhood.[40]

This divide grows out of a basic fault line that Ann Snitow identified as running through the history of feminism. What do feminists want? Do we want to do away with the category of woman—minimize the significance of sex differences and claim our rights on the basis of our essential sameness with men? Or do we want to claim the identity of woman, valorize women's culture and organize on the basis of our commonalities as women?

The fault line is especially "sore" in feminist discussions of mothering. We are reluctant to give up the idea that motherhood is special. Pregnancy, birth, and breast-feeding are such powerful bodily experiences, and the emotional attachment to the infant so intense, that it is difficult for women who have gone through these experiences and emotions to think that they do not constitute unique female experiences that create an unbridgeable gap between men and women. Further, as the first generation of second-wave feminists learned, employment in a competitive, hierarchical workplace has not fostered the sense of fulfillment and empowerment that some anticipated. Indeed, the alienation many experienced led them to reinstall family, children, and motherhood as important realms of personal satisfaction. Even those who are highly critical of the way motherhood has been distorted by patriarchal, capitalist ideology, tend to romanticize the experience of motherhood, using the same language of naturalism that they deplore as sexist when used by antifeminists. Moreover, given the hegemony of sexist ideology, motherhood is often the only basis for women to claim status and privilege. The paradox is that, in order to claim positions of power and influence, women have to accommodate prevailing notions that women possess special knowledge or moral qualities by virtue of being mothers. Such claims reinforce the very ideology that justifies women's subordination, that is, the notion that women are essentially different from men and thus should be relegated to specific functions in society. Motherist movements on behalf of peace and community empowerment illustrate both the efficacy and limitations of organizing women on the basis of their special status as mothers.

The notion that women are "peacemakers" because of their role as mothers has been the basis of women taking leadership in peace movements. Using motherhood as authorization, women have called for disarmament in the name of children. In "Feminist Perspectives on Mothering and Peace," Linda Rennie Forcey says that the idea that women are essentially different from men—more nurturing and caring—serves as a consciousness-raising tool, promoting solidarity among women for collective action. She cautions however that this view poses two problems: it limits women's power by reinforcing patriarchal ideology, and it fails to take into account differences among women. In her study of mothers and sons she found that many women encouraged their sons to join the military because they saw this as the only means to shift the intolerable burden of sole responsibility for mothering. Barbara Omolade points out that for some minority communities, the military may represent one of the few routes to gain access to education and benefits. Thus, African-American mothers have a legacy of support for the military because it offers their sons and daughters economic opportunity and social status which are unavailable to them in civilian society.[41]

A case which clearly illustrates both the efficacy of organizing on the basis of women's commonalities as mothers, and the limitations it imposes on women's actions, is the case of Mothers of East Los Angeles (MELA). This organization was formed to oppose the construction of a prison and a toxic waste incinerator in a Chicano community. Father Moretta, the priest who organized the group, commented that he focused his efforts on the women because they would be "cooler and calmer than the men." A member, Aurora Castillo, argued "Mothers are for the children's interest, not for self-interest; the governor is for his own political interest." These comments indicate that though the rhetoric of self-sacrificing motherhood offers a culturally sanctioned rationale for organizing, it also reinforces patriarchal ideology and traditional gender hierarchy. This became apparent when the group adopted the strategy of offering higher offices, such as secretary, to women. Erlinda Robles, a member, later commented, "At the time we thought it was a natural way to get fathers involved. . . . But now that I think about it, a woman could have done the job just as well."[42] MELA did succeed in blocking construction of the toxic waste incinerator. It is not clear whether mothers could be organized to speak out for their own needs as individuals (that is, as women) as opposed to the needs of their children or the community.

Motherist movements draw on a long tradition of "women's culture," which in turn grows out of a history in which survival depended on mutual support and cooperation among women, and in which women were excluded from "men's world." Because of the way motherist movements, such as MELA, rely on and reinforce culturally defined oppositions between men and women, however, it might be asked whether they are feminist. Ann Snitow indicates that motherism and feminism share certain goals and visions. Motherists fall on one side of the fault line, the side that celebrates women's cultures, and values the ways women differ from men. However, it appears that a motherist vision does not include the aspirations of that side of feminism that wants to do away with defining women primarily in terms of reproduction and mothering responsibilities.

Would a strategy of asserting women's essential sameness with men have more radical potential? Ann Oakley notes, for example, that challenges to medicalization of childbirth could be based, not on the claim that mothers are special kinds of people, but on the grounds that women are people with basic human rights to dignity, privacy, and freedom from assault. Yet this claim might be of limited significance in a situation where "patients" generally are not accorded much dignity, privacy, or freedom from assault. Barbara Katz Rothman, in her article in this volume, suggests that the strategy of asserting the essential sameness of men and women is as problematic as making claims based on the specialness of women, if the sameness means adopting male standards as the norm. Rothman argues that this is precisely what liberal feminism has been most successful in accomplishing—extending to women the "right" to be like men. Thus, for example, the central concept of patriarchy, the importance of the seed, has been retained by extending it to women. Women's claims to their children are recognized not on the basis of their providing nurturance, but because they provide the egg as the equivalent of the father's seed.

This line of reasoning helps explain court rulings in disputes between surrogate mothers and couples who have contracted for their services. A court ruled that Anna Johnson, a surrogate who signed a contract to carry and give birth to a child conceived from another woman's egg, had no parental rights because she was not the biological parent of the child.[43] Analyzing another more famous surrogate trial—the Baby M case—Barbara Katz Rothman argues that if paternity/maternity were defined as a social relationship of caring, then the relationship that pregnant women develop in carrying a fetus for nine months would establish their rights as mothers.[44] Men would establish their paternity through the relationship with the woman carrying the child. Rothman calls for the same standard of a "relationship of caring" to define paternity and maternity. However since the act of carrying a fetus establishes a relationship and men are obviously disqualified from such a direct relationship, in fact Rothman does not completely avoid privileging motherhood as a special and unique status.

This observation is not meant as a criticism of Rothman, because no one has been able to resolve the dilemma. It may not be resolvable: women's relationship to mothering seems both different from and (potentially) the same as men's, just as any particular woman's relationship to mothering is both the same and different from that of other women.

I will not attempt to resolve the seeming contradiction. The social constructionist view implies that searching for universals that characterize mothers and mothering is probably fruitless. For example, even the definition of mothering as involving a concern with preserving life always has to be qualified. I was reminded of this while listening to a radio discussion between a Christian Science practitioner, a physician, and various callers. One caller described an incident in which one of her schoolmates died in a diabetic coma after his Christian Science parents decided to have him forego insulin and rely on spiritual healing. She condemned the parents as negligent for putting their religious beliefs ahead of the life of their child. In responding to this and other cases, the practitioner asserted that Christian Science parents love their children and want to preserve their lives. However, they are equally concerned about their children's spiritual state. Moreover since they believe that death means passage to a higher state, death is not the worst fate. I cite this because it is a case where ordinary people in the same culture—the majority of Christian Scientists are middle and upper class—can have very different interpretations of what maternal protection constitutes. Usually those who refute the concept of "maternal thinking," the notion that mothers are concerned about preserving their children's lives, point to extreme or pathological examples, such as child abuse, slavery, or situations of extreme starvation or poverty. Here we see that people in nonextreme circumstances can both cherish their children and assert priorities that may take precedence over preserving their lives.

Looking at the historical and social specificity of mothering draws our attention to the importance of social contexts and of human agency within those contexts. We can recognize both differences and commonalities arising from people's actions within similar and dissimilar contexts. We do not have to suppress or minimize differences among women and/or mothers to develop a sense of community, or to engage in collective action to nurture growth and preserve human life. As Elsa Barkley Brown notes, difference may be viewed as interdependence, not separation. Therefore community is built on difference as well as sameness.[45] Our goals in putting together this volume were to draw attention to this diversity of mothering and of the contexts in which people mother, to restore agency to a central place, and to raise questions. We invite you to plunge in and see what questions individual chapters and the volume as a whole raise for you.

Notes

I wish to thank Grace Chang for her many contributions to this essay. I am also grateful to Linda Forcey, Gary Glenn, Barbara Laslett, and Carole Turbin for reading and commenting on earlier drafts of this essay.

1. Don Lattin, "Bishops Re-open Debate Over Women Priests," *San Francisco Chronicle* (November 18, 1992), p. A2.

2. Kristin Luker, *Abortion and the Politics of Motherhood* (Berkeley: University of California Press, 1984), p. 214.

3. Martha Minow, "Adjudicating Differences: Conflicts Among Feminist Lawyers," in Marianne Hirsch and Evelyn Fox Keller, *Conflicts in Feminism* (New York & London: Routledge, 1990), pp. 150–163. See also Lise Vogel, "Debating Difference: Feminism, Pregnancy, and the Workplace," *Feminist Studies* 16, No. 1 (Spring 1990), pp. 9–32.

4. e.g., Elaine Draper, "Fetal Exclusion Policies and Gendered Constructions of Suitable Work," *Social Problems* 40, 1 (February 1993) pp. 90–107. Such debates among feminists are not new. During the early years of the twentieth century, advocates for women workers took opposing sides in the debate over protective labor legislation for women. Laws limiting work hours and regulating working conditions of women workers were justified on the grounds of protecting mothers and potential mothers, but their impact was to restrict women's employment opportunities. See Susan Lehrer, *Origins of Protective Legislation for Women* (Albany: State University of New York Press, 1987).

5. Schwartz did not use the term "mommy track" in her article, but the separate track was so dubbed in the popular media. See Felice N. Schwartz, "Management Women and the New Facts of Life," *Harvard Business Review* 67, No. 1 (1989), pp. 65–76. For a popular account, see Ellen Hopkins, "Who is Felice Schwartz and Why is She Saying These Terrible Things About Us?," *Working Woman* (October 1990), pp. 116–118, 148.

6. Alison M. Jaggar, *Feminist Politics and Human Nature* (Totowa, NJ: Rowman and Allanheld, 1983), p. 256.

7. Barbara Laslett, personal communication.

8. See, for example, Barbara Laslett and Johanna Brenner, "Gender and Social Reproduction: Historical Perspectives," *Annual Review of Sociology* 15 (1989), pp. 381–404; Joan Scott, "Gender: A Useful Category of Historical Analysis," *American Historical Review* 91 (December 1986), pp. 1053–1075.

9. R. W. Connell, *Gender and Power: Society, the Person and Sexual Politics* (Stanford, Cal.: Stanford University Press, 1987), p. 140.

10. Nancy Chodorow, *The Reproduction of Mothering* (Berkeley, University of California Press, 1978); Nancy Chodorow, *Feminism and Psychoanalytic Theory* (Berkeley: University of California Press, 1989).

11. Sarah Ruddick, "Maternal Thinking," *Feminist Studies* 6, No. 2 (Summer 1980), pp. 342–367.

12. An example of how heated the debate can become is the exchange between Katha Pollitt and readers in response to her article, "Marooned on Gilligan's Island: Are Women Morally Superior to Men?," in *The Nation* (December 28, 1992), pp. 799–806. The exchange occured in the letters to the editor section in *The Nation* (March 8, 1993), pp. 290, 319–320.

13. Bonnie Thornton Dill, "Our Mother's Grief: Racial Ethnic Women and the Maintenance of Families," *Journal of Family History* 13, (1988), 415–431.

14. Evelyn Nakano Glenn, "Racial Ethnic Women's Labor: The Intersection of Race, Gender and Class Oppression," *Review of Radical Political Economy* 17, No. 3 (1985), pp. 86–108.

15. See Deborah Gray White, *Ar'n't I a Woman: Female Slaves in the Plantation South* (New York: Norton, 1985), on shared mothering among bondswomen; and Carol Stack, *All Our Kin* (New York: Harper and Row, 1974) on shared mothering among low-income urban Blacks in the 1970s.

16. Evelyn Nakano Glenn, "From Servitude to Service Work: Historical Continuities in the Racial Division of Women's Work," *Signs* 18, No. 1 (Fall, 1992), pp. 1–43.

17. See Barbara Katz Rothman, *Recreating Motherhood* (New York: Norton, 1989), pp. 198–220, for a discussion of the managerial mother.

18. Deborah King, "Sarah and her Handmaid: Race and Class in Surrogate Motherhood," paper presented at the conference, "Contested Terrains: Constructions of Motherhood," Sojourner Center, State University of New York at Binghamton, October, 1990.

19. Timothy Diamond, *Making Gray Gold: Narratives of Nursing Home Care* (Chicago: University of Chicago Press, 1992).

20. C.f. Barbara Field, "Slavery, Race and Ideology in the United States of America," *New Left Review* 181 (1990), pp. 110, 112.

21. Ann Oakley, *Woman's Work: The Housewife, Past and Present* (New York: Pantheon Books, 1974), p. 186.

22. In a study of the history of this concept, Diane E. Eyer *Mother-Infant Bonding: A Scientific Fiction* (New Haven, CT: Yale University Press, 1993) notes that the evidence for bonding was slim—an original study involving twenty-eight mothers, analogies from studies of attachment and rejection in nonhuman mammals, and interpretations of infants in pathological situations—yet the theory of bonding had major impacts.

23. Firestone characterized giving birth as akin to "shitting a pumpkin." Shulamith Firestone, *The Dialectic of Sex* (New York: Bantam Books, 1970 and reprinted by Morrow, 1993).

24. Adrienne Rich, *Of Woman Born* (New York: Norton, 1976).

25. Ann Oakley, "Feminism, Motherhood and Medicine—Who Cares?," in Juliet Mitchell and Ann Oakley, eds., *What is Feminism?* (Oxford: Basil Blackwell, 1986), p. 137.

26. Nancy Chodorow with Susan Contratto, "The Fantasy of the Perfect Mother," in Nancy Chodorow, *Feminism and Psychoanalytic Theory* (New Haven, CT: Yale University Press, 1989), pp. 79–96. They refer to the spate of writings in late 1970s that included

Dorothy Dinnerstein, *The Mermaid and the Minotaur* (New York: Harper and Row, 1976); Nancy Friday, *My Mother/Myself* (New York: Dell, 1977); Jane Lazarre, *The Mother Knot* (New York: Dell, 1976); and Adrienne Rich, *Of Woman Born* (New York: Norton, 1976).

27. Regarding wet-nursing, see, for example, Edward Shorter, *The Making of the Modern Family* (New York: Basic Books, 1975), especially pp. 175–190. For a discussion of the issue of the supposed unitary interest of the household, and of the actual predominance of men's interest that this notion disguises, see Richard Curtis, "Household and Family in Theory on Inequality," *American Sociological Review* 51 (1986), pp. 168–183.

28. Joan W. Scott, "Deconstructing Equality-Versus-Difference: Or the Uses of Post-Structuralist Theory for Feminism," in Marianne Hirsch and Evelyn Fox Keller, eds., *Conflicts in Feminism* (New York and London: Routledge, 1990), p. 137.

29. For accounts of the transition, see, e.g., Nancy Cott, *The Bonds of Womanhood* (New Haven, CT: Yale University Press, 1977), especially pp. 87–92; Carl Degler, *At Odds Women and Family from the Revolution to the Present* (New York: Oxford University Press, 1984); Ruth Schwartz Cowan, *More Work for Mother: The Ironies of Household Technology from the Open Hearth to the Microwave* (New York: Basic Books, 1983); and Jeanne Boydston, *Home and Work: Housework, Wages, and the Ideology of Labor in the Early Republic* (New York: Oxford University Press, 1990).

30. See Ellen Ross, "Labour and Love: Rediscovering London's Working-Class Mothers, 1870–1918," in Jane Lewis, ed., *Labour and Love: Women's Experience of Home and Family, 1850–1940* (Oxford: Basil Blackwell, 1987), pp. 73–98.

31. Elizabeth Pleck, "A Mother's Wages: Income Earning Among Married Italian and Black Women, 1896–1911," in Nancy F. Cott and Elizabeth H. Pleck, eds., *A Heritage of Her Own: Toward a New Social History of American Womanhood* (New York: Touchstone, 1979), pp. 343–366.

32. Adrienne Rich, *Of Woman Born;* and Ann Oakley, "Feminism, Motherhood and Medicine—Who Cares?".

33. Carlos G. Velez-I, "Se Me Acabo La Cancion: An Ethnography of Non-Consenting Sterilizations Among Mexican Women in Los Angeles" in Margarita Melville and eds., *Twice a Minority: Mexican American Women* (St. Louis: Mosby) 1980; and Angela Y. Davis, *Women, Race and Class* (New York: Vintage, 1983), pp. 202–221.

34. Linda Gordon, *Woman's Body, Woman's Right* (New York: Penguin, 1977), especially pp. 286–290.

35. Minna Davis Caulfield, "The Family and Cultures of Resistance," *Socialist Revolution* 20 (1975), pp. 67–85.

36. Mimi Abramovitz, *Regulating the Lives of Women: The Social Functions of Public Welfare* (Boston: South End Press, 1983); see also Frances Fox Piven and Richard A. Cloward, *Regulating the Poor: The Functions of Public Welfare* (New York: Random House, 1971); and Sylvia A. Law, "Women, Work, Welfare and the Preservation of Patriarchy," *University of Pennsylvania Law Review* 131, No. 6 (1983), pp. 1249–1339.

37. George J. Sanchez, " 'Go After the Women': Americanization and the Mexican Immigrant Woman, 1915–1929," in Ellen Carol DuBois and Vicki L. Ruiz, *Unequal Sisters* (New York and London: Routledge, 1990), pp. 250–263.

38. Firestone, *The Dialectic of Sex,* p. 17.

39. Nancy Tanner, "Matrifocality in Indonesia and Africa and Among Black Americans" in Michelle Zimbalist Rosaldo and Louise Lamphere, eds., *Woman, Culture and Society* (Stanford, CA: Stanford University Press, 1974), pp. 129–157; Judith K. Brown, "Iroquois Women: An Ethnohistoric Note" in Rayna R. Reiter, ed., *Toward an Anthropology of Women* (New York: Monthly Review Press, 1975), pp. 235–251; Sherry B. Ortner, "Female to Male as Nature is to Culture?" in Rosaldo and Lamphere, pp. 67–88; Michelle Zimbalist Rosaldo, "Woman, Culture and Society: A Theoretical Overview," in Rosaldo and Lamphere, pp. 17–42; Mary O'Brian, *The Politics of Reproduction* (Boston: Routledge & Kegan Paul, 1981).

40. Rich, *Of Woman Born* p. 11.

41. Barbara Omolade, "We Speak for the Planet," in Adrienne Harris and Ynestra King, eds., *Rocking the Ship of State: Toward a Feminist Peace Politics* (Boulder, Colo.: Westview, 1989) p. 184.

42. Mary Pardo, "Mexican American Women Grassroots Community Activists: Mothers of East Los Angeles," *Frontiers* vol. XI, No. 1 (1990), pp. 1–7.

43. Harriet Chiang, "Surrogate Mother Custody Case Argued in State High Court," *San Francisco Chronicle* (February 3, 1992), p. A5.

44. Barbara Katz Rothman, *Recreating Motherhood* (New York: Norton, 1989).

45. Elsa Barkley Brown, "Weaving Threads of Community: The Richmond Example," presented at the Southern Historical Association 54th Annual Meeting, Norfolk, Virginia, November 12, 1988.

Part I

CHALLENGING UNIVERSALISM: DIVERSITY IN MOTHERING

Chapter 2

KINSCRIPTS: REFLECTIONS ON FAMILY, GENERATION, AND CULTURE

Carol B. Stack and Linda M. Burton

People do not necessarily do for kin what they are supposed to do, but they understand *what* they are supposed to do, and *when* they are supposed to do it; and they know their kin *will* summon them some day. Not long ago a friend, a distinguished professor who was one of five children from a Southern sharecropping family, called to say: "Carol, I've been given ten hours notice that my sister's two children are coming on the train to live with me!" She had been drafted by her older sister to care for these children. It did not matter that she was in the process of finishing a book and preparing for a major international conference. She lamented that over her protests her sister said firmly: "It's your turn."

This chapter presents a framework for examining how individuals and families as multigenerational collectives work out family responsibilities. We provide a useful lens for viewing how work and responsibility concerning the care of children is delegated: in particular, with respect to children born to young mothers. This paper draws upon a broad variety of examples from diverse family situations as a way of thinking about multigenerational families and child care across the life span. We introduce kinscripts, a framework representing the interplay of family ideology, norms, and behaviors over the life course. Kinscripts encompass three culturally defined family domains: kin–work, which is the labor and the tasks that families need to accomplish to survive from generation to generation; kin–time, which is the temporal and sequential ordering of family transitions; kin–scription, which is the process of assigning kin–work to family members

The kinscripts framework is derived in part from the family life course perspective,[1] studies of kinship,[2] and literature on family scripts.[3] The principal basis of kinscripts, however, is our ethnographic research, conducted between 1968 and 1990, with urban and rural, low–income, multigenerational, Black, extended families in the Northeast, Southeast, and Midwest portions of the United States. Case history data on families involved in these ethnographic studies are used to illuminate components of the kinscripts framework where appropriate.

The kinscripts framework was developed to organize and interpret qualitative observations of (a) the temporal and interdependent dimensions of family role transitions; (b) the creation and intergenerational transmission of family norms; and (c) the dynamics of negotiation, exchange, and conflict within families as they construct the life course. This framework is based on the premise that families have their own agendas, their own interpretation of cultural norms, and their own histories.[4] Families assist individual members in constructing their personal life courses, but in the process families as collectives create a life course of their own.[5]

The kinscripts framework can be applied across race, ethnicity, social class, and to the range of family forms existing in contemporary American society. Typically, the conceptual frameworks used to interpret the life course of kin are derived from explorations involving white, middle–class families. Kinscripts, in contrast, is an example of a framework that is derived from the study of low–income Black families, but offers insights for study of mainstream families as well.

KINSCRIPTS

Family Scripts

The concept of scripts as used in the family therapy literature is also an integral part of the kinscripts framework. Family scripts prescribe patterns of family interaction.[6] They are mental representations that guide the role performances of family members within and across contexts.

The kinscripts framework extends the notion of scripts to the study of the family life course. Specifically, kinscripts focus on the tensions that are produced and negotiated between individuals in families in response to scripts. These dynamics are discussed in the context of three, culturally defined, family domains: kin–work, kin–time, and kin–scription.

Kin–work

Kin–work is the collective labor expected of family–centered networks across households and within them.[7] It defines the work that families need to accomplish to endure over time. The family life course is constructed and maintained through kin–work. Kin–work regenerates families, maintains lifetime continuities, sustains intergenerational responsibilities, and reinforces shared values. It encompasses, for example, all of the following: family labor for reproduction; intergenerational care of children or dependents; economic survival, including wage and nonwage labor; family migration and migratory labor designated to send home remittances; and strategic support for networks of kin extending across regions, state lines, and nations.

Kin–work is distributed in families among men, women, and children. Samuel Jenkins, a seventy–six–year–old widower in Gospel Hill, provided his own interpretation of kin–work. After Samuel's oldest daughter died, his granddaughter Elaine moved in with him, along with her three children: A six–month– old baby, a two–year– and a three–year–old. Samuel is raising these children. Elaine, he says, is running the streets and not providing care. When asked why he is parenting his grandchildren, he said:

> There ain't no other way. I have to raise these babies else the service people will take 'em away. This is my family. Family has to take care of family else we won't be no more

Janice Perry, a thirteen–year–old pregnant girl from Gospel Hill, described her rather unique kin–work assignment. Her contribution to the family, as she understood it, was through reproduction. She states:

> I'm not having this baby for myself. The baby's grandmother wants to be a "mama" and my great-grandfather wants to see a grandchild before he goes blind from sugar. I'm just giving them something to make them happy.

Janice's mother, Helen, comments further:

> I want this baby. I want it bad. I need it. I need to raise a child. That's my job now. My mama did it. It's my turn now.

Samuel Jenkins, Janice Perry, and Helen Perry have clear notions of kin–work within families. While their individual family circumstances are different, kin–work for each one of them is tied to providing care across generations, and maintaining family traditions and continuity.

Kin-work is the consequence of culturally constructed family obligations defined by economic, social, physical, and psychological family needs. Henry Evans, thirty–eight–year–old resident of New Town,[8] a Northeastern Black community, provided a very clear profile of his assigned kin-work. He noted that his kin-work emerged from the physical and psychological needs of his family members. Henry was the only surviving son in his family. His mother had given birth to eleven other sons, all of whom were stillborn or died shortly after birth. At the time of his interview, Henry was providing care for his father, who had recently suffered a heart attack, his thirty–six–year old sister, who was suffering from a chronic neuromuscular disease, and his forty–year–old sister and her four children. When asked about his family duties, he remarked:

> I was designated by my family as a child to provide care for all my family members. My duties read just like a job description. The job description says the following: one, you will never marry; two, you will have no children of your own; three, you will take care of your sisters, their children, your mother, and your father in old age; and four, you will be happy doing it.

Henry went on to discuss how his commitment to the family life course took precedence over his personal life goals:

> Someone in my family must be at the helm. Someone has to be there to make sure that the next generation has a start. Right now, we are a family of codependents. We need each other. As individuals, my sisters and father are too weak to stand alone. I could never bring a wife into this. I don't have time. Maybe when the next generation (his sister's children) is stronger, no one will have to do my job. We will redefine destiny.

The life situation of Henry Evans is not an unfamiliar one. Hareven,[9] in detailed historical analysis of families who worked for the Amoskeag Company in Manchester, New Hampshire, provides poignant examples of how, for many individuals, the demands of kin–work supersede personal goals.[10] Comparable evidence is noted in Plath's[11] in–depth interview study of contemporary Japanese families. In each cultural context, across historical time, kin–work was described as self–sacrificing, hard work—work designed to insure the survival of the collective.

Kin–time

Kin–time represents the temporal scripts of families. It is the shared understanding among family members of when and in what sequence role transitions and kin–work should occur. Kin–time encompasses family norms concerning the timing of such transitions as marriage, childbearing, and grandparenthood. It includes temporal guides for the assumption of family leadership roles and caregiving responsibilities. The temporal and sequencing norms of kin–time are constructed in the context of family culture. Consequently, for some families, these norms may not be synonymous with the schedules of family life course events inferred from patterns assumed to exist in larger society.

Stack's[12] ethnographic study of the migration of Black families to and from the rural South provides an example of the relationship between kin–time and kin–work. Two aspects of kin–work are highlighted—reproduction and migration. The timing and sequencing of reproduction and migration is such that young adults first have children and then migrate to the North to secure jobs and send money back home. Their young children are left behind in the South to be reared by grandparents or older aunts and uncles. After an extended period of time, the migrating adults return to the South and, for some, their now young-adult children repeat the cycle—they bear children and migrate North.

The temporal sequencing of reproduction and migration in these families reflects a scripted family life course involving cooperative action among kin. Family members must be willing to assume economic and child care responsibilities according to schedule. Individuals in families, however, do not always adhere to kin–time. A young adult may choose not to migrate, another may leave home but fail to send remittances, and yet others may return home sooner than expected. These individuals are considered insurgent by kin and may create unexpected burdens that challenge family resilience.

Kin–time also demarcates rites of passage or milestones within families, including the handing down of familial power and tasks following the death of family elders. For example, in the Appalachian mountains in the southeastern United States, older women proclaim those few years after the death of their husbands, when they alone own the family land, as the time they have the most power in their families. The grown children and nearby community members observe, in a timely fashion, the activities of these elderly rural women. It was still common lore in the 1980s that the year such an older, widowed woman announces plans for planting her last garden is the last year of her life. That year kin vie for their inheritances. Thus, the life course of families, which involves a scripted cycle of the relegation of power through land ownership, continues to unfold.

Kin–scription

It is important to understand how power is brought into play within the context of kin–time and kin–work. The question this raises is summed up in the tension reflected in kin–scription. Rather than accept the attempts of individuals to set their own personal agendas, families are continually rounding up, summoning, or recruiting individuals for kin–work. Some kin, namely women and children, are easily recruited. The importance women place on maintaining kin ties and fostering family continuity has been assiduously documented.[13] Placing preeminent emphasis on kin–keeping—the undertakings necessary to keep family con-

nected and family traditions transmitted—women often find it difficult
to refuse kin demands.

The life course of a young woman, Yvonne Carter, who lives in Gospel
Hill, offers an example of the interplay of power, kin–scription, and the
role of women. When Yvonne's first love died fourteen years ago, she
was twenty–one. At thirty–five, she recounted how the years had un-
folded:

> When Charlie died, it seemed like everyone said, since she's not getting
> married, we have to keep her busy. Before I knew it, I was raising kids,
> giving homes to long lost kin, and even helping the friends of my mother.
> Between doing all of this, I didn't have time to find another man. I bet
> they wouldn't want me and all my relatives anyway.

How relatives collude to keep particular individuals wedded to family
needs—a chosen daughter in Japan,[14] a chosen son in rural Ireland,[15]—
confirms Yvonne Carter's suspicion: she has been recruited for specific
kin–work in her family.

Recruitment for kin–work is one dimension of power in kin–scription.
Exclusion from kin–work is another, as this profile of Paul Thomas, a
thirty–six–year–old resident of Gospel Hill, illustrates.

Paul Thomas, down on his luck, out of sorts with his girlfriend, and
the oldest of seven children, had just moved back into his mother Mattie's
home when he was interviewed. Eleven of Mattie's family members live
in her two–bedroom apartment. The family members include Paul's two
younger brothers (one who returned home from the service and moved
in with his new wife and child), an unmarried sister, a sister and her
child, and a pregnant sister with her two children. Paul reported finding
his move back home, the result of repeated unemployment, particularly
difficult under these living conditions.

After Paul moved back home, Mattie characterized Paul's history
within the family as follows:

> Paul left this family when he was thirteen. I don't mean leave, like go away,
> but leave, like only do the things he wanted to do, but not pay attention
> to what me or his brothers and sisters wanted or needed. He took and took,
> and we gave and gave all the time. We never made him give nothing back.

In Mattie's view, her son Paul abandoned the family early on, claiming
rights, but not assuming responsibilities. On a later visit to Mattie's apartment, family members gathered in the living room were asked a rather
general question about doing things for kin. Paul stood up to speak.
Addressing this question, with anger and entitlement in his voice, he said:

> I come back only for a little while. I am the outsider in the family. The

black sheep. I belong, but I don't belong. Do you understand what I mean? I am only important because my mother can say, I have a son, and my sisters can say, I have a brother. But it doesn't mean anything. I can't do anything around here. I don't do anything. No one makes me. My sisters know what they have to do. They always have. They know their place! Now that I'm getting old I've been thinking that someway I'll make my place here. I want Ann (his sister) to name her baby after me. I'm begging you, Ann. Give this family something to remember that I'm part of it too.

Renegade relatives such as Paul attest to subtle dynamics that challenge their places within families. These relatives may inadvertently play havoc with family processes while simultaneously attempting to attach themselves to family legacies.

When kin act out or resist procedures to be kept in line, families have been known to use heavy-handed pressures to recruit individuals to do kin-work. However, kin may be well aware that family demands crisscross, and that it is impossible for the individual summoned to do kin-work to satisfy everyone. In particular, those family members assigned to do kin-work cannot be in two places at once. Adults, and even children under such circumstances, may be left to choose between conflicting demands. Stack's study of family responsibilities assumed by children in the rural, Southeastern community of New Jericho provides an example of competing demands placed on adolescents as they are recruited for family tasks

In New Jericho, multiple expectations are transmitted to children whose parents migrated from the rural South to the Northeast. It is not unusual for adolescents, skilled at child care and other domestic activities, to be pulled in a tug-of-war between family households in the North and South. Kin at both locations actively recruit adolescents to move with them or join their households. Parents in the North and grandparents in the South are the main contenders. Children find themselves deeply caught in a web of family obligations. At eleven years of age, Jimmy Williams was asked to move to Brooklyn to help his parents with their new baby. But his grandmother needed his help in rural North Carolina. Jimmy responded by saying:

I think I should stay with the one that needs my help the most. My grandmother is unable to do for herself, and I should stay with her and let my mother come to see me.

In this example, Jimmy was conscripted by two households within the family network. The decision Jimmy made to remain with his grandmother punctuates the leeway given to the children to make judgments in the context of personal and family interests. In a similar situation, young Sarah Boyce said:

I'll talk to my parents and try to get them to understand that my grand-parents cannot get around like they used to. I want to make an agreement to let my brother go to New York and go to school, and I'll go to school down here. In the summer, I will go and be with my parents, and my brother can come down home

Children are conscripted to perform certain kin tasks that are tied to the survival of families as a whole. Definitions of these tasks are transmitted through direct and indirect cues from family members. Jimmy and Sarah responded to the needs of kin, taking advantage of the flexibility available to them in negotiating the tasks. That same flexibility is not always available for adults. The life situation of Sandra Smith provides an example.

Sandra Smith, married and a mother, found herself pressed between the demands of kin in her family of origin and her in-laws in Gospel Hill. She states:

I'm always the one everybody comes to to take care of children. My mother expects me to raise my sister's three kids. My mother-in-law calls upon me to mind my nieces and nephews while she takes it easy. She expects me to kiss her feet. I won't do it, none of it, everybody can go to hell.

Sandra, in fact, did refuse kin-work. When asked what impact her choice would have on her situation in the family, she said:

It means I won't have nobody. But so what, they need me more than I need them.

Pressed between opposing sets of demands and resentments that build up over the years, refusal to do kin-work is a choice some individuals opt for. Refusal, however, may be costly, particularly for those individuals who are dependent on the economic and emotional resources of kin.

DISCUSSIONS

The examples of kin-work, kin-time, and kin-scription provided in this discussion are drawn primarily from our ethnographic studies of low-income, multigenerational, Black families. The examples illuminate extraordinary situations of individuals embedded in families that have scripted life courses. Not all families, unlike those described here, have such well-defined family guidelines. The family guidelines that exist for those who live in Gospel Hill, New Jericho, and New Town emerge out of extreme economic need and an intense commitment by family members to the survival of future generations.

The kinscripts framework is useful for exploring the life course of the families highlighted in this discussion, but it can also be applied to families that construct their life course under different circumstances. Kinscripts is particularly suited to exploring the effects that certain individuals within families have on the life course of kin. In all families, across racial, ethnic, and socioeconomic groups, there are individuals who cannot be counted on to carry out kin tasks; who leave the family fold for reasons of personal survival; who remain as dependent insiders within families, making excessive emotional and economic demands on family members; and who return to the bosom of kin because of personal experiences such as unemployment, homelessness, divorce, or widowhood. From each angle, and in a diversity of family systems, the life course of kin through kin-work, kin-time, and kin-scription are affected by the personal agendas of family members.

Consider, for example, how the kinscripts framework might be used in exploring the life course of a kin network in which one of its members is experiencing divorce. Divorce is a fairly common experience in mainstream American families.[16] Under such circumstances, an adult child with dependent children may return to the home of his or her parents. The return home may put the scripted life course of kin in disarray, necessitating that collective family notions of kin-work, kin-time, and kin-scription be reconstructed. In terms of kin-work, grandparents, who in the past may have assumed a less active role in the rearing of their grandchildren, may now be expected to take on a more formal surrogate parent role.[17] With respect to kin-time, family members may delay certain transitions in response to the divorce. For example, an older parent might put off retirement for a few years to generate enough income to help an adult child reestablish himself or herself financially. Kin-scription may also be revised. The adult child experiencing the divorce may have been the family kin-keeper—that is, the person in the family charged with organizing family reunions, documenting family history, and negotiating conflicts between relatives. Given the change in this kin-keeper's life course, these duties may have to be reassigned to another family member.

Kinscripts can also be applied to explorations of the relationship between broader social conditions, unemployment, and the life course of kin. Under ideal conditions, unemployed family members are absorbed by kin as best they can. Given severe socioeconomic conditions, however, tensions between individual needs and kin-work, kin-time, and kin-scription may emerge. Again, the family life course may have to be redesigned. For example, low-income families attempting to absorb down-and-out members, or homeless mothers and children, find that sometimes in the face of economic cutbacks and emotional crisis they must, however reluctantly, "let go" of family members who cannot pull their weight. When public welfare support decreased in the 1980s, it produced a remarkable increase in families with these experiences. Stressful economic conditions decrease both individuals' and families' ability to perform effectively. Certain economic and political changes can disrupt kin-time, delaying family milestones such as childbearing and adding complexity to family timetables, and can inhibit kin–work and kin–scription, thereby increasing tensions between the individual and family life course. The kinscripts framework, drawing on the life course perspective, is attentive to exploring these issues in the context of social change.

Another application of the kinscript framework is seen in the study of family members who leave the fold of kin. Under certain circumstances, particularly in the case of a dysfunctional family, an individual may temporarily dissociate himself from kin as a means of personal survival, and then return to the fold having learned new family skills. Within the context of the kinscripts framework, several questions might be addressed: (a) What implications does the individual's exit from the family have on kin–work, kin–time, and kin–scription? (b) How does the individual negotiate reentry to the kin network? (c) What effect does that individual's reentry have on the family's restructuring of the life course?

In summary, our contention is that kinscripts can be a useful framework for research in which the basic questions concern how families and individuals negotiate, construct, and reconstruct the life course. The utility of this framework is found in observing the interplay of three culturally defined family domains—kin–work, kin–time, and kin–scription.

CONCLUSION

This chapter suggests a way of thinking about the life course of individuals embedded within the life course of families. The kinscript framework is conceptually grounded in the life course perspective, studies of kinship, and the literature on family scripts; as such, many of the ideas outlined here are not new. What is new, however, is the union of these various perspectives in the domains of kin–work, kin–time, and kin–scription.

In addition to describing three domains of the family life course, kinscripts represent an attempt to use knowledge generated from the study of Black, multigenerational families to formulate a framework that can be useful for the study of families in general. Minority families have historically experienced issues such as the juggling of work and family roles for women, single parenthood, extended family relationships, and poverty, that mainstream families have only recently been attentive to. Important lessons can be learned through exploring these issues in the context of the life course of minority families. These lessons can provide critical insights into the life course of the variety of family forms existing in contemporary American society.

Notes

The research reported in this paper was supported by grants from the Rockefeller Foundation and the Guggenheim Foundation to the first author, and by the National Science Foundation (RII-8613960), the Brookdale Foundation, the Center for the Study of Child and Adolescent Development, The Pennsylvania State University, a FIRST Award from the National Institute of Mental Health (No. R29MH46057-01), and a William T. Grant Faculty Scholars Award to the second author. This paper was partially prepared while the authors were Fellows at the Center for Advanced Study in the Behavioral Sciences. We are grateful for financial support from the John D. & Catherine T. MacArthur Foundation, the Spencer Foundation, and the Guggenheim Foundation. We also wish to thank Robert Weiss, Gunhild Hagestad, Ann Crouter, Jean Lave, Blanca Silvestrini, Judy Stacey, Brad Shore, Jane Ifekwunigwe, Cindy Brache, and Caridad Souza for their helpful comments on an earlier draft. The authors are grateful to the *Journal of Comparative Family Studies* for permission to reprint portions of their article, "Kinscripts," vol. XXIV, 1993.

1. See Aldous, Joan, "Family development and the life course: Two perspectives on family change," *Journal of Marriage and the Family* 52 (3)(1990), pp. 571–583; Elder, Glen H., Jr., "Families and lives: Some developments in life-course studies," *Journal of Family History* 12 (1987), pp. 179–199; Hagestad, Gunhild O., "Social perspectives on the life course," in Robert K. Binstock and Linda K. George, eds., *Handbook of Aging and the Social Sciences,* Third Edition, (New York: Academic Press, 1990); Hareven, Tamara K., *Family Time and Industrial Time: The Relationship Between the Family and Work in a New England Industrial Community* (New York: Cambridge University Press, 1982); and Hareven, Tamara K., "Historical changes in the social construction of the life course," *Human Development* 29 (3)(1986), pp. 171–180.

2. See Aschenbrenner, Joyce, 1975. *Lifelines: Black Families in Chicago* (New York: Holt, Rinehart, and Winston, 1975); Di Leonardo, Micaela, "The female world of cards and holidays: Women, families, and the work of kinship." *Signs: Journal of Women in Culture and Society* 12 (1986), pp. 440–453; Hinnant, John, "Ritualization of the life cycle," in C. L. Fry and J. Keith, eds., *New Methods for Old Age Research* (Mass: Bergin and Garvey, 1986); Stack, Carol, *All Our Kin* (New York: Harper Row, 1976).

3. Byng-Hall, John, "The family script: A useful bridge between theory and practice," *Journal of Family Therapy* 7(1985), pp.301–305; Byng-Hall, John, "Scripts and legends in families and family therapy," *Family Process* 27(1988), pp. 167–179; and Steiner, C. M., *Scripts People Live: Transactional Analysis of Life Scripts* (New York: Grove Press, 1976).

4. See Hagestad, Gunhild O., "Dimensions of time and the family," *American Behavioral Scientist* 29(1986), p. 679–694; Reiss, David, *The Family's Construction of Reality* (Cambridge, MA: Harvard University Press 1981); Reiss, David, and Mary Ellen Oliveri, "The family's construction of social reality and its ties to its kin network: and explorations of causal direction," *Journal of Marriage and the Family* 45(1983), pp. 81–91; and Tilly, Charles, "Family history, social history, and social change," *Journal of Family History* 12(1987), pp. 320–329.

5. Watkins, Susan C., "On measuring transitions and turning points," *Historical Methods* 13(3)(1980), pp. 181–186.

6. Byng-Hall, John, "Scripts and legends in families and family therapy," *Family Process* 27(1988), pp. 167–179; and Ferreira, A. J., 1963. "Family myth and homeostasis," *Archives of General Psychiatry* 9(1963), pp. 457–463.

7. Di Leonardo, Micaela, "The female world of cards and holidays."

8. Burton, Linda M., and Robin L. Jarrett, "Studying African-American family structure and process in underclass neighborhoods: Conceptual considerations." Unpublished manuscript. Pennsylvania State University, 1991.

9. Hareven, Tamara K., *Family Time and Industrial Time*

10. Hareven, Tamara K., and Randolph Langenbach, *Amoskeag* (New York: Pantheon, 1978.

11. Plath, David, *Long Engagements* (Stanford, CA: Stanford University Press, 1980).

12. Stack, Carol B., *Call To Home: African Americans Reclaim the Rural South* (New York: Basic Books, forthcoming).

13. Dressel, Paula L., and Ann Clark, "A critical look at family care," *Journal of Marriage and the Family* 52 (3) (1990), pp. 769–782; Gilligan, Carol, *In a Different Voice* (Cambridge, MA: Harvard University Press, 1982); Hagestad, Gunhild O, "The aging society as a context for family life," *Daedalus* 115(1986), pp. 119–139.

14. Plath, David, *Long Engagements*.

15. Scheper-Hughes, Nancy, *Saints, Scholars and Schizophrenics* (Berkeley, CA: University of California Press, 1979).

16. Anspach, Donald F., "Kinship and divorce," *Journal of Marriage and the Family* 38(1976), pp. 323–335; Hagestad, Gunhild O., and Michael S. Smyer, "Dissolving long-term relationships: Patterns of divorcing in middle age," in S. Duck, ed., *Personal Relationships, vol. 4: Dissolving Personal Relationships* (London: Academic Press, 1982), pp. 155–188; and Norton, A. J., and J. E. Moorman, "Current trends in marriage and divorce among American women," *Journal of Marriage and the Family*, (1987), pp. 3–14.

17. Johnson, Colleen L., "Active and latent functions of grandparenting during the divorce process," *The Gerontologist* 28(2), (1988), pp. 185–191.

Chapter 3

SHIFTING THE CENTER: RACE, CLASS, AND FEMINIST THEORIZING ABOUT MOTHERHOOD

Patricia Hill Collins

> I dread to see my children grow, I know not their fate. Where the white boy has every opportunity and protection, mine will have few opportunities and no protection. It does not matter how good or wise my children may be, they are colored.
>
> an anonymous African-American mother in 1904,
> reported in Lerner, 1972 p. 158.

For Native American, African-American, Hispanic, and Asian-American women, motherhood cannot be analyzed in isolation from its context. Motherhood occurs in specific historical situations framed by interlocking structures of race, class, and gender, where the sons and daughters of white mothers have "every opportunity and protection," and the "colored" daughters and sons of racial ethnic mothers "know not their fate." Racial domination and economic exploitation profoundly shape the mothering context, not only for racial ethnic women in the United States, but for all women.[1]

Despite the significance of race and class, feminist theorizing routinely minimizes their importance. In this sense, feminist theorizing about motherhood has not been immune to the decontextualization of Western social thought overall.[2] While many dimensions of motherhood's context are ignored, the exclusion of race and/or class from feminist theorizing generally (Spelman 1988), and from feminist theorizing about motherhood specifically, merit special attention.[3]

Much feminist theorizing about motherhood assumes that male domination in the political economy and the household is the driving force in family life, and that understanding the struggle for individual autonomy in the face of such domination is central to understanding motherhood (Eisenstein 1983).[4] Several guiding principles frame such analyses. First, such theories posit a dichotomous split between the public sphere of economic and political discourse and the private sphere of family and household responsibilities. This juxtaposition of a public, political economy to a private, noneconomic and apolitical, domestic household allows work and family to be seen as separate institutions. Second, reserving the public sphere for men as a "male" domain leaves the private domestic sphere as a "female" domain. Gender roles become tied to the dichotomous constructions of these two basic societal institutions—men work and women take care of families. Third, the public/private dichotomy separating the family/household from the paid labor market shapes sex-segregated gender roles within the private sphere of the family. The archetypal white, middle-class nuclear family divides family life into two oppositional spheres—the "male" sphere of economic providing and the "female" sphere of affective nurturing, mainly mothering. This normative family household ideally consists of a working father who earns enough to allow his spouse and dependent children to withdraw from the paid labor force. Due in large part to their superior earning power, men as workers and fathers exert power over women in the labor market and in families. Finally, the struggle for individual autonomy in the face of a controlling, oppressive, "public" society, or the father as patriarch, comprises the main human enterprise.[5] Successful adult males achieve this autonomy. Women, children, and less successful males, namely those who are working-class or from racial ethnic groups, are seen as dependent persons, as less autonomous, and therefore as fitting objects for elite male domination. Within the nuclear family, this struggle for autonomy takes the form of increasing opposition to the mother, the individual responsible for socializing children by these guiding principles (Chodorow 1978; Flax 1978).

Placing the experiences of women of color in the center of feminist theorizing about motherhood demonstrates how emphasizing the issue of father as patriarch in a decontextualized nuclear family distorts the experiences of women in alternative family structures with quite different political economies. While male domination certainly has been an important theme for racial ethnic women in the United States, gender inequality has long worked in tandem with racial domination and economic exploitation. Since work and family have rarely functioned as dichotomous spheres for women of color, examining racial ethnic women's experiences reveals how these two spheres actually are interwoven (Glenn 1985; Dill 1988; Collins 1990).

For women of color, the subjective experience of mothering/motherhood is inextricably linked to the sociocultural concern of racial ethnic communities—one does not exist without the other. Whether because of the labor exploitation of African-American women under slavery and its ensuing tenant farm system, the political conquest of Native American women during European acquisition of land, or exclusionary immigration policies applied to Asian-Americans and Hispanics, women of color have performed motherwork that challenges social constructions of work and family as separate spheres, of male and female gender roles as similarly dichotomized, and of the search for autonomy as the guiding human quest. "Women's reproductive labor—that is, feeding, clothing, and psychologically supporting the male wage earner and nurturing and socializing the next generation—is seen as work on behalf of the family as a whole, rather than as work benefiting men in particular," observes Asian-American sociologist Evelyn Nakano Glenn (1986, p. 192). The locus of conflict lies outside the household, as women and their families engage in collective effort to create and maintain family life in the face of forces that undermine family integrity. But this "reproductive labor" or "motherwork" goes beyond ensuring the survival of one's own biological children or those of one's family. This type of motherwork recognizes that individual survival, empowerment, and identity require group survival empowerment, and identity.

In describing her relationship with her "Grandmother," Marilou Awiakta, a Native American poet and feminist theorist, captures the essence of motherwork.

Putting my arms around the Grandmother, I lay my head on her shoulder. Through touch we exchange sorrow, despair that anything really changes.

Awiakta senses the power of the Grandmother and of the motherwork that mothers and grandmothers do.

"But from the presence of her arms I also feel the stern, beautiful power that flows from all the Grandmothers, as it flows from our mountains themselves. It says, "Dry your tears. Get up. Do for yourselves or do without. Work for the day to come." (1988, p. 127)

Awiakta's passage places women and motherwork squarely in the center of what are typically seen as disjunctures, the place between human and nature, between private and public, between oppression and liberation. I use the term "motherwork" to soften the existing dichotomies in feminist theorizing about motherhood that posit rigid distinctions between private and public, family and work, the individual and the collective, identity as individual autonomy and identity growing from the collective self-determination of one's group. Racial ethnic women's mothering and work experiences occur at the boundaries demarking these dualities. "Work for the day to come," is motherwork, whether it is on behalf of one's own biological children, or for the children of one's own racial ethnic community, or to preserve the earth for those children who are yet unborn. The space that this motherwork occupies promises to shift our thinking about motherhood itself.

SHIFTING THE CENTER: WOMEN OF COLOR AND MOTHERWORK

What themes might emerge if issues of race and class generally, and understanding of racial ethnic women's motherwork specifically, became central to feminist theorizing about motherhood? Centering feminist theorizing on the concerns of white, middle-class women leads to two problematic assumptions. The first is that a relative degree of economic security exists for mothers and their children. The second is that all women enjoy the racial privilege that allows them to see themselves primarily as individuals in search of personal autonomy, instead of members of racial ethnic groups struggling for power. It is these assumptions that allow feminist theorists to concentrate on themes such as the connections among mothering, aggression, and death, the effects of maternal isolation on mother-child relationships within nuclear family households, maternal sexuality, relationships among family members, all-powerful mothers as conduits for gender oppression, and the possibilities of an idealized motherhood freed from patriarchy (Chodorow and Contratto 1982; Eisenstein 1983).

While these issues merit investigation, centering feminist theorizing about motherhood in the ideas and experiences of African-American, Native American, Hispanic, and Asian-American women might yield markedly different themes (Andersen 1988; Brown 1989). This stance is to be distinguished from one that merely adds racial ethnic women's experiences to preexisting feminist theories, without considering how these experiences challenge those theories (Spelman 1988). Involving much more than simply the consulting of existing social science sources, the placing of ideas and experiences of women of color in the center of analysis requires invoking a different epistemology. We must distinguish between what has been said about subordinated groups in the dominant discourse, and what such groups might say about themselves if given the opportunity. Personal narratives, autobiographical statements, poetry, fiction, and other personalized statements have all been used by women of color to express self-defined standpoints on mothering and motherhood. Such knowledge reflects the authentic standpoint of subordinated groups. Therefore, placing these sources in the center and supplementing them with statistics, historical material, and other knowledge produced to justify the interests of ruling elites should create new themes and angles of vision (Smith 1990).[6]

Specifying the contours of racial ethnic women's motherwork promises to point the way toward richer feminist theorizing about motherhood. Themes of survival, power, and identity form the bedrock and reveal how racial ethnic women in the United States encounter and fashion motherwork. That is to understand the importance of working for the physical survival of children and community, the dialectical nature of power and powerlessness in structuring mothering patterns, and the significance of self-definition in constructing individual and collective racial identity is to grasp the three core themes characterizing the experiences of Native American, African-American, Hispanic and Asian-American women. It is also to suggest how feminist theorizing about motherhood might be shifted if different voices became central in feminist discourse.

MOTHERWORK AND PHYSICAL SURVIVAL

When we are not physically starving we have the luxury to realize psychic and emotional starvation. (Cherrie Moraga 1979, p. 29.)

Physical survival is assumed for children who are white and middle-class. The choice to thus examine their psychic and emotional well-being and that of their mothers appears rational. The children of women of color, many of whom are "physically starving," have no such choices however. Racial ethnic children's lives have long been held in low regard: African-American children face an infant mortality rate twice that for white infants; and approximately one-third of Hispanic children and one-half of African-American children who survive infancy live in poverty. In addition racial ethnic children often live in harsh urban environments where drugs, crime, industrial pollutants, and violence threaten their survival. Children in rural environments often fare no better. Winona LaDuke, for example, reports that Native Americans on reservations often must use contaminated water. And on the Pine Ridge Sioux Reservation in 1979, thirty-eight percent of all pregnancies resulted in miscarriages before the fifth month, or in excessive hemorrhaging. Approximately sixty-five percent of all children born suffered breathing problems caused by underdeveloped lungs and jaundice (1988, p. 63).

Struggles to foster the survival of Native American, Hispanic, Asian-American, and African-American families and communities by ensuring the survival of children comprise a fundamental dimension of racial ethnic women's motherwork. African-American women's fiction contains numerous stories of mothers fighting for the physical survival both of their own biological children and of those of the larger Black community.[7] "Don't care how much death it is in the land, I got to make preparations for my baby to live!" proclaims Mariah Upshur, the African-American heroine of Sara Wright's 1986 novel *This Child's Gonna Live* (p. 143). Like Mariah Upshur, the harsh climates which confront racial ethnic children require that their mothers "make preparations for their babies to live" as a central feature of their motherwork.

Yet, like all deep cultural themes, the theme of motherwork for physical survival contains contradictory elements. On the one hand, racial ethnic women's motherwork for individual and community survival has been essential. Without women's motherwork, communities would not survive, and by definition, women of color themselves would not survive. On the other hand, this work often extracts a high cost for large numbers of women. There is loss of individual autonomy and there is submersion of individual growth for the benefit of the group. While this dimension of motherwork remains essential, the question of women doing more than their fair share of such work for individual and community development merits open debate.

The histories of family-based labor have been shaped by racial ethnic women's motherwork for survival and the types of mothering relationships that ensued. African-American, Asian-American, Native American and Hispanic women have all worked and contributed to family economic well-being (Glenn 1985; Dill 1988). Much of their experiences with motherwork, in fact, stem from the work they performed as children. The commodification of children of color, starting with the enslavement of African children who were legally "owned" as property, to the subsequent treatment of children as units of labor in agricultural work, family businesses, and industry, has been a major theme shaping motherhood for women of color. Beginning in slavery and continuing into the post-World War II period, Black children were put to work at young ages in the fields of Southern agriculture. Sara Brooks began full-time work in the fields at the age of eleven, and remembers, "we never was lazy cause we used to really work. We used to work like men. Oh, fight sometime, fuss sometime, but worked on" (Collins 1990, p. 54).

Black and Hispanic children in contemporary migrant farm families make similar contributions to their family's economy. "I musta been almost eight when I started following the crops," remembers Jessie de la Cruz, a Mexican-American mother with six grown children. "Every winter, up north. I was on the end of the row of prunes, taking care of my younger brother and sister. They would help me fill up the cans and put 'em in a box while the rest of the family was picking the whole row" (de la Cruz 1980, p. 168). Asian-American children spend long hours working in family businesses, child labor practices that have earned Asian Americans the dubious distinction of being "model minorities." More recently, the family-based labor of undocumented racial ethnic immigrants, often mother-child units doing piecework for the garment industry, recalls the sweatshop conditions confronting turn-of-the-century European immigrants.

A certain degree of maternal isolation from members of the dominant group characterizes the preceding mother-child units. For women of color working along with their children, such isolation is more appropriately seen as reflecting a placement in racially and class stratified labor systems than as a result of a patriarchal system. The unit may be isolated, but the work performed by the mother-child unit closely ties the mothering experiences to wider political and economic issues. Children, too, learn to see their work and that of their mother's not as isolated from wider society, but as essential to their family's survival. Moreover, in the case of family agricultural labor or family businesses, women and children work alongside men, often performing the same work. If isolation occurs, the family, not the mother-child unit, is the focus of such isolation.

Children working in close proximity to their mothers receive distinctive types of mothering. Asian-American children working in urban family businesses, for example, report long days filled almost exclusively with work and school. In contrast, the sons and daughters of African-American sharecroppers and migrant farm children of all backgrounds have less access to educational opportunities. "I think the longest time I went to school was two months in one place," remembers Jessie de la Cruz. "I attended, I think, about forty-five schools. When my parents or my brothers didn't find work, we wouldn't attend school because we weren't sure of staying there. So I missed a lot of school (de la Cruz 1980, p. 167–8)." It was only in the 1950s in fact, that Southern school districts stopped the practice of closing segregated Black schools during certain times of the year so that Black children could work.

Work that separated women of color from their children also framed the mothering relationship. Until the 1960s, large numbers of African-American, Hispanic, and Asian-American women worked in domestic service. Even though women worked long hours to ensure their children's physical survival, that same work ironically denied mothers access to their children. Different institutional arrangements emerged in these mothers' respective communities, to resolve the tension between maternal separation due to employment and the needs of dependent children. The extended family structure in African-American communities endured as a flexible institution that mitigated some of the effects of maternal separation. Grandmothers are highly revered in Black communities, often because grandmothers function as primary caretakers of their daughters' and daughter-in-laws' children (Collins 1990). In contrast, exclusionary immigration policies that mitigated against intergenerational family units in the United States led Chinese-American and Japanese-American families to make other arrangements (Dill 1988).

Some mothers are clearly defeated by the demands for incessant labor they must perform to ensure their children's survival. The magnitude of their motherwork overwhelms them. But others, even while appearing to be defeated, manage to pass on the meaning of motherwork for survival to their children. African-American feminist June Jordan remembers her perceptions of her mother's work:

> As a child I noticed the sadness of my mother as she sat alone in the kitchen at night. . . . Her woman's work never won permanent victories of any kind. It never enlarged the universe of her imagination or her power to influence what happened beyond the front door of our house. Her woman's work never tickled her to laugh or shout or dance. (Jordan 1985, p. 105)

But Jordan also sees her mother's work as being essential to individual and community survival.

> She did raise me to respect her way of offering love and to believe that hard work is often the irreducible factor for survival, not something to avoid. Her woman's work produced a reliable home base where I could pursue the privileges of books and music. Her woman's work invented the potential for a completely new kind of work for us, the next generation of Black women: huge, rewarding hard work demanded by the huge, different ambitions that her perfect confidence in us engendered. (Jordan 1985, p. 105)

MOTHERWORK AND POWER

Jessie de la Cruz, a Mexican-American migrant farm worker, experienced firsthand the struggle for empowerment facing racial ethnic women whose daily motherwork centers on issues of survival.

> How can I write down how I felt when I was a little child and my grandmother used to cry with us 'cause she didn't have enough food to give us? Because my brother was going barefooted and he was cryin' because he wasn't used to going without shoes? How can I describe that? I can't describe when my little girl died because I didn't have money for a doctor. And never had any teaching on caring for sick babies. Living out in labor camps. How can I describe that? (Jessie de la Cruz 1980, p. 177)

A dialectical relationship exists between efforts of racial orders to mold the institution of motherhood to serve the interests of elites, in this case, racial elites, and efforts on the part of subordinated groups to retain power over motherhood so that it serves the legitimate needs of their communities (Collins 1990). African-American, Asian-American, Hispanic, and Native American women have long been preoccupied with patterns of maternal power and powerlessness because their mothering experiences have been profoundly affected by this dialectical process. But instead of emphasizing maternal power in dealing with father as patriarch (Chodorow 1978; Rich 1986), or with male dominance in general (Ferguson 1989), women of color are concerned with their power and powerlessness within an array of social institutions that frame their lives.

Racial ethnic women's struggles for maternal empowerment have resolved around three main themes. First is the struggle for control over their own bodies in order to preserve choice over whether to become mothers at all. The ambiguous politics of caring for unplanned children has long shaped African-American women's motherwork. For example, the widespread institutionalized rape of Black women by white men, both during slavery and in the segregated South, created countless biracial children who had to be absorbed into African-American families and communities (Davis 1981). The range of skin colors and hair textures in contemporary African-American communities bears mute testament to the powerlessness of African-American women in controlling this dimension of motherhood.

For many women of color, choosing to become a mother challenges institutional policies that encourage white, middle-class women to reproduce, and discourage and even penalize low-income racial ethnic women from doing so (Davis 1981). Rita Silk-Nauni, an incarcerated Native American woman, writes of the difficulties she encountered in trying to have additional children. She loved her son so much that she only left him to go to work. "I tried having more after him and couldn't," she laments.

> "I went to a specialist and he thought I had been fixed when I had my son. He said I would have to have surgery in order to give birth again. The surgery was so expensive but I thought I could make a way even if I had to work 24 hours a day. Now that I'm here, I know I'll never have that chance." (Brant 1988, p. 94).

Like Silk-Nauni, Puerto Rican and African-American women have long had to struggle with issues of sterilization abuse (Davis 1981). More recent efforts to manipulate the fertility of women dependent on public assistance speaks to the continued salience of this issue.

A second dimension of racial ethnic women's struggles for maternal empowerment concerns the process of keeping the children that are wanted, whether they were planned for or not. For mothers like Jessie de la Cruz whose "little girl died" because she "didn't have money for a doctor," maternal separation from one's children becomes a much more salient issue than maternal isolation with one's children within an allegedly private nuclear family. Physical and/or psychological separation of mothers and children, designed to disempower individuals, forms the basis of a systematic effort to disempower racial ethnic communities.

For both Native American and African-American mothers, situations of conquest introduced this dimension of the struggle for maternal empowerment. In her fictional account of a Native American mother's loss of her children in 1890, Brant explores the pain of maternal separation.

> It has been two days since they came and took the children away. My body is greatly chilled. All our blankets have been used to bring me warmth. The women keep the fire blazing. The men sit. They talk among themselves. We are frightened by this sudden child-stealing. We signed papers, the agent said. This gave them rights to take our babies. It is good for them, the agent said. It will make them civilized. (1988, p. 101).

A legacy of conquest has meant that Native American mothers on "reservations" confront intrusive government institutions such as the Bureau of Indian Affairs in deciding the fate of their children. For example, the long-standing policy of removing Native American children from their homes and housing them in reservation boarding schools can be seen as efforts to disempower Native American mothers. For African-American women, slavery was a situation where owners controlled numerous dimensions of their children's lives. Black children could be sold at will, whipped, or even killed, all without any recourse by their mothers. In such a situation, getting to keep one's children and raise them accordingly fosters empowerment.

A third dimension of racial ethnic women's struggles for empowerment concerns the pervasive efforts by the dominant group to control the children's minds. In her short story, "A Long Memory," Beth Brant juxtaposes the loss felt by a Native American mother in 1890 whose son and daughter had been forcibly removed by white officials, to the loss that she felt in 1978 upon losing her daughter in a custody hearing. "Why do they want our babies?" queries the turn-of-the-century mother. "They want our power. They take our children to remove the inside of them. Our power" (Brant 1988, p. 105). This mother recognizes that the future of the Native American way of life lies in retaining the power to define that worldview through the education of children. By forbidding children to speak their native languages, and in other ways encouraging children to assimilate into Anglo culture, external agencies challenge the power of mothers to raise their children as they see fit.

Schools controlled by the dominant group comprise one important location where this dimension of the struggle for maternal empowerment occurs. In contrast to white, middle-class children, whose educational experiences affirm their mothers' middle-class values, culture, and authority, the educational experiences of African-American, Hispanic, Asian-American and Native American children typically denigrate their mothers' perspective. For example, the struggles over bilingual education in Hispanic communities are about much more than retaining Spanish as a second language. Speaking the language of one's childhood is a way of retaining the entire culture and honoring the mother teaching that culture (Morago 1979; Anzaldua 1987).

Jenny Yamoto describes the stress of continuing to negotiate with schools regarding her Black-Japanese sons.

> I've noticed that depending on which parent, Black mom or Asian dad, goes to school open house, my oldest son's behavior is interpreted as disruptive and irreverent, or assertive and clever. . . . I resent their behavior being defined and even expected on the basis of racial biases their teachers may struggle with or hold. . . . I don't have the time or energy to constantly change and challenge their teacher's and friends' misperceptions. I only go after them when the children really seem to be seriously threatened. (Yamoto 1988, p. 24)

In confronting each of these three dimensions of their struggles for empowerment, racial ethnic women are not powerless in the face of racial and class oppression. Being grounded in a strong, dynamic, indigenous culture can be central in these women's social constructions of motherhood. Depending on their access to traditional culture, they invoke alternative sources of power.[8]

"Equality per se, may have a different meaning for Indian women and Indian people," suggests Kate Shanley. "That difference begins with personal and tribal sovereignty—the right to be legally recognized as people empowered to determine our own destinies" (1988, p. 214). Personal sovereignty involves the struggle to promote the survival of a social structure whose organizational principles represent notions of family and motherhood different from those of the mainstream. "The nuclear family has little relevance to Indian women," observes Shanley. "In fact, in many ways, mainstream feminists now are striving to redefine family and community in a way that Indian women have long known" (p. 214).

African-American mothers can draw upon an Afrocentric tradition where motherhood of varying types, whether bloodmother, othermother, or community othermother, can be invoked as a symbol of power. Many Black women receive respect and recognition within their local communities for innovative and practical approaches not only to mothering their own "blood" children, but also to being othermothers to the children in their extended family networks, and those in the community overall. Black women's involvement in fostering Black community development forms the basis of this community-based power. In local African-American communities, community othermothers can become identified as powerful figures through their work in furthering the community's well-being (Collins 1990).

Despite policies of dominant institutions that place racial ethnic mothers in positions where they appear less powerful to their children, mothers and children empower themselves by understanding each other's position and relying on each other's strengths. In many cases, children, especially daughters, bond with their mothers instead of railing against them as symbols of patriarchal power. Cherrie Moraga describes the impact that her mother had on her. Because she was repeatedly removed from school in order to work, by prevailing standards Moraga's mother would be considered largely illiterate. But she was also a fine storyteller, and found ways to empower herself within dominant institutions. "I would go with my mother to fill out job applications for her, or write checks for her at the supermarket," Moraga recounts.

> We would have the scenario all worked out ahead of time. My mother would sign the check before we'd get to the store. Then, as we'd approach the checkstand, she would say—within earshot of the cashier—"oh, honey, you go 'head and make out the check,' " as if she couldn't be bothered with such an insignificant detail. (1979, p. 28)

Like Cherrie Moraga and her mother, racial ethnic women's motherwork involves collaborating to empower mothers and children within structures that oppress.

MOTHERWORK AND IDENTITY

> Please help me find out who I am. My mother was Indian, but we were taken from her and put in foster homes. They were white and didn't want to tell us about our mother. I have a name and maybe a place of birth. Do you think you can help me? (Brant 1988, p. 9)

Like this excerpt from a letter to the editor, the theme of lost racial ethnic identity and the struggle to maintain a sense of self and community pervade many of the stories, poetry and narratives in Beth Brant's volume, *A Gathering of Spirit*. Carol Lee Sanchez offers another view of the impact of the loss of self. "Radicals look at reservation Indians and get very upset about their poverty conditions," observes Sanchez.

> But poverty to us is not the same thing as poverty is to you. Our poverty is that we can't be who we are. We can't hunt or fish or grow our food because our basic resources and the right to use them in traditional ways are denied us. (Brant 1988, p. 165)

Racial ethnic women's motherwork reflects the tensions inherent in trying to foster a meaningful racial identity in children within a society that denigrates people of color. The racial privilege enjoyed by white, middle-class women makes unnecessary this complicated dimension of the mothering tradition of women of color. While white children can be prepared to fight racial oppression, their survival does not depend on gaining these skills. Their racial identity is validated by their schools, the media, and other social institutions. White children are socialized into their rightful place in systems of racial privilege. Racial ethnic women have no such guarantees for their children; their children must first be taught to survive in systems that oppress them. Moreover, this survival must not come at the expense of self-esteem. Thus, a dialectical relationship exists between systems of racial oppression designed to strip subordinated groups of a sense of personal identity and a sense of collective peoplehood, and the cultures of resistance extant in various racial ethnic groups that resist the oppression. For women of color, motherwork for identity occurs at this critical juncture (Collins 1990).

"Through our mothers, the culture gave us mixed messages," observes Mexican-American poet Gloria Anzaldua. "Which was it to be—strong, or submissive, rebellious or conforming?" (1987, p. 18). Thus women of color's motherwork requires reconciling contradictory needs concerning identity. Preparing children to cope with and survive within systems of racial oppression is extremely difficult because the pressures for children of racial ethnic groups to assimilate are pervasive. In order to compel women of color to participate in their children's assimilation, dominant institutions promulgate ideologies that belittle people of color. Negative controlling images infuse the worlds of male and female children of color (Tajima 1989; Collins 1990; Green 1990). Native American girls are encouraged to see themselves as "Pocahontases" or "squaws"; Asian-American girls as "geisha girls" or "Suzy Wongs"; Hispanic girls as "Madonnas" or "hot-blooded whores"; and African-American girls as "mammies", "matriarchs" and "prostitutes." Girls of all groups are told that their lives cannot be complete without a male partner, and that their educational and career aspirations must always be subordinated to their family obligations.

This push toward assimilation is part of a larger effort to socialize racial ethnic children into their proper, subordinate places in systems of racial and class oppression. Since children of color can never be white, however, assimilation by becoming white is impossible despite the pressures. Thus, a second dimension of the mothering tradition involves equipping children with skills to confront this contradiction and to challenge systems of racial oppression. Girls who become women believing that they are only capable of being maids and prostitutes cannot contribute to racial ethnic women's motherwork.

Mothers make varying choices in negotiating the complicated relationship of preparing children to fit into, yet resist, systems of racial domination. Some mothers remain powerless in the face of external forces that foster their children's assimilation and subsequent alienation from their families and communities. Through fiction, Native American author Beth Brant again explores the grief felt by a mother whose children had been taken away to live among whites. A letter arrives giving news of her missing children.

> This letter is from two strangers with the names Martha and Daniel. They say they are learning civilized ways. Daniel works in the fields, growing food for the school. Martha is being taught to sew aprons. She will be going to live with the schoolmaster's wife. She will be a live-in girl. What is live-in girl? I shake my head. The words sound the same to me. I am afraid of Martha and Daniel. These strangers who know my name. (Brant 1988, pp. 102–103)

Other mothers become unwitting conduits of the dominant ideology. Gloria Anzalduce (1987, p. 16) asks:

> How many time have I heard mothers and mothers-in-law tell their sons to beat their wives for not obeying them, for being *hociconas* (big mouths), for being *callajeras* (going to visit and gossip with neighbors), for expecting their husbands to help with the rearing of children and the housework, for wanting to be something other than housewives?

Some mothers encourage their children to fit in, for reasons of survival. "My mother, nursed in the folds of a town that once christened its black babies Lee, after Robert E., and Jackson, after Stonewall, raised me on a dangerous generation's old belief," remembers African-American author Marita Golden.

> Because of my dark brown complexion, she warned me against wearing browns or yellow and reds . . . and every summer I was admonished not to play in the sun "cause you gonna have to get a light husband anyway, for the sake of your children." (Golden 1983, p. 24)

To Cherrie Moraga's mother,

> On a basic economic level, being Chicana meant being "less." It was through

my mother's desire to protect her children from poverty and illiteracy that we became "anglocized"; the more effectively we could pass in the white world, the better guaranteed our future. (1979, p. 28).

Despite their mothers' good intentions, the costs to children taught to submit to racist and sexist ideologies can be high. Raven, a Native American woman, looks back on her childhood:

I've been raised in white man's world and was forbade more or less to converse with Indian people. As my mother wanted me to be educated and live a good life, free from poverty. I lived a life of loneliness. Today I am desperate to know my people. (Brant 1988, p. 221)

To avoid poverty, Raven's mother did what she thought best, but ultimately, Raven experienced the poverty of not being able to be who she was.

Still other mothers transmit sophisticated skills to their children, enabling them to appear to be submissive while at the same time to be able to challenge inequality. Willi Coleman's mother used a Saturday-night hair-combing ritual to impart a Black women's standpoint to her daughters:

Except for special occasions mama came home from work early on Saturdays. She spent six days a week mopping, waxing and dusting other women's houses and keeping out of reach of other women's husbands. Saturday nights were reserved for "taking care of them girls' " hair and the telling of stories. Some of which included a recitation of what she had endured and how she had triumphed over "folks that were lower than dirt" and "no-good snakes in the grass." She combed, patted, twisted and talked, saying things which would have embarrassed or shamed her at other times. (Coleman 1987, p. 34)

Historian Elsa Barkley Brown captures this delicate balance that racial ethnic mothers negotiate. Brown points out that her mother's behavior demonstrated the "need to teach me to live my life one way and, at the same time, to provide all the tools I would need to live it quite differently" (1989, p. 929).

For women of color, the struggle to maintain an independent racial identity has taken many forms: All reveal varying solutions to the dialectical relationship between institutions that would deny their children their humanity and institutions that would affirm their children's right to exist as self-defined people. Like Willi Coleman's mother, African-American women draw upon a long-standing Afrocentric feminist worldview, emphasizing the importance of self-definition, self-reliance, and the necessity of demanding respect from others (Terborg-Penn 1986; Collins 1990).

Racial ethnic cultures, themselves, do not always help to support women's self-definition. Poet and essayist Gloria Anzaldua, for example, challenges many of the ideas in Hispanic cultures concerning women. "Though I'll defend my race and culture when they are attacked by non-*mexicanos*, ... I abhor some of my culture's ways, how it cripples its women, *como burras,* our strengths used against us" (1987, p. 21). Anzaldua offers a trenchant analysis of the ways in which the Spanish conquest of Native Americans fragmented women's identity and produced three symbolic "mothers." *La Virgen de Guadalupe,* perhaps the single most potent religious, political and cultural image of the Chicano people, represents the virgin mother who cares for and nurtures an oppressed people. *La Chingada (Malinche)* represents the raped mother, all but abandoned. A combination of the other two, *La Llorona* symbolizes the mother who seeks her lost children. "Ambiguity surrounds the symbols of these three 'Our Mothers,' " claims Anzaldua.

> In part, the true identity of all three has been subverted—*Guadalupe,* to make us docile and enduring, *la Chingada,* to make us ashamed of our Indian side, and *la Llorona* to make us a long-suffering people. 1987, p. 31)

For Anzaldua, the Spanish conquest, which brought racism and economic subordination to Indian people, and created a new mixed-race Hispanic people, simultaneously devalued women:

> No, I do not buy all the myths of the tribe into which I was born. I can understand why the more tinged with Anglo blood, the more adamantly my colored and colorless sisters glorify their colored culture's values—to offset the extreme devaluation of it by the white culture. It's a legitimate reaction. But I will not glorify those aspects of my culture which have injured me and which have injured me in the name of protecting me. (Anzaldua 1987, p. 22)

Hispanic mothers face the complicated task of shepherding their children through the racism extant in dominant society, and the reactions to that racism framing cultural beliefs internal to Hispanic communities.

Many Asian American mothers stress conformity and fitting in as a way to challenge the system. "Our parents are painted as hard workers who were socially uncomfortable and had difficulty expressing even the smallest opinion," observes Japanese-American Kesaya Noda, in her autobiographical essay "Growing Up Asian in America" (1989, p. 246). Noda questioned this seeming capitulation on the part of her parents: " 'Why did you go into those camps,' I raged at my parents, frightened by my own inner silence and timidity. 'Why didn't you do anything to resist?' " But Noda later discovers a compelling explanation as to why Asian-Americans are so often portrayed as conformist:

> I had not been able to imagine before what it must have felt like to be an American—to know absolutely that one is an American—and yet to have almost everyone else deny it. Not only deny it, but challenge that identity with machine guns and troops of white American soldiers. In those circumstances it was difficult to say, "I'm a Japanese-American." "American" had to do. (1989, p. 247)

Native American women can draw upon a tradition of motherhood and woman's power inherent in Native American cultures (Allen 1986; Awiakta 1988). In such philosophies, "water, land, and life are basic to the natural order," claims Winona LaDuke.

> All else has been created by the use and misuse of technology. It is only natural that in our respective struggles for survival, the native peoples are waging a way to protect the land, the water, and life, while the consumer culture strives to protect its technological lifeblood. (1988, p. 65)

Marilou Awiakta offers a powerful summary of the symbolic meaning of motherhood in Native American cultures. "I feel the Grandmother's power. She sings of harmony, not dominance," offers Awiakta. "And her song rises from a culture that repeats the wise balance of nature: the gender capable of bearing life is not separated from the power to sustain it" (1988, p. 126). A culture that sees the connectedness between the earth and human survival, and sees motherhood as symbolic of the earth itself, holds motherhood as an institution in high regard.

CONCLUDING REMARKS

Survival, power and identity shape motherhood for all women. But these themes remain muted when the mothering experiences of women of color are marginalized in feminist theorizing. Feminist theorizing about motherhood reflects a lack of attention to the connection between ideas and the contexts in which they emerge. While such decontextualization aims to generate universal "theories" of human behavior, in actuality, it routinely distorts, and omits huge categories of human experience.

Placing racial ethnic women's motherwork in the center of analysis recontextualizes motherhood. While the significance of race and class in shaping the context in which motherhood occurs remains virtually invisible when white, middle-class women's mothering experiences assume prominence, the effects of race and class on motherhood stand out in stark relief when women of color are accorded theoretical primacy. Highlighting racial ethnic mothers' struggles concerning their children's right to exist focuses attention on the importance of survival. Exploring the dialectical nature of racial ethnic women's empowerment in structures of racial domination and economic exploitation demonstrates the need to broaden the definition of maternal power. Emphasizing how the quest for self-definition is mediated by membership in different racial and social class groups reveals how the issues of identity are crucial to all motherwork.

Existing feminist theories of motherhood have emerged in specific intellectual and political contexts. By assuming that social theory will be applicable regardless of social context, feminist scholars fail to realize that they themselves are rooted in specific locations, and that the specific contexts in which they are located provide the thought-models of how they interpret the world. While subsequent theories appear to be universal and objective, they actually are partial perspectives reflecting the white, middle-class context in which their creators live. Large segments of experience, specifically those of women who are not white and middle-class, have been excluded (Spelman 1988).

Feminist theories of motherhood are thus valid as partial perspectives, but cannot be seen as *theories* of motherhood generalizable to all women. The resulting patterns of partiality inherent in existing theories, such as, for example, the emphasis placed on all-powerful mothers as conduits for gender oppression, reflect feminist theorists' positions in structures of power. These theorists are themselves participants in a system of privilege that rewards them for not seeing race and class privilege as being important.

Theorizing about motherhood will not be helped by supplanting one group's theory with that of another; for example, by claiming that women of color's experiences are more valid than those of white, middle-class women. Varying placement in systems of privilege, whether race, class, sexuality, or age, generates divergent experiences with motherhood; therefore, examination of motherhood and mother-as-subject from multiple perspectives should uncover rich textures of difference. Shifting the center to accommodate this diversity promises to recontexualize motherhood and point us toward feminist theorizing that embraces difference as an essential part of commonality.

Notes

1. In this essay, I use the terms "racial ethnic women" and "women of color" interchangeably. Grounded in the experiences of groups who have been the targets of racism, the term "racial ethnic" implies more solidarity with men involved in struggles against

racism. In contrast, the term "women of color" emerges from a feminist background where racial ethnic women committed to feminist struggle aimed to distinguish their history and issues from those of middle-class, white women. Neither term captures the complexity of African-American, Native American, Asian-American and Hispanic women's experiences.

2. Positivist social science exemplifies this type of decontextualization. In order to create scientific descriptions of reality, positivist researchers aim to produce ostensibly objective generalizations. But because researchers have widely differing values, experiences, and emotions, genuine science is thought to be unattainable unless all human characteristics except rationality are eliminated from the research process. By following strict methodological rules, scientists aim to distance themselves from the values, vested interests, and emotions generated by their class, race, sex, or unique situation. By decontextualizing themselves, they allegedly become detached observers and manipulators of nature. Moreover, this researcher decontextualization is paralleled by comparable efforts to remove the objects of study from their contexts (Jaggar 1983).

3. Dominant theories are characterized by this decontextualization. Boyd's (1989) helpful survey of literature on the mother-daughter relationship reveals that while much work has been done on motherhood generally, and on the mother-daughter relationship, very little of it tests feminist theories of motherhood. Boyd lists two prevailing theories, psychoanalytic theory and social learning theory, that she claims form the bulk of feminist theorizing. Both of these approaches minimize the importance of race and class in the context of motherhood. Boyd ignores Marxist-feminist theorizing about motherhood, mainly because very little of this work is concerned with the mother-daughter relationship. But Marxist-feminist analyses of motherhood provide another example of how decontextualization frames feminist theories of motherhood. See, for example, Ann Ferguson's *Blood at the Root: Motherhood, Sexuality, and Male Dominance* (1989), an ambitious attempt to develop a universal theory of motherhood that is linked to the social construction of sexuality and male dominance. Ferguson's work stems from a feminist tradition that explores the relationship between motherhood and sexuality by either bemoaning their putative incompatibility or romanticizing maternal sexuality.

4. Psychoanalytic feminist theorizing about motherhood, such as Nancy Chodorow's groundbreaking work, *The Reproduction of Mothering* (1978), exemplifies how decontextualization of race and/or class can weaken what is otherwise strong feminist theorizing. Although I realize that other feminist approaches to motherhood exist, see Eisenstein's 1983) summary for example, I have chosen to stress psychoanalytic feminist theory because the work of Chodorow and others has been highly influential in framing the predominant themes in feminist discourse.

5. The thesis of the atomized individual that underlies Western psychology is rooted in a much larger Western construct concerning the relation of the individual to the community (Hartsock 1983). Theories of motherhood based on the assumption of the atomized human proceed to use this definition of individual as the unit of analysis, and then construct theory from this base. From this grow assumptions based on the premise that the major process to examine is one between freely choosing rational individuals engaging in bargains (Hartsock 1983).

6. The narrative tradition in the writings of women of color addresses this effort to recover the history of mothers. Works from African-American women's autobiographical tradition, such as Ann Moody's *Coming of Age in Mississippi*, Maya Angelou's *I Know Why the Caged Bird Sings*, Linda Brent's *Narrative in the Life of a Slave Girl*, and Marita Golden's *the Heart of a Woman* contain the authentic voices of Black women centered on experiences of motherhood. Works from African-American women's fiction include Sarah Wright's *This Child's Gonna Live*, Alice Walker's *Meridian*, and Toni Morrison's *Sula* and *Beloved*. Asian-American women's fiction, such as Amy Tan's *The Joy Luck Club* and Maxine Kingston's *Woman Warrior*, and autobiographies such as Jean Wakatsuki Houston's *Farewell to Manzanar* offer a parallel source of authentic voice. Connie Young Yu

(1989) entitles her article on the history of Asian-American women "The World of Our Grandmothers," and proceeds to recreate Asian-American history with her grandmother as a central figure. Cherrie Moraga (1979) writes a letter to her mother as a way of coming to terms with the contradictions in her racial identity as a Chicana. In *Borderlands/La Frontera,* Gloria Anzaldua (1987) weaves autobiography, poetry and philosophy together in her exploration of women and mothering.

7. Notable examples include Lutie Johnson's unsuccessful attempt to rescue her son from the harmful effects of an urban environment in Ann Petry's *The Street*; and Meridian's work on behalf of the children of a small Southern town after she chooses to relinquish her own child, in Alice Walker's *Meridian.*

8. Noticeably absent from feminist theories of motherhood is a comprehensive theory of power and explanation of how power relations shape theories. Firmly rooted in an exchange-based marketplace, with its accompanying assumptions of rational economic decision-making and white, male control of the marketplace, this model of community stresses the rights of individuals, including feminist theorists, to make decisions in their own self-interests, regardless of the impact on larger society. Composed of a collection of unequal individuals who compete for greater shares of money as the medium of exchange, this model of community legitimates relations of domination either by denying they exist or by treating them as inevitable but unimportant (Hartsock, 1983).

REFERENCES

Allen, Paula Gunn. 1986. *The Sacred Hoop: Recovering the Feminine in American Indian Traditions.* Boston: Beacon.

Andersen, Margaret. 1988. "Moving Our Minds: Studying Women of Color and Reconstructing Sociology." *Teaching Sociology* 16 (2), pp. 123–132.

Anzaldua, Gloria. 1987. *Borderlands/La Frontera: The New Mestiza.* San Francisco: Spinsters.

Awiakta, Marilou. 1988. "Amazons in Appalchia." In Beth Brant, ed., *A Gathering of Spirit.* Ithaca, NY: Firebrand, pp. 125–130.

Boyd, Carol J. 1989. "Mothers and Daughters: A Discussion of Theory and Research." *Journal of Marriage and the Family* 51, pp. 291–301.

Brant, Beth, ed. 1988. *A Gathering of Spirit: A Collection by North American Indian Women.* Ithaca, NY: Firebrand.

Brown, Elsa Barkley. 1989. "African-American Women's Quilting: A Framework for Conceptualizing and Teaching African-American Women's History." *Signs* 14 (4), pp. 921–929.

Chodorow, Nancy. 1978. *The Reproduction of Mothering.* Berkeley, CA: University of California Press.

———, and Susan Contratto. 1982. "The Fantasy of the Perfect Mother." In Barrie Thorne and Marilyn Yalom, eds., *Rethinking the Family: Some Feminist Questions.* New York: Longman, pp. 54–75.

Coleman, Willi. 1987. "Closets and Keepsakes." *Sage: A Scholarly Journal on Black Women* 4 (2), pp. 34–35.

Collins, Patricia Hill. 1990. *Black Feminist Thought: Knowledge, Consciousness and the Politics of Empowerment.* New York: Unwin Hyman//Routledge.

de la Cruz, Jessie. 1980. "Interview." In Studs Terkel, ed., *American Dreams: Lost and Found.* New York: Ballantine.

Davis, Angela Y. 1981. *Women, Race, and Class.* New York: Random House.

Dill, Bonnie Thornton. 1988. "Our Mothers' Grief: Racial Ethnic Women and the Maintenance of Families." *Journal of Family History* 13 (4), pp. 415–431.

Eisenstein, Hester. 1983. *Contemporary Feminist Thought.* Boston: G. K. Hall.

Ferguson, Ann. 1989. *Blood at the Root: Motherhood, Sexuality, and Male Dominance.* New York: Unwin Hyman/Routledge.

Flax, Jane. 1978. "The Conflict between Nurturance and Autonomy in Mother-Daughter Relationships and within Feminism." *Feminist Studies* 4 (2), pp. 171–189.

Glenn, Evelyn Nakano. 1985. "Racial Ethnic Women's Labor: The Intersection of Race, Gender and Class Oppression." *Review of Radical Political Economics* 17 (3), pp. 86–108.

———. 1986. *Issei, Nisei, War Bride: Three Generations of Japanese American Women in Domestic Service.* Philadelphia: Temple University Press.

Green, Rayna. 1990. "The Pocahontas Perplex: The Image of Indian Women in American Culture." In Ellen Carol DuBois and Vicki Ruiz, eds., *Unequal Sisters.* New York: Routledge, pp. 15–21.

Hartsock, Nancy. 1983. *Money, Sex and Power.* Boston: Northeastern University Press.

Jordan, June. 1985. *On Call.* Boston: South End Press.

LaDuke, Winona. 1988. "They always come back." In Beth Brant, ed., *A Gathering of Spirit.* Ithaca, NY: Firebrand, pp. 62–67.

Lerner, Gerda. 1972. *Black Women in White America.* New York: Pantheon.

Moraga, Cherrie. 1979. "La Guera." In Cherrie Moraga and Gloria Anzaldua, eds., *This Bridge Called My Back: Writings By Radical Women of Color.* Watertown, MA: Persephone Press, pp. 27–34.

Noda, Kesaya E. 1989. "Growing Up Asian in American." In Asian Women United of California, eds., *Making Waves: An Anthology of Writings By and About Asian American Women.* Boston: Beacon, pp. 243–50.

Rich, Adrienne. 1986 [1976]. *Of Woman Born: Motherhood as Institution and Experience.* New York: W. W. Norton.

Shanley, Kate. 1988. "Thoughts on Indian Feminism." In Beth Brant, ed., *A Gathering of Spirit.* Ithaca, NY: Firebrand, pp. 213–215.

Smith, Dorothy E. 1990. *The Conceptual Practices of Power: A Feminist Sociology of Knowledge.* Boston: Northeastern University Press.

Spelman, Elizabeth V. 1988. *Inessential Woman: Problems of Exculsion in Feminist Thought.* Boston: Beacon Press.

Tajima, Renee E. 1989. "Lotus Blossoms Don't Bleed: Images of Asian Women." In *Asian Women United of California, eds., Making Waves: An Anthology of Writings By and About Asian American Women.* Boston: Beacon, pp. 308–317.

Terborg-Penn, Rosalyn. 1986. "Black Women in Resistance: A Cross-Cultural Perspective." In Gary Y. Okhiro, ed., *In Resistance: Studies in African, Caribbean and Afro-American History.* Amherst: University of Massachusetts Press, pp. 188–209.

Wright, Sarah. 1986. *This Child's Gonna Live.* Old Westbury, NY: Feminist Press.

Yamoto, Jenny. 1988. "Mixed Bloods, Half Breeds, Mongrels, Hybrids . . ." In Jo Whitehorse Cochran, Donna Langston and Carolyn Woodward, eds., *Changing Our Power: An Introduction to Women's Studies.* Dubuque, IO: Kendall/Hunt, pp. 22–24.

Yu, Connie Young. 1989. "The World of Our Grandmothers." In Asian Women United of California, eds., *Making Waves: An Anthology of Writings By and About Asian American Women.* Boston: Beacon, pp. 33–41.

Chapter 4

DIVERTED MOTHERING: REPRESENTATIONS OF CAREGIVERS OF COLOR IN THE AGE OF "MULTICULTURALISM"

Sau-ling C. Wong

INTRODUCTION

A white couple vacation in Jamaica to recuperate from the death of their infant daughter. They come upon a wonderful black maid, who intuitively nurtures them with good food and good counsel. They bring her home to a Baltimore suburb, where she becomes their son's best friend, teaches him Jamaican patois, and helps him survive his parents' breakup. In turn, the boy shares her secret.

In New York's dingy, crowded Chinatown, an aged Chinese acupuncturist/herbalist uses his magic to heal a neurotic white woman disenchanted with her pampered, Upper East Side life. Under the wise tutelage of the Oriental, she recovers her altruistic instincts, renounces her privileges, leaves her greedy, overbearing husband, and goes to India to help Mother Teresa.

In 1940s Atlanta, an old black chauffeur serves a peevish, stubborn Jewish widow with endless patience; over the decades, weathering the racial tensions of the Civil Rights era, they develop a friendship. The white woman's son and daughter-in-law, well-to-do but weary of meeting her emotional and physical demands, eventually put her into a rest home. Now accepted as her "best friend," the chauffeur visits his former employer and spoonfeeds her like a baby.

A loft-dwelling yuppie couple in New York become separated by death when the man is killed in a mugging. An irrepressibly spunky black woman, a smalltime crook reluctantly turned medium, transmits messages of love and warning from the man's ghost, saving his girlfriend from the murderous villains responsible for the young corporate banker's death.

A black maid decides to take part in the Montgomery Bus Boycott of 1955. By doing so, she effects an awakening in her bridge-playing, Junior League white mistress. The white wife, at first motivated by self-interest to give the maid rides, learns to rebel against patriarchal restrictions and joins the Civil Rights struggle in solidarity with her housekeeper.

In Los Angeles, a black towtruck driver saves a stranded white motorist from teenage black thugs; he continues to be the rescuee's confidant and counselor after the midnight encounter. (Meanwhile, other middle-class, middle-aged whites are similarly sent into shock by escalating urban violence.) Nourished by the towtruck driver's friendship, the white man resolves his existential/family crisis. The two families, one black, one white, take a trip to the Grand Canyon together.

In Seattle, a retarded black handyman rescues a white middle-class family from an ax-wielding nanny, a blue-eyed blonde driven psychopathic by her sudden and simultaneous loss of husband, wealth, child (miscarriage), and fertility (hysterectomy). (He has remained loyal even after having been framed by the nanny and wrongfully dismissed from the household.) After the evil nanny dies by impalement on a white picket fence, the black man is allowed to hold the baby from whom he is formerly barred.

A soap opera actress is paralyzed from the waist down in a car accident; lonely and embittered, she returns to her childhood home in Louisiana. After wearing out a series of candidates, she hires a live-in black nurse who is her match in tender-toughness. Initial edginess and antagonism between the two women give way to friendship.

The above situations are all drawn from American films made in the late 1980s and early 1990s—*Clara's Heart* (directed by Robert Mulligan, 1988); *Alice* (directed by Woody Allen, 1991); *Driving Miss Daisy* (directed by Bruce Beresford, 1990); *Ghost* (directed by Jerry Zucker, 1990); *The Long Walk Home* (directed by Richard Pearce, 1991); *Grand Canyon* (directed by Lawrence Kasdan, 1992); *The Hand That Rocks the Cradle* (directed by Curtis Hanson, 1992); and *Passion Fish* (directed by John Sayles, 1993). These films vary greatly in genre and tenor, spanning satire and romance, pop thriller and heavy-handed morality play, zany comedy and delicate character study, with fantasy and magic occasionally thrown in. Some of the stories are set in an earlier historical period while others are contemporary. Yet they share in common the figure of the caregiver of color: a man or woman from a racial minority (mainly African American), meager in worldly possessions and lowly of status but capable of nurturing his or her white patrons, even rescuing them from acute, at times life-threatening, crises. Some of these caregivers are male. Yet their function vis-a-vis their white employers is markedly "maternal," that is, associated with qualities traditionally ascribed to exemplary mothers: understanding, enabling, protective, steadfast, forgiving, free from bitterness even in the face of outright mistreatment by their misguided charges.

Mothering is not only dispersed among both sexes but also concentrated in a racially/ethnically stigmatized group: although white mothers are on view as well, their mothering is often portrayed as inadequate, at least temporarily. Yet the effective mothering is shown as primarily cross-racial/cross-ethnic: what happens in the caregiver's own family—if one exists—is either peripherally mentioned or else overlooked by mainstream reviewers.

How do we read this phenomenon that became noticeable during and immediately following the Reagan-Bush era—this recurrent appearance of the caregiver of color in the American popular imagination? Is it a reflection of socioeconomic realities? Is it an expression of ideological imperatives, and if so, what and whose? Is it a symbolic projection peculiar to our time, or is it a reincarnation of earlier American representations of mothering? How do we contextualize it and interpret it?

In the following essay, I will attempt to answer the above questions through a contextualized analysis of selected recent films featuring "motherly" caregivers of color of both genders. I argue that, in a society undergoing radical demographic and economic changes, the figure of the person of color patiently mothering white folks serves to allay racial anxieties: those who fear the erosion of their dominance and the vengeance of the oppressed can exorcise their dread in displaced forms. (Hence the appearance of the feminized/desexualized black male caregiver, where a biologically female character—an updated black mammy—might at first glance seem more relevant.) Furthermore, by conceding a certain amount of spiritual or even physical dependence on people of color—as helpers, healers, guardians, mediators, educators, or advisors—without ceding actual structural privilege, the care-receiver preserves the illusion of equality and reciprocity with the caregiver. In the process, what might be called *diverted mothering* results: time and energy available for mothering are diverted from those who, by kinship or communal ties, are their more rightful recipients; or else the perpetuation of the caregiver's family is made problematic in other ways. Attention is also diverted from the true nature of this kind of mothering arrangement, especially its hidden power differential.

I argue that the recurrence of diverted mothering in late 1980s–early 1990s filmic representations is homologous with a larger, contemporaneous cultural phenomenon: the increasing domestication of the initially activist concept of multiculturalism, so that the cultural productions of racial/ethnic Others are now appropriated as life-enhancing "enrichment" for whites sensible of their group's decline. Thus people of color collectively become "*ideological caregivers*" for whites, in addition to being their literal caregivers in the childcare, healthcare, nursing home, and housekeeping industries. "Ideological caregiving" is typically depicted in a benign light in mass culture, with emphasis placed on the benefits accruing to the care-receiver, the volitional participation of the caregiver, and the general mutuality of the exchange. This wish-fulfilling picture expediently flattens the complex social and emotional dynamics generated when mothering is performed by those who are stigmatized and disenfranchised, in virtually every other context, by the care-receivers. Yet mainstream reception of the caregiver films indicates an inclination to accept the wish-fulfillment while resisting efforts to reinstate the subordinate's perspective.

It should be noted that in the following analysis, *caregiving* and *mothering,* obviously not synonymous, will be used loosely as overlapping terms. Yet it is not from indulgence in sensationalistic rhetoric that I speak of caregivers of color in contemporary cultural representations, even the male ones, as variations on the figure of the mother. Caregiving— a wide range of activities, paid or unpaid, organized or informal, public or private, "encompassing both instrumental tasks and affective relations" and designed to "sustain life, nurture the weak, and respond to the needs of intimates"[1]—is not a biologically mandated monopoly of women, let alone mothers. On the other hand, whether from some essentialistic predisposition or from patriarchal socialization (or a combination of both), women, especially mothers, have historically been and continue to be primary providers of care in most societies in the world.

This is a connection well recognized by feminist theorists as well as analysts of caregiving. Nancy Chodorow explores it in her *The Reproduction of Mothering.* Sara Ruddick posits the concept of "maternal thinking" to describe the unity of reflection, judgment and emotion required in competent caregiving (Ruddick cited in Abel and Nelson, 5). An ethnographer of the nursing home industry, Timothy Diamond, notes that "mother's wit," or "maternal feelings and skills"—not just "mother wit," which merely "connotes native intelligence irrespective of gender"[2]—is an indispensable element of elderly care; this is true even when the aides' officially acknowledged duties consist of menial, seemingly mechanical, ones like changing bedpans and mopping the floor. Similarly, domestics are hired not just for their skills in performing practical chores (housecleaning, ironing, cooking, etc.) but often also for their ability to provide "motherly" emotional sustenance to members of the employer's family.[3]

By electing not to make a scrupulous distinction between caregiving and mothering when I discuss the figure of the caregiver of color, I aim to draw attention to the depth of gender conditioning in the concept of caregiving, an activity of which both genders are physically capable.[4] Moreover, I wish to stress that, in so far as race or ethnicity in American society can be said to be "always already" gendered as well,[5] representations of how mothering responsibilities are distributed among various groups demarcated by race/ethnicity and gender may correspond to economic realities in oblique or incomplete ways. To a significant degree, the need for ideological defusion and containment informs the translation of material particularities into identifiable topoi in cultural texts.

DIVERTED MOTHERING IN HISTORICAL CONTEXT

Diverted mothering, as a historical, institutional reality, can be traced to at least slavery times, when the care of white plantation owners' children by black women took precedence over care of their own children, who were subject to sale and dispersion as soon as they were old enough to be economically valuable. (As a symbolic construct, the notion of people of color as mothers can be read in early American depictions of the American land as a welcoming Indian princess/mother.[6] After Emancipation, black women were disproportionately concentrated in domestic service. David Katzman notes that a married black domestic typically saw her children once every two weeks, leaving them in the care of the husband or older siblings, while remaining on call around the clock for the employer's children.[7] Representations of diverted mothering are traced in detail in Trudier Harris's *From Mammies to Militants: Domestics in Black American Literature*. In particular, her analysis of Ann Petry's 1946 novel *The Street*, in which Lutie Johnson loses her son Bob to street crime, and Toni Morrison's 1970 novel *The Bluest Eye*, in which Pauline Breedlove rejects her daughter Pecola in favor of the Fishers' "little pink-and-yellow girl," demonstrates how, be it reluctantly or readily, the black mother finds her strengths and skills channeled to serve the white family.[8] A study of domestics in contemporary American society, Judith Rollins's *Between Women: Domestics and Their Employers* (1985), finds a repetition of the pattern of diverted mothering: one black maid, for example, is forbidden by her mistress from taking a phone call from the former's sick son.[9]

In recent decades, as a growing number of caregiving tasks were incorporated into profit-making, bureaucratically managed capitalist enterprises (e.g., nursing in hospitals; elderly care in retirement homes), diverted mothering has been perpetuated by below-subsistence pay, society's lip service to the nobility of caregiving notwithstanding. The situation of a "professional caregiver" calling upon relatives to take care of her children, as she herself takes care of others for minimum wage, is not uncommon. One nursing home attendant comments: "At home it's just me and my husband. If I had children I couldn't afford to work here. I'd have to go on welfare or get an extra job."[10] Family childcare, though allowing a mother to stay home with her young child, creates diverted mothering as well in that the provider's time and energy have to be shared among the paying children, over whom she has limited authority if also limited responsibility; this leads to conflicts in her feelings and her concept of mothering.[11]

Since women predominate in occupations like hospital and private nursing care, daycare, geriatric care, disabled care, and related human services, the above observations apply to both white and racial/ethnic women. However, it is crucial to recognize that women of color (including immigrant women from the Third World) have increasingly become the mainstay of the caregiving industries and thus the chief victims of diverted mothering. For example, Filipino women are heavily employed as hospital nurses.[12] Likewise, in the nursing home industry, which functions as a link in a "world economic labor force," foreign-born women from Haiti, the West Indies, Jamaica, Ghana, Nigeria, Mexico, Puerto Rico, India, South Korea, China, the Philippines, and other parts of the Third World form a veritable "United Nations" of workers, adding to the presence of native-born African-American women.[13] A similar picture emerges for daycare and housekeeping, as the recent controversy over Clinton's aborted nomination of Zoe Baird for attorney general so vividly shows; women of color, including undocumented aliens, are widely recruited into a semi-underground economy to support white middle-class women and their careers.[14] In "day work," a field traditionally dominated by black women, foreign-born female domestics are taking over.[15]

All in all, as Evelyn Nakano Glenn so pointedly observes

> Whereas the wife-mother roles of white working class women were recognized and accorded respect by the larger society, the maternal and reproductive roles of racial ethnic women were ignored in favor of their roles as workers. The lack of consideration for their domestic functions is poignantly revealed in the testimony of black domestics . . . who were expected to leave their children and home cares behind while devoting full time to the care of the white employer's home and children. Similarly, Chinese and

Mexican-American women and children were treated as units of labor, capable of toiling long hours without regard for their need for private life.[16]

While diverted mothering is a documentable social fact of long standing in the United States, its cultural manifestations are more difficult to characterize. Even as clichéd a type as the black mammy—perhaps the originary figure of diverted mothering—is open to permutations, sometimes quietly shaped by fluctuations in the reigning ethos, at other times given subtle shadings by an actor's skills, or else overtly modified by a writer's parodic or revisionist interventions.[17] In the late 1980s–early 1990s American filmic representations of the caregiver of color, direct allusions to recent demographic and economic changes in the caregiving industries, such as those outlined above, are conspicuously absent. In particular, the caregivers of color's increasing participation in (and exploitation by) the capitalist economy is routinely downplayed in favor of informal or incidental employment as well as retainer-like personal service; it is also muted by temporal displacement: relocating the setting to an earlier period in American history (*Driving Miss Daisy; The Long Walk Home*). Most intriguingly, gender displacement obscures the centrality of mothering—the fact that white individuals and families are preserved by people of color physically and spiritually—in the interracial relationships in these films.

Since space limitations preclude a sustained analysis of all the films featuring the caregiver of color, I will use a close reading of *The Hand That Rocks the Cradle* to develop a framework for understanding the dynamics of diverted mothering, meanwhile drawing parallels and contrasts to the others. *The Hand That Rocks the Cradle,* being a piece of unabashedly mass-oriented entertainment, is especially amenable to such an investigation.

THE HAND THAT ROCKS THE CRADLE AND THE MAMMY THAT DOESN'T ROCK THE BOAT

When *The Hand That Rocks the Cradle* appeared in early 1992, reviewers were quick to identify the topical "women's issues" that propel the plot: sexual molestation; fertility, sterility and the biological clock; a middle-class mother's desire to have a career; the scarcity of reliable childcare. Most of their attention is riveted on Peyton, the chillingly beautiful and well-mannered nanny, and her relationship to Claire, the hapless young matron; comparison to anti-feminist *Fatal Attraction* (directed by Adrian Lyne, 1988) is virtually obligatory. A *Time* review refers to Peyton as "the ultimate Other Woman" out to strip her rival of husband, children,

and middle-class comforts.[18] *Newsweek* calls the film "a thriller that can-
nily toys with the fears and guilts of baby-boomer moms"[19]: look what
happens when a modern mother neglects her natural duties by paying
someone else to perform them! Lizzie Francke announces in *Sight and
Sound*: "[The film's] moral is simple: women beware women, and guard
your family with your life."[20] It is true that racial issues are not entirely
ignored. Francke describes the character of the black handyman as a new
Uncle Tom, "the kind of faithful servant that Bill Robinson might have
portrayed in the 1930s."[21] Vincent Canby, in *The New York Times,* ex-
presses disgust at the treatment of Solomon as "a yard slave for the
1990s."[22] Still, race is no more than touched on; it seems taken for granted
by all that Solomon's role is minor and mechanical, unrelated to the main
"women's story" except as narrative convenience to bring on the thrills
and bring out the guilt.

Yet the reincarnation of a hoary American stereotype may not be as
residual and incidental as it may seem. In some ways, it can be argued
that it is the gender story that is peripheral to the racial story in *The
Hand That Rocks the Cradle.* In fact, in so far as race and class disadvantages overlap, there is also a subtextual class story as well. The real
villain who needs to be feared, but is here symbolically disarmed through
the mental retardation and devotion of the handyman, is the underclass
black male on whose back the Bartels's dream life is built.

As Elayne Rapping suggests, *The Hand That Rocks the Cradle* belongs
with films like *Grand Canyon* and *Cape Fear* (directed by Martin Scors-
ese, 1992) to form a subgenre, the "yuppie horror films." These are films
that proclaim: "The 1980s ride is over. The vandals are at the gates, and
they've got a grudge that's been building for a long, long time. It won't
be long before they come for you."

> Peyton—racist, manipulative, greedy, pathological—now that's a woman
> who has lived through the 1980s and been transformed by them. Her ug-
> liness is the ugliness of the Reagan-Bush era with its nasty way of pitting
> us all against each other—especially the poor, women, and minorities—as
> we scramble for the few crumbs left after the lucky top dogs finish their
> gargantuan meal of imported delicacies.[23]

The Hand That Rocks the Cradle, in that unerringly masterful way that
products of mass culture often display, has done such a thorough job of
conflating "the poor, women, and minorities" that only a few months
before Los Angeles erupted in flames in response to the first Rodney King
verdict, the "vandals at the gate" could be left unidentified, or misiden-
tified, by the majority of viewers. Class conflict is softened by making
the villainess an accidentally dispossessed former yuppie with few gen-

eralizable, class-based grievances. As for racial anxieties, they are exorcised by attenuating the impoverished black male into a sweet, docile caregiver. The interplay between the two women, if not a mere red herring, does distract attention from potentially more alarming possibilities.

While sweet, trusting Claire is, on the most obvious level, Good Girl to Peyton's Bad Girl in the gender dichotomy, in other ways Peyton's true double (both as complement and as antithesis) is not Claire but Solomon. Peyton's white skin, blond hair, and middle-class polish contrast with Solomon's black skin, social ineptness, and lack of education, but both are hired caregivers in the service of the biological mother; each spends considerable time with one of the children, from vastly different motives. Both are "atypical" compared to the demographic profile of today's nanny, who is increasingly likely to be a foreign-born woman of color.[24] Such slippage from sociological average is often, though far from always, a sign of ideological recoding at work. The most telling details that betray Solomon's symbolic kinship to Peyton are from the beginning and ending sequences of the film. When he first reports to work, he is mistaken for a prowler. After his identity has been verified, he is eager to hold the new baby, but Claire refuses, lamely citing agency regulations as an excuse. At the end, for risking his life to save the family, he is rewarded with an offer to hold the baby, which he gratefully accepts. Thus despite his gender, Solomon is revealed to be a version of the mammy, whose key function is ensuring the survival and prosperity of the employer's family.

What ideological purpose is fulfilled by the intricate doubling of gender, racial features, and class status in Solomon and Peyton? Toni Morrison, writing of the Clarence Thomas-Anita Hill hearings, remarks:

[B]lack people, as a group, are used to signify the polar opposites of love and repulsion. On the one hand, they signify benevolence, harmless and servile guardianship, and endless love. On the other, they have come to represent insanity, illicit sexuality, and chaos.[25]

When the "black," especially "black male," traits of "insanity, illicit sexuality, and chaos" are attributed to Peyton, Solomon is left with "benevolence, harmless and servile guardianship, and endless love." Thus is the menace of the angry urban black male nullified in fantasy. The sequence that introduces the story, showing a hooded black man peeking at a white family through the kitchen window of a perfect suburban home, articulates a nightmare of white America more profound and terrifying than the speakable one about the deranged nanny—so profound and terrifying, in fact, that it cannot be explored, only alluded to in disguised form. The Bartels, consciously or subconsicously knowing that their affluent lifestyle rests on an exploited multiethnic workforce, assuage their guilt with liberal sentiments and make a feeble gesture toward social responsibility through the hiring of Solomon, a member of the most disenfranchised group. But collective reconciliation would have been impossible; indeed, even a direct admission of the very existence of this group would have been too intolerable. Hence Solomon's potential for aggressiveness must be neutralized through mental retardation, an individual misfortune that provides a rationalization for his general unemployability.

Though Solomon is male, he represents diverted mothering in that the possibility for the reproduction of black families is abolished by his retardation. He is shown with no other social attachments than to the Bartels and no interest whatsoever in the opposite sex. Thus desexualized, no longer a threat to either the white man's power or the white woman's sexual purity, he is allowed to exercise his (now "her"?) mothering talents on the white family.

In short, the operative racial fantasy in *The Hand That Rocks the Cradle* is to see people of color as white people's natural caregivers and to envision both as being engaged in a common social enterprise (building the house and planting the garden). Such a fantasy even pays tribute to the "primitive" by giving Solomon, namesake of the Biblical king, instinctive wisdom to see through the nanny's ruses, a welcome corrective to the over-wrought, over-developed 1980s. As the economic division of labor gives whites a raison d'etre for their privilege (*noblesse oblige*), the spiritual division of labor contributes to a liberal vision of multiculturalism: the diverse faculties and energies of people of color, through a rhetoric of mutual benefit, are appropriated to accomplish a national agenda tuned to the interests of the dominant group. By conveniently conflating the "taking caring of" performed by people of color for pay with emotional "caring about" enjoyed by the employers, this fantasy creates an obfuscated patron-client relationship that imputes complicity in the system to the caregiver while overlooking the existence and consequences of diverted mothering.[26]

The above analysis of displacement and fantasy may strike some as making too much of a minor character whose actions do not even amount to a subplot. Yet it is precisely in the nature of *diversion* that judgments like "major" and "minor" get pronounced without regard for the social positioning of the evaluator; the presumed universality of white interests gives an air of inevitability to the supporting role of "minorities." Certainly even a slick thriller like *The Hand That Rocks the Cradle,* no more than other products of popular culture made possible by complex social organizations, cannot be boiled down to a single simplistic formula. The feminist/anti-feminist concerns in the film are not merely a coverup for the fantasy of harmonious multiculturalism, nor are they any less "real" by being more explicitly advanced. These and other discursive elements co-exist, but the superficially discounted ones are the ones that need to be recuperated, the slippages and absences scanned for "unspeakable" meanings, through an examination of context and reception.

MISS DAISY'S KIN VERSUS HOKE COLBURN'S KIN

The same is true of other films featuring caregivers of color referred to at the beginning of this essay. Highly uneven in conceptualization and execution, none of them can be mechanistically "decoded," especially when the pretensions to serious social commentary in some are not unfounded. The actor's or actress's art can also lend dimensions to a situation that in synopsis sounds corny, even absurd. Yet the constituents of diverted mothering identified through a close reading of *The Hand That Rocks the Cradle* are undeniably present in them, in various intensities and combinations.

The gender displacement so vital to the multifaceted horror of *The Hand That Rocks the Cradle* does not appear in as neat a form (doubles competing for the same object of care) in any of the other films under discussion. Still, the chauffeur in *Driving Miss Daisy* and the towtruck driver in *Grand Canyon,* like Solomon the handyman, are "male mammies" of sorts in spite of their plausibly male occupations. This is especially clear when, at the end of *Driving Miss Daisy,* Hoke Colburn is shown coaxing and spoonfeeding a recalcitrant Miss Daisy as if she were a baby. The male gender of the towtruck drive, Simon, is important in *Grand Canyon* for highlighting the Good Nigger/Bad Nigger distinction: the responsible, employed black man can be counted on to protect the white man by disowning and repelling certain members of his "own kind"—the shiftless, predatory criminals of the decaying inner city. The former must take on "feminine," indeed "maternal," attributes like gentleness, compassion, empathy, and selflessness for this differentiation to take hold.

Broadening the inquiry from gender displacement to feminization, we may note that desexualization takes place in several of the films. Hoke's age not only removes the threat of interracial sexual attraction (Miss Daisy's age could have the same effect too) but reduces him to his job performance. In *Alice,* the advanced age of Dr. Yang, the acupuncturist/herbalist, combines with the historical emasculation of Chinese men to make his intrusion into Alice Tate's personal life (including her sex life) safe. At one point, a distraught Alice visits Dr. Yang's home/office at night and enters a room crowded with sleeping Chinese men. The scene is so devoid of even latent sexual threat that the men's bodies could have been sacks of potatoes. Early on in their occupational history in America, Chinese men were confined to "women's work"—laundry and cooking—for whites; the image of Chinese men in American popular culture has been heavily feminized as well, associated with passivity and weakness. Woody Allen's 1991 version of the Chinese male is, however, not a sidekick or a buffoon. Dr. Yang is a mother figure: he soothes Alice's aches and pains, patiently listens to her problems, gives her license as well as guidance to experiment with her life. In helping a white woman against white patriarchy, he echoes the Chinese man in D. W. Griffith's classic *Broken Blossoms* (1919), a spiritual-minded exile who platonically adores a white girl abused by her brutal father and gets himself killed for attempting to defend her. Both are the white woman's ally (is it from similarity of temperament or of fate?); only Dr. Yang, for reasons that will be discussed later in this essay, is no longer presented as a fellow victim but as a protector. Interestingly, even in *Grand Canyon,* where Simon is delineated as a more rounded character, he has to be partially desexualized by having a blind date—a black woman—arranged by his solicitous white friend, Mack, so that his libidinal needs can be channeled *intra*-racially.

Despite the black characters' romance as well as substantial episodes about the black families (Simon's, his sister's, his girlfriend Jane's), the focus of *Grand Canyon* is on the crisis of continuance in the white nuclear family, in a manner recalling the emphasis on the survival of the children (especially the baby) in *The Hand That Rocks the Cradle.* Claire's (Mack's wife's) miraculous discovery of the foundling in the bushes, and her subsequent adoption—infinitely agonized over, as befits the gravity of the choice—are portrayed as an answer to individual psychological needs (the midlife crisis, the empty nest syndrome). Yet in a larger sense the episode functions to assure that the white family is given a second chance. In the same vein, after being chastened by a mugger's shooting, Mack's friend Davis, a screenwriter, accedes to his girlfriend's near-hysterical yearning to get married and have kids. *Clara's Heart* begins with the death of the Harts' baby, so that the first child's survival and growth become all the more crucial; the parents fail in the end to hold the family together, but David Hart must go on (assisted by Clara, of course). In *Ghost,* the aborted potential of the white yuppie family (through death) is partially redeemed by the ministrations of Oda Mae Brown, the medium.

Elsewhere, even if biological threat is absent, the white family is shown to be in crisis: despite its financial success, genuine connection between members is lacking, so that the emotional labor of people of color has to be called upon. Alice's marriage is on the rocks, with both husband and wife turning to affairs while the children are gotten out from underfoot by maids and chauffeurs. Miss Daisy's only son and daughter-in-law prefer acting out the conventional script of success to spending time with the old lady. In *The Long Walk Home,* Miriam Thompson appears to have an enviable marriage and family; under stress, though, the husband is unmasked as a tyrannical bully. May-Alice in *Passion Fish,* has no family to turn to after her accident; only an abandoned family estate awaits.

In all these films, a diffuse sense of infirmity and loss of control is common. Impaired mobility on the part of white characters, whether from accident (*Passion Fish*), violence (*Grand Canyon*), or old age (*Driving Miss Daisy*), externalizes the perception of beleaguerment and paralysis experienced by the white American population in the late 1980s and early 1990s, when the fact of racial/ethnic diversity no longer brooked denial, the cultural monopoly of whites was fast being eroded, the ravages of Reaganomics, especially in the cities, were coming home to roost, and the United States' reverses in the world economy began to look irreversible.

As the image of the penny in *Ghost* insinuates, there is a critique of Reagan-Bush era materialism and heartlessness implicit in these films' exposé of the middle-class white family's failures. This implicitness was soon to give way to a full-blown appreciation of the magnitude of the decline. In 1993, Clinton notwithstanding, the likes of *Falling Down,* director Joe Schumacher's study of a regular white guy driven to destructive rage; David Gates's *Newsweek* cover story on "white male paranoia"; and anthropologist Katherine S. Newman's study of suburban whites, *Declining Fortunes: The Withering of the American Dream,* are trumpeting the message of doom to the American public.[27] Nevertheless, such a critique tends to be offset in most of the films by a subtle suggestion that since the caregivers of color are, in comparison to their white charges, less cursed with greed, and moreover have intangible advantages to make up for their tangible deprivation, they belong where they are on the economic ladder. Not that the caregivers are innocent of monetary concerns: they cannot be, given their financial dependence. Even the long-suffering Hoke has to have the shrewdness to haggle with Miss Daisy's son for a raise, and Oda Mae Brown makes no bones about her love of money. Yet their desire for money are carefully differentiated from the whites' "rational" acquisitive ambitions—the stuff that powers the nation's economic institutions—which the characters of color are never shown to covet. Instead, for indifferent material returns, they offer their patrons retainer-like personal service beyond the call of duty, sometimes persisting long after their occupational tenure, in defiance of Clara's wry response to David's pledge of eternal friendship: "Always is much longer than you're going to need me."

As Abel and Nelson point out,

In practice, caregiving often cannot be disentangled from personal service. In a society riven by divisions of class, race, and gender, relationships of mutuality are difficult to achieve. In both the domestic domain and the waged labor force, most caregivers are members of subordinate groups, who provide care from compulsion and obligation as well as warmth and concern.[28]

Yet it is precisely "relationships of mutuality" and "warmth and concern" that American audiences are most predisposed to see in the caregiver films, accounting in no small measure for their general popularity. Given the precariousness of blood ties in the white family, where love is often revealed to be predicated on subordination (typically of women), one is led to wonder what grounds there are for believing that the *paid* caregiver's subordination consistently leads to heartfelt affection. Still, this is what reviewers are most inclined to register and commend whenever the film permits character development beyond the stage-machinery use of caregivers of color.

For example, a recurrent theme in reviews of *Driving Miss Daisy* is that the rich and understated acting by Jessica Tandy and Morgan Freeman portrays a touching friendship beyond social barriers, taking the film beyond didacticism. The *Time* review is typical: the film "aspires more to complex observation of human behavior than to simple moralism about it."[29] Many other critics follow a similar emphasis on the reciprocity of affection and common humanity, based on the principal actors' superb skills.[30] *The New Yorker*'s venerable Pauline Kael goes so far as to see "love between blacks and whites" and describes Hoke as using his "wiles" to "court" Miss Daisy and "win [her] acceptance," overlooking the role of economic necessity in the 25-year "courting."[31]

In this heartwarming chorus, a detail is nearly completely overlooked: toward the end of the film, we discover Hoke to have his own family, and an apparently successful one at that: he speaks of a daughter who attended Spelman, and his granddaughter waits for him in the car. This is the same Hoke who is depicted as better family than Miss Daisy's own family. Where, when and how did he raise his family? What, as Helen Vann and Jane Caputi put it in a finely contextualized critique citing the servants' own tales, is the "untold underside" of the story?[32] Diverted mothering is clearer than ever when we realize how, in the reviewers' rush to endorse personal transcendence of social code as a solution to America's racial ills, the caregiver's caregiving for his own kin is left out of the picture.

Of the films cited, only *The Long Walk Home* makes an effort to

reinsert the diverted mothering and bring it to the audience's consciousness. When Odessa Cotter, the black maid, decides to join the bus boycott,
she has to spend much more time and energy to keep her job, walking
nine miles roundtrip in addition to putting in a full day of cooking and
housecleaning. As a result of sheer exhaustion, her own mothering suffers.
Everyone in the family becomes edgy and dispirited despite the presence
of a supportive husband/father. The daughter is assaulted by rampaging
white teenagers, the son gets into trouble for fighting, and the entire family
is thrown into nervous disarray, weakened by both external menace and
internal tension. The film's attempted recuperation of diverted mothering
predictably tries the mainstream media's patience. *Newsweek*'s David
Ansen faults screenwriter John Cork for "[failing] in his attempt to bring
Odessa's family fully to life—they remain, all-too-familiarly idealized,
noble icons."[33] The *New York Times*'s Janet Maslin writes: "The film
insists on stacking its deck to sanctify the Cotter family as fully as possible."[34] Presumably, the *Miss Daisy*-type formula, in which the black
caregiver's family is conveniently expunged, is considered morally more
sophisticated.

Whoopi Goldberg, who plays Odessa, admits in an interview that she
clashed with director Richard Pearce on a few occasions by "insisting
that the film remain a story about the blacks and not veer too far toward
the perspective of the white housewife."[35] Whatever the degree of Goldberg's success, it is clear that a trans-racial message of feminist sisterhood
is much more palatable to a mass audience than a "story about the
blacks." Thus Ansen prefers to praise the screenwriter's recognition of
"the connection between Miriam's servitude to her husband and Odessa's
servitude as a maid."[36] In a pattern familiar from our foregoing analysis
of *The Hand That Rocks the Cradle,* a certain amount of displacement
occurs, this time in age (Odessa is not much older than Miriam), so that
the mothering of the maid is partially veiled. Once again, the illusion of
mutuality is preserved, the white patron's personal betterment kept on
center-stage. In *Passion Fish,* the comparable age of May-Alice and her
black nurse, Chantelle, also accentuates sisterhood at the expense of the
paid caregiving relationship.[37]

IDEOLOGICAL CAREGIVING IN THE AGE OF
"MULTICULTURALISM"

That there is a hidden power differential in these superficially reciprocal
relationships can be more keenly appreciated if we take an exchange
between caregiver and care-receiver and imagine inverting it. For example, when in emotional need, Mack in *Grand Canyon* makes quite

free of Simon's work time; for the price of a breakfast, the towtruck driver shares his life experiences and dispenses therapy. Can we readily visualize this happening in reverse? Can a distraught Simon simply show up in Mack's office with its spectacular view of the Los Angeles skyline and demand a heart-to-heart talk on life's profundities? Can we imagine Miss Daisy spoonfeeding Hoke if the latter is incapacitated before she is? What are the invisible boundaries of these "mutual" friendships of which mainstream reviewers make so much?[38]

Collectively, the employees of color in the films under discussion—portrayed as slimmed-down, mostly smartened-up, often age-matched modern-day mammies, unfazed by exploitation, devoted to their bosses' well-being—are made into "ideological caregivers." Their chief raison-d'etre is to reassure their white patrons that the latter's interests will not be threatened by America's rapid transformation into an ethnically diverse society. The placement of caregivers of color in a position of mothering is, at first glance, a compliment no one should be churlish enough to refuse. Why quarrel with attributions of fuller vitality, deeper empathy, more gratifying interpersonal relationships, level-headedness, courage, instinctive wisdom, selflessness, indifference to the allures of wealth and power—in general, firmer moral fiber than that of middle-class whites made shallow and effete by the good life? Yet upon reflection, one discovers that the superficial concession of white emotional and spiritual dependence does not alter the economic dependence of the caregivers of color. It is the latter that makes the former possible, while the former justifies the continuation of the latter, in an arrangement I have elsewhere called a "psycho-spiritual plantation system."[39] Under this system, whatever spiritual superiority the caregiver actually or allegedly possesses functions mainly as a *resource,* subject to appropriation to salve the insecurities of the master/mistress.

When this concept is broadened beyond thematics to include audience-author relationships, one can see diverted mothering in the overwhelming popularity among white readers, especially white women with feminist sympathies, of mother-daughter stories by women of color writers, such as Maxine Hong Kingston's *The Woman Warrior,* Toni Morrison's *Beloved,* and Amy Tan's *The Joy Luck Club* and *The Kitchen God's Wife.* Based on a presumption of a sisterhood of equals, this appropriative reception is oblivious to the inverse relationship between political power and cultural visibility pointed out by anthropologist Renato Rosaldo.[40] Elements of cultural resistance and survival, of self-preservation and community-building, in these mother-daughter texts are ignored, overpowered by the white reader's penchant for deriving inspiration and little else from the struggles of the marginalized.[41]

Indeed, as George Yúdice notes, the very concept of marginality, from which the insurgent practices known collectively as "multiculturalism" drew their initial strength, has become "inflated to such proportions that it loses its critical edge, its contribution to concrete struggles against oppression and domination."[42] By the late 1980s, "multiculturalism" had become incorporated into liberal pluralism, often envisioned as an "I'm OK, you're OK" conversational sharing between diverse groups whose uneven positioning in the social hierarchy is never acknowledged.[43] What Hazel Carby, in a British context, identifies as a "normative pluralism" based on a merely "assumed consensus of social interests, problems, and solutions" describes equally well the variety of "multiculturalism" that has taken hold in the United States.[44] From the agendas of this tamed version of "multiculturalism" issues of structural, material inequities are noticeably absent.[45] Instead, the "culture" of a minority is typically commodified and promoted for consumption much like ethnic cuisine, or else easy conflations are made between the increased ethnic diversity of the work force (mainly in non-managerial positions) and the greater opportunities for cultural enjoyment by the privileged group through canon expansion.[46] In higher education, models of "mutual enhancement" are being developed to address problems resulting from ethnic diversity, with the express intent of "minimiz[ing] the issue of scarce resources";[47] minority literatures are readily appropriated as "enrichment" for the dominant culture, with little respect for the works' historical and political specificities.[48] In short, equality of exchange and mutuality of benefit—or the impression thereof—have become the defining characteristics of a co-opted "multiculturalism" in the Reagan-Bush era and its aftermath. These are, of course, the very qualities found to be salient in the representations of mothering in the films discussed in this essay. The "multiculturalist's" erasure of the difference between choosing to learn another's culture for enrichment and having to do so for survival—a necessity with which people of color are painfully familiar—likewise parallels the films' tendency to impute *voluntarism* to the caregivers despite the latter's obvious economic dependence. Thus both in the films' thematization of mothering and in their reception by establishment critics and mainstream viewers, the contours of contemporary American "multiculturalism" are replicated and reinforced.

ASIAN IMMIGRANT WOMEN CAREGIVERS' NARRATIVES: SOME COMPLEMENTARY READINGS OF DIVERTED MOTHERING

Our analysis of representations of caregivers of color would not be complete without an account of diverted mothering as represented from the caregiver's perspective. This being a vast topic that must be left to another study, however, its dimensions can only be hinted at here by reference to a handful of Asian immigrant women's narratives. Published in the late 1980s and early 1990s like the films discussed above, these afford interesting points of contrast and comparison, since as a group Asian immigrant women occupy a place in America's material and symbolic economy quite different from that of blacks. Because of the history of Orientalism and the "model minority" myth, Asian women are often seen as "naturally" qualified to provide white society with domestic, sexual and emotional services. Immigrant status further encourages exoticization. That diverted mothering is found in such disparate discursive locations suggests that it is a paradigmatic experience for American people of color in the late 1980s and early 1990s.

Bharati Mukherjee's novel *Jasmine*[49] is about an illegal alien from India who makes her way across a decaying America and undergoes several transformations, among them nanny for a New York couple; commonlaw wife to an Iowa banker; and, upon the man's crippling, his disability nurse supplying exotic Indian dishes and athletic sex. Populated by West Indian nannies in Manhattan, Asian doctors in the American heartland, and Latino dishwashers all over, Jasmine's world fits Newman's description of "our multi-ethnic American culture." Nevertheless, narrated from the point of view of the caregiver who may or may not be in love with her wheelchair bound husband—we are never quite sure since the narrator, like any good survivor, plays it close to her chest—Jasmine's story of cross-cultural encounters has a tone that is far from celebratory. A calculated unreadability pervades the protagonist's choices, mixing grimness and exhilaration, prudence and abandon.

Wanwadee Larsen's *Confessions of a Mail Order Bride: American Life Through Thai Eyes*[50] is an autobiographical account of a Thai "mail order bride" who marries a white man sight unseen as a way of fleeing troubles in her homeland, only to find a pothead upon arrival. Over the years, with "Oriental" (her own description) cunning and patience, she proceeds to wean the family's breadwinner from his addiction and make him grow up. Like Mukherjee's fictional tribute to survival, but much more crudely written, *Confessions* mixes several genres (among them the immigrant success story and "cultural pornography"), showing the ambivalence of a caregiver at once dependent on her husband for economic support and saddled with the responsibility of mothering him from a position of racial subservience. Vietnamese American Le Ly Hayslip Hayslip, in her autobiographical *Child of War, Woman of Peace,*[51] speaks of having to marry older white men out of economic necessity and mother them as they age or suffer emotional breakdowns, a task which cuts into time for her own sons and forces alienation from her Vietnamese friends. Later in her life, practicing healing on American veterans of the Vietnam War while making a living as a restaurant and electronic assembly line worker, Hayslip exemplifies the combination of spiritual superiority and material subordination typical of the "psycho-spiritual plantation system."

The uneasy assemblage of contradictory discourses in these three texts—feminist and Orientalist, resisting and accommodating, cultural nationalist and American patriotic—betrays an effort (only partially successful) to assert agency within the caregiving framework and to arrest and reclaim diverted mothering. Reception to these works, not surprisingly, divides largely along racial/ethnic lines: mainstream critical acclaim for *Jasmine* for its complexity, alongside scorn for a "sellout" from Indian and Indian American readers; adoption of Hayslip's books for an Oliver Stone film countered by the fury of the Vietnamese refugee community. As Viet Thanh Nguyen points out, Hayslip's autobiographies, like much Vietnamese American cultural production, are easily absorbed into the discourse of healing over the Vietnam War, all the more valued because forgiveness from a former "enemy" is such a powerful assuager of guilt.[52] Thus, even with racial/ethnic writers' works less subject to mass cultural tastes than films, and even when racial anxieties associated with the group are weaker than for blacks, "ideological caregiving" and "multiculturalist" appropriative moves are at work.

CONCLUSION

In the last chapter of *Motherhood and Representation: The Mother in Popular Culture and Melodrama,* E. Ann Kaplan tracks and classifies a fascinating array of "motherhood discourses" in the 1980s and 1990s from popular culture, pegging them to social and technological changes such as the consolidation of consumerism, the rise in female employment, and innovations in reproductive technology.[53] My analysis of "diverted mothering" and "ideological caregiving" may be seen as augmenting and modifying a project of this kind, by broadening the concept of mothering to include the assignment of caregiving tasks to men; by affirming the connectedness of gender and race/ethnicity; by demonstrating the importance of considering race/ethnicity in motherhood discourses; and by positing "ideological caregiving" as a phenomenon of renewed relevance to a nation growing in ethnic and cultural diversity.

Notes

My sincerest thanks to Evelyn Nakano Glenn, editor of this volume, who encouraged me to develop this essay from some of the ideas on motherhood expressed in my " 'Sugar Sisterhood': Situating the Amy Tan Phenomenon"; and who referred me to social science sources that strengthened my understanding of caregiving. I also thank Grace Chang for her patient assistance in this project; Janie Har for generously volunteering her time to research reviews of the cited texts; and Helen Jun for helping me complete last-minute tasks. Victor Bascara, Viet Thanh Nguyen, and Christine So all contributed to my analysis of caregiving by sharing their unpublished papers (on *Broken Blossoms, Confessions of a Mail Order Bride,* and Le Ly Hayslip's two autobiographies respectively); their insights did much to confirm my initial "hunches" about the significance of the topic. I am grateful to David Palumbo-Liu for directing me to readings on the state of "multiculturalism" and generously sharing his research and writing on the subject; and to Ed Guerrero for a stimulating conversation on *Gremlins II* several years ago which sharpened my interest in reading popular films.

1. Emily K. Abel and Margaret K. Nelson, eds., *Circles of Care: Work and Identity in Women's Lives* (Albany: State University of New York Press, 1990), pp. 11–22, 4.

2. Timothy Diamond, *Making Gray Gold: Narratives of Nursing Home Care* (Chicago and London: University of Chicago Press, 1992), p. 17.

3. Judith Rollins, *Between Women: Domestics and Their Employers* (Philadelphia: Temple University Press, 1985), pp. 118–122, 214.

4. On this point, see also Janet Finch and Dulcie Groves, eds., *A Labour of Love: Women, Work, and Caring* (Boston: Routledge, 1983); Berenice Fisher and Joan Tronto, "Toward a Feminist Theory of Caring," in Abel and Nelson, *Circles of Care;* and Marjorie L. DeVault, *Feeding the Family: The Social Organization of "Caring" as Gendered Work* (Chicago: University of Chicago Press, 1991).

5. In my "Ethnicizing Gender: An Exploration of Sexuality as Sign in Chinese Immigrant Literature" in Shirley Goek-lin Lim and Amy Ling eds., *Reading the Literatures of Asian America* (Philadelphia: Temple University Press, 1992), p. 111, I have argued that both the "ethnicizing of gender" and the "gendering of ethnicity" take place in American cultural productions. While the former may be prevalent among immigrant writers, for whom gender functions as a natural category to explain their cross-ethnic experiences, the latter is familiar to American "domestic" minorities as a process whereby "white ideology assigns selected gender characteristics to various ethnic Others to create a coherent, depoliticized, and putatively self-explanatory mythic account of American institutions and operations."

6. Werner Sollors, *Beyond Ethnicity: Consent and Descent in American Culture* (New York: Oxford University Press, 1986), p. 77.

7. David Katzman, *Seven Days a Week,* cited in Evelyn Nakano Glenn, "Racial Ethnic Women's Labor: The Intersection of Race, Gender and Class Oppression," *Review of Radical Political Economics* 17 No. 3 (1985), p. 102.

8. Trudier Harris, *From Mammies to Militants: Domestics in Black American Literature* (Philadelphia: Temple University Press, 1982), pp. 59–69, 87–100.

9. Rollins, *Between Women,* pp. 144–145.

10. Diamond, *Making Gray Gold,* pp. 43–45.

11. Margaret K. Nelson, "Mothering Other's Children: The Experiences of Family Day Care Providers," in Abel and Nelson, *Circles of Care,* pp. 210–232.

12. Jeannine Grenier, "Nurses from Manila," *Union* (October–November 1988), p. 26;

Tomoji Ishi, "Politics of Labor Market: Immigrant Nurses in the United States," paper presented at the annual meeting of the American Sociological Association, Atlanta, 1988.

13. Diamond, *Making Gray Gold,* pp. 38–42.

14. Melinda Beck et al., "The Parent Trap: It's Hard to Follow the Law and Easy to Get Good, Illegal Child Care," *Newsweek* February 1, 1993, pp. 34–37.

15. Rollins, *Between Women,* p. 69.

16. In this passage "reproductive labor" refers not to procreation but the Marxist-feminist concept of "the physical and emotional maintenance of current workers and the nurturing and socializing of future workers" (Glenn, "Racial Ethnic Women's Labor," pp. 102, 104). See also Nancy Chodorow, *The Reproduction of Mothering: Psychoanalysis and the Sociology of Gender* (Berkeley: University of California Press, 1978), pp. 35–38; and Evelyn Nakano Glenn, "From Servitude to Service Work: Historical Continuities in the Racial Division of Paid Reproduction Labor," *Signs: Journal of Women in Culture and Society* 18, No. 1 (1992), pp. 1–43.

17. Donald Bogle, *Toms, Coons, Mulattoes, Mammies, and Bucks: An Interpretive History of Blacks in American Films* (New York: The Viking Press, 1973), pp. 9, 45–47, 57–60, 62–68, 82–94; see also Harris, *From Mammies to Militants.*

18. Richard Schickel, "The Ultimate Other Woman," *Time* January 20, 1992, p. 58.

19. David Ansen, "Every Parent's Nightmare: Evil Nanny Wreaks Havoc on Yuppie Household," *Newsweek* January 20, 1992, p. 60.

20. Lizzie Francke, *Sight and Sound* May 1992, p. 51.

21. *Ibid.*

22. Vincent Canby, "Help Wanted: A Nanny, Duplicity and Malice Req'd.," *The New York Times* January 10, 1992, p. C8.

23. Elayne Rapping, "Yuppie Horror Films," *The Progressive* June 1992, pp. 34–35.

24. Beck et al., "The Parent Trap."

25. Toni Morrison, "Introduction: Friday on the Potomoc," in Morrison, ed., *Race-ing Justice, En-gendering Power: Essays on Anita Hill, Clarence Thomas, and the Construction of Social Reality* (New York: Pantheon Books, 1992), p. xv.

26. My distinction between "taking care of" and "caring about" borrows from but does not completely adhere to Fisher and Tronto's thesis that four intertwining components make up caregiving: caring about, taking care of, caregiving, and care-receiving. Their usage of "caring about" is broader than the commonsense one of love or affection; their term refers to a general process of "[selecting] and [attending] to the features of our environment that bear on our survival and well-being" ("Toward a Feminist Theory of Caring," 41).

27. David Gates, "White Male Paranoia," *Newsweek* March 29, 1993, pp. 48–53; Katherine S. Newman, *Declining Fortunes: The Withering of the American Dream* (New York: Basic Books, 1993).

28. Abel and Nelson, *Circles of Care,* p. 7.

29. Schickel, "The Ultimate Other Woman."

30. E.g., Richard A. Blake, "Relationships," *America* February 10, 1990, p. 127; John Simon, "Minority Reports," *National Review* February 19, 1990, p. 58; and James M. Wall, "Films of Power and Grace in '89," *The Christian Century* January 24, 1990, pp. 67–68.

31. Pauline Kael, *The New Yorker,* December 25, 1989, pp. 74–76.

32. Helene Vann and Jane Coputi, "*Driving Miss Daisy*: A New 'Song of the South,'" *Journal of Popular Film and Television* (Summer 1990), p. 82.

33. David Ansen, "History a la Hollywood: Civil Rights and Wrongs," *Newsweek* January 14, 1991, p. 54.

34. Janet Maslin, "A Personalized View of the Civil Rights Struggle," *The New York Times* December 21, 1990, p. C28. See also Richard Corliss's scornful dismissal of the film in his "Dole List," *Time* December 17, 1990, p. 92.

35. Paul Chutkow, "Remembering Whoopi," *Vogue* January 1991, p. 180.

36. Ansen, "History a la Hollywood," p. 54.

37. David Ansen, "A Southern Soap Sans Suds," *Newsweek* January 11, 1993, p. 52; Ben Brantley, review of *Passion Fish, Elle* March 1993, p. 88; Joan Juliet Buck, "Funy Folk," *Vogue* February 1993, pp. 91, 94, 96; and Richard Corliss, "Dole List," *Time* December 17, 1990, p. 92.

38. The assumed unidirectional nature of caregiving is also made clear when one reads these realistic films against *Gremlins II* (Joe Dante, 1990), a contemporaneous science fiction horror film allegorizing the dangers of immigration and ethnic empowerment gone awry. In *Gremlins II*, the white protagonist acquires a cute, harmless-looking furry creature from a Chinatown shop (read: Third World intruder) and is warned against feeding it or giving it water after certain hours. When he takes pity on the creature and plays "caregiver," however, the creature multiplies uncontrollably; murderous gremlins take over the entire city, imitate human dress and cultural practices, and hold a press conference asking for recognition of their "ethnic group."

39. This is a phrase I first used in my paper " 'Sugar Sisterhood': Situating the Amy Tan Phenomenon," presented at the "After Orientalism: East Asia in Global Cultural Criticism" conference, University of California, Berkeley, April 1992.

40. Renato Rosaldo, *Culture and Truth: The Remaking of Social Analysis* (Boston: Beacon Press, 1989), p. 202.

41. This idea has been developed in greater detail in my " 'Sugar Sisterhood.' "

42. George Yúdice, "Marginality and the Ethics of Survival," in Andrew Ross (for the Social Text collective), ed., *Universal Abandon? The Politics of Postmodernism* (Minneapolis: University of Minnesota Press, 1989), pp. 214–215.

43. Yúdice, ibid., p. 215.

44. Hazel Carby, "Multi-Culture," *Screen Education* 34 (1980), p. 64. The fact that even a neoconservative like Nathan Glazer can claim to be a champion of multiculturalism is an indication of how innocuous the terms of contention have become: see his "In Defense of Multiculturalism," The *New Republic* (September 2, 1991), pp. 18–22.

45. George Yúdice, "We Are *Not* The World," *Social Text* 31/32 (1992), p. 205.

46. Katherine Newman, "MELUS Invented: The Rest Is History," *MELUS* 16.4 (Winter 1989–1990), pp. 99–113; see especially her roll-call of multiethnic attendants—dressmaker, gas station attendant, dentist, etc. (p. 108)—which has strong overtones of personal service.

47. See, for example, Institute for the Study of Social Change, *The Diversity Project: Final Report* (Berkeley: University of California, Berkeley, 1991), p. 53.

48. E. San Juan, Jr., "The Cult of Ethnicity and the Fetish of Pluralism: A Counterhegemonic Critique," *Cultural Critique* (Spring 1991), pp. 215–229.

49. Bharati Mukherjee, *Jasmine* (New York: Grove Weidenfeld, 1989).

50. Wanwadee Larsen, *Confessions of a Mail Order Bride: American Life Through Thai Eyes* (New York: Harper Paperbacks, 1989).

51. Le Ly Hayslip (with James Hayslip), *Child of War, Woman of Peace* (New York: Doubleday, 1993). Her first autobiography is *When Heaven and Earth Changed Places* (New York: Plume, 1989), which is mostly about her life in Vietnam.

52. Private communication.

53. E. Ann Kaplan, *Motherhood and Representation: The Mother in Popular Culture and Melodrama* (London and New York: Routledge, 1992).

References

Abel, Emily K., and Nelson, Margaret K., eds. *Circles of Care: Work and Identity in Women's Lives.* Albany: State University of New York Press, 1990.

Ansen David. "History a la Hollywood: Civil Rights and Wrongs." Review of *Come See the Paradise* and *The Long Walk Home. Newsweek* January 14, 1991, 54.

——. "Every Parent's Nightmare: Evil Nanny Wreaks Havoc on Yuppie Household." Review of *The Hand That Rocks the Cradle. Newsweek* January 20, 1992, 60.

——. "A Southern Soap Sans Suds." Review of *Passion Fish. Newsweek* January 11, 1993, 52.

Beck, Melinda et al. "The Parent Trap: It's Hard to Follow the Law and Easy to Get Good, Illegal Child Care." *Newsweek* February 1, 1993, 34–37.

Blake, Richard A. "Relationships." Review of *Driving Miss Daisy* and *Enemies: A Love Story. America* February 10, 1990, 127.

Bogle, Donald. *Toms, Coons, Mulattoes, Mammies, and Bucks: An Interpretive History of Blacks in American Films.* New York: The Viking Press, 1973.

Brantley, Ben. Review of *Passion Fish. Elle* March 1993, 88.

Buck, Joan Juliet; "Funy Folk." Review of *Passion Fish* and *Olivier, Olivier. Vogue* February 1993, 91, 94, 96.

Canby, Vincent. "Help Wanted: A Nanny, Duplicity & Malice Req'd." Review of *The Hand That Rocks the Cradle. The New York Times* January 10, 1992, C8.

Carby, Hazel. "Multi-Culture." *Screen Education* 34 (1980): 62–70.

Chodorow, Nancy. *The Reproduction of Mothering: Psychoanalysis and the Sociology of Gender.* Berkeley: University of California Press, 1978.

Chutkow, Paul. "Remaking Whoopi." *Vogue* January 1991, 178–182.

Corliss, Richard. "Dole List." Review of *The Long Walk Home. Time* December 17, 1990, 92.

DeVault, Marjorie L. *Feeding the Family: The Social Organization of "Caring" as Gendered Work.* Chicago: University of Chicago Press, 1991.

Diamond, Timothy. *Making Gray Gold: Narratives of Nursing Home Care.* Chicago and London: University of Chicago Press, 1992.

Finch, Janet, and Groves, Dulcie, eds. *A Labour of Love: Women, Work, and Caring.* Boston: Routledge and Kegan Paul, 1983.

Fisher, Berenice, and Tronto, Joan. "Toward a Feminist Theory of Caring." In Abel and Nelson, 35–62.

Francke, Lizzie. Review of *The Hand That Rocks the Cradle. Sight and Sound* May 1992, 51.

Gates, David. "White Male Paranoia." *Newsweek* March 29, 1993, 48–53.

Glazer, Nathan. "In Defense of Multiculturalism." *The New Republic* September 2, 1991, 18–22.

Glenn, Evelyn Nakano. "Racial Ethnic Women's Labor: The Intersection of Race, Gender and Class Oppression." *Review of Radical Political Economics.* 17.3 (1985): 86–108.

——. "From Servitude to Service Work: Historical Continuities in the Racial Division of Paid Reproductive Labor." *Signs: Journal of Women in Culture and Society.* 18.1 (1992): 1–43.

Grenier, Jeannine. "Nurses from Manila." *Union* October–November 1988, 26.

Harris, Trudier. *From Mammies to Militants: Domestics in Black American Literature.* Philadelphia: Temple University Press, 1982.

Hayslip, Le Ly. With Jay Wurts. *When Heaven and Earth Changed Places.* New York: Plume, 1989.

————. With James Hayslip. *Child of War, Woman of Peace.* New York: Doubleday, 1993.

Institute for the Study of Social Change. *The Diversity Project: Final Report.* Berkeley: University of California Press, November 1991.

Ishi, Tomoji. "Politics of Labor Market: Immigrant Nurses in the United States." Paper presented at the annual meeting of the American Sociological Association, Atlanta, 1988.

Kael, Pauline. Review of *Driving Miss Daisy. The New Yorker* December 25, 1989, 74–76.

Kaplan, E. Ann. *Motherhood and Representation: The Mother in Popular Culture and Melodrama.* London and New York: Routledge, 1992.

Katzman, David. *Seven Days a Week: Women and Domestic Service in Industrializing America.* New York: Oxford University Press, 1978.

Kingston, Maxine Hong. *The Woman Warrior: Memoirs of a Girlhood among Ghosts.* New York: Knopf, 1976.

Larsen, Wanwadee. *Confessions of a Mail Order Bride: American Life Through Thai Eyes.* New York: Harper Paperbacks, 1989.

Maslin, Janet. "A Personalized View of the Civil Rights Struggle." Review of *The Long Walk Home. The New York Times* December 21, 1990, C28.

Morrison, Toni. *The Bluest Eye.* New York: Holt, Rinehart and Winston, 1970.

————. *Beloved.* New York: Knopf, 1987.

————. "Introduction: Friday on the Potomac." In Morrison, ed., *Race-ing Justice, Engendering Power: Essays on Anita Hill, Clarence Thomas, and the Construction of Social Reality.* New York: Pantheon Books, 1992. vii–xxx.

Mukherjee, Bharati. *Jasmine.* New York: Grove Weidenfeld, 1989.

Nelson, Margaret K. "Mothering Others' Children: The Experiences of Family Day Care Providers." In Abel and Nelson, 210–232.

Newman, Katharine S. *Declining Fortunes: The Withering of the American Dream.* New York: Basic Books, 1993.

Newman, Katharine. "MELUS Invented: The Rest Is History." *MELUS* 16.4 (Winter 1989–1990): 99–113.

Petry, Ann. *The Street.* 1946; rpt. Boston: Beacon Press, 1985.

Rapping, Elayne. "Yuppie Horror Films." *The Progressive* June 1992, 34–35.

Rollins, Judith. *Between Women: Domestics and Their Employers.* Philadelphia: Temple University Press, 1985.

Rosaldo, Renato. *Culture and Truth: The Remaking of Social Analysis.* Boston: Beacon Press, 1989.

San Juan, E., Jr. "The Cult of Ethnicity and the Fetish of Pluralism: A Counterhegemonic Critique." *Cultural Critique* Spring 1991, 215–229.

Schickel, Richard. "The Ultimate Other Woman." Review of *The Hand That Rocks the Cradle. Time* January 20, 1992, 58.

Simon, John. "Minority Reports." *National Review* February 19, 1990, 58.

Sollors, Werner. *Beyond Ethnicity: Consent and Descent in American Culture.* New York: Oxford University Press, 1986.

Tan, Amy. *The Joy Luck Club.* New York: Putnam, 1989.

————. *The Kitchen God's Wife.* New York: Putnam, 1991.

Vann, Helene, and Caputi, Jane. "*Driving Miss Daisy*: A New 'Song of the South.' " *Journal of Popular Film and Television* Summer 1990, 80–82.

Wall, James M. "Films of Power and Grace in '89." Review of *Driving Miss Daisy* and others. *The Christian Century* January 24, 1990, 67–68.

Wong, Sau-ling Cynthia. "Ethnicizing Gender: An Exploration of Sexuality as Sign in Chinese Immigrant Literature." In Shirley Geok-lin Lim and Amy Ling, eds., *Reading the Literatures of Asian America.* Philadelphia: Temple University Press, 1992. 111–129.

————. " 'Sugar Sisterhood': Situating the Amy Tan Phenomenon." Paper presented at the "After Orientalism: East Asia in Global Cultural Criticism" conference, University of California, Berkeley, April 1992.

Yúdice, George. "Marginality and the Ethics of Survival." In Andrew Ross (for the Social Text collective), ed., *Universal Abandon? The Politics of Postmodernism.* Minneapolis: University of Minnesota Press, 1989. 214–236.

————. "We Are *Not* The World." *Social Text* 31/32 (1992): 202–216.

Part II

IDEOLOGY AND THE CONSTRUCTION OF MOTHERHOOD

Chapter 5

AN ANGLE OF SEEING: MOTHERHOOD IN BUCHI EMECHETA'S *JOYS OF MOTHERHOOD* AND ALICE WALKER'S *MERIDIAN*

Barbara Christian

Pathlet . . . leading home, leading out
Return my mother to me.[1]

Stella Ngatho, (b. 1953)
Kenya

momma
teach me how to hold a new life
momma
help me
turn the face of history
to your face.[2]

June Jordan (b. 1936)
Afro-America

Motherhood is a major theme in contemporary women's literature, the "unwritten story" just beginning to be told. The primacy of motherhood for women is a value that societies, whatever their differences, share. Yet, as Adrienne Rich emphasizes in *Of Women Born,* while motherhood is the shared universal experience of woman, the institution of motherhood has been and is under male control, even as the *potential* of women to be mothers conditions their entire lives.[3] Thus the meaning of motherhood has usually been interpreted by societal institutions which, as far as we know, have always been under male authority.

In exploring the theme of motherhood in the Ibo Nigerian writer Buchi Emecheta's novel, *The Joys of Motherhood,* and the African-American writer Alice Walker's novel, *Meridian,* I am interested in the shift in our

angle of seeing, from male perspectives to that of women, and also in
these two writers' common African cultural roots, that is, their people's
experiences of enslavement, racism, sexism, and colonialism as these
experiences affect their respective interpretations of motherhood. An examination of such cultural roots is particularly important, I believe, since
American feminism has itself been concerned with the institution of
motherhood primarily from a Eurocentric perspective. As a result, most
feminist critiques have not taken into account distinctions in the meaning
of motherhood for different peoples, and thus have tended to present a
monolithic view of this institution so vital to our understanding of woman's relationship to her society.[4]

The concept of motherhood is of central importance to the philosophies
of both African and African-American peoples. Critic Andrea Benton
Rushing reminds us of the Yoruba proverb, "Mother is Gold," and says
"portraits of Black women in African poetry seem to radiate from that
hub."[5] Rushing also reminds us that "the prevalent image of Black women
in African-American poetry and literature is that of mother."[6] Recent
criticism on African-American writing reiterates this point, that motherhood is central to such narratives as Harriet Jacobs's *Incidents in the
Life of A Slave Girl,* (1861) as well as to contemporary novels such as
Toni Morrison's *Beloved* (1987).[7]

In Africa, a continent with a multiplicity of social structures, the significance of motherhood is a "universal" value, perhaps because of shared
spiritual beliefs. John Mbiti, an African anthropologist, tells us in his
African Religions and Philosophies that without descendants, an African
spiritual existence is nullified, since the dead of this earthly plane continue
to exist in another dimension—as long as they are remembered and called
upon. A person's immortality depends not only on his progeny, but also
on whether he has descendants who *remember* him.[8] That spiritual belief
is at the core of contemporary novelist Toni Morrison's *Beloved,* a mag-
nificent indication of this belief's persistence in African America.[9]

The African mother is a spiritual anchor; thus she is greatly respected
in African societies. By giving birth to children, African women ensure
their people's continuity, both in the here and in the hereafter. But if the
African woman was "barren," she was an outcast in her society.[10] Thus
the high regard for mothers in African society has both positive and
negative effects for women, circumscribing them even as it honors them.

Yet African women in many traditional societies were not defined only
by their position as mother and wife. Their contributions to the household
were indispensable, and their status was often higher than that of their
European counterparts, whose centrality in production was fast undermined by Europe's Industrial Revolution. Generally speaking, precolon-
ial African women had the "right to own and acquire property that was
separate from that of their husbands."[11] Because women in these societies

were irrevocably joined to their natal family, rather than to their husband's family, they had a certain degree of autonomy.[12] They had their own women's societies, as well, even after the advent of colonialism. African women could call upon their sisters with whom they had been initiated, in organizations like the Nigerian *mikiri,* to act together as a political force. African women, then, were able to participate in leadership positions in the religious and political life of their communities.[13]

However, these women lost many of their traditional rights when European colonialism imposed its cultural gender constraints. In being relegated more and more to the "private sphere," African women, like Nnu Ego in Emecheta's *Joys of Motherhood,* lost access to the economic independence they were entitled to in traditional societies, even as they continued to experience the limitations that had always been a part of their role.[14] For example, although African women had been major actors in the overthrow of colonialism in many capitalist African societies such as Nigeria, they have been virtually excluded from the money economy that grew out of colonialism.[15] Undoubtedly, the intersection of traditional values which both respected mothers yet restricted them, and the colonial system which denied them traditional rights and relegated them to the silence of "privacy" have gravely affected the meaning of motherhood in these African societies.

The mother figure in African-American communities is also greatly respected, because the very lineage of "Blacks" in the United States is determined by the status of the mother. According to the custom of mother-right during the period of American slavery, if a woman was Black, her child was Black, and therefore born into slavery, while if a woman was white, her child was white and therefore free.[16] It is through the slave mothers that the very concept of the African-American came into being.

Because of slavery, African-American motherhood became a battleground for racist and sexist ideology. Slave women were valued not only for themselves, but for their capacity to breed, that is, their ability to produce and nurture children until the children could become producers for the society. At the same time, since slave families were often separated, the role of the mother took on tremendous importance within slave communities. She was often the only one in a position to even attempt to safeguard her children's spiritual as well as physical survival. Because of the history of slave mothers, the idea that mothers should live lives of sacrifice has come to be seen as the norm in many African-American communities, an idea Alice Walker explores in *Meridian.*[17] While the centrality of motherhood to African-American culture probably has its roots in African culture, this root is strengthened by the precarious position in which the African-American community, and therefore mothers and children, are situated in the U.S.

African-American mothers also have had to function within the ethos of prevailing ideas of motherhood in the dominant American society, where women are expected to be "the angel of the home," and not to be involved in the "productive" forces necessary to the society's well-being, except in the sacred realm of the home. While Black women were stereo-typed as the strong mammy figure, white women were characterized as the norm, that is, subordinate in the home.[18] This schema continues to generate tremendous contradictions for African-American mothers, who must, of necessity, be producers both within and without the home, and who are often punished, as in the Moynihan Report's myth of the Black matriarch, for being "too strong," or too concerned with their own class mobility, as in the recent film "Boyz in the Hood," by the African-Amer-ican director John Singleton.[19]

African-American motherhood can thus be seen as contested terrain involving three distinct points of view—the African-American commu-nity's view of motherhood; the white American view of motherhood; and the white American view of Black motherhood. These points of view intersect to produce a distinctly complex ideology of African-American motherhood, which simultaneously sanctifies and denigrates African-American mothers, even as the institution of motherhood is honored in the general society.

The Joys of Motherhood and *Meridian* are novels primarily concerned with the complexity of these ideologies of motherhood. What distin-guishes the works of these particular writers is that they share a profound belief in the value of women, whether they are mothers or not. They also believe that a people's awareness of the value of women's humanity will ultimately and substantively transform their societies.

Through their many novels, both Emecheta and Walker have chal-lenged prevailing views of motherhood held by their respective societies. They have also graphically presented their own view of the experience of motherhood in contrast to the literary tradition that preceded them. Their critiques of their societies are not located solely in the particular books on which I will concentrate. Certainly Emecheta's novel *Second Class Citizen* (1975) is as much an exposé of West African views on motherhood as is *The Joys of Motherhood* (1979). Walker's *The Third Life of Grange Copeland* (1970), as well as her later novel, *The Color Purple* (1982), look carefully at aspects of motherhood in the Southern U.S. that the previous literature had not approached. But *The Joys of Motherhood* and *Meridian* have as a dominant theme an appraisal of the ideology of motherhood within the context of changing forces in Nigeria of the 1930s and 1940s and the Southern U.S. of the 1950s and 1960s, times when these societies were forging strong movements of liberation. At the same time, these authors dramatize the changes that affect their mother-protagonists in the context of history, in the light of a tradition that informs their central characters.

Thus, each author begins her novel in the middle of her character's story, then takes us back in time, before she brings us into the present. We meet Nnu Ego, Emecheta's protagonist, as she hysterically runs through the streets of 1930s Lagos to throw herself into the river. We have no idea why she is so crazed. Gradually we move from an outside view of her, a view that sees her as crazy, to an inside view, where her mad action makes perfect sense within the context of her tradition. Meridian, too, seems crazed when we meet her, as she leads a motley crew of Black children in 1970 up against a tank in a small Southern town, so that they might claim their "right" to see Marilene O'Shay, a mummy of a dead white woman, who was killed by her husband for her adultery, and who now is fraudulently billed by her husband as the Twelfth Wonder of the World. While Walker uses comic slapstick and Emecheta melodrama, both authors initially present their mother-protagonists as outwardly crazy.

Also, the initial scene in each novel not only underscores the irony of their protagonists' situations, but also gives us a sense of their respective societies. As Nnu Ego runs through the streets of Lagos, it is clear that we are in a city and not a village. Yet as we listen to her thoughts, she draws us back to her village, Ibuza, and to the story of her *chi,* her personal god, whom she sees as her tormentor. While Nnu Ego is caught between an unfamiliar urban culture and the clearly established patterns of village life, Meridian is, in the 1970s, enacting a ritual of the early 1960s. Truman, her comrade of that period who observes her crazy action, puts it succinctly when he tells her that "When things are finished it is best to leave."[20] Meridian's response—"And pretend they were never started?"[21]—is the prelude to a journey back in time. Like Emecheta, Walker places her analysis of motherhood in the context of a tradition that must be understood before it can be assessed.

The first chapter of *The Joys of Motherhood* is called "The Mother," as Emecheta immediately signals to her readers that Nnu Ego's attempt at suicide is, in some way, related to that condition. Emecheta reinforces that view by calling her second chapter "The Mother's Mother," as Nnu Ego recalls her history through her mother and her mother's mother. Although it is not immediately obvious that one of Walker's major concerns is motherhood, she too moves backward in time through Meridian's recent past to that of her mother and her mother's mother. In both novels, a portion of a history of a people is seen, not through battles or leaders, but through the history of the mothers. This thematic element is an important one in articulating the ideology of motherhood in both societies and the ways in which these mothers experience it.

The mothers of both protagonists had a lasting effect on their daughters' psyches and on their lives. Central to both novels is how the mother-daughter relationship is critical to the society's continuation of the ideology of motherhood. Ona, Nnu Ego's mother, had been an extraordinary woman in that she refused to marry Nnu Ego's father, Agbadi, although he was a great chief and was passionately in love with her. She is described by Emecheta as "a very beautiful young woman who managed to combine stubbornness with arrogance.[22] She does not marry because her father, who deeply cherishes her, vowed that "his daughter was never to stoop to any man."[23] That is, to any man but him. For she is free to have men, but if she bears a son, he would take her father's name, thereby giving him the son he had never had.

Ona then becomes, in a real way, her own father's replacement for a son, since her womb might "rectify the omission nature had made."[24] In relating Ona's story, Emecheta immediately gives us a lesson about the value of sons for a woman as well as a man. When she describes Ona as haughty and vibrant, we begin to sense that this woman is allowed to behave more like a man than a woman, for she, too, does not want to "stoop to any man." Marriage, not sex, is the condition that demands submission. Yet although she will not marry and does have a sexual life, Ona is beholden to her father, thus maintaining the rule of men in her tradition.

Emecheta weaves proverbs throughout her novel to indicate how her characters' sense of life is rooted in time immemorial. It is a tradition so unquestioned that variations on it are possible for haughty women such as Ona. Yet Ona is also subject to the laws of "nature." Caught between her father and her lover's wishes, she comes to stay with Agbadi when he has been critically wounded in a hunt, and is seduced by him on the very night that his senior wife dies. It is at this woman's funeral that a slave girl, who is destined by tradition to be buried with her mistress, fights back and has to be clubbed into her grave. And it is at this moment that Ona becomes ill. Later, it is discovered that she is pregnant, and when her daughter Nnu Ego is born with a lump on her head, the *dibia* declares, "This child is the slave woman who died with your senior wife, Agunwa."[25] Because Nnu Ego has to pacify her *chi* who was buried in her father's village, her mother Ona finally has to leave her father's house and live with Agbadi, unless she chooses to give up her child. Emecheta adds a further note to the story. Not long after Ona comes to live with Agbadi, she dies in childbirth, making Agbadi pledge that he will allow their daughter "to have a life of her own, a husband if she wants one. Allow her, she tells him, to be a woman."[26]

In this ballad of a tale, Emecheta stresses certain elements essential to the ideology of motherhood in her tradition. Although Ona is allowed to deviate somewhat from tradition, her story is set within the context of a firmly held belief that a women's primary function is that of being a mother, particularly of sons. Ona must be subject, if not to a husband, then to a father, to whom she might give sons. Another element that appears at first to be contradictory is Emecheta's emphasis on Ona's haughtiness, which attracts Agbadi rather than repels him. Gradually we see that it is her independent spirit that spurs him to make her dependent, to conquer her sexually and to make her a mother. It is her motherhood that forces her to give up her independence and finally kills her. The third element is the emphasis Emecheta places on the slave girl, on women as slaves, which she develops in another of her novels, *The Slave Girl* (1977). That both Ona, her mother, and the slave girl, her *chi,* are women who will not submit easily to the authority of tradition does not auger well for Nnu Ego. It is not surprising, then, that she leads a conflicted life, especially around the issue of motherhood.

In contrast to Emecheta's use of proverbs in her tale about Nnu Ego's mother, Walker does not immediately draw us into Meridian's mother's story. Rather she creates a quilt, a joining of diverse pieces into a coherent pattern, that is both a history of African-American mothers in the South, as well as Meridian's personal past. One consistent motif in the pattern is the violence that U.S. society inflicts on its children, especially its Black children.

After we observe Meridian's crazy act at the beginning of the novel, we are reintroduced to her. This time she is a student at a Black women's college in the early 1960s, witnessing one of any number of TV funerals in "a decade marked by death. Violent and inevitable."[27] This short, charged scene is juxtaposed with the college student Meridian's attempt to help "The Wild Child, a young girl who had managed to live without parents, relatives, or friends for all of her thirteen years,"[28] and who somehow becomes pregnant. In contrast to the dead national leaders on TV this child is insignificant. Without a mother, no one feels responsible for her, and she, too, dies violently. Within the pattern of the TV funerals and this child's funeral, Walker stitches the folktale of the Sojourner, the most beautiful magnolia tree on the campus. This story takes us back to Africa and to the violence of U.S. slavery, for the beauty of the tree is attributed to its root, a slave woman's clipped-out tongue that is buried under it.

Louvenia is symbolic of Meridian's original maternal ancestors, for she comes from West Africa and was brought to America a slave. Her West African family's "sole responsibility was the weaving of intricate tales with which to entrap people who hoped to get away with murder."[29] But in America, this gift of storytelling and justice-giving results in the loss of her tongue. In burying it, she preserves her history, for she knows that "Without one's tongue in one's mouth or in a spot of one's own choosing, the singer in one's soul was lost forever, to grunt and snort through eternity like a pig."[30] But even this story of one of our mothers, a history Louvenia literally takes great pains to preserve, is violated. In that decade of death, protesting students at Meridian's campus cut down the Sojourner after the funeral procession of The Wild Child is refused admittance to the school chapel. Only after Walker has demonstrated that it is sometimes Black women who deny our own maternal history (often unintentionally) does she introduce Meridian Hill's mother. Unlike Ona's people, this society takes care neither of its children nor its history.

Mrs. Hill's story is both similar to and different from Ona's. There is, indeed, a clearly established tradition in the U.S that prescribes marriage and motherhood as the primary functions of women. But while the Ibuza have clearly *articulated* precepts, American society is both rigid and indirect in its prescriptions. American women, even African-American women, appear to have choice, when they may not.

Meridian's "mother was not a woman who should have had children."[31] Unlike Ona, she "had known the freedom of thinking out the possibilities of her life."[32] But after tasting her independence as a schoolteacher, she wanted "more of life to happen to her."[33] Unlike Ona, who could, within West African tradition, experience passion and love without marriage, Mrs. Hill began to believe that she was missing something in life, some "secret mysterious life,"[33] which mothers were experiencing. Thus she marries Meridian's father and becomes pregnant, believing that this will add something to her personal life. "She could never forgive her community, her family, the whole world, for not warning her against children,"[35] and for not at least allowing her "to be resentful that she was caught."[36] For this woman, motherhood meant "becoming distracted from herself."[37] Unlike Ona, she does not physically die from motherhood, but she passes onto her daughter that sense of guilt for having "shattered her emerging self."[38] Appropriately, the chapter in which Meridian remembers her mother's experience of motherhood and her own experience of being a daughter is called "Have You Stolen Anything?" It is no wonder, then, that Meridian, like Nnu Ego, has deep conflicts around the issue of motherhood.

Although Meridian's mother has not been given information about the restrictions of motherhood, both she and her daughter are told about its glory. Thus, Meridian's conflict is further exacerbated by her knowledge of her maternal ancestors—mothers who were slaves and who were often denied their children; mothers who did anything and everything to keep their children. Like Nnu Ego, who is tormented by her *chi,* a slave girl forced to die. Meridian is tormented by the memory of those slave mothers who had to starve themselves to death to feed their children. She feels that these women "had persisted in bringing them all (the children, the husband, the family, the race) to a point far beyond where she, in her mother's place, her grandmother's place, her great-grandmother's place would have stopped."[39]

In her recounting of Meridian's maternal history, Walker emphasizes certain elements characteristic of the African-American ideology of motherhood. Like the Ibuza society, motherhood is the prescribed role for women in American society, but this prescription is not so much ritualized as it is enforced by the limited options available to women. Little is known by young women about what motherhood will really mean for them, the most important omission being that they, not the society, will be totally responsible for their children. Further, because of the history of slave mothers, such sanctification surrounds African-American motherhood that the idea that mothers should live lives of sacrifice has come to be seen as the norm. Another element that Walker stresses is significantly different from Emecheta's emphasis. For in America, racism results in violence inflicted upon Black children in society, while in Ibuza children are beloved. Both authors, however, show how the women in their respective societies are valued only in relation to the men in their lives, and finally because of the children they bear, and how this value demands a giving up of their independence, of their personal life.

In both novels, the daughters are left motherless; one, because her mother dies, the other because her mother is psychologically incapable of mothering her. The stories of the protagonists' mothers, interestingly enough, demonstrate not only their lasting effect on their daughters, but also their inability to mother their daughters. They embody Adrienne Rich's assertion that "the loss of the daughter to the mother, the mother to the daughter is the essential female tragedy."[40] Especially poignant in *Joys of Motherhood* and *Meridian* is the way in which Nnu Ego and Meridian characterize their mothers' histories as processes that they cannot or will not repeat. Yet, because these motherless daughters will become mothers, they have few clues as to how to positively change those aspects of that history that are unacceptable to them. In both novels, the mothers' daughters are left with fathers who give them the love they need. As a result, they come to identify more with their fathers than their mothers.

After her initial "crazy" appearance in the novel, Nnu Ego is reintroduced to us—this time as an adolescent girl lighting her father's pipe and listening to his friend's traditional greeting: "My daughters, you all will grow to rock your children's children."[41] Even her name symbolizes her relationship with her father, for she is called *Nnu Ego* because she is priceless to her father, even more than twenty bags of cowries. He is so devoted to her that, like Ona's father, he is reluctant to give her to another man and must be nudged by his friends to do so. But although her father gives her in marriage to another man, Nnu Ego does not conceive a child. She is told that "the slave woman who was her *chi* would not give her a child because she has been dedicated to a river goddess before Agbadi took her away in slavery."[42] Finally, Nnu Ego's husband takes a second wife, who conceives immediately. Shamed by her barrenness, Nnu Ego becomes ill and is finally returned to her father's house. In trying to appease her *chi,* Agbadi even "stopped dealing in slaves."[43] As Nnu Ego is recovering in her father's house, she reminds him of her mother, Ona.

> In Nnu Ego were combined some of Ona's characteristics and some of his. She was more polite, less abusive and aggressive than Ona, and unlike her had a singleness of purpose, wanting one thing at a time and wanting it badly. Whereas few men could have coped with, let alone controlled Ona, this was not the case with Nnu Ego.[44]

And in describing Agbadi's reaction to his daughter's plight, Emecheta adds:

> Agbadi was no different from many men. He himself might take wives and then neglect them for years, apart from seeing that they each received their one yam a day; he could bring his mistress to sleep with him right in his courtyard while his wives pined and bit their nails for a word from him. But when it came to his own daughter, she must have a man who would cherish her.[45]

Agbadi's effect on his cherished daughter is to render her a suitable wife, submissive and delightful, and because she does not experience the ordinary domestic relationship of her father to her mother, she is not aware of what mettle a wife or mistress must have in order to be cherished. Unlike Ona, who did not wish to stoop to any man, Nnu Ego lights her father's pipe. While he cherishes the daughter whose life he can determine, he neglects his wives, unless, like Ona, they resist his "natural authority." Without the arrogant Ona to guide her, at least by opposing through her haughtiness the traditions of Ibuza, Nnu Ego does not see the contradictions in her position. Thus, when her father arranges another marriage for her, her response is "Maybe the next time I come back, I shall come with a string of children,"[46] as she accepts whole-heartedly the traditions of her society. Her former husband's response to their separation summarizes the difference between Ona's and Agbadi's untraditional relationship and Nnu Ego's and his. After her bride price is returned, he consoled himself, "Let her go, she is as barren as a desert."[47]

In repeatedly reminding us of Nnu Ego's *chi,* Emecheta made a further comment on societal contradictions in Ibuza. This slave girl's fate is tragic because Agbadi's senior wife falls suddenly ill and dies. The chief's wife dies, it is said, because she hears her husband making love to Ona in their courtyard. Nnu Ego's existence, then, is due to a series of traditionally correct acts that are unjust. In the novel, her *chi's* revenge represents the tangle of human emotions—contradictions in the society around being a mother, a wife, and a slave—states of mind that are intertwined in Emecheta's narrative.

When Nnu Ego meets her new husband in the chapter "The First Shocks of Motherhood," she naturally compares him to her father. Her assessment of Nnaife is not only a personal one, it is based on her people's concept of manhood. But Nnaife does not live in the village; as a black man in Lagos, he can only be a houseboy, "a womanmade man,"[48] in contrast to the proud men of Ibuza who are farmers and hunters. In describing Nnu Ego's reaction to her womanlike husband, Emecheta is not only demonstrating the difference between the father-daughter and the husband-wife relationship, she is also commenting on the shift from traditional rural life to urban life, where racism pervades the entire social fabric. All the wives in Lagos see that their husbands accept their status, seeing only the "shining white man's money."[49]

But while Nnu Ego must adjust to these new mores, she is still expected to abide by the traditional prescription that she is an incomplete woman unless she is a mother. While disgusted by her new husband, she consoles herself by hoping that she may become pregnant. Emecheta emphasizes how powerful is this balm by inserting in the narrative Nnu Ego's dream that her *chi* hands her a baby boy by the banks of the stream in Ibuza. Thus Nnu Ego, although she may live in the city, is still compelled by the traditional norms of her village. When she becomes angry with Nnaife because he is not like her father, he reminds her "Remember, though, without me, you could not be carrying that child."[50] Although her father had helped to give her life, it is her husband who allows her to give life. Thus Agbadi, in spite of all his love and concern for his daughter, cannot alter the path of womanhood that the society expects of her, nor can he guide her through its many pitfalls.

Meridian, too, has a loving relationship with her father, who, unlike her mother, has a gentle temperament. Placed next to "Have You Stolen Anything," the chapter "Indians and Ecstasy" focuses on Meridian's relationship with her father, thus providing some comparison between this woman's responses to her parents. Mr. Hill is introduced to us as a man who is tenderly concerned with Indians, the original inhabitants of this continent. He gives the land he "holds," an Indian burial ground called Sacred Serpent, to an Indian as an attempt to right some of the wrongs of history and as an admission that "we were part of it."[51] Meridian's mother's objection to his "foolishness" is contrasted to his humaneness, his ability to mourn the injustices of the past.

Meridian describes her father as "a wanderer, a mourner, a man who could *cry* over the terrible deeds committed against others."[52] But even in this section, devoted to him, Walker emphasizes Meridian's maternal history, for it is Feather Mae, Mr. Hill's grandmother, on whom the chapter concentrates. Through her father, Meridian learns of this woman who refused to eat food "planted over other folks' bones,"[53] who "renounced all religion that was not based on the experience of physical ecstasy,"[54] who "loved walking nude about her yard,"[55] and who "worshipped only the sun."[56] Like their maternal ancestor, Meridian and her father experience physical ecstasy at the Sacred Serpent's coiled tail. This experience is their "tangible connection to the past."[57] Feather Mae is a womanly model, other than her mother, who is accessible to the developing Meridian.

Other than this intense scene, however, Meridian's father barely seems to touch her life. He scarcely appears again in the novel. And even in this instance, he is unable to effect any change, for the government moves the Indian off the land and turns it into an amusement park. Despite their experience at Sacred Serpent, he is not able to alter Meridian's movement into womanhood, so that she might resist the limited societal patterns prescribed for women. Thus "English Walnuts," the chapter that follows, "Indians and Ecstasy," which is about Meridian's initiation into sexual relationships with men, is also a comment on her relationship with her father.

Meridian always has to have a boyfriend, because "mainly it saved her from the strain of having to respond to other boys or even noting the whole category of men. This was worth a great deal, because she was afraid of men."[58] In contrast to the physical ecstasy she experienced with her father, sex for her is "not pleasure, but a sanctuary"[59] from the social behavior expected of an unattached woman. Unlike her father, Eddie, the man she marries, has little depth; like her father, he treats her with "gentleness and respect." When their marriage has fallen apart, Meridian describes Eddie as someone who "would always be a boy. Not that she knew what a man should be; she did not know."[60] She sees all of her male peers as boys who would never grow up, who would always be "fetching and carrying and courteously awaiting orders from someone above."[61] Just as racism affects the black men of Lagos, so that they do the work of slaves, so it affects the young men of Meridian's generation. Both Nnu Ego and Meridian react to their condition in the same way, perceiving their mates as less then men, not only because of the work they do, but because the attitude they exhibit is one of acceptance without protest.

The men Meridian comes to know do not have her father's depth, nor even his capacity to "mourn" the injustices of the society. The sexual relations she experiences with them grow out of the sordid character her society attributes to sex, and are essentially different from the sacred experience she had with her father in Sacred Serpent, when "the body seemed to drop away and only the spirit lived, set free in the world."[62] Only with Truman, in the early days of the civil rights movement, does Meridian come close to this experience, for she felt "they were absolutely together,"[63] "that they were at a time and place in History that forced the trivial to fall away."[63] But even her experience of unity with Truman, a man she describes as "unlike any other black man she knew, a man who fought against obstacles, a man who could become anything,"[65] is changed when they become sexually involved. Although she experiences physical sensation with him, their sexual relationship is a coming apart, rather than a coming together, as she is reduced, even in her own mind, to a physical object. Although their relationship, as well as her relationship with her husband Eddie, results in the conception of a child, Meridian does not experience physical ecstasy nor union with them as she had with her father. Having experienced that knowledge, she, like her maternal ancestor Feather Mae, understands that freedom and union are simultaneously possible. Thus, it is through her father, ineffectual though he might be, that the seeds for her pilgrimage toward wholeness are sown.

Like Nnu Ego's father, Meridian's father gives her love and tenderness—even more, the possibility of vision. Like Agbadi, Mr. Hill cannot guide her through the precarious path of womanhood. It is from their mothers that these young women must receive that knowledge, otherwise they must chart their own paths, stumbling over the same ruts that might have hindered their mothers, possibly never being able to rise from the fall, nor understand where they are. Both Emecheta and Walker infer through the narrative and structure of their novels that the knowledge their young mothers need has been denied them because prevailing thought about motherhood is couched either in mystical language or in terms of endurement.

Meridian's and Nnu Ego's first experiences of motherhood are both similar and different, in much the same ways that their cultures are similar and different. In contrast to Nnu Ego, who marries in order to have children so that "her old age would be happy, that when she died, there would be someone left behind to refer to her as "mother,"[66] the teenage Meridian marries because she gets pregnant. Without marriage, mothers are socially unacceptable in U.S. society. Sex for Meridian is a sanctuary from social pressure, which unfortunately results in pregnancy; sex for Nnu Ego is a sanctuary, because it leads to pregnancy. For neither woman is sex pleasure or self-fulfilling, nor does it bring them closer to their husbands. After Nnu Ego becomes pregnant she and her husband started "growing slightly apart. Each was in a different world."[67] Eddie complains that after their marriage, Meridian's legs are "like somebody starched them shut."[68] Her disinterest in sex leads him to find a woman who loved sex, even as his wife thinks of motherhood as a "ball and chain."[69] For Nnu Ego's society, the purpose of sex is children, while in Meridian's world, pleasure is the expectation. But she is unable to experience that pleasure, since it also is characterized for a woman as "giving in." Thus, constraints about sex in both societies affect these two women's experience of it. Sex's primary effect, wanted or not, is a child.

The initial experience of mothering has a different value for these two women. For Nnu Ego it is her fulfillment as a woman, while for Meridian it is the means by which she becomes further cut off from life. In the chapter "The Happy Mother," Walker describes the teenager Meridian's experience of motherhood as "slavery." Although she was told by everyone that she was an exemplary young mother, it took "everything she had to tend to the child."[70] In rejecting the possibility that she might resent her child, Meridian begins to think of suicide as a possibility—blaming herself for her inability to enjoy the hassles of "happy motherhood." She is cut off from the world, left alone with her baby's needs and the TV set. On the other hand, Nnu Ego's delivery of a baby boy, a son, inspires her to vow that she will "start loving her husband for he had made her a real woman."[71] She becomes a part of the community of women who help her deliver the baby, although Nnaife was not awakened on the night that the baby was born. But in contrast to the patterns of her village, she must immediately go back to her petty trading, coming home to feed her baby at lunch. It is on one of these days that she finds her son dead and runs through the streets of Lagos to throw herself into the river.

Although each woman puts a different value on motherhood, they both experience the same feelings of guilt about their inability to perform its duties correctly. Both women are driven to thoughts of suicide—one, because she is locked out from the world as a result of her responsibility for her child's need; the other, because she believes her child dies since she must leave him to work in the world. Ironically, although no one is aware of Meridian's thoughts of suicide, Nnu Ego's people find her attempt at suicide understandable when they hear her child has died. "They all agreed that a woman without a child for her husband was a failed woman."[72]

While Nnu Ego waits for the day when she might again bear a child, Meridian becomes more involved in the world as a participant in the civil rights movement. It is through this involvement that she receives a scholarship to college, an event that precipitates the decision that will affect her entire life. She must choose between keeping her child and going to college, since mothers are not allowed there, their fate in life having already been decided. The chapter "Battle Fatigue," in which Meridian and her mother confront each other on this decision, is at the core of Walker's discussion of the ideology of motherhood in the Black South.

"Battle Fatigue" begins with our introduction to Truman Held, "the first of Civil Rights workers to mean something to Meridian"[73] and continues with a description of their unifying experience in a demonstration against the town's segregated hospital facilities. Juxtaposed with their attempt to improve the health of the community is Mrs. Hill's castigation of her daughter for wasting her life in this way. Mrs. Hill's comments, which invoke tradition—that things should be as they have always been—are a subtle preparation for the climactic action in this chapter—Meridian telling her mother that she will give up her son so that she can go to college.

It is important that, in order to confront the mother, Meridian brings two women with her: Delores Jones, a movement worker, and Nelda Henderson, an old classmate. Meridian needs these sisters, of distinctly different orientations to support her. The intrepid Delores is clear, her voice an indication of change: "You have a right to go to college,"[74] she tells Meridian. On the other hand, Nelda Henderson's voice is from the past. Her history informs the discussion, for she had borne the burden of helping her mother care for her five younger brothers and sisters and was herself pregnant at fourteen. She'd had little information, if any, about sex and pregnancy; she resents Mrs. Hill, her neighbor, for not giving her the information she needed to get through her adolescence. Despite her awareness that Meridian has an opportunity to open up her life, Mrs. Hill is adamant in her condemnation of her daughter:

> "It's just selfishness. You ought to hang your head in shame. I have six children," she continued self-righteously, "though I never wanted to have any. And I raised every one myself."[75]

Meridian's confrontation with her mother is followed by her own conflicted thoughts about her decision. She gave her son away "believing she had saved a small person's life."[76] But although she knows he is better cared for by others than he would have been by her, she feels "condemned, consigned to penitence for life,"[77] for she has committed the ultimate sin against Black motherhood. She knows that freedom for Black women had meant that they could keep their own children, while she has given hers away, and she therefore feels unworthy of her maternal history. The chapter ends as she goes to college, where she begins to hear "a voice, that cursed her existence; an existence that could not live up to the standard of motherhood that had gone before."[78] The appearance of this voice is the first indication of the spiritual degeneration that will, a year later, result in her "madness."

What Walker does in "Battle Fatigue" is to present in a succinct way the essence of African-American motherhood as it has been passed on. At the center of this construct is a truth that mothers during slavery did not have their natural right to their children and did everything, including giving up their lives, to save them. From this truth, however, a moral dictum has developed, a moral voice that demands that African-American mothers, whatever the changed circumstances of their lives, take on the sole responsibility for children. One result of this rigid position is the guilt that permeates parent-child relationships. For although some women, like Mrs. Hill, raised their own children, they did not want them and thus poisoned their development. Although Meridian saved her own child from those thorns of guilt, she cannot save herself. Only her mother or a mother figure can save her from her own judgment. But both women are trapped by the myth of motherhood, and cannot help each other. The moral choice that Meridian makes saves her child, but not herself. Ironically, although she believes she has sinned against her maternal history, she belongs to it, for she is willing to die on account of her child. Her spiritual degeneration results in a kind of madness as well as the deterioration of her body.

Nnu Ego also goes "mad" when she loses her child, and her body also begins to deteriorate. "She had to face the fact that not only had she failed as a mother, she had failed in trying to kill herself and had been unable even to do that successfully."[79] Her husband continually calls her a "mad woman," and she herself begins to believe in her madness. She is saved from her deterioration by two events: a visit from one of her sisters, a woman with whom she was initiated, who supports her and lifts her spirit, and by a dream of her *chi*.

This dream is significantly different from her first dream, when she had just arrived in Lagos. In this one her *chi* hands her "dirty chubby babies," tells her "You can have as many of those as you want. Take them," and laughs as she disappears.[80] Nnu Ego realizes that she may be pregnant and that she should be happy. But the dream also makes her ponder her fate, for it challenges her desire to want children without question. Motherhood, her *chi* seems to say, will be my ultimate revenge on you, the woman whose father caused my death. She responds to her own fear with the traditional recipe: to have a son, like her father, "who would fulfill her future hopes and joys."[81]

Nnu Ego does have a son, but this time she does not trade, fearful that something terrible might happen to him. Although she suffers from her lack of money, she consoles herself with the belief that "never mind, he will be grown soon and clothe you and farm for you, so that your old age will be sweet."[82] What she gives up in this new urban setting is her traditional right to earn her own income. She recalls that "in Ibuza women made a contribution, but in urban Lagos, men had to be the sole providers; this new setting robbed the woman of her useful role."[83] But Nnu Ego resolves to accept this new way of life, since it is the only guarantee she has that she can look after their son. Thus, Nnu Ego, in contrast to Meridian, becomes increasingly cut off from the world and becomes more dependent on her husband. Her "madness" manifests itself in her acceptance of her condition, the years of self-sacrifice for her "dirty chubby babies" that comprise her entire life.

As a result of their circumstances, Nnu Ego and Meridian cope with the restrictive aspects of motherhood in totally different ways. Meridian has the option to go to college. But in order to expand her life, she must give up her child, not only physically but psychologically. She must be a virgin, with no knowledge of sex, if she is to become a part of that community of learners. The knowledge of sex for women in U.S. society is seen as undesirable, unless tempered by the institution of marriage. Motherhood outside marriage is a sign of transgression rather than ful-fillment. Mrs. Hill invokes this point of view when she tells Meridian, "I always though you were a *good* girl and all the time you were fast."[84] This precept is adhered to, even as men of all types and ages pursue sex with women. Thus, at her college, Meridian must be seen as a virgin, "as chaste and pure as the driven snow."[85] In spite of the attention she re-ceives from Truman, a sophisticated Black man, she knows that "had she approached him on the street dragging her child with her by the hand, he would never have glanced at her. For him she would not even have existed as a woman he might love."[86]

Meridian's motherhood puts her beyond the pale—of advancement or of love. But so does the use of birth control, for it involves knowledge about sexuality. In the novel, no adult, not even Mrs. Hill, gives Meridian information about sex or the prevention of pregnancy—even as the mother knows the drastic changes that motherhood will impose on her daughter. Her attitude, as well as society's, is summarized in her words— "Everybody else that slips up like you did *bears* it."[87] Even the doctor who performs an abortion on Meridian when she becomes pregnant by Truman concludes that if such an operation is needed, his patient must be "fast." "I could tie your tubes," he chopped out angrily, "if you'll let me in on some of all this extracurricular activity."[88]

Nnu Ego's society relates to a woman's knowledge of sexuality in a different way. Agbadi says of his virgin daughter, "There is nothing that makes a man prouder than to hear that his daughter is virtuous." But he adds, "When a woman is virtuous, it is easy for her to conceive."[89] Virginity, then, is linked to the capacity to conceive, and when Nnu Ego does not conceive a child, the fault, of course, being hers, her father can return her bride price and she can be engaged to another man. The fact that she is not a virgin does not interfere with her new marriage. But if she had conceived a child, her marriage would not have been so easily dissolved. Thus, motherhood, not sexual intercourse, is the seal of mar-riage in Ibuza society. It is *the necessary* state of being for a woman.

Because children are the primary reason for marriage, prevention of conception, regardless of the family or of the woman's situation, is not important. Emecheta stresses the rigidity of this position by emphasizing

the economic precariousness of Nnu Ego and Nnaife's family. When
Nnaife's white boss leaves Lagos, he loses his job and must depend upon
Nnu Ego's tiny income from trading. Ironically, at this time she becomes
pregnant. Nnaife's response indicates that motherhood is not as blessed
as tradition might decree: "What type of *chi* have you got when you were
desperate for children, she would not give you any; now that we cannot
afford them, she gives them to you."[90] Nnu Ego is blamed for becoming
pregnant, just as she had been blamed for not becoming pregnant. Her
children might starve, but she will continue to have more, seeing them
as a mother's "investment." She will deny herself everything, will almost
die from giving birth, but she will continue to have children. Nnaife will
take on other wives so that he might guarantee himself even more children. Nnu Ego's reaction to the arrival of Nnaife's second wife underscores the toll that motherhood has taken:

> Nnu Ego felt that she should be bowing to this perfect creature—she who
> had once been acclaimed the most beautiful woman ever seen. What had
> happened to her? Why had she become so haggard, so rough, so worn. . . .[91]

But she knows she cannot protest even to her father, for he would respond
with the proverb, "What greater honor is there for a woman to be a
mother and now you are a mother."[92] Motherhood for Nnu Ego, then,
regardless of what toll it takes, is an honor and is to be endured at
whatever cost. When she and her co-wife cannot get enough money from
Nnaife to run the house—for women are dependent on men in Lagos—
it occurs to her that she "was a prisoner, imprisoned by her love for her
children."[93] Ironically, her honor, her investment becomes her imprisonment.
  Meridian, too, for a time, is imprisoned by her love for her children,
the one she gives away, the one she aborts. Obsessed by her guilt, she
thinks constantly of her mother, as "Black Motherhood personified and
of that great institution she was in terrible awe, comprehending as she
did the horror, the narrowing of perspective for mother and for child, it
had invariably meant."[94] She loses her hair, has severe headaches and
terrible dreams, until finally she temporarily loses her sight and becomes
paralyzed. Only then does she experience ecstasy, this time from suffering
rather than from pleasure. She does not recover from her illness until
she is absolved by Miss Winter, her music teacher. A symbol of Meridian's mother, Miss Winter responds to Meridian's statement when she
is in a dreamlike state—"Mama I love you. Let me go."—with the necessary words, "I forgive you."[95] This absolution gives Meridian the permission to go on the quest that will occupy the rest of the novel, a quest
that will take her beyond the society's narrow meaning of the word *mother*

as a physical state and expand its meaning to those who create, nurture, and save life in social and psychological as well as physical terms.

The points of view of Emecheta and Walker on the possibilities of change available to their mother-protagonists are completely different. While Meridian perceives herself as having sinned against her maternal tradition, she is able, in the context of the civil rights movement, to probe the meaning of motherhood. Nnu Ego, on the other hand, is trapped in herself by traditional norms and by the lack of a social movement that might give her insight into her own condition.

Thus, Nnu Ego's life deteriorates, until by the end of the novel she ends her life alone, expecting to hear from her sons in America and Canada. Because her family is dispersed, she goes back to her village, Ibuza, where she becomes slightly mad, until one night, "she died quietly there with no child to hold her hand and no friend to talk to her."[96] Emecheta quietly adds that "Nnu Ego had been too busy building up her joys as a mother"[97] to indulge in friendship. The novel ends ironically as her children come home and build her a shrine. Although many people agreed that she had given all to her children, they mitigate this sacrifice by pointing out that "the joy of being a mother was the joy of giving all to her children."[98] Because of this, her family and tribeswomen are angry that she never answered the prayers of people who called upon her. In death as well as life, Nnu Ego does not fulfill the prescriptions of motherhood.

Although Emecheta's novel ends tragically, she indicated that some change is taking place in relation to the status of women. Nnu Ego's daughter, Kehinde, goes against her father's wishes, runs away to marry a man from another tribe, and seems to build a life for herself. But even here, Nnu Ego is the one who suffers, for her husband, angered by the loss of his daughter's bride price, assaults the young man and is hauled off to jail. Because they do not understand the laws of their country, Nnaife and Nnu Ego effectively condemn themselves. In honestly recounting her years of sacrifice, the years her husband spent in the army, the money she saved to send her sons to school, her insistence on her husband's ownership of their family, she exposes the tragedy of her own life. Her confusion is succinctly contained in one of her last statements; "Why were they all laughing at me. Things surely have changed, but Nnaife still owns us, does he not?"[99] A "backward woman," she is blamed for the destruction of her family, for Kehinde's bad behavior, for her husband's imprisonment, her son's departure to the West. Kehinde's farewell to her mother is true irony: "Mother, pray for us, that our life will be as productive and fertile as yours."[100]

In contrast, Meridian does not follow the traditional pattern of her mothers. Within the context of the civil rights movement, a movement opposed to the fragmentation of violence and committed to the wholeness of creativity, she is able to probe the meaning of motherhood, not solely in a biological context, but in terms of justice and love. As she struggles through her own atonement, she becomes a "man/woman person with a shaved part in close-cut hair, a man's blunt face and thighs, a woman's breast,"[101] who owns nothing and wanders through the land, listening to the people, being close to them and helping them "to get used to using their voice." In the final chapter of the novel, "Release," she becomes *strong* enough to return to the world, not strong in the sense of her mothers' sacrifices, but in the sense of her understanding of the preciousness of life. She passes on her struggle to Truman, who understands that the "sentence of bearing the conflict in her own soul which she had imposed on herself, and lived through must now be borne in terror"[102] by us all. In passing this struggle for understanding to a man, Walker infers that the need for understanding of creativity and life in both men and women is a prerequisite for revolutionary change.

Although Meridian's journey is a painful one, she is able, partly because of the existence of a social movement among her people, to struggle in order to rise up and bring back the truth of her personal discovery. In that sense, she is a hero in the classical sense. Unlike the antiheroes of much contemporary literature who are alienated from self and society, Meridian "slouches off the victim role to reveal her true powerful and heroic identity."[103]

On the other hand, Emecheta's rendition of Nnu Ego's life is that of a victim who has yet to articulate her victimization, a necessary step for change. She is destroyed by this lack of consciousness and by the silence in her society, where the personal lives of women and wider social change have yet to be related. *The Joys of Motherhood* protests the lack of value Nnu Ego's society places on her life; Walker's *Meridian* both protests Meridian's powerlessness and traces her journey to spiritual health. Although similar in their thrust against the restrictions placed on mothers, these two novels are extremely different in the presentation of the particular state of women's development, the particular historical moment in their respective societies.

Emecheta's *Joys of Motherhood and Walker's Meridian* substantiate much of the ideology of motherhood in their societies, even as they illuminate their effects on women. Both authors clearly perceive that motherhood is the primary function expected of women—that women are often reduced to this function, are not seen as complex human beings, and as a result have inferior status in their societies. They both insist that such reductionism occurs because women have little knowledge of or control over societal structures that interpret this aspect of their potentiality. As a result, women themselves internalize these values without being aware of the dire effects they will have on their lives. Both writers also agree that motherhood is not an issue of the individual; it is an ideology that is interwoven into every aspect of society's basic structures. The forms of these two novels reiterate the power of these structures, even as they emphasize the value of women's culture.

By weaving proverbs into the narrative of *Joys of Motherhood,* Emecheta shows us how tradition had decreed that motherhood is a necessary state for African women. The novel has the quality of an oral tale; its plot and characters are subordinated to a world view incorporated in the proverbs, an oral form of transmitting values. In compiling the innumerable succinct statements on motherhood in Ibuza tradition, Emecheta also juxtaposes them with the reality of the new urban life to which they have little applicability. But in literally separating these sayings from the societal layers of Ibuza life, Emecheta also heightens the way they restrict women's lives in traditional societies as well. Thus, the saying on which the book is centered—"The joy of being a mother is the joy of giving all to your children"—is set in such relief in the novel that we feel the impact of religion, custom, myth, economics, and politics in its formulation. And we understand how important it is for the novelist to break through the many layers of the societal language about motherhood because of the power of these often repeated statements. Thus, Emecheta does not include in the novel coping mechanisms, such as women's organizations, that might obscure the primary tenets of motherhood as she perceives them.

The question of whether the oral tradition, represented by the proverbs, is the domain of all the folk, the property of men, or the remnant of a post-mother-centered society is not dealt with in this particular novel of Emecheta's. There is, however, some indication in her other novels, especially in *The Bride Price* (1976), that the oral tradition was partially created by women in a context that, at one time, was of some benefit to them.

Just as Emecheta uses an indigenous African form in the construction of her novel, in *Meridian,* Walker uses the form of the quilt, the Southern African-American women's creation of functional beauty out of the discarded pieces of their society. She connects the many aspects of the experience and ideology of motherhood in the South, and shows how complex is the design. Her restructuring of the design emphasizes the way in which certain motifs of maternal history, the focus on sacrifices as a means to goodness, disguise other motifs, that unjust sacrifice may also be a means to death, to stifling self-righteousness and to guilt. The tension between a maternal history when "extreme purity of life was compelled by necessity" and the present era, "an age of choice"[104] for which mothers fought, is one of the major axes of *Meridian.*

But Walker goes a step further. She sees the waste inherent in a society that is fragmented at every level by hierarchical concepts of gender, race, and class, concepts that result in violence and are opposed to the unifying truth that is Nature. Thus, *Meridian* is a novel dedicated to the need for making connections between the many aspects of society, if "One Life" is to be cherished. Like Emecheta, Walker does not condemn motherhood, rather she respects it so much that she condemns society's use of mothers for its own ends, even as it takes no responsibility for their lives.

Both Emecheta and Walker are mothers. Their own personal experiences of motherhood have surely sharpened their insights into the ideology of motherhood that restricts women. One feels Emecheta's urgency in her novels, some of which are dedicated to her children, to expose the plight of African mothers. Most of her work is concerned with the dilemma of young girls becoming mothers, either in traditional settings as in *The Slave Girl* and *The Bride Price,* or in the transition from traditional to modern life, as in *In The Ditch* (1972), *Second Class Citizen,* (1975), *Joys of Motherhood,* and *Double Yoke* (1983). And in most of her novels, she also demonstrates the impact of colonialism, whether the characters understand it or not, on mothers, even as they are restricted internally by their own culture.

Walker's novels also focus on mothers. In the *Third Life of Grange Copeland* (1970), both Margaret and Mem Copeland are violently destroyed by the incredible burden of motherhood that Black and white society imposes on them. Her third novel, *The Color Purple,* presents many types of mothers: Celie, a child who has children conceived in rape that are taken away from her; Shug, who leaves her children partly because of her lover's treatment of her; Sophie, who is taken away from her children when she is unjustly imprisoned by whites; Nettie, to whom Celie's children are given. In all of Walker's novels, violence is inflicted upon Black mothers and children precisely because they are powerless in Black and white society, have little control over their lives, and are clearly not valued.

Although the state of motherhood restricts women in these authors' novels, it also gives them insight into the preciousness of life. In her essay "*One* Child of One's Own," Walker tells that her daughter's "birth was the incomparable gift of seeing the world at quite a different angle than before and judging it by standards that would apply far beyond my natural life."[105] And as she points out in her review of Emecheta's *Second Class Citizen,* "Emecheta is a writer and a mother and it is because she is both, that she writes at all."[106]

While both writers clearly see the experience of motherhood as a profound one, they protest its use by society as a means to ends other than the value of human life, including and especially their own. Because women are reduced to the function of mother, which often results in their loss of sense of self, the gift of seeing the world from that angle is lost to them and their communities.

So Emecheta stresses in *Joys of Motherhood* the inherent waste of Nnu

Ego's life *and* the contribution that such an awareness of self might have been to her society. Walker attempts to demonstrate the struggle of her protagonist to penetrate the death-producing ideology of motherhood in which her society is embedded, so that she might "judge the world by standards that would apply beyond her natural life." Nonetheless, that personal struggle occurs within the context of a societal struggle for freedom, suggesting that Meridian's quest cannot, if it is to be successful, be a purely individualistic one. This point becomes even more clear if one looks at Walker's first novel, where Mem Copeland resembles Nnu Ego in that she initially internalizes her society's value system. But when, out of pure necessity, she begins to question and resist those values, she is destroyed. Like Nnu Ego, she is a victim without awareness, without a language through which she can forge understanding with others like herself.

Thus, the importance of societal change, rather than solely individual awareness, in transforming society's ideology of motherhood, is one of the major themes of these novels. Both Walker and Emecheta establish the relationship between slavery, racism, and the oppression of women in constructing their novels. Emecheta makes clear distinctions between an indigenous African slavery and the racism that the European colonialists inflicted on all Africans. In both phenomena, the slave or the African is reduced to a function, to a thing for use, in much the same way that her protagonist is reduced to the function of mother. In all three states of mind, the people in power construct myths as to why slaves or Africans or women should enjoy being a function. *Joys of Motherhood* protests the interrelationship between these states of mind and the language within which they are embedded, which result in a sense of inferiority in the slave's mind, the African's mind, the Ibuza woman's mind. Her novel focuses on breaking through this state of mind—hence her presentation of Nnu Ego as a woman whose tragedy is her lack of self-awareness, her loss of *her* sense of her right to life.

Walker also shows the relationship between slavery, racism, and the oppression of women. But because of the particular history of African-Americans, she gives Meridian historical models to which she can turn, as well as cultures that have consistently opposed fragmentation. Her use of Native American culture as well as African-American culture emphasizes the need for a point of view that values *all life* rather than some life. But even within these cultural contexts, women who have resisted the norm are compelled to a "purity of life." While celebrating her maternal ancestors' strength and sacrifice, Walker also insists that mothers have a right to a fullness of life, and that sacrifice should be a means to more life rather than an end in itself. Further she demonstrates that if the ideology of motherhood in African-American culture does not value women, that culture loses the particular gift of seeing the world from the angle of continuation, a necessary attitude for any meaningful struggle toward health and freedom.

These two novels express, in their different ways, two fundamental ideas. While acknowledging the respect for motherhood that African and African-American cultures proclaim, the authors insist that women be valued for themselves, and not reduced to a function, a thing. On the other hand, both writers see that motherhood provides an important insight into the preciousness, the value of life, which is the cornerstone of the value of freedom. They are also clear about the fact that this particular way of seeing the world does not necessarily proceed from being a biological mother; rather, it is a state of mind that women can lose if biological motherhood is legislated or forced upon them as their necessary state, a state in which they are restricted by being responsible for society's children. It is the entire society that must take on that angle of seeing the world, of judging its development from the standard of the value and continuity of all life.

It is this truth Emecheta and Walker, among other African and African-American women writers, express about the value of motherhood. Thus, motherhood includes not only the bearing of children, but the resistance against that which would destroy life and nurturance of that which would support and develop life. For them, feminism is inseparable from the struggle of the living to be free, and freedom cannot exist unless women, mothers or not, are free to pursue it.

Notes

1. Stella Ngatho, "Footpath," in Joanna Bankier and Deidre Lashgari, eds., *Women Poets of the World* (New York: Macmillan, 1983), p. 289.

2. June Jordan, "Trying to Get Over," in her *Things I do in the Dark* (New York: Random House, 1977), p. 37.

3. See: Adrienne Rich, *Of Women Born* (New York: Bantam Books, 1976).

4. In her essay, "*One* Child of One's Own," Alice Walker discusses the tendency of many white feminists to devalue mothers. See Alice Walker, "*One* Child of One's Own" in her *In Search of Our Mothers' Gardens: Womanist Prose* (New York: Harcourt Jovanich, 1983).

5. Andrea B. Rushing, "Images of Black Women in Modern African Poetry: An Overview," in Roseann Bell, Bettye Parker and Beverley Guy-Sheftall, eds., *Sturdy Black Bridges* (New York: Anchor Press/Doubleday, 1979), p. 19.

6. Andrea Benton Rushing, "Images of Black Women in Afro-American Poetry," in Filmoina Chioma Steady, ed., *The Black Women Cross-Culturally* (Cambridge, MA: Schenkman, 1981), p. 404.

7. See: Joanna Braxton, "The Mother Figure in Afro-American Literature," in Jeanna Braxton, ed., *Wild Women of the Whirlwind* (New Brunswick, NJ: Rutgers U. Press, 1990).

8. John Mbiti, *African Religious and Philosophy* (New York: Doubleday Anchor, 1970), p. 33.

9. See: Barbara T. Christian, "Fixing Methodologies," *Cultural Critique* (Spring, 1993).

10. Mbiti, p. 144.

11. Nancy J. Hafkin and Edna G. Bay, *Women in African: Studies in Social and Economic Change* (Palo Alto: Stanford University Press, 1976), p. 6.

12. See: Nancy J. Hafkin and Edna G. Bay, *Women in Africa.*

13. Ibid., p. 5.

14. See: Leith Mullings, "Women and Economic Change in Africa," in Haftin and Bay *Women in Africa.*

15. Ruth Simms, "The African Woman Entrepenuer, " in Filomena Chioma Steady, ed., *The Black Woman Cross-Culturally,* p. 150.

16. See: Barbara T. Christian, "Shadows Uplifted," in her *Black Women Novelists, 1892–1976,* (Westport, Conn: Greenwood Press, 1980).

17. See: Gloria I. Joseph and Jill Lewis, *Common Differences: Conflicts in Black and White Feminist Perspectives* (New York: Doubleday Anchor, 1981), for further discussion of this issue.

18. *Ibid.*

19. See: Carrie Allen McCray, "The Black Woman and Family Roles," in La Frances Rodgers-Rose, ed., *The Black Woman* (Beverly Hills: Sage Pubulications, 1980).

20. Alice Walker, *Meridian* (New York: Harcourt Brace Jovanovich, 1976), p. 13.

21. Ibid., p. 13.

22. Buchi Emecheta, *The Joys of Motherhood* (New York: George Brazillier, 1979), p. 11.

23. Ibid., p. 12.

24. Ibid., p. 12.

25. Ibid., p. 27.

26. Ibid., p. 28.

27. Walker, *Meridian*, p. 21.

28. Ibid., p. 23.

29. Ibid., p. 31.

30. Ibid., p. 34.

31. Ibid., p. 39.

32. Ibid.

33. Ibid.

34. Ibid., p. 40.

35. Ibid.

36. Ibid.

37. Ibid.

38. Ibid., p. 41.

39. Ibid., p. 121.

40. Rich, *Of Woman Born*, p. 240.

41. Emecheta, *The Joys of Motherhood*, p. 29.

42. Ibid., p. 31.

43. Ibid., p. 35.

44. Ibid., p. 36.

45. Ibid.

46. Ibid., p. 39.

47. Ibid.

48. Ibid., p. 42.

49. Ibid., p. 51.

50. Ibid., p. 46.

51. Walker, *Meridian*, p. 47.

52. Ibid., p. 46.

53. Ibid., p. 49.

54. Ibid., p. 50.

55. Ibid.

56. Ibid.
57. Ibid., p. 51.
58. Ibid., p. 54.
59. Ibid., p. 55.
60. Ibid., p. 64.
61. Ibid.
62. Ibid., p. 51.
63. Ibid., p. 80.
64. Ibid.
65. Ibid., p. 96.
66. Emecheta, *The Joys of Motherhood,* p. 54.
67. Ibid., p. 52.
68. Walker, *Meridian* p. 57.
69. Ibid., p. 63.
70. Ibid.
71. Emecheta, *The Joys of Motherhood,* p. 53.
72. Ibid., p. 62.
73. Walker, *Meridian,* p. 79.
74. Ibid., p. 83.
75. Ibid., p. 86.
76. Ibid., p. 87.
77. Ibid., p. 88.
78. Ibid.
79. Emecheta, *The Joys of Motherhood,* p. 72.
80. Ibid., pp. 77–78.
81. Ibid., p. 79.
82. Ibid., p. 80.
83. Ibid., p. 81.
84. Alice Walker, *Meridian,* p. 87.
85. Ibid., p. 89.
86. Ibid., p 141.
87. Ibid., p. 84.
88. Ibid., p. 112.
89. Emecheta, *The Joys of Motherhood,* p. 31.
90. Ibid., p. 91.
91. Ibid., p. 118.
92. Ibid., p. 119.
93. Ibid., p. 137.
94. Walker, *Meridian,* p. 123.
95. Ibid.
96. Emecheta, *The Joys of Motherhood,* p. 224.
97. Ibid.
98. Ibid.
99. Ibid., p. 218.
100. Ibid., p. 223.
101. Walker, *Meridian,* p. 217.
102. Ibid., p. 228.
103. Carol Pearson and Katherine Pope, *The Female Hero in American and British Literature* (New York: R. R. Booker, 1981), p. 13.
104. Walker, *Meridian,* p. 123.
105. Alice Walker, *In Search of Our Mothers Gardens: Womanist Prose,* p. 369.
106. Ibid., p. 67.

Chapter 6

LOOK WHO'S TALKING, INDEED: FETAL IMAGES IN RECENT NORTH AMERICAN VISUAL CULTURE

E. Ann Kaplan

The unprecedented proliferation of films about babies and parents in the 1980s signified, in the imaginary terrain, societal changes in the wake of the sixties women's liberation movements. What is at stake is traditional late-Western "motherhood ideology," implicit in the construct of the modern nuclear family. This family, articulated in Rousseau's 1772 volume, *Emile,* assumes the father at work in the public sphere, the mother at home, nurturing the children, until her educational and moral role is taken on by a male tutor (later the grammar school). In this family, sex is the forbidden, excluded terrain (Kaplan, 1992).

Some women's demands, from the sixties on, for liberation from the necessity to mother and nurture, for active sexual lives and choice of sexual object, for work lives devoted to fulfilling projects, have greatly stressed the North American social imaginary. By the "social imaginary," I reference the sphere of often unconscious mental images and concepts of the "right and proper life" in North American culture. Such mental images and constructs are passed down interpersonally from generation to generation, but have also been reinforced in popular and then mass culture, where literal images bolster mental ones. This imaginary has long relied on confronting constructs of mother-in-the-family to keep at bay fears about death, destruction, degeneration. It is an imaginary to which peoples in other nations have been exposed through North American popular culture, and it often lures people to America. It is also an imaginary that oppresses minority groups in America too poor or disadvantaged to attain an approximation of the imaginary family.

Both men and women are implicated in the comforting imaginary constructs of the ideal nuclear family: Hence my reference above to "some" women's liberatory demands. There is no consensus among North American women generally, and certainly not among feminists, about why women desire the biological child (and use reproductive technologies to obtain it), about how (or if) sex, work, and motherhood should be combined, or about what should happen to the nuclear family. North American men, meanwhile, are being newly implicated as these issues increasingly impact on men's lives, especially on their own needs to combine sex, work, and fatherhood. Nevertheless, the issues have specific significance for women, partly for biological reasons (it is still women's bodies that gestate the zygote and fetus, and that give birth), and partly because of the long and tenacious traditional constructions of the feminine role in North America.

At the end of the eighties, Hollywood responded to the disturbance about parenting, work, sex, and the family on the level of the imaginary, by producing a host of films about fathers (at the beginning and end of the decade), later about mothers, babies, and, finally, about parenting more generally. One theme is the threat of female sexuality to motherhood, as in *The Good Mother* (1988) and *Fatal Attraction* (1988). In this construct, often destructive female sexuality is located in the career woman. This figure is no longer the dried up, homely, spinster type of earlier Hollywood constructs, but is closer to the forties *femme fatale.* She combines two negative female constructs—sexuality and career. A second theme is satisfaction in motherhood and the impossibility of combining motherhood and work, as in *Baby Boom* (1989), *The Good Mother* (1988), and *Stella* (1990). Usually work is reduced merely to putting bread on the table, rather than being an activity that is meaningful to the mother in its own right. The discourse establishes mothering as the only fulfilling role for women. A third theme is fathers taking up new roles because women abandon babies, as in *Three Men and a Baby,* (1988), or showing what fathering demands of men, as in *Parents* (1990), or *She's Having a Baby* (1990). Rarely do films deal fully with what *mothering* actually demands or means, although *The Good Mother, Baby Boom,* and *Stella* make gestures in this direction.

Finally, there is a new interest, not only in babies themselves, but in the fetus. The fetus is now given a voice, made to speak; and it threatens to displace the mother in original ways. This final Hollywood concern is linked to increasing focus on inception, gestation, and birth, as seen in surrogacy debates and in discussions of new reproductive technologies. These come on top of debates about life within the womb, fueled in recent years by antiabortion groups.

Confronting scholars and requiring analysis is a new "interpellation of the fetus," to borrow a concept from Louis Althusser, the influential sixties revisionist and post structuralist Marxist. By "interpellation" Althusser meant the process through which a subject is "called" or "hailed" into being via dominant ideology (Althusser, 1969). Dominant institutions demand certain kinds of subjects at specific historical moments, and these institutions produce discourses, which in turn produce the needed kinds of subjects. An example is the recent "hailing" of the fetus as a subject because it satisfies certain cultural needs. Earlier the fetus was merely an object, or a part of the mother's body. Where before there was one subject, and one body (the woman's, in pregnancy, carrying a developing extra part), suddenly there are two subjects, two bodies, from the moment of conception. Scholars face a major constitutive alteration in thinking about both what a "body" is and what a "subject" is. Where before there were no boundaries between mother and fetus (they were thought of as one body), suddenly boundaries, difference, and conflicting rights separate the two.

In terms of the science discourse, it appears that a new part of the human (in this case, specifically female) body had come into view because technologies exist to make it visible and manipulable. An analogy may be found in the eighteenth-century "discovery" that is the brain, and not the heart (as Renaissance doctors thought) that registers emotions and that controls our thought processes. With brain research also, a new part of the body comes into view. But it is the discursive process through which new objects are constituted (be it the "brain" or the "fetus"), and how such objects may become "subjects," that concerns the cultural studies scholar.

As part of that effort, in this chapter I explore the discursive processes through which the fetus became interpellated in the post-World War II period. At the same time, I examine categories relating to images of the fetus, such as subjectivity, humanness, whiteness, and salvation. My work is grounded in feminist, cultural studies and psychoanalytic perspectives, leaving aside, for now, historical analyses such as those being undertaken by Susan Squier (1991). While I am sensitive to hierarchical gender relations, I am also unable to deal fully with links between increasing fetal discourse and the construction of the white, imperial subject. This work also needs complementing by attention to meanings women themselves assign to fetal images (Petchesky, 1987; Rapp, 1984).

I aim to problematize, and thereby uncover, the dominant categories, and to discuss their implications and their contradictions. Why is the fetus being interpellated—that is, called into being, hailed as a "subject"—in the ways we find it? What is the relation between this interpellation and motherhood ideology? How do we account for the contradictions? One of my primary interests is in how current representations of the fetus in select dominant forms manifest, and give meanings to, such contradictory discourses. A crucial aspect of fetal images in journalism, and in

Hollywood comedies about fetuses, is their uniform whiteness—a sign of how dominant discourses assume whiteness as a universal, as well as of how dominant media seek to address mainly white audiences.

Cultural studies scholars have long theorized that popular representations provide some evidence for what preoccupies the social imaginary in specific historical moments. The requirement that productions relayed through the commercial media (film, TV) command an audience large enough to make handsome profit means that producers keep their senses honed to the social imaginary. They consider it their business to know what fantasies, fears, and desires preoccupy most people in a given period. In addition, producers keep their pulse on the moment, so as to anticipate the next fashion before it gels, thereby being the first to provide desired representation.

While some cultural studies scholars go on to study what specific uses receivers of images make of them, my concern in this chapter is with research that makes a point of teasing out the underlying forces setting media discourses in play. Analysis of these power hierarchies shows which discourses are privileged, which are marginalized and which are excluded altogether. It is then possible to deduce the cultural needs that produce certain discourses, and the specific political interests they serve. Since commercial products present discourses as though they operate merely on the individual level (that is, as though all were a matter of personal character, individual choice, or fate), scholars have to locate that discourse itself as ideology. It is true that dominant media are not monolithic (many different, contradictory discourses may be seen at work at the same time) (Stam, 1988); and the sheer enormity of production increasingly guarantees gaps and spaces for some alternate discourses and for subversive audience use of cultural productions (Feuer, 1989). But unconscious cultural constraints still function to prevent expression of certain kinds of image. The absence of nonwhite fetuses as mentioned above, for example, can be attributed to such unconscious cultural constraints, if not to racism.

Subcultural or marginalized groups such as minorities, women, gays and lesbians, which Jane Feuer (1989) and others label "interpretative communities," may, as Feuer has argued, make new use of popular materials. Feuer shows how these communities defuse ideologic messages in such materials, and incorporate them into new imaginary constructs, as, for example, gay groups did in their "camp" *Dynasty* Night Parties. Similarly, many nonwhite audiences evidently make their own empowering uses of white cultural productions, as hooks (1990) has shown in discussing fifties television shows and films. But this does not mean that it is not important to explore the investments in positions that texts themselves stake out on the level of the unconscious; or to seek out displacements of anxiety about woman in the construction of specific images.

North American capitalism, in its search for new markets and its uncanny method of co-opting subversive discourses, has transformed many of the sixties oppositional positions into dominant ones; blurring distinctions and boundaries, and eliminating the sense of an "outside" distinct from the dominant culture. Hence, there is increasing confusion between the "popular" and the "oppositional" text; or between "dominant" and "marginal" cultures. I here discuss commercial texts whose sites of production offer differing discourses on sex, work, and motherhood, although, for the most part, they reveal unconscious, white, patriarchal desires regarding these issues.

In what follows, I distinguish four groups of commercial fetal images that serve different ends. I label them cosmic entity; perfected being; full-blown subject; and safe haven. They all share a crucial feature: the presenting of the fetus as already human, white, and a subject. The most graphic examples of what I mean are routine drawings of the fetus in seemingly innocuous articles about fetal surgery or other matters in newspapers like the *New York Times*. The images depict the fetus as a small human with all the outward signs that mark it as such: eyes, nose, hands, fingers, legs, feet, toes. Often, the fetus has a little smile on its lips, and a peaceful, babylike look. In addition, these sketches in newspapers always image the "baby" as white and sexless, but somehow implicitly "male."

We all know that zygotes of thirty days, six weeks or even later, at a stage when it was called an embryo and is ready for complex operations, do not really have such human expressions. But depicting the zygote this way, in pictures far larger than actual size, instigates the same feelings in the viewer as would a picture of an actual baby. The representational qualities of largeness, whiteness, and humanness become moral determiners, misleading readers/viewers about the *actual* status of the zygote, and negating race/gender specificities. These support Susan Squier's argument that fetal images embody not only the bourgeois subject, but its linked white, imperialist, and male subject. (Squier, forthcoming,). Each of the following groups of images imply such a subject, even when quite indirectly. It would seem that at the very moment the centrality of the white, male, bourgeois subject is being challenged, it returns in the rather unlikely guise of the fetus.

COSMIC ENTITY

In the first group of commercial images we find the fetus as cosmic entity, made possible through an interaction between a new fetal interpellation, and developing medical and photographic technologies. From the sixties on, photography, sonar systems, microcopy, and medical science together have brought new awareness of, and knowledge about, life in the mother's womb. The famous Swedish photographer, Lennart Nilsson, provides an interesting example of how technologies developed originally in the sphere of medicine for *medical* purposes can be used (and abused) through their dissemination in popular forms.

Nilsson has devoted his career to capturing on film the "mystery of life" in the womb. His first series of black-and-white, with some color, photos about conception and gestation were produced in 1965 in his book, *A Child Is Born*. This rapidly became a best-seller, and has been through many editions since. But the most extensive popularization of the images was their reproduction in *Life* magazine on April 30 of the same year. They created a sensation in relaying images of the sperm penetrating the egg, and of the almost daily growth of the fetus in the uterus. While Nilsson's *A Child Is Born* ran on two tracks, one of which was that of the mother-in-the-world, the tracks were not united. The images posited two distinct, disconnected realms: inside the mother's body and the mother-in-the-world. This second track, significantly, is almost completely lost in the *Life* popularized version.

Again significantly, his second series of incredibly lush and highly polished color photos, this time about not only the very moment of conception but the following days, appeared in August 1990, also in *Life* magazine, at the time when antiabortion activities were intensifying. The new focus, in *Life*'s words, is on "the earliest and least understood moment of creation." The introduction praises Nilsson's use of high-tech tools, and his devotion to seeing inside woman that entails rushing off to hospitals at any hour in order to get a good picture. But it is the *quality* of the photos that is significant: these are not "scientific" images, untouched; but rather highly produced images. The actual photos, I am assured by professors of microcopy, would have been a bland greyish, blueish color, unlikely to attract buyers of *Life* magazine. Nillson's photos have been elaborately and dramatically colorized—the reds, deep blues, orange, purple—all are added precisely to make the photos attractive and appealing in a way that "nature" (the real inside of woman) would not be.

Both series of photos, but particularly the later ones, are made to suggest the abstract, cosmological import of the creation of life. Through incredible magnification, the brightly colored images of swirls and folds, and the planetlike fertilized egg, are made to look like images of outer space—conception on the grand scale. The images present the fetus-as-miracle, as the wonder of Man (sic), far beyond the mundane scale of a simple, ordinary, female body. They now are imbued within an ideological discourse that differs from that of the original medical context, although one might find common links in the marginalizing of the mother's body and subjectivity.

PERFECTED BEING

A second group of images shows the fetus as perfected being. This discourse has been developed in both popular science fiction and the science film and horror genres, where the fetus is relied on to fill fantasies of perfectibility. *2001: Space Odyssey* was one of the earliest films to make use of fetal imagery to connote rebirth, renewal, the future for Mankind. The film ends with an image of the planet, Earth (which looks similar to Nilsson's planet "eggs"), in front of which appears, in close-up, a fetal image. This image is held on the screen until the very end, and is meant to suggest hope for the future.

Later films became obsessed with a similar image. Recall the fetal-like appearance of the aliens in films like *Close Encounters of the Third Kind*; or the utopian desire to create a more beneficent being through intercourse between a computer and a human, as in a film like *Demon Seed* (1977). The relevant sequence toward the end of *Demon Seed* starts with the computer shutting itself down, and saying "Why did I want a child? So that I too could be immortal." It is important to note here the marginalization of the mother in the birth process, and the fanatical will of the husband to keep the new being alive against the "mother's" wishes. The mother wants to kill the fetus because she believes it is monstrous—a violation of nature. But the husband, in the tradition of the Hollywood scientist—who always puts science or the possibility of new knowledge before humane considerations, including even the health and safety of humans—is determined to help the fetus survive precisely because it is the product of computer and human, and will, he thinks, have untold technological potentials.

In these popular, patriarchal texts, focus on the fetus manifests an urge to make the perfect being that will save Mankind (sic). Barbara Creed (1992) has analyzed fetal images in the horror film—usually the genre for such perfection fantasies—while critics like Susan Squier are currently at work on fetal images and concepts in history and fiction (1992), attempting to locate some of the early beginnings for utopian urges.

FULL-BLOWN SUBJECT

A third set of images focus on the fetus as full-blown subject. This was already clear in an aspect of Nilsson's work different from, if not contradictory to, the cosmic one noted above. Nilsson's images, and the text accompanying them, suggest the incipient *humanity* of the fetus from the earliest days. Nilsson stresses the little shapes that will become eyes, or ears, or other organs. The emphasis is all on the baby-to-be read back into the zygote. Further, the fact that this is all taking place in the mother's body is ignored. The photos have no boundary to them that might represent the limit of the mother's womb or fallopian tubes; that body is nowhere in sight, but is rather the repressed, nonrepresented, vessel for the growing "baby."

The photos, together with increasing medical access to and knowledge about, the fetus and its development, fed the militant antiabortionists' campaign (Ginsburg, 1989). Images like those featured in *Life* magazine, together with the ones in the antiabortion film *The Silent Scream,* encouraged the spectator to identify with the fetus as *subject,* initiating privileging of the fetus over, if not to the exclusion of, the mother. By the early eighties, the fetus-as-subject from the moment of conception was so overemphasized that it even became ripe for satire, as in Gary Trudeau's comic strip of a *Silent Scream II,* this time about a twelve-*minute* pregnancy, reprinted in *Ms* magazine (November 1985).

This new fetal subjectivity has entered journalist discourse, as many *New York Times* images and accompanying articles about fetal surgery show. The enlarged images of the surgeon obtaining access to the fetus do not even include the mother's body. The images show the surgeon's implements entering the womb as if the womb were located in space, floating unattached to anything (*New York Times,* May 1990). Discussion of the surgery mentions nothing about discomfort to the mother in whose body this is taking place. The mother is *assumed* to be at her fetus's behest, and safely located in nuclear family.

Fetus-as-subject threatens to displace the mother in film. Titles for Amy Heckerling's 1990 comedy, *Look Who's Talking,* emerge over representation of the moment of conception. Spectators are shown the inside of what we later realize is the heroine's body; an egg matures and drops into the fallopian tube. The camera then pans right to focus on the adulterous couple ostensibly at work but about to have sex. The camera pans left again, now imaging sperm racing through the fallopian tubes. The sperm are given male voices, which sound like men chasing, and competing for, women in a dance hall. The "winner" is seen diving into the egg, while tones of satisfaction fill the sound track.[1]

In *Look Who's Talking,* the camera continues periodically to take us into the heroine's womb, where the *male* fetus talks to us about what it feels like there. The world as seen by the fetus returns as the heroine struggles with her baby's father over whether or not to marry. Things the heroine does are registered by the fetus in the womb. The birth is presented from the fetus' perspective, and after birth the baby continues to talk to the viewer, as if he is a fully cognizant being from the start. He even has opinions about the heroine's boyfriends, and helps her choose the right one. While this makes for good comedy, the underlying significance of displacing the mother-as-subject, and of assigning to fetus and baby thoughts and perceptions of adulthood should not be taken lightly.[2]

I have elsewhere discussed the Heckerling follow-up, *Look Who's Talking, Too* (Kaplan, 1992), where the fetus this time was female. Let me note that such American comedies about babies and parenting can be read as reflecting a healthy playing with mother/father constructs. In addition, contradictory discourses are at work: the film's heroine is, after all, a woman who works, is gutsy, answers back, and decides to go it alone and have the baby when the father takes another girlfriend. Yet, this new, independent "mother" is not the film's main subject. Nor does the reading about a healthy play with stereotypes in a postmodern way mitigate the problems: the comedies I have in mind are not ultimately postmodern because narratives do not leave things ambiguous, undecided. Rather they make a choice for heterosexuality, for closure, and for conventional mother/father positions. As Bakhtinians have noted, comic reversals alone do not entail subversion (White and Stallybrass, 1988; Stam, 1963).

The same representation of the fetus as a person may be found in the "My Bundle Baby" doll recently given media attention. This doll sits in a pouch of soft material that has strings and may be tied around the child's waist, like an apron. Traditional ideas of the family and woman-as-mother underlie the toy, and are evident in the quotes by Ms Gibbs, company spokeswoman, who says: "By making a little girl feel what it is like to be pregnant, we have taken nurturing play one step closer to the magic of motherhood." What is not commented upon by either the manufacturers or the psychologists interviewed is the elision of difference between "baby" and "fetus" on which so much of the antiabortion debate depends. This "fetus" is fully clothed in the pouch (the photograph chosen for the newspaper shows a "fetus" that looks like a little girl, but when the child gets the doll, s/he does not know what gender the "baby" is until the pouch is unzipped), and has features and expression much like those in the slides and the movie. The "Mommy-To-Be" doll followed, featuring a doll whose pregnant body can be dismantled to produce the "baby" from inside.[3] (This doll, significantly, comes in both black and white forms, showing, perhaps, a new awareness of the usual limitation of the fetus to "whiteness"). Both dolls encourage young children to think that "fetus" equals "baby," and may promote automatic antichoice sentiments.

Since surrogacy intensifies in its own way the focus on the fetus as "baby/person," and paradoxically marginalizes the woman, let me focus for a moment on this issue. Two books by mother-surrogates (those by Elizabeth Kane, 1988, and Mary Beth Whitehead, 1989) show the women happily subordinating themselves to the experience of carrying the fetus. Both women accept the belief that the prime and only worthwhile experience for women is bearing children and staying at home with them. Whitehead's volume in particular exemplifies an anti-career-woman discourse, as I have detailed elsewhere (Kaplan, 1992). While some feminists support women's rights both to act as surrogates and to engage a woman to bear a child, others fear that the practice of surrogacy can result in exploitation of some women by other women. The fears are that society's acceptance of surrogacy will inaugurate and naturalize the hiring out of women's uteruses. The fantasy of "baby farms" (Murphy, 1984) where Third World women would bear babies for wealthy American couples, lead some feminists to stand behind Mary Beth's legal position advocating banning surrogacy.

The phenomenon of the intense desire for pregnancy and a baby was exemplified in the TV film, *Baby M.* The fetus is interpellated by the film in the section where Mary Beth and the Sterns see the sonar image of the fetus. Important is the fetishistic structure to the "gaze" at the fetus: By this, I mean the psychoanalytic and Marxian process by which an object endowed with libidinal meanings that eliminate its actual functions or reasons for being.[4] One is most familiar with this process in advertisements, in which the (male) viewer cathects to the image of a sexy woman's body. Since this body is linked to the object being advertised, the desire slips over to the object, which can be bought, and which the viewer confuses with the woman, and his desire for her. The viewing male subject's erotic desire eliminates the divide between himself and the woman, whom he possesses in his fantasy, and can keep on possessing if he buys the car. Similar analyses of Hollywood films and the "male gaze" have shown how this gaze eliminates the subject/object divide through the male subject's taking in of the female film object to himself via the gaze (Kaplan, 1983).

In the TV film, *Baby M,* arguably something similar happens with the fetishization of the fetus. In the sequence where "Mary Beth" goes to her doctor for the sonargram, accompanied by the "Sterns," viewers are shown the delighted response to the image by Mr. Stern. In this shot, he looks across Mary Beth's body to the ultrasound on the screen. The narrative illustrates Mr. Stern's bonding to the baby, whereas Mary Beth's body is visually alienated from itself. The womb is on the monitor, out there, while her body lies nearby on the bed. Everyone's eyes turn to the monitor, and away from Mary Beth. The fetus has now been "seen," made an object of the gaze, possessed by all those watching. It is the object of everyone's desire; the hoped-for one that all yearn toward, as against either of the two mothers in the scene. Although the fetus is "differently real" to Mary Beth, too, after her seeing the sonar image, it has already been real because her body has been involved. The film refuses to dwell on the new meanings to Mary Beth that the fetal imagery produces. An attention to feminine experience would explore such meanings, as Rapp (1984) and Petchesky (1987) have begun to do.

But the fetus is also now a commodity: it has, after all, been produced as an object to "sell," an object of exchange. Mr. Stern's cathecting to the fetus is to a desired object that he is buying. Mary Beth's lack of similar delight in the fetal image marks her realization of her own cathexis to the fetus, her wish not to "sell" the product.

SAFE HAVEN

The final set of images evidences, arguably, an unconscious association between the fetus/womb and the idea of a safe haven. A 1991 Volvo advertisement may support the theory that the fetus symbolizes safety. I read this advertisement rather differently from how Jennifer Taylor (1992) does. The ad, as presented in *Harper's* magazine, consists of a large, black-and-white image of a fetus. The caption, in big black letters, reads: IS SOMETHING INSIDE TELLING YOU TO BUY A VOLVO? Beneath this line is a small photograph of a gray Volvo, and to the right of the Volvo logo, in very small print because it is so familiar in Volvo ads, the line "A Car You Can Believe In." It is this line, despite its smallness, that is an important component of the ad's meaning. The ad seems to say: Just as you can believe in the fetus—just as you can trust that it is in a safe place—so you can trust that in the Volvo you will be save—as safe as in the womb. In other words, mother/home, fetus/womb, passenger/Volvo are linked concepts and images. But it is extremely significant that the first, mother/home, is no longer viable (*it can't after all be trusted*), and must be replaced with fetus/womb. Nevertheless, while the fetus/womb apparently replaces mother/home, it in fact re-evokes it. The loss of the one is being recuperated through the recourse to the other.

Contradictions emerge, however, because this conception of the fetus/womb as "safe" is itself problematic. The idea of the womb as safe has been threatened by the media attention to women's abuse of their wombs (Terry, 1989). Such discourse has given rise to the demands made on mother-surrogates to control their diet and so forth, while pregnant (Hartouni, 1991). Nevertheless, for many, the womb has become the new safe haven in a heartless world.

The thesis of the fetus fulfilling needs for something that evokes *safety*— in an era when the home can no longer be relied upon—ties together many of the other images. The need for safety, a secure place, emerges from the anxiety produced by women's changing roles in the wake of the sixties. Arguably, fetal interpellation evidences the anxiety underlying the varied, even contradictory, motherhood discourses in America today. It seems a desperate response to several interconnected crises produced partly through the new freedoms women won in the sixties and seventies. This period saw a spectacular reorientation of consciousness (at least in America) *toward* woman that put women nearer the male centerpoint.

Fetal interpellation challenges that new female centrality: it constructs another subject—one cleverly linked to woman, and hard for her to reject or contest (as she had done in relation to male subjects). When central, the fetus renders unimportant woman's work, sex, *and* mother subjectivities: her body (assumed to be in the home, in heterosexual marriage) is now to be in the service of the fetus.

Culture now imposes constraints on this body, dictating what the mother will, or will not, use her body for. The mother's body is increasingly regulated, and public signs proliferate warning against pregnant women drinking, smoking, or taking drugs of any kind. No longer is the womb the safe, idyllic sanctuary it has long been mythically celebrated for. On the contrary, following a change in medical thought, the womb is constituted as a dangerous place for the fetus. The placenta's membrane is no longer conceived as an impermeable barrier to harmful substances; now the mother's toxins (drugs, alcohol, viruses) may infect the fetus. As a result, the mother becomes a slave to her fetus, while her body becomes the site for surveillance by the social apparatus. Obviously, as I and others have noted, poor, minority, and working-class women are the prime targets of the most virulent forms of surveillance and control during pregnancy. Such women are routinely accused of placing the fetuses they carry at risk (Katz Rothman, 1990; Kaplan, 1992; Terry, 1992).

The new freedoms middle-class women have won, including freedom not to bear children, or to combine children with full-blown careers, have produced a gap, a space, where there was once the long-held idea of home as haven in a heartless world. The new-won female freedoms, together with the increase in divorce, left many middle class homes with single parents, and many males without the wives who have traditionally retrieved their lost "mothers" for them. Essential to the mythic ideal home—the US fantasy—was the mother-wife secure in it, nurturing husband and children alike. If that home cannot be relied upon, the cultural imaginary seeks another image of this safe place. Some of the deep interest in the fetus in the womb that technology now allows us to see—to witness, even to experience, through identification with the camera and ultrasound image—can be ascribed to the search for a safe place. The focus on the fetus as hero, as savior of mankind, is a response to the greater economic reliance of males on women, and the greater demand for men to function within the hitherto "feminine" domestic sphere, in an era when opportunities for male heroism are fewer. While the mother has disappointed in the home, so the fetus—linked with technology—comes to symbolize not only the missing "safety" but also new and better worlds beyond the domestic.

CONCLUSIONS

The fetus fulfills people's (mainly males') need for a hero, the new savior of mankind, delivering us from all the messes we have made and from overdependence on mother. The fetus is incorporated as part of man's (sic) ongoing dream to make the perfect being that will deliver humankind from seemingly insuperable global dilemmas—a dream that includes eliminating woman's role in reproduction. Recall how the computer in *Demon Seed* said it desired a child to make it, too, immortal. Such abstract motivation for the child seems a male construct: women rarely announce this sort of reason for having children (Hoffman and Hoffman, 1976).

Fetal preoccupation is the latest form of the age-long male utopian urge to control reproduction (Fox Keller, 1976) and to control the body, perhaps to the extent of eliminating it altogether. While some 1970s radical feminists like Shulamith Firestone also fantasized ridding women of the need to gestate fetuses, the end of such fantasies was arguably quite different from the end in male fantasies (See Kaplan, 1992). Medical science and patriarchal culture long to control an aspect of nature that has hitherto been mysterious, and has involved men only peripherally. Women, on the other hand, wished (and may still wish) to be freed from the necessity to carry the burden of pregnancy and childbirth. Artificial wombs would, indeed, give women wanting children a choice about pregnancy and childbirth. Male culture desires control over something men cannot naturally do; female culture desires liberation from something women have hitherto *had* to do. The two desires are different.

In many films, like *Demon Seed,* depiction of reproductive technologies that no longer require woman's body *per se,* but only her extractable eggs, may indicate a renewed desire to write the woman out of the story (except, once more, as an unquestioned patriarchal function), or to marginalize and negate her subjectivity. It is largely males who fantasize getting rid of the body, however (Kaplan, 1992). New communications technologies, such as virtual reality, are motivated by male urges to make literal Hegel's idea of "Mind contemplating itself as Mind." The apparently healthy elimination of gender difference in such a concept may, in fact, reinscribe male desire.

The attempt to figure forth the fetus as already human, white and a subject reveals the underlying need for freshness and a look toward a better future world, while at the same time making the mother secondary—less important, and now in the service of the fetus-subject. The way that images of the fetus repress the woman and her body would support the scientific fantasy that the mother is no longer essential—that she can indeed be rendered irrelevant. One of the benefits of the nineteenth-century reification of the mother had been the new status accorded her—a status lacking in earlier eras. The late-twentieth-century displacement of the mother reworks earlier discourses on the separateness of mother and child, such as were evident in the Catholic doctrine that "person-hood" is established at the moment of conception. It also reworks the medieval concept of the homunculus in the man's sperm. The homun-culus, once planted in the woman's womb, develops into the person, leaving the mother as merely an incubator, rather than generating the child together with the father.[5]

Films like Heckerling's and *Baby M* discussed above reflect a new kind of marginalizing of the mother as a result of new imaging technologies, and the coexistence of contradictory discourses, such as a series of sen-timentalizing motherhood fantasies in Hollywood films (Kaplan, 1991, 1992) alongside discourses encouraging poor and welfare women to start work. Reproductive technologies involve contradictions, as a *New York Times* article (May 26, 1992) makes clear. The headline, "Cost of High-Tech Fertility: Too Many Tiny Babies," belies the underlying force of the article, which is the technological lengths to which women will go in order to have the biological children they yearn for. But another contra-diction exists in the way the front-page photo for the article shows three women literally overtaken by the nine babies they are holding on their laps. Not exactly the sentimental motherhood ideal.

Previous feminist discourses about the mother, going as far back as Adrienne Rich's pioneering *Of Woman Born* (1976), have explored the simultaneous idealization and marginalization of the mother within pa-triarchal capitalism. Fetal interpellation reworks this paradigm, only now with a cruel twist. Previously, although the mother was overinstalled in the symbolic, motherhood at least gave women an opportunity to gain attention, to fulfill an important function for the aristocracy and then the bourgeoisie (that is, reproduction of the class), and, at times, to gain a certain amount of power within the home, despite its constraints. Fetal interpellation displaces many of these "benefits" onto the fetus—now made a subject in its own right, as I have shown. The mother *herself* is no longer important: it is what she carries that matters. In other words, the mother's own body, and along with it, her subjectivity, are sidelined to make the fetus central. While the mother's body still bears the burdens it did before, these burdens are not the central focus. Fetal interpellation, thus, displaces the mother even further from the center.

The feeling of "safety" is what the mother-in-the-home traditionally provided for men. The desire to eradicate the need for the woman herself in reproduction would seem to expose man's bitter disappointment with woman. Since she has let man down, the unconscious narrative goes, let's try to do without her altogether. Through new technologies, let's construct new cyborgian worlds in which gender difference is eradicated and men are finally comfortable.

The possibility that women may stand to gain from some of these moves requires another level of analysis. Theories now being developed, of motherhood as an interpersonal possibility or as intersubjective agency, are attractive, if somewhat utopian (Mann, forthcoming). Women, along with others, may be fascinated with the fetus' *liminality*— its being an entity between life and not-life, human and not-human.[6] I have here only presented a critique of how commercial patriarchal culture represents, and has taken up, the fetus to serve its own needs. Women's science fiction (especially writers like Marge Piercy, Naomi Mitchison, Octavia Butler) has presented yet other utopian visions of how the female body may be liberated by new technologies, and of how new genetic research may eliminate oppressive gender binaries (Haraway, 1985, 1989, 1991; Kaplan, 1992). But that, as they say, is another story.

Notes

1. It is interesting to contrast this sequence with that in Woody Allen's *Everything You Wanted to Know About Sex,* where the sperm are being mobilized for release. You may recall how Allen himself plays the one sperm extremely anxious about being released into the vagina! Heckerling may be deliberately evoking Allen's sequence by having *her* sperm be unambiguously virile. (I want to thank Krin Gabbard for pointing out the analogy with Allen's film.)

2. Such assignment could theoretically involve a certain empowerment of children, but the way in which the scenes are done is closer to exploitation of the child actors.

3. I want to thank Susan Squier for drawing my attention to the ad for this doll, which I had not yet seen.

4. The deep interest in the fetus is, indeed, extreme enough to be called "fetishization." Both Freud and Marx theorized the fetish in linked, if ultimately different ways. As Laura Mulvey (1990) has pointed out, in Marx's concept of commodity fetishism, an abstract quality (eroticism, status, power) is added to a material thing (the object to be consumed), which conceals the labor power involved in the commodity's production. In a sense, this is what happens with the fetus: the fetus stands for humanity, status, the future, while the costly, painstaking, and commodified processes of its production (via new technologies) are repressed. The images in the *New York Times* articles and the ultra-sound image in *Baby M* fulfill this fetish function.

For Freud, the fetish stands in for the penis, and prevents man from recognizing castration. It is an unconscious way of coping with fear of loss that has been displaced into the penis. That fear of loss is now remedied by recourse to the fetus: the fetus becomes the fetish-object to cover not castration *per se,* but loss of the nurturing mother. The mother who refuses to stay in the home is now the *castrating* mother, the castrator, as Barbara Creed has argued (1992). One male defense against this now castrating (as against *castrated*) mother is to replace her with the fetus. The other sets of images—the Volvo ad, the Heckerling film—manifest this Freudian kind of fetus-fetish.

5. I want to thank Evelyn Nakano Glenn for pointing out these earlier discourses to me.

6. Indeed, as we become more and more interested in, and close to being, not-humans, like computers or cyborgs, so interest in the fetus grows as a different kind of not-human from the technological one. The interface between computer and women in *Demon Seed* in this sense seems to anticipate many fitting twenty-first-century interests and fantasies.

Clearly, feminists need to develop ongoing work about *women's* appropriation of fetal images (see Petchesky, 1987; Taylor, 1992); to analyze conflicting feminist responses to reproductive technologies and their logical need for the family (see Barrett and McIntosh); and to explore non-commercial art works that deal with these issues (such as Martha Rossler's fascinating *Baby S/M* video). I have only here had time to explore and theorize briefly dominant images produced in dominant institutions, and to hypothesize their possible meanings. These are perspectives that will be continued in future research.

REFERENCES

Althusser, Louis. 1971. "Ideology and Ideological State Apparatuses." In *Lenin and Philosophy and Other Essays* trans. Ben Brewster. New York and London: Monthly Review Press.
Barrett, Michèle, and Mary McIntosh. 1982. *The Anti-Social Family*. London: NLB.
Butler, Octavia. 1987. *Dawn*. The Xenogensis Trilogy. Vol. 1. New York: Warner Books.
Creed, Barbara. 1992. *Monstrous Women*. Dissertation. Australia: La Trobe University.
Fuer, Jane. 1989. "Reading *Dynasty*: Television and Reception Theory." *South Atlantic Quarterly* 88 (2), pp. 443–460.
Ginsburg, Faye D. 1989. *Contested Lives: The Abortion Debate in an American Community*. Berkeley: U. California Press.
Haraway, Donna. 1985. "A Manifesto for Cyborgs: Science, Technology, and Socialist Feminism in the 1980s." In *Socialist Review* 80, pp. 65–108.
———. 1989. "The Biopolitics of Postmodern Bodies: Determinations of Self-Immune System Discourse." In *Differences: A Journal of Feminist Cultural Studies* 1 (1), pp. 3–43.
Hartouni, Valerie. 1991. "Containing Women: Reproductive Discourse in the 1980s." In Constance Penley and Andrew Ross, eds., *Technoculture*. Minneapolis, MN: U. Minnesota Press.
Hoffman, Lois W. and Martin L. Hoffman. 1973. "The Value of Children to Parents," in James T. Fawcett, ed., *Psychological Perspectives on Population*. New York: Basic Books, pp. 19–76.
hooks, bell. 1990. *Yearning: Race, Gender, Culture*. Boston, MA: South End Press.
Jameson, Fredric. 1984. "Postmodernism and the Logic of Late-Capitalism." *New Left Review* No. 146.
Kane, Elizabeth. 1988. *Birth Mother*. New York: Harcourt, Brace, Jovanovich.
Kaplan, E. Ann. 1983. *Women and Film: Both Sides of the Camera*. London and New York: Methuen. See especially Chapter One, "Is The Gaze Male?"
Kaplan, E. Ann. 1991. "Sex, Work and Motherhood: The Impossible Triangle (With Reference to Post 1960s USA Film and Fiction)." In *Journal of Sex Research* 27 (3) (August), pp. 409–425.
———. 1992. *Motherhood and Representation: The Mother in Popular Culture and Melodrama*. London and New York: Routledge.
Katz Rothman, Barbara. 1989. *Reproducing Motherhood: Ideology and Technology in a Patriarchal Society*. New York: Norton.
Keller, E. Fox. 1986. "Making Gender Visible in the Pursuit of Nature's Secrets," In T. de Lauretis (ed.), *Feminist Studies/Critical Studies*. Bloomington, Indiana: Indiana U. Press.
Mann, Pat. 1993. "A Cyborgian View of Motherhood." Unpublished paper.
Mitchison, Naomi. 1985 (1962). *Memoirs of a Spacewoman*. London: The Woman's Press.

Mulvey, Laura. 1990. "The Theme of Fetishism in Sembene's *Xala*." Paper read at The Humanities Institute, Stony Brook.

Murphy, Julie. 1984. "Egg Farms." In R. Arditti, Renate Duelli Klein and Shelley Minden, eds., *Test-Tube Women: What Future for Motherhood?* London: Pandora Press.

Nilsson, Lennart. 1965 (1977; 1990; 1993) *A Child Is Born*. New York: Delacourte.

Petchesky, Rosaling. 1987. "Fetal Images: The Power of Visual Culture in the Politics of Reproduction." *Feminist Studies* 13 (2), pp. 263–92.

Piercy, Marge. 1976. *Woman on the Edge of Time*. New York: Knopf.

Rapp, Rayna. 1984. "XYLO: A True Story," in Rita Arditti, Renate Duelli Klein and Shelley Minden, eds., *Test-Tube Women: What Future For Motherhood?* London: Pandora Press, pp. 310–320.

Rich, Adrienne. 1976. *Of Woman Born. Motherhood as Experience and Institution*. New York: Norton.

Rorvik, David M. 1971. *As Man Becomes Machine: The Evolution of the Cyborg*. New York: Doubleday.

Rossler, Martha. 1990. Video *Baby S/M*. Distributor: Women Make Movies.

Stam, Robert. 1988. "Mikhail Bakhtin and Left Cultural Critique." In E. Ann Kaplan, ed., *Postmodernism and Its Discontents: Theories and Practices*. London: Verso, pp. 116–145.

Squier, Susan. 1991. "Fetal Voices: Speaking for the Margins Within." *Tulsa Studies* 10 (1) (Spring), pp. 17–30.

———. Forthcoming. *Babies and Bottles*.

Taylor, Jennifer. 1992. "The Public Fetus and the Family Car: From Abortion Politics to a Volvo Advertisement." *Public Culture* 4 (2) (Spring), pp. 67–80.

Terry, Jennifer. 1989. "The Body Invaded: Medical Surveillance of Women as Reproducers." *Socialist Review* 19 (Summer), pp. 26–32.

———. 1992. "Criminalization of Pregnancy." Paper read at Conference on "Reproductive Technologies: Narratives, Gender, Culture." Stony Brook Humanities Institute.

White, Allon and Peter Stallybrass. (1986) *The Politics and Poetics of Transgression*. London: Methuen.

Whitehead, Mary Beth. 1989. *A Mother's Story*. New York: St. Martin's Press.

Chapter 7

BEYOND MOTHERS AND FATHERS: IDEOLOGY IN A PATRIARCHAL SOCIETY

Barbara Katz Rothman

Something has gone seriously awry in our cultural understanding of motherhood in America. We find ourselves surrounded by contradictions that would give George Orwell pause: the return of the midwife, and the rise of the cesarean section; cigarette ads, clearly aimed at young women, carrying a warning that smoking harms fetuses; the infant formula companies distributing sample packages of formula for new mothers, labeled "In support of your decision to breast feed." An angry Black social worker says of a grieving white woman whose Black foster child was taken away after three years: "She had no right to love that child. It was just a *job*." Much the same is said of a pregnant woman who is not the "mother" of the fetus in her belly, because it was contracted to be there. Childbearing at forty is chic, at fifty is the new frontier, at eighteen is pathetic. Murphy Brown is supposed to be the epitome of something.

To understand it, to explain it, we need to step back and try to disentangle the contradictions. When we do, we find ourselves unweaving the strands of a fabric, understanding the pattern as we work it backwards to the underlying threads. American motherhood now rests on three deeply rooted ideologies that shape what we see and what we experience, three central threads of motherhood: an ideology of patriarchy; an ideology of technology; and an ideology of capitalism. As these three come together, with all of their multiplicity of meaning, they give us the shape, and the discordance, of our experience—the fabric of motherhood.

As used in this chapter, ideology is the way a group looks at the world, the way it organizes its thinking about the world. An ideology can let us see things, but it can also blind us, close our eyes to our own lived reality, our own experiences, our own bodies. The ideologies of patriarchy, technology, and capitalism gives us our vision of motherhood while they block our view, give us a language for some things while they silence us for others.

The ideology of patriarchy is perhaps the easiest to understand of the three ideologies that shape motherhood. More than half the world has another reality called women's reality to contradict it. But women's reality is not the dominant ideology, and women's view of the world is overruled by men's view. Motherhood in a patriarchal society is what mothers and babies signify to men. For women this can mean too many pregnancies or too few; "trying again" for a son; covering up male infertility with donor insemination treated as the deepest darkest secret; having some of our children called "illegitimate"; not having access to abortions we do want; being pressured into abortions we may not want. The ideology of capitalism, that goods are produced for profit, is also something clear to us; we know that some societies avoid the profit motive, and that most societies feel there should be *some* limits to how much of life should be viewed as a commodity. It may seem farfetched to apply this ideology to motherhood and to children. But the family has always been an economic unit as well as a social and psychological unit. What is new, perhaps, is the shift from children as workers to children as commodities, accompanying the change in the family from its role as a unit of production to its new role as a unit of consumption.[1] Finally, the ideology of technology shapes motherhood. No longer an event shaped by religion and family, having a baby has become part of the high-tech medical world. But as an ideology, a way of thinking, technology is harder to pin down, so pervasive has it become in Western society. The ideology of technology encourages us to see ourselves as objects, to see people as made up of machines and part of larger machines. It is this mechanization that connects the ideology of patriarchy with capitalism, to create a worldview.

This chapter addresses each of these ideologies as separate ways of thinking; then, most importantly, it turns to the ways they weave together to create a pattern, a fabric, both a curtain and a cage.

THE IDEOLOGY OF PATRIARCHY

The term "patriarchy" is often used loosely as a synonym for "sexism," or to refer to any social system where men rule. The term technically means "rule of fathers," but in its current practical usage it more often refers to any system of male superiority and female inferiority. But male dominance and patriarchal rule are not quite the same thing, and when the subject is motherhood, the difference is important.

Patriarchal kinship is the core of what is meant by patriarchy: the idea that paternity is the central social relationship. A very clear statement of patriarchal kinship is found in the Book of Genesis, in the "begats." Each man, from Adam onward, is described as having "begat a son in his likeness, after his image." After the birth of this firstborn son, the men are described as having lived so many years and having begat sons and daughters. The text then turns to that firstborn son, and in turn his firstborn son after him. Women appear as the "daughters of men who bore them offspring." In a patriarchal kinship system, children are born to men, out of women. That is, women, in this system, bear the children of men.

While all societies appear to be male dominated to some degree, not all societies are patriarchal. In some, the line of descent is not from father to son, but along the lines of the women. These are called "matrilineal" societies: it is a shared mother that makes for a shared lineage or family group. Men still rule in these groups, but they do not rule as fathers. They rule the women and children who are related to them through their mother's line. Women in such a system are not a vulnerability, but a source of connection. As anthropologist Glenn Petersen says, in a matrilineal system "women, rather than infiltrating and subverting patrilinies, are acknowledged to produce and reproduce the body of society itself."[2] People are not men's children coming through the bodies of women, but the children of women.

In a patriarchal system, in contrast, the essential concept is the "seed," the part of men that grows into the children of their likeness within the bodies of women. Such a system is inevitably male dominated, but it is a particular kind of male domination. Men control women as daughters, much as they control their sons, but they also control women as the mothers of men's children. It is women's motherhood that men must control to maintain patriarchy. In a patriarchy, because what is valued is the relationship of a man to his sons, women are a vulnerability that men have: to beget these sons, men must pass their seed through the body of a woman.

In a patriarchal system, when people talk about blood ties, they are talking about a genetic tie, a connection by seed. In a mother-based system, the blood tie is the mingled blood of mothers and their children: children grow out of the blood of their mothers, of their bodies and being. The shared bond of kinship comes through mothers. The maternal tie is based on the growing of children. The patriarchal tie is based on genetics, the act of impregnating.

Each of these ways of thinking leads to different ideas about what a person is. In a mother-based system, a person is what mothers grow—people are made of the care and nurturance that bring a baby forth into the world, and turn the baby into a member of the society. In a patriarchal system, a person is what grows out of men's seed. The essence of the person, what the person really is, is there in the seed when it is planted in the mother. Early scientists in Western society were so deeply committed to the patriarchal concept that it influenced what they saw. One of the first uses of the microscope was to look at semen and see the little person, the homunculus, curled up inside the sperm. And in 1987 the director of a California sperm bank distributed T-shirts with a drawing of sperm swimming on a blue background accompanied by the words "Future People." Out of the patriarchal focus on the seed as the source of being, on the male production of children from men's seed, has grown our current, usually far more sophisticated thinking about procreation.

Modern procreative technology has been forced to go beyond the sperm as seed, however. "Daddy plants a seed in Mommy" won't work any more; modern science has had to confront the *egg* as seed also. Scientific thinking cannot possibly hold on to old notions of women as nurturers of men's seeds. The doctor who has spent time "harvesting" eggs from women's bodies for *in vitro* fertilization fully understands the significance of women's seed. But that does not mean we no longer continue to think of the seed as the essence of being. It is not the end of the belief that the seeds, the genes, are everything, that they are all that really matters in the making of a baby, that they are what *real* kinship is based on.

The old patriarchal kinship system had a clear place for women: they were the nurturers of men's seeds, the soil in which seeds grew, the daughters who bore men offspring. When forced to acknowledge that a woman's genetic contribution is equal to a man's, Western patriarchy was in trouble. *But the central concept of patriarchy, the importance of the seed, was retained by extending the concept to women.* Valuing the seed of women extends to them some of the privileges of patriarchy. That is, when the significance of women's seed is acknowledged in their relationship with their children, women, too, have paternity rights in their children. In this modified system, based on the older ideology of patriarchy, women, too, can be seen to own their children, just like men do. Unlike what happens in a mother-based system, however, this relationship between women and their children is not based on motherhood *per se*, not on the unique nurturance, the long months of pregnancy, the intimate connections with the baby as it grows and moves inside her body, passes through her genitals, and sucks at her breasts. Instead, women are said to own their babies, have "rights" to them, just as men do: based on their seed. This does not end patriarchy, and it does not end the domination of the children of women by men. Instead, by maintaining the centrality of the seed, the ideology maintains the rights of men in their children, even as it recognizes something approaching equal rights of women in their children. Since men's control over women and the children of women is no longer based simply on men's (no longer) unique seed, men's economic superiority and other privileges of a male-dominated social system become increasingly important. Children are, based on the seed, presumptively "half his, half hers"—and might as well have grown in the backyard. Women do not gain their rights to their children in this society as *mothers*, but as father equivalents, equivalent sources of seed.

The ideology of patriarchal society thus goes much deeper than male dominance. It means far more than just having men in charge, or men making more decisions than women do. The ideology of patriarchy is a basic worldview, and in a patriarchal system that view permeates all of our thinking. In our society, the ideology of patriarchy provides us with an understanding not only of the relations between women and men, but also of the relations between mothers and their children.

In a patriarchal society, men use women to have their children. A man can use this woman or that woman to have *his* children. He can hire this woman or that woman to substitute for one or another aspect (biological, social, or psychological) of the mothering his child needs. From the view of the man, his seed is irreplacable; the mothering, the nurturance, is substitutable.

And from the woman's point of view? We can use this man's sperm or that one's to have our children. With this or that man as father, our bellies will swell, life will stir, milk will flow. We may prefer one man's seed to another, just as a man may prefer one woman's nurturance to another for his child, but they are substitutable, they are interchangeable. For a man, what makes the child *his* is his seed. For women, what makes the child ours is the nurturance, the work of our bodies. Wherever the sperm came from, it is in our bodies that our babies grow, and it is our physical presence and nurturance that make our babies ours. But is that inevitable? Did not some women substitute other women's bodies when they hired wet nurses? Don't some women substitute other women's arms, other women's touch, when they hire housekeepers and baby-sitters and day-care workers? And now the new procreative technology lets us cut our seeds loose from our bodies, and plant them in other women's bodies. The seed, the egg, of one woman can be brought to term in the body of another.

We have a technology that takes Susan's egg and puts it in Mary's body. And so we ask, *who* is the mother? Who is the surrogate? Is Mary substituting for Susan's body, growing Susan's baby for Susan? Or is Susan's egg substituting for Mary's, growing into Mary's baby in Mary's body? Our answer depends on where we stand when we ask the question.

When we accept the patriarchal valuing of the seed, there is no doubt— the real mother, like the real father, is the genetic parent. When we can contract for pregnancy at the present rate of ten thousand dollars, we can choose which women to substitute for us in the pregnancy. The brokers have books of pictures of women for potential parents to choose from, to take this woman or that woman to carry the pregnancy, to nurture the seed.

But for which women are these substitutes available? Who can afford to hire substitutes for the various parts of mothering? The situation today is exactly what it has been historically: women of privilege, wealthy or fairly wealthy women, hiring the services of poor, or fairly poor, women. Upper-class women can have some of the privileges of patriarchy. Upper-class women can buy some of the privileges of their paternity, using the bodies of poorer women to "bear them offspring." And upper-class women can, as they so often have, be bought off with these privileges, and accept men's worldview as their own. And so we have women, right along with men, saying that what makes a child one's own is the seed, the genetic tie, the "blood." And the blood they mean is not the real blood of pregnancy and birth, not the blood of the pulsing cord, the bloody show, the blood of birth, but the metaphorical blood of the genetic tie.

This is the ultimate meaning of patriarchy for mothers: seeds are precious; mothers are fungible.

THE IDEOLOGY OF TECHNOLOGY

In technological society we apply ideas about machines to people, asking them to be more efficient, productive, rational and controlled. We treat our bodies as machines, hooking them up to other machines, monitoring and managing bodily functions. When a doctor manages a woman's labor, controlling her body with drugs and even surgery, it is to make her labor more efficient, predictable, rational. And so it is when mothers and fathers push their babies into a schedule, so that feeding the baby meshes into the nine-to-five day. Books like *Toilet Training in One Day* show us how to "train" our children efficiently. When we think of our *relationships* with our children as a job to be done well, we are invoking the ideology of technology.

To do these parenting tasks efficiently, we divide them up into their component parts, organize them, systematize them, rationalize, *budget* our time, *order* our day, *program* our lives. All of this rationalizing, reducing, dividing, systematizing, organizing, in the name of efficiency, however, does harm to the human spirit. Clearly, not everything is best viewed as a resource.

The most obvious application of the technological ideology to motherhood has occurred in the medicalization of pregnancy and of childbirth. From the medical management of pregnancy, with its new, quality-control technology of prenatal diagnosis, through the rigidly monitored control of women's labor, the focus is on the "mechanics" of production, and not the social transformation of motherhood. It is as if biology were beyond culture, beyond ideology. The "mechanism" of contraception, the "mechanics" of labor, the "programming" of genetic development—these things are often seen as simple biological givens with which we must cope. But remember, that is the nature of ideology: the constructs look like common sense, the ideas are obvious, the descriptions are simply how things are, "naturally."

In our society, when we look at what we know, what our taken-for-granted reality about physical motherhood is, we are looking at medical ideology, a particular type of mechanical thinking, of technological ideology. Medical ideology is deeply rooted in the mind-body dualism expressed by Descartes: the body is a machine, the structure and operation of which falls within the province of human knowledge, as distinguished from the mind.

In the management of childbirth we see the ideology of technology played out, in all its inhumane absurdity. Pregnant women become workers in an unskilled assembly line, conceptualized as machines, containers holding precious, genetic material. What is it like to be the laborer in such a factory? Sheila Kitzinger, the extraordinary childbirth educator writes:

> Grateful as most women are for all this care and awed by the advanced technology, it is not difficult to understand how a woman can feel that she is merely a container for a fetus, the development and safe delivery of which is under the control of obstetric personnel and machinery, and that her body is an inconvenient barrier to easy access and the probing of all those rubber gloved fingers and the gleaming equipment, and even—ridiculous, but we are talking about *feelings*—that if she were not around the pregnancy could progress with more efficiency.[3]

It is not only the body that we treat as mechanical, but the social order as well. Rather than seeing society as an organic, deeply interconnected whole, technological ideology encourages us to see society as a collection of parts. Liberal philosophy, the intellectual underpinning of the American Revolution and American government, is the articulation of the technological ideology in the social order.

Carolyn Merchant's work *The Death of Nature* traces the development of a mechanical order in Western society to replace the organism of earlier times. She argues that whereas in the time of the Renaissance the earth was perceived as "alive and considered to be a beneficent, receptive, nurturing female,"[4] by the seventeenth century the worldview had changed, and the machine became the metaphor. "As the unifying model for science and society, the machine has permeated and reconstructed human consciousness so totally that today we scarcely question its validity. Nature, society, and the human body are composed of interchangeable atomized parts that can be repaired or replaced from the outside." This "removal of animistic, organic assumptions about the cosmos constituted the death of nature—the most far-reaching effect of the scientific revolution."[5]

The rise of mechanism, as Merchant calls technological ideology, laid the foundation for a new social order in which the relationship between mind and body, person and society was to be reevaluated. "A new concept of the self as a rational master of the passions housed in a machine-like body began to replace the concept of the self as an integral part of a close-knit harmony of organic parts united to the cosmos and society."[6]

The difficulty in reconciling the image of people as "atomized parts" with our very real desire for community, for interconnectedness between people, remains one of the ongoing problems of liberal society. This was addressed in *Habits of the Heart*, a book about the conflicts American society has structured between individualism and commitment. The authors describe modernity as a "culture of separation,"[7] America as a world in which "it became clear that every social obligation was vulnerable, every tie between individuals fragile."[8]

And against this, we have motherhood, the physical embodiment of connectedness. We have in every pregnant woman the living proof that individuals do not enter the world as autonomous, atomistic, isolated beings, but begin socially, begin connected. And we have in every pregnant woman a walking contradiction to the segmentation of our lives: pregnancy does not permit it. In pregnancy the private self, the sexual, familial self, announces itself wherever we go. Motherhood is the embodied challenge to liberal philosophy, and that, I fear, is why a society founded on and committed to liberal philosophical principles cannot deal well with motherhood.

When the authors of the American Constitution declared "All men are created equal," they were drawing on this philosophical tradition of the Enlightenment. What made that statement reasonable was that the equality they spoke of was of the mind, of the rational being. Certainly some men were weak and some strong, some rich and some poor—but all shared the human essence, the rational mind. The extension of such "equality" to Blacks and to women is based on the claim that these groups, too, share the essence of humanity, the rational mind—housed, in the "accident of birth," in the body of the Black, the body of the woman. And it is that same belief that underlies the endless stream of movies and stories about the computer or robot, the machine, that learns to think and to feel, and so becomes essentially human—and ultimately tragic.

If we believe, then, as this liberal philosophic tradition holds, that what is especially valuable about human beings is the capacity for rationality, then the ordering, rationalizing, and purposeful efficiency of technology will be seen as good. But hand in hand with the valuing of rationality is a "theoretical disdain for the significance of the body," and a disdain for physical work in preference for "mental" work. The latter, dividing the physical from the mental work, and then using machines and people interchangeably to do the menial physical work, is the essence of technological organization.

In American society, blue-collar work is less valued than is managerial work. The white collar is a status symbol for having risen above the work of the body. The repair people who work on office copiers come in dressed as managers—white shirt and jacket, carrying a briefcase. To do the work, the briefcase unfolds to a tool bag, and the white shirt-sleeves get rolled up, but dressing in washable work clothes and carrying a tool bag, however much more practical, would be demeaning. Physical labor, the work of the hands and the bodies, is of low status.

This division of labor is a particular problem for women as mothers: mothers *do* the physical work of the body, we *do* the "menial" work of body maintenance. Thus women become identified with the physical, the body, and men with the higher, the rational. The distinction between menial physical labor and highly valued rationality goes a long way toward explaining the utter disdain with which a laboring woman may be strapped down and ignored or even insulted, while the doctor who "manages" her labor—reading her chart and ordering others to carry out his decisions—is held in such high esteem. Or similarly, why the woman who produces perfect nourishment from her body is seen as cowlike, animalistic in a negative way, while the pediatrician who "prescribes" a "formula" deserves such respect—and high pay.

The mind-body dualism has consequences at the macro level as well: viewing the body as a machine encourages us to see it as a resource to be used. If the mind and rationality are held as "above" the body, it becomes relatively easy to see the body as a resource for the use of the mind, and specifically, women's reproductive bodies as "societal" resources. So if the factories or the armies need fodder, women's bodies are the resources from which the young are produced. And if there are too many mouths to feed then the bodies are to be idle, like factories closed until inventories are reduced.

Here we have the ubiquitous problem of reconciling individual freedom and social order. In China, an increasingly technological society without the liberal tradition, the solution is simple: the needs of the society determine the rights of the individual, and the "one-child" policy is enacted. In the United States, such a policy would not be tolerated. And yet the birth rate does fluctuate with social need. In all kinds of ways people do what society needs them to do, and do so seemingly out of choice. What can we make of the choices of women to be used by the social order?

Because of their respect for the individual judgment of rational people, in principle "liberals are committed to the belief that individuals are fulfilled when they are doing what they have decided freely to do, however unpleasant, degrading or wrong this may appear to someone else."[9] The hook here is the notion of *freely chosen*. Thus, "informed consent" becomes a crucial American legal concept: if one consents or agrees to something *rationally*, then one accepts the consequences. But liberal thinking, with its emphasis on rationality, does not seem equipped to understand the more subtle forms of coercion and persuasion, whether psychological or economic, so the "choices" people make out of their poverty or need, choices individuals may experience as being coerced, liberals tend to see as being freely chosen. To take a simple example: advertising campaigns that are shown to be highly effective in getting a targeted population to start smoking, such as those campaigns aimed at young women, are legal—as long as the ads include the information that cigarette smoking may be hazardous to your health.

The liberal position on prostitution is an even better example of how these ideas about mind-body dualism and individual choice come together:

> Liberals do not conceive one's body to be an essential part of oneself, so there seems to be no reason why one's sexual services may not just as well be sold as one's other abilities. Indeed, the propriety of selling one's intellectual capacities might be more problematic, on liberal grounds, than the sale of one's sexual services.[10]

The liberal vision of a better world does not inherently preclude people experiencing their bodies as salable commodities.

The extension is easily made from sexual prostitution to what some call "reproductive prostitution," the hiring of "surrogate" mothers. Here is what John Robertson, a liberal legal scholar, has to say about that:

> Baby selling laws prohibit fees for adoption in order to protect the child from unfit parents and the mother from exploitation and coercion. But these concerns do not apply to surrogate gestators who freely choose this reproductive role before pregnancy occurs, uninfluenced by the stigma of illegitimacy or the financial burdens of single parenthood. An acceptable system of paid surrogacy must assure that the surrogate is fully informed, has independent legal counsel, and has made a deliberative choice. There is also no fear that surrogates will be drawn primarily from poorer groups, who will serve the rich with their bodies as well as their housekeeping and childbearing services. Indeed, money is likely to be a prime motive to the decisions of women to serve as surrogates, but other factors are reported to play a role. It is not apparent that only poor women will select that occupation, much less that the operation of a labor market in this area is more unjust than labor markets in other areas.[11]

Surrogacy is then an "occupation" and a "reproductive role," freely chosen. The only protections needed are to make sure that the surrogate is operating "rationally"—informed, with counsel, making a deliberative choice. The patent absurdity of claiming fairness because wealthy, well-educated women have the same rights to be surrogates and poor women have the rights, although not at all the means, to hire surrogates slides by.

In sum liberal philosophy is an articulation of the values of technological society, with its basic themes of order, predictability, rationality, control, rationalization of life, the systematizing and control of things and people as things, the reduction of all to component parts, and ultimately the vision of everything including our very selves, as resources.

THE IDEOLOGY OF CAPITALISM

From the standpoint of the ideology of technology, we have seen that motherhood is perceived as work, and children as a product produced by the labor of mothering. Mother's work and mother's bodies are resources out of which babies are made. From the standpoint of the market, however, not all work is equally valuable, and not all products are equally valued. In other words there is not a direct relationship between the value of the worker and the value of the product.

What is essential to capitalism is the accumulation and investment of capital, of wealth, by people who are in a position to control others. Under capitalism, workers do not own or control the products of their own labor. This means we are no longer talking about mothers and babies at all—we are talking about laborers and their products. Babies, at least healthy white babies, are very precious products these days. Mothers, rather like South African diamond miners, are the cheap, expendable, not-too-trustworthy labor necessary to product the precious products.[12] This is where it is all heading; the commodification of children and the proletarianization of motherhood. This is the end result of the evolution of these three ideological perspectives. This is what ties together the patriarchal and technological ideologies with the recreation of motherhood.

Because capitalism is complex, both as system and as ideology, here I will focus on only one essential aspect—the extension of ownership or property relations. There is a great deal of modern social criticism that claims the ways in which ownership has been extended is at best inappropriate, and too often morally wrong. For example, ecologists argue that it is inappropriate to think we can own the land, the waters: the earth, they claim—significantly—is our *mother*, not our property. The actual word *property* gets used relatively infrequently in discussions of human relations. More often the term is *rights*. Janet Farrell Smith says:

"A right can be interpreted as an entitlement to do or have something, to exclude others from doing or having something or as an enforceable claim.[13] What happens, then, when we start thinking of motherhood itself in terms of property? There are two directions in which property rights have extended that are directly relevant to motherhood: rights of ownership of one's own body, and rights to one's own child.

The way an ideology works is to focus our attention in certain ways, to give us a point of view, a perspective—often expressed in language as metaphor. People do not necessarily talk of or even actively think of their bodies or their children as *property* in the sense of real estate. As Smith points out, "In applying a property model to parenting, it is important to remember that a parent may not literally assert that a child is a piece of property, but may work on assumptions analogous to those which one makes in connection with property."[14]

Within the American system, intelligent feminist use of the individualist ethos has been invaluable in assuring women's rights in procreation. Once women themselves are recognized as full citizens, then individual women must be accorded the same rights of bodily autonomy and integrity that men have. For women, that means sexual and procreative autonomy. Because it is her body, she cannot be raped. Because it is her body, she cannot be forced to bear pregnancies she does not want. Because it is her body, she cannot be forced to abort pregnancies she does not want.

This does not mean that women are not forced by circumstance into these very situations and eventualities. It only means that the society will not use the official power of the state to force her. Women are in fact prevented from having abortions they might want by family pressure, by economic circumstances, by religious and social pressures. And women are forced into having abortions they might not want to have because of poverty, because of lack of services for children and mothers, because of lack of services for disabled children and adults. By offering amniocentesis to identify fetuses who would have disabilities, and by cutting back on services for disabled children and their families, we effectively force women to have selective abortions.

Because of our current battles over the right to abortion, Americans tend to think of the state as "permitting" women to have abortions, as if the drive for continuing pregnancies came from the state, and the drive for abortions from women. In fact, the legal protection works also to permit women not to have abortions. When women's ownership rights over their bodies are lost, the rights to have and the rights *not* to have abortions are likewise lost. Such was the case in Nazi Germany, where some abortions were indeed forced, but it is equally true that women lost the right to have the abortions they themselves chose, the abortions they as individual women felt they needed.

In American society, when we bring it back to the simple legal questions—who can force an abortion or forcibly prevent one—we wisely retreat to safety, calling forth our most sacred value. It's *her* body. We invoke a higher power, the power of ownership.

This then is the way that women have been able to combine dominant American liberal philosophy with capitalist ideology to our benefit. We've made use of the mind-body dualism, to allow a view of the body as owned, like a shelter which houses the more important mind. If one claims rationality for women—the essential liberal claim for all people—then simple fairness gives women the same rights of bodily ownership that men have, and the very high value of ownership, of property rights, is then turned to the advantage of women, who can claim exclusive rights to our own bodies. In the name of ownership, women have demanded access to contraception, sterilization, and abortion. And given the prevailing liberal philosophy, we've gotten those rights to control our fertility—although given the capitalist class system, we have fared less well with access to the necessary means.

While the "owned-body" principle has worked for women in avoiding motherhood, it is less clear how it can be made to work to empower women as mothers. Our bodies may be ours, but given the ideology of patriarchy, the bodies of mothers are not highly valued. The bodies are just the space in which genetic material matures into babies. In a patriarchal system, even if women own their bodies, it may not give them any real control in pregnancy. Women may simply be seen to own the space in which the fetuses are housed. This is the argument on which attempts to control women's behavior during pregnancy are based: owning her own body is not enough to assure her civil liberties if her body is believed to contain the property of someone else, somebody else's baby.

Of course, if women's bodies are understood to be the space in which sperm and egg grow to be a baby, and women are understood to be the owners of that space, then the acceptance of "surrogacy" follows logically, almost inevitably. The woman can rent out space in her body just as she can rent out the spare back bedroom. And she will have no more ownership rights over the inhabitants of that space in her body than over the boarder in her home. Whether she chooses to "rent" or not, the state can claim rights of passage through her body in the interests of the "citizens" within.

REWEAVING THE FABRIC

From these ideologies of patriarchy, technology, and capitalism we get the supportive fabric for the strange patterns we see emerging. In varying combinations, with sometimes one thread dominating, and sometimes another, these patterns explain things as disparate as genetic testing, including prenatal diagnosis for selective abortion; micro and macro level eugenics programs; reproductive technologies that commodify and commercialize babies and pregnancy, including breast milk substitutes, "gestational surrogacy," electronic fetal monitoring, and eight-thousand-dollars-a-cycle *in vitro* fertilization; minimum wage for child care; the "mommy track"; the simultaneous commercialization and politicization of abortion; and—well, you get the picture.

Over the years many of us have railed against each of these emerging patterns. We have made Luddite-sounding noises about routine ultrasound, overly medicalized births, the false promises and dangerous drugs of infertility treatments; we have tilted at the windmills of "surrogacy," and of "affordable" child care. But our real concerns must go deeper. Our question must be: How best to create a supportive fabric for intimate human relations, including that most intimate of human relations that is motherhood, that is not blinded by the limitations of the ideologies of patriarchy, technology, and capitalism, and that is truly feminist in all its complexity.

The simplest and least threatening version of feminism is to ask for what is seen in North America as simple *fairness*. Even lots of Americans who would never, ever think of themselves as actually being feminists nonetheless expect fairness for women. Demands for fairness are generally based on insistence that prevailing liberal ideals be applied to women: ideals like equal pay for equal work. Since we are living in a society founded on liberal principles, it is liberal feminism that comes closest to mainstream values, and consequently often sounds like the very voice of reason, especially when juxtaposed with the more "strident" feminist positions.

Liberal feminism has its roots deep in American culture, with the feminists we have always had with us, as far back as Abigail Adams, who requested that the framers of the Constitution "remember the ladies." The liberal feminists, in asking that the ladies be remembered, are not so much offering a critique of American life and values as they are seeking full access. As Alison Jaggar writes:

> Liberal philosophy emerged with the growth of capitalism. It raised demands for democracy and political liberties that often expressed deeply held moral convictions about the inherent equality of men. . . . Consistently over the centuries, feminists have demanded that the prevailing liberal ideals should also be applied to women.[15]

Liberal feminism works best to defend women's rights to be like men, to enter into men's worlds, to work at men's jobs for men's pay, to have the rights and privileges of men. But what of our rights to be *women?*

The liberal argument, the fairness argument, the equal rights argument, these all begin to break down when we look at women who are, or are becoming, mothers. A woman lawyer is exactly the same as a man lawyer. A woman cop is just the same as a man cop. And a pregnant woman is just the same as . . . well, as, uh, . . . It's like disability, right? Or like serving in the army? Pregnancy is just exactly like pregnancy. There is nothing else quite like it. That statement is not glorification or mystification. It is a statement of fact. Having a baby grow in your belly is not like anything else one can do. It is unique.

The question is: how can uniqueness be made to fit into an equality model? Strangely enough, albeit for different reasons, both patriarchal ideology and liberal feminist thinking have come to the same conclusion about what to do with the problem of the uniqueness of pregnancy—devalue it; discount it so deeply that its uniqueness just doesn't matter. In strongly patriarchal systems, as described earlier, the genetic tie for men is the most important parental tie: women grow men's children, what Caroline Whitbeck calls "flower pot theory of pregnancy."[16] Men have the seeds and women are the flower pots. Liberal feminists, seeking equality and recognition of women's rationality and rights, claim equality of parenthood between men and women. Women too have seed, they argue, and men too can nurture children. Men cannot nurture with their bodies, not with their blood or their milk as women do—but that is just menial, body work. What matters is that both parents have seeds. Children are "half hers, half his." Instead of a flower pot, the woman is seen as an equal contributor of seed—and the baby might just as well have grown in the backyard. It is, after all, only women's bodily experience that is different from men's.

Liberal feminism does not challenge the mind-body dualism posited by and embedded in liberal philosophy, and so falters on the same grounds as discussed earlier. It has no place for the inherent physicality of gestation and lactation, and no respect for the "menial" work of body maintenance, the *mothering* work of early childhood.

Equal rights sounds good, and in many ways it is a fine goal, and one that has yet to be achieved for any of these groups: radical minorities, old people, women, disabled people. But a focus on "rights" ignores *needs*. Special attempts to get help based on need is called "reverse discrimination." Women as mothers are especially hard hit by this narrow equal rights approach. For one thing, those individuals who are not yet rational—our babies and children—need an awful lot of care and attention, and that falls to our lot. Liberal thinking, including liberal feminism, is a bit shy on what to do with the children—and the other deeply needy people. Even achieving a liberal goal of including men as child-tenders does not solve the problem: it remains individualized, privatized.

The second way that women as mothers are particularly hard hit by the "equality" approach of liberalism is that our specific needs as mothers are not taken into account. The liberal argument for formal equality has simply no place for the special needs of any group, including mothers. The *reductio ad absurdum* of formal equality for mothers, as Jaggar points out, is the 1976 Supreme Court decision in the case of *Gilbert v. General Electric Company*.[17] The case was brought by the women employees, claiming sex discrimination because the disability benefits package at GE excluded pregnancy-related disabilities. The Supreme Court, in what Meredith Gould has called the "pregnant person school of thought,"[18] ruled that it was not sex discrimination. One physical condition had been removed from coverage, that's all. The discrimination, if such it was, was against *pregnant persons*, not against *women*.

For those people (and they may be the most traditional of conservatives or the most radical of feminists) who want to see women—our bodies, ourselves, our sexuality, or motherhood—treated with respect, liberal feminism fails. Clearly, while feminists are good and strong critics of patriarchal society, they do not fight the ideologies of technology or capitalism. The ideologies of patriarchy, technology, and capitalism support each other, prop each other up, but they are not the same thing. And so fighting one does not destroy the others.

It is the nature of this complex worldview, constructed of interlocking ideologies, that we cannot see through it clearly. And so we fear to pick at the fabric, fear to pull at the individual loose threads for fear of falling into some abyss. If we challenge any piece of the system, other pieces block our way. When we challenge technological ideology, people hear the sound of the baby being chucked out with the bathwater, fear and return of the angel of death hovering at every birth, fear unchecked fertility and untreatable infertility, women captured and held hostage to some mad biology. When we challenge ownership models of bodily integrity, we hear the enormous fear of someone else claiming ownership. So deep the ownership model lies that the only askable question seems to be: *whose* property? When we challenge patriarchal models of genetic-based parenthood, we hear the fears of women of privilege who have gained for themselves some of the privileges of patriarchy—often at the expense of other women, particularly women of color.

What if we genuinely valued that work that is motherhood? What if we valued intimacy and nurturance, and human relationships, not just as means toward some end, but in themselves? Would such a valuing privilege women as mothers—but simultaneously lock out nonmothering women and all men? I genuinely do not think so. Such a valuing would open up, and not close down, acts of nurturance and caring, free up, and not constrain, the gender boundaries of intimacy we now face. It would expand, and not restrict, the very definition of mothering.

Mothering is an activity, a project. Sara Ruddick has described "maternal thought," the intellectual work of mothering, the attitudes, the values—in essence, the *discipline* of mothering.[19] That motherhood is a discipline does not mean that all who engage in it achieve its goals—not any more than all scientists live up to the demands of the discipline of science, or achieve its goals. But motherhood, Ruddick reminds us, is not just a physical or emotional relationship—it is *also* an intellectual activity. It is this unity of reflection, judgment, and emotion that she calls "maternal thinking."

Looking at motherhood this way, as a discipline, a way of thinking, a response to the needs and demands that exist outside of the mother, shifts our focus from who the mother is to what she is doing. Who she *is*, who she feels herself to be, is deeply gender based: she is a woman, a mother. What she is *doing* is not gender based: the similarities in behavior of mothers has more to do with the similarities in their situations, in the demands they face from their children and from their societies, than it has to do with the similarities in the women. And so the person engaged in this discipline of motherhood need not be a mother, need not be a woman, to engage in these activities, this way of thought and practice that is mothering.

The social relationship of parenting, of nurturing, and of caring needs a social base, not a genetic one. Through their pregnancies, women begin to establish that base. Through their relationships with women, and then with children, men too can establish that base. Pregnancy is one of the ways that we begin a social relationship with a child, but obviously not the only one.

If women are not to drop from exhaustion and lose all pleasure in life, someone is going to have to help with the kids. If women are sharing their lives, and sharing their children, with someone, then that is the obvious person to share the work of child care. For some it is a lesbian partner, for some it is one's own mother, and for many of us it is our husband. It is not by virtue of their paternity, their genetic ties to children, that men have an obligation to rear and to nurture them, but by virtue of their social relationship. If someone, man or woman, is going to be the life partner, the mate, of a woman who mothers, then that person must share the child care. And in turn it is by sharing the care and rearing of the children that the partner comes to have a place in the life of the child. We have to move beyond a paternity standard to a standard of nurturance.

Mothers also need men who can mother because we *ourselves* need that mothering—women are tired of mothering the whole world. Mothering, like everything else in life, is best learned by doing. Mothering women have taught many of us the skills of listening to what is said and to what is not said. In mothering we hone our empathic abilities, learn to understand the vulnerability in others without profiting from it. The experience of mothering teaches people how to be more emotionally and intellectually nurturant, how to take care of each other. It is not the only way we learn that lesson, but it is hard to mother and not learn it.

Mothering teaches us physical nurturance. Having nurtured the literally unselfconcious child, we are more competent, more confident providing other kinds of intimate, physical care. I remember my own awkwardness providing "nursing" care to my mother during an illness of hers in my adolescence. I compare that with the competence with which I can now, after mothering, provide such care. And I particularly remember my husband's awkwardness providing such care to me before our first child, and the skill and ease with which he does it now. Nursing me through my first labor, he was infinitely well-meaning. Nursing me through my second, he knew what he was doing. He had been nurturing for seven years of nursing earaches, bellyaches, changing diapers, calming night terrors, holding pans for vomit, taking out splinters, washing bloody wounds. He had grown accustomed to the sheer physicality of the body, the sights and sounds and smells. More essentially, what I showed him in my pain and my fear was not foreign—he saw the baby, the child in me, not the one I was birthing, but the one I myself am, and he nursed it. Now *that* is a man to enter old age with.

If men are not providing this kind of care, learning these skills, with their children, they're not going to be much help with their elderly fathers, or with their own sick wives. When women do all the mothering, it's not just the child care the men are being excused from—it's all of the intimate care women end up providing for children, for men, and for each other.

And finally, men should join women in mothering because it is the only way to avoid recreating the gender and class system and still live together. We can pool our resources, join together in infinite varieties of social arrangements to rear our children, but we must not recreate endlessly the separate worlds of power and of care. We must not do this in any of its guises: not as separate public and private worlds, not as separate worlds of men and of women. It is morally wrong to have children raised by one group for another group, whether it is Mrs. John Smith raising John Smith Jr. in her husband's image, slave nurses raising their masters, or hired caregivers raising the children of dual-career couples.

Caring people can and do raise whole and healthy children, and they do it across lines of gender, class, and race. It is not that the children are "subhuman," but that we ask them to turn away from humanity, away from care, and toward power. We do that whenever we separate the world into the kinds of people who take care of children and the kinds of people who rule the world.

In this I share a vision with Sara Ruddick. With her, I look forward to a day when:

there will be no more "fathers," no more people of either sex who have power over their children's lives and moral authority in their children's world, though they do not do the work of attentive love. There will be mothers of both sexes who live out a transformed maternal thought in communities that share parental care—practically, emotionally, economically and socially. Such communities will have learned from their mothers how to value children's lives.[20]

And in so doing we will learn to value all of our lives—and that is still what I think the women's movement is about.

Notes

1. For a fuller discussion of the changing economic value of children, see Viviana A. Zelizar, *Pricing the Priceless Child* (N.Y.: Basic Books, 1985).

2. Glenn Petersen, "Ponepean Matriliny: Production, Exchange and the Ties that Bind," *American Ethnologist* vol. 9 No 1, 1982, p. 141.

3. Sheila Kitzinger, *Women as Mothers: How They See Themselves in Different Cultures* (N.Y.: Vintage Books, 1978), p. 74.

4. Caroline Merchant, *The Death of Nature: Women, Ecology and the Scientific Revolution* (San Francisco: Harper and Row, 1980), p. 28.

5. Ibid., p. 185.

6. Ibid., P. 214.

7. Robert N. Bellah, Richard Madsden, William M. Sullivan, Ann Swidler, and Steven M. Tipton, *Habits of the Heart: Individualism and Commitment in American Life* (Berkeley CA: University of California Press, 1985), p. 277.

8. Ibid., p. 276.

9. Alison M. Jaggar, *Feminist Politics and Human Nature* (Totowa NJ: Roman and Allenheld 1983), p. 186.

10. Ibid., p. 174.

11. John Robertson, "Embryos, Families and Procreative Liberty: The Legal Structure of the New Reproduction," in *Southern California Law Review* vol. 59 no. 5, July 1986, p. 1022.

12. I want to express my appreciation to the Texas midwife who found it so hard to understand how babies could be valued and mothers not—reminding me again why I so deeply value midwives; and to the other Texas midwife in the audience who gave us the example of the South African diamond miners.

13. Janet Farrell Smith, "Parenting and Property," in Joyce Treblicot, ed., *Mothering: Essays in Feminist Theory* (Totowa NJ: Rowman and Allenheld, 1984), p. 202.

14. Ibid., p. 201.

15. Alison M Jaggar, op cit., p. 27.

16. Caroline Whitbeck, "Theories of Sex Difference," in *The Philosophical Forum*, vol. 5, (1973) pp. 1-2.

17. Jaggar, p. 42.

18. Meredith Gould, 1980. "Reproducing Gender: The sociology of Constitutional Adjudication," unpublished doctoral dissertation, New York University.

19. Ruddick, Sara, "Maternal Thinking," in Joyce Treblicot, ed. *Mothering: Essays in Feminist Theory* (Totowa NJ: Rowman and Allenheld, 1983).

20. Ibid., p. 227.

Part III

DECOMPOSING MOTHERHOOD: FUSIONS AND DICHOTOMIES

Chapter 8

MOTHERS ARE NOT WORKERS: HOMEWORK REGULATION AND THE CONSTRUCTION OF MOTHERHOOD, 1948–1953

Eileen Boris

When is a mother a homemaker and when is she a worker? Who determines her identity? Who sets the meanings of motherhood? The history of industrial homework provides a rich arena to explore the social construction of motherhood. Homework is waged labor that occurs at the site of unpaid family labor; in casual conversation, we would say it is work that takes place at home. Whether in the form of the sewing of garments, the sorting of wires, or the typing of papers, homework during the past century has appeared as a type of mother's labor, one where activities for the family and waged work flow into each other.

Engaged in mostly by women, and predominantly by mothers of small children, homework has reflected the sexual division of labor and the construction of gender that defines women's subordinate position in both the family and the labor market as "natural." Its very existence derived from the acceptance of separate spheres as normative by employers, family, and women themselves. When earning wages at home, women seemed not to be breadwinners but rather mothers making good use of their extra time. Homework employers drew upon women's position as mothers to justify low pay, long hours, and irregular work; conditions that trade unionists and reformers labeled exploitative and sought to prohibit. Interestingly, it was the construction of motherhood that provided the rhetoric through which all sides of the debate—employers, trade unionists, reformers, and the state—struggled over the matter of industrial homework.[1]

Homework emerged as a political issue during the late nineteenth century, with the various factions all defending motherhood. Employers and reformers alike agreed that mothers should remain at home with their children; they disagreed only as to whether industrial labor should be part of that home environment. Proponents of the system, particularly contractors and other homework employers, argued that it allowed mothers to fulfill familial duties. Opponents, most vigorously the women of the National Consumers' League, believed that homework commercialized the home, motherhood, and child life. It should be noted, however, that the reformers initially focused on its peril to the middle-class consumer from disease and dirt rather than its harm to homeworking families from long hours and low wages. It wasn't until the New Deal that they began to combine moral and economic arguments. Early on, they argued for legislation that would protect motherhood by ending the substandard wages and hours of homework while shielding factory workers and their employers from its unfair competition. Then, with World War II, homework opponents who were part of the Women's Bureau coalition changed their stance, contending that women's successful entrance into factories refuted the charge that mothers could not leave the home for waged labor. The coalition still preferred a family wage for men, or a mother's pensions for women without men, over wage labor by mothers; but, they argued, women forced by circumstance into the labor force did deserve the best wages and working conditions possible and not the exploitation of homework. This pragmatic approach to the issue of home work broke the ideological identification of mothers with the home, even as the Women's Bureau support for homework bans reinforced the separation of home from work, and mother from worker.[2]

The century-old debate about homework raises interesting questions about the social construction of motherhood and women's work. Did homework destroy the home by commercializing the relationship of mother and child, as mothers drew their children into their tasks? Or did homework provide the means for worthy women to supplement their husband's earnings, provide for their families, or gain a higher standard of living? Did homework allow mothers to earn wages without sacrificing their children to other care? Or were these mothers being exploited? Did mothers' attempt to combine wage earning and dependent care, in order to create an advantageous working structure for themselves, undermine the wages, hours, and working conditions of factory and office workers? Did they work at home because they wanted to stay there, or because employers structured the job market in such a way that their choices were limited? Whose definition of homework, whose portrait of the mother who earned at home, would compose the public narrative of their lives?

Whether homeworkers considered themselves mothers who labored for their families or workers who happened to labor at home generated little discussion, because public debates over the homework problem presented few voices of homeworkers. Instead, employers, contractors, government administrators, reformers, and trade unionists spoke for the homeworker, interpreting her words and actions, fashioning a meaning to meet their own agendas even when occasionally recording her words. Indeed, she became a medium through which questions of profit and loss, authority and subordination, power and control became resolved. Descriptions of homeworkers embedded others' assumptions about the family economy, mothers' care of children, women's relation to the wage system, and the position of women in society.

This essay focuses on one incident in the political struggle over homework regulation that reveals the ways in which the mother as worker became defined: the debate over homework regulation in the direct mail industry in New York City and suburbs between 1948 and 1953. What happened can be quickly summarized. New York State had the most comprehensive homework law; it allowed the Industrial Commissioner to restrict or prohibit homework if he found the law to be detrimental to the health of an industry and its workers. Local 16 of the United Office and Professional Workers of America (UOPWA)—one of the left-wing unions that soon would be expelled from the CIO for refusal to certify itself free of Communist leadership[3]—initiated a complaint to the New York State Department of Labor (NYDOL) in 1948. After a series of public hearings and private meetings with the union, unionized employers in the Direct Mail Master Contract Association, and disgruntled contractors and small businessmen (United Addressers Association), the Commissioner of Labor issued an order in July 1950 that severely restricted home typing. About forty small employers appealed the order to the State Board of Standards and Appeals and essentially stayed its enforcement. But before the board ever decided this case, the State legislature amended the homework law in March 1953 to exclude typists, bookkeepers, and stenographers from its operations.[4]

This incident illuminates one of the ways that women's status as mothers and the conditions under which they labored stood at the heart of political discourse in Cold-War America. In debating whether clerical work could be regulated under an industrial homework law, business proponents of homework associated motherhood with patriotism and protection of the American way. But rather than representing simply a defense of traditional gender roles, the homeworking mother offered an updated version of domesticity, one that celebrated a "work ethic for women"[5] even if their work remained confined to the home. The free market allowed a woman the freedom to choose homework, to stay at home to fulfill her responsibilities to family. Opponents of homework, on the other hand, offered a version of motherhood freed from economic exploitation, but focused on homeworkers as victims or victimizers.

Mother and worker became oppositions despite the mother-worker becoming the subject/object of both labor reform and employer strategies.

THE GENDERED ECONOMY OF HOMEWORK

Before analyzing the debate over homework in the direct mail industry, we need to situate the discourse;[6] we need to turn to the structure of clerical work, especially in the direct mail industry, in the early postwar years. This was a period of rapid demobilization, when decline in basic manufacturing caused layoffs of women like Rosie the Riveter from well-paying industrial jobs, and forced their return to the pink-collar ghetto of women's work. Trade unions were militant, including those in the female-dominated service industries, where members walked out of department stores, hotels and restaurants, and telephone exchanges. Although women reformers were promoting equal pay for equal work, most Americans desired to form families and have children in the aftermath of depression and war, to move away from the inner city. The turbulence of the late 1940s, when many feared a renewed economic collapse and others looked forward to expanding opportunities, generated public actions to improve the possibilities for a fulfilling domestic life.[7]

The growth in clerical work was part of that new world. In 1947 it composed the largest occupation for women, with over four million out of a total of sixteen million employed in the labor force. Although nearly half of married women workers, a quarter of all working women, were clerical workers or operatives, clerical workers were younger than other working women. Of all clerical workers in the late forties, thirty seven percent were single, twenty three percent married, and nineteen percent widowed or divorced.[8]

The married woman worker, exhaustively researched by the Women's Bureau in the 1920s and thirties, remained a social problem; sympathetic experts wondered whether such women were "neglecting, or discharging inefficiently, responsibilities that are theirs by virtue of their marital and parental status"; and, if not, were they hurting themselves through lack of leisure?[9] In 1946, the Bureau of the Census reported that when children were small, women tended to leave the labor force. Most married women who worked did so to support themselves and others. Yet such women did not fully control their choices. As a number of studies revealed, hiring and dismissal practices discriminated against married and older women in office work. Despite the high turnover rate among young clerical workers, who, without financial or professional incentives, left to marry and have children, many employers judged married and older woman workers to be less desirable.[10]

Transformation of clerical work, with the growth of the modern corporation and the mechanization of copying, had precluded substantial increases in homework. Prior to the introduction of typewriters in the 1880s, "deserving" widows had received copy work to do at home, especially from government agencies. Into the twentieth century, some married women performed clerical work at home for former employers. These employers often gave the impression that such work, allotted on an ad hoc basis, was out of the kindness of their hearts and their own sense of largesse. After all, the overall function of their typing, filing, and other office work was to centralize and dispatch information efficiently and aid managers on a daily basis. Not until the 1940s, when war demands for female labor lead to a shortage of typists, did clerical homework emerge as a problem for the direct mail industry, however.[11]

Consisting of letter shops that reproduced letters by hand or machine prior to addressing and mailing them, and "list houses" that compiled and sold or rented mailing lists, the direct mail industry was an early form of business service. Housed in lofts, direct mail houses resembled printing factories more than offices. The work, even the contractors admitted, was "dull, repetitive and not too stimulating," especially for the typists who had to produce three- and four-line address. Rush orders and overnight deadlines contributed to an irregular flow of work, with production bottlenecks often developing at the typing stage, especially for smaller shops that lacked sufficient personnel. Although some companies tried overtime and additional shifts, many turned to homework or homework contractors for flexibility to meet the varying volume of business. They complained of a shortage of typists, but in the late forties, low wages and poor working conditions, well below office work, undoubtedly had much to do with their inability to recruit sufficient workers.[12]

The industry had employed some homeworkers since the 1920s, but most firms preferred inside workers whom they could count upon to get out production rapidly and efficiently. The 1940s witnessed not only a turn toward homework but the growth of the "homework contractor" who, located in residential areas of Queens and Brooklyn, drew upon neighborhood housewives for a labor force. Contracting intensified competition, and, in a scenario common to the garment trades, led to price-cutting, and ultimately to lower piece-rates for homeworkers and layoffs or lower rates for inside workers.[13] Between May and October of 1948, for example, the number of homeworkers actually increased by thirty percent while the number of shop typists (mostly women) declined by two percent.[14] Interestingly, printerlike operations performed by men experienced about a seventeen percent growth rate. Compared with the eighty four cents an hour for inside typists, homeworkers earned on the average only sixty eight cents; and this does not account for the added cost of typewriters, repairs, and utilities for the home/workplace. The earnings of homeworkers averaged nearly a third less than the $1,755 gained by shopworkers employed more than thirty nine weeks a year. It should be noted, however, that fewer than half of the homeworkers interviewed by the NYDOL worked that many weeks in the preceding year. This is another indication of the high turnover of homeworkers and their intermittent use by employers.[15]

The meagerness of the women's annual earnings reminds us that homeworking was neither the only nor the major activity of these women; they were housewives and mothers. Typists, like other homeworking women, generally were married and felt they had to stay at home to care for their children and elders while they supplemented their husbands' earnings. Only thirteen percent claimed that they could leave home for shop work. Compared to other homeworkers, these women had fewer children (one or two, with the youngest between two and six in half the families),[16] were more likely to be native-born,[17] and usually had a high school education. In addition, most had been clerical workers prior to marriage and with a median age of thirty six, were older than the average office worker, whose median age was just less than thirty. This was similar to women in the direct mail shops, where the average age was thirty seven.[18] Direct mail typists differed from those in the office, who were younger, often more skilled, perhaps more attractive, and certainly more mobile. The social conditions that shaped choice separated the two groups of clerical workers. As a counselor at the Y.W.C.A. Employment Service explained, many women looking for work "had expressed a strong prejudice against letter shop work because of the pressure and the piece rates prevalent in the industry . . . before [they]) would take letter shop jobs they would accept lower paying office work." Clerical workers preferred the office to the factory; even those laboring at home did not have to put up with the awful conditions of the direct mail lofts.[19]

While most husbands of homeworkers were employed, they were nonmanagerial white-collar workers, craftsmen and operatives, transportation and utility workers, policemen, and firemen—workers in occupations that by themselves usually were inadequate to maintain high enough living standards in the inflation-prone late forties. Only one in twelve was a professional or proprietor. Earnings for husbands averaged $65.52 a week, with thirteen percent earning less than fifty dollars, and six percent with earnings of at least ninety dollars. About one in five families had income from additional adults in their households, and a few others, from pensions and rents. Most homemakers and their families lived in suburban New York or outside of Manhattan—in Flushing, Brooklyn, or Long Island, their place of residence reflecting urban expansion and population diffusion, as well as the movement of second- and third-generation white ethnics from the inner city.[20]

According to the Department of Labor, homeworkers worked "because they needed the money," with a mere seven percent claiming "they were working to keep busy or to save money for luxury items." Bureau investigators constructed the case of Mrs. K., "a secretary for 10 years before her marriage," as typical:

> Her family included two young sons, aged 11 and 5½ years, and her husband, who was employed as a maintenance mechanic at $60 a week. She had been doing addressing homework for a year before the interview. She reported, "Last year I wanted to get bicycles for Christmas for my boys. Now the money goes for food and clothing."

Clearly then, spiraling costs of food, clothing, and other basic items pushed at least some mothers into the labor market.[21]

By itself, however, economic need has never accounted for why some women do homework and others go to the shop or factory. About a quarter of mail-order shops in the survey instituted one shift, either from one to five p.m. or from two to six p.m., to be staffed by housewives.[22] Presumably these women could go to Manhattan where the firms were located because they had child care alternatives. Homeworkers not only preferred the location of their labor, but contractors organized their businesses around the availability of such a labor force. Employer demand as much as worker supply shaped the homework system.[23]

COMPETING CONSTRUCTIONS OF MOTHERHOOD

Representations of homework reflected competing political and economic interests. The debate over homework regulation in the direct mail industry overlapped with U.S. entry into Korea, a timing that partially explains the resulting discourse. Because the union initiating restriction, the UOPWA, was "Communist-influenced," business supporters of homework linked patriotism, motherhood, and freedom to work at home. UOPWA leaders and the Women's Bureau coalition continued to portray the homeworker as a victim whose labor violated domesticity. Most homework opponents refused to consider the homeworker as a worker; those who did also relied upon a general understanding of domestic virtue to attack employers who would dare exploit such mothers. In the renewed consumer culture of the postwar years, trade unionists also viewed the homeworker as a selfish woman who took work and decent wages away from real workers (men and single women) in order to satisfy unnecessary longings. In the portrait drawn by contractors, on the other hand, mothers put their children before their jobs; they were not really serious about work. Homework employers held contradictory representations: Although they would agree that pitiful need pushed some to homework, their interest lay in emphasizing the worthiness of homeworking mothers in order to counter attacks by reformers.

Henry Hoke, editor of the industry's trade journal, *The Reporter of Direct Mail Advertising*, and John J. Patafino of Ambassador Letter Service Co., one of the leaders of the United Addressers Association, organized a letter-writing campaign through which employers and their workers complained to the Governor, the State legislature, and the Department of Labor.[24] Although some of these letters captured individual circumstances, their similarity of rhetoric and charges—by women and men, homeworkers and employers—both attested to their origins and created a distinct discourse. One correspondent graphically expressed ideas promoted by Hoke:

> While our neighborhood boys are fighting Communism in far away Korea, we at home are being Sovietized by the Reds in our midst, who forbid thousands of Americans with initiative to make an honest dollar at home without being supervised by Commissioner Edward Corsi [of the Department of Labor] and his representatives, who will, by this law, be permitted to violate the privacy of American homes to tell us what we may or may not do.

As another letter writer put it, "The general feeling is . . . this definitely breaks the ice for Sovietizing the American home under a Commissar." The order, in short, was "most un-American." A Brooklyn homeworker expressed this antistatist individualism in a manner that emphasized her role as mother (just as some men stressed their parental role): "True my two little girls are not dependent on my working for their daily bread, but that is of no concern of theirs [the state]. Just as it would be no concern of theirs if my children were destitute." Attacks on homework regulation were part of a position of persistent objection to state interference in the economy.[25]

Despite upholding the home as a private space, a site free from state intervention, the letter writers' interpretation of domesticity did not call for a retreat into an isolated suburban ranch house—what some historians have labeled the dominant theme during the early Cold-War years.[26] It was rather a paean to the self-sacrificing, hardworking mother; thus representing a postwar discourse that shunned the idle bridge player and lauded the woman who combined part-time wage labor or community service with motherhood.[27] In opposition to one particular aspect of the proposal, a small a businessman protested to the Industrial Commissioner:

> This Order . . . is unfair, not only to small businesses employing less than five workers, but unfair to women with small children who, in these troubled

times when their husbands are in military service, must supplement their income through earnings from clerical work which they can perform in their homes.

In a letter to Governor Dewey, a homeworker combined arguments about women's necessity with the motif of "a man's home is his castle":[28]

In these days of rising prices and steadily increasing cost of living I can see no reason why the great State of New York should object to a wife helping out, in her own small way, to increase the family income. My husband's salary has not increased in any like proportion—and we need what small income I am able to make from this homework. . . . Why should the State of New York suddenly try to regulate our home life—or what we do with our own time in our own houses?

Countering a central theme of homework opponents, she argued, "This homework is not 'slave labor'. . . ." Here we find a women identifying as wife and not mother, justifying her efforts because of the needs of her spouse, not her child. But another homeworker made the connection that women social investigators and opponents of homework had been emphasizing since the turn of the century when she claimed:

We work to supplement the small incomes of our husbands so that we can give our children the necessities of life. Some, unfortunately have no husbands and depend on what they earn to support their families.[29]

Clearly, mothers worked for their children and their families—this characterization justified homework and, in fact, made the homework contractor into a kind of savior, one who kept such women from charity or welfare. Women preferred work to the public dole, a situation that for many was all too real, as one deserted mother who supplemented her secretarial job with home typing related:

I would not be working at all if the laws of New York State were such as to bring back a husband who deserted us two years ago after twenty-two years of marriage. He took a new Chrysler car with him and is now living in California with the other woman. He sends $48.00 a month for the support of his boy; pays no Doctors or Dentists' bills and buys no clothing. He now claims he has been unemployed. . . . I haven't received a cent, although I have a separation action pending. . . . It seems very easy for the State to enforce a law forbidding you to earn a few extra dollars but the District Attorney or the Judge of a Court can't make a husband take care of his legal family properly but allow him to remain out of the State absolutely free to come and go and not pay a cent to us.

Women resented a state that worked against their interests as mothers but allowed a man who failed in his obligations to children and wife "to do as he pleases," as another divorced homeworking mother complained to the Governor. But it was not just basic survival items that these post-war mothers defined as needs. As one woman put it, "I . . . sought out this position as homeworker so I could be with my son. It provided him with the little things a boy desires plus building his education."[30] One contractor interpreted needs in the renewed consumer society by arguing that women worked:

> to buy little necessities like a television set up so that they can watch . . . while they are typing—that is all true—for all our women do need these little necessities of life or they wouldn't have them if they did not do typing.[31]

In letters of support to government officials, then, homeworkers appeared "self-reliant," "skilled," "not . . . under pressure," and working "at their convenience."[32] They were needy but hard workers who put home, children, and husbands first. Proponents of the homework ban, in contrast, portrayed such women as victims of exploitation, as workers for pin money, or both. The *New York Post* labor columnist declared, "Young housewives, particularly in Queens, are being exploited to an increasing degree by New York companies which pay them sweatshop wages for typing at home." At the public hearing on homework in the direct mail industry in May, 1949, a representative from the U.S. Women's Bureau repeated their long-standing claim "that homeworkers are exploited," while the Executive Secretary of the New York Women's Trade Union League classified these clerical homeworkers as industrial workers, envisioning the same kinds of "sanitary, health and child labor" abuses that accompanied homework elsewhere. In addition, she argued, homeworkers depressed wages without any accompanying social benefit.[33]

According to male trade unionists, the home typists engaged in anti-social behavior. They followed the practice of other homeworkers and involved their children, who carried boxes of envelopes and sometimes even helped in the typing. While employers saw nothing wrong with children aiding their mothers to bring work home, trade unionists and women reformers pounced upon this as an evil. Jack Greenspan, the chief organizer of Local 16, UOPWA, embraced the myth of the male breadwinner to argue that because most homeworkers were housewives "with children, whose husbands *work*," they really did not need the income. They took jobs away from those "who urgently need jobs, in order to merely supplement their own income." As a male typist and UOPWA member exclaimed:

> To hear some people speak about homeworkers needing money—they do

not need it worse than typists do. . . . So far as the cruelty of depriving
homeworkers of needed work, I say we need work as much as they do.

In this representation, the homeworking mother became a designing
woman, who through carelessness or selfishness has forced the real workers, those who derive their full maintenance from their wages, to seek
unemployment insurance or welfare, as the meagerness of her piece-rate
drove down shop workers' earnings and transferred work from shop to
home.[34]

Ironically, homework employers actually reinforced this image when
they attempted to reject any comparison of their establishments with
sweatshops. They claimed that "the homeworkers are very largely home
owners, working in comfortable, airy, healthful, sanitary homes, under
pleasant working conditions, of assured privacy, and with freedom to
work in such spare time as is available." The contractors contended that
"their little stand in the dining room" or living room took up little space.
No one would use child labor because the work required too much skill,
they insisted, even as they admitted to its mechanical quality. In a series
of descriptions that government attorneys found contradictory, homeworkers were characterized by contractors as:

Wives, Sisters, mothers of fighting men in Korea;
Women whose husbands need a little more money to pay current
bills and taxes;
Pregnant women who urgently need money;
Women with old or sick relatives who cannot leave home;
Women with babies or children who must stay at home;
Women who have reached retirement age and cannot live on their
security checks;
Women who are not well enough to go out to work;
Older women, ex-office workers, striving to help their children or
grandchildren.

Thus contractors, when protesting the loss of earnings that regulation
would bring, also portrayed the homeworker as victim, a worthy but poor
woman trying to keep hunger from the door. But rather than belonging
to the old, ill, destitute, deserted, or war widowed, Department of Labor
researchers discovered that most homeworkers were "relatively young
married women with small children who cannot or do not wish to travel
to offices to work." They were, in other words, neither desperate nor well-
off.[35] The UOPWA, as we have seen, equally distorted the needs of these
families when it contended that such married women did not need jobs.

Only the Congress of American women, another organization in the
Communist Party orbit, which claimed three hundred thousand female
members, accurately recognized the relation between women who worked

at home and those in the shops. It opposed "any attempt to pit the housewives' income needs against the wage standards of the working women" by skillfully deploying the language of domesticity and motherhood. Defining her group's objective as "improving the lot of women as workers, mothers, and citizens," spokeswomen Haloise Moorehead argued for a guaranteed right to work for all women, regulated wage and working standards, and "proper nursery school facilities." The Congress of American Women supported the restrictive order "because we consider homework to be inimical to the interests of women as wage-earner and as *mothers*" (emphasis added.) Like pro-labor feminists and women reformers, Moorehead drew upon the image of the home turned into a sweatshop to attack economic exploitation of women workers. For her, mothers were workers.[36]

In hearings on the proposed order, contractors clearly defined homeworkers as housewives and mothers whom they happened to employ, rather than as workers. These women, they charged, were neither steady nor dependable. "To get out 1600 to 2000 you got to have five homeworkers to give you that amount of envelopes in a week, because, at the most they do it in their spare time and if you get good ones, you might get 3000 and inside you would get 10,000," one employer asserted.[37] As the lawyer for the United Addressers Association complained, if they had the space and available typists, inside workers were preferable because an "order has to be finished in a week, the typing has to be finished in three days and the homeworker may not be feeling well or going to a movie or visiting relatives, she holds it back." That is, homeworkers typed during their "odd moments or half hours" because care of children and housework were their priorities.[38]

Homeworkers were mothers, then, who could not drag their children on the subway to pick up work in New York; therefore, they worked locally for contractors. According to one such deployer of neighborhood women, "They push a baby buggy with one kid in the back and the other kid on the side and they pick up a thousand envelopes and dump it into the carriage and wheel it home." These employers assumed that mothers alone cared for children. They countered union claims that women desired to work in offices with "—well, how in the world can they if they have children. How can they? The only time they can come is at night and . . . they have too much to do at night to bother with typing." As if they were not typing at home in the evenings![39]

Homeworkers were also "girls," like other women workers, no matter their age. Despite praise of mothers who contributed to the family economy, contractors held deeply misogynist views. Not only did they refuse to view homeworkers as serious and trustworthy workers, they heaped scorn on "girls [who] come in from offices, they want to work in an office, they are expert typists," as one put it. "They work for half an hour and say 'this is too hard.'" Another argued that you couldn't pay "girls" on a weekly basis because "they will talk in the shop and you can't run the business on that basis." The image of the "average typist," "slated for 40 hours a week," who "puts in three and the rest of the time she spends out in the wash room" justified their turn to homeworkers. This picture also defined what employers meant by labor shortage: a lack of women willing to work under the terms offered. Contractors seemed to share the attitude of one man who protested the homework order out of fear that it would interfere with "the prerogative" of "business men, and professional men . . . of having typing done at home by women who cannot work full time in an office." Homeworkers/women/mothers existed for their convenience.[40]

This identification of homeworker with mother and housewife provided the basis by which the employment status of these women workers was mystified. As the Director of the American School of Business Administration complained to the Industrial Commissioner:

> Any regulation that would arbitrarily give these outside addressers the status of employee—subject to unemployment insurance and other employee benefits—would create an incongruous situation. These individuals—whose primary occupation is that of housewife—certainly cannot be considered as being unemployed when they are not doing addressing work for us. They may be performing such services for other organizations, or they may choose to be *idle.* (emphasis added)

When not doing homework, women became "idle," the Director continued. Because family obligations inclined addressers not to accept as much work as this employer was willing to offer, he classified them as "independent contractors," or workers not subject to FLSA, unemployment, social security, or other state protections. For other employers, the rhythms of the work, done without immediate supervision and presumably at the workers' own pace in her own time, justified that designation. These rhythms derived, of course, from the position of the worker as housewife and mother, the very factor behind both her availability as homework labor and her attractiveness to employers. As the lawyers for the giant, interstate R.H. Donnelly Corporation concluded in a brief against providing unemployment insurance to homeworkers:

> It is a well known fact that clerical homeworkers are invariably former stenographers or typists whose principal occupation has changed to that of housewife. It is because these people cannot accept definite working hours that they rent or purchase typewriters and set themselves up as home typists in which capacity they can work solely at their own convenience free from direction, supervision or control.

Some contractors attempted to argue that home clerical work should not be regarded as industrial homework because "the type of work is easy and genteel"; others drew upon the task-oriented and less routinized world of housework to obscure the employer-employee relationship.[41]

Homeworkers may have been mothers, but the simple truth is they were employees too. In 1952, the Unemployment Insurance Appeal Board rejected this separation of mother from worker by considering only the conditions under which employment took place. It reversed an earlier decision and defined homeworkers as employees, not independent contractors. It cited how the employer checked the typewriter, demanded work be redone, and gave further directions by phone. The Board explained that such workers "do not have their own established places of business; . . . are subject to discharge by appellant and are under its direction and control to an extent sufficient to establish an employer-employee relationship." Noting that some supervision existed, especially as to the manner and acceptability of the work, and that piece-rate payment failed to determine status, the Board affirmed an employee relationship.[42]

Mothers, after all, could be workers even if the state legislature soon would affirm the contractor's position that clerical homeworkers could not be regulated under the industrial homework law. At stake was also that status of clerical workers inside the direct mail houses. Even the big unionized employers feared that if this industry had been defined as industrial for homework regulation, such typists would come under the hours, wage, and other labor legislation for women, which exempted office workers from coverage.[43]

CONCLUSION

Mothers continued to type at home in increasing numbers during the 1950s, when business services represented the growth area for homework. These women expressed the same reason for the site of their labor as had those working for the direct mail houses: "need to stay home to care for young children." As long as their labor remained hidden in the home and appeared not to violate labor standards (which neglected comparable clerical jobs anyway), even opponents of the evils of homework lauded their supplementing family income. Certainly the changing political economy of white-collar work found a flexible labor force in white women removed by housing patterns from employment choices and tied down with mother-care of children. Homework as a form of part-time labor fitted into their life pattern: paid labor before marriage, interruption with the birth of their first child, and return to nondomestic employment after the last child started school. Despite the conservative political and ideological climate of the time, women during their childbearing years increasingly entered the labor force. Employers continued to be central in determining the location of their labor.[44]

By depending on the identification of homeworker as mother, neither side in the regulatory debate of forty years ago addressed the conditions of homeworking mothers. Women like Mrs. K. had to type envelopes to make ends meet without much guarantee that the work would be there for her tomorrow at the same rate. Without child care or other employment options, mothers made the best out of what they had. Neither trade unionists nor most organized women's groups ever proposed alternatives for homeworkers; their concern ended with the stopping of an exploitative labor system rather than the organizing of homeworkers or the improving of their labor standards. Only the Congress of American Women recognized the need for an alliance between homeworking women and those who labored in shops and offices. It alone challenged the false division between mother and worker. Trade unionists, other women advocates, and employers reinforced this separation, albeit in a manner to buttress opposing positions.

Such constructions of motherhood not only denied the labors of mothers, but maintained the dichotomous thinking central to the inequalities that structure women's lives. By viewing the home and workplace as separate spheres, such thinking obscured the connection between productive and reproductive labor. Women's position in the paid labor force has always depended on their position within the home; and also on their racial ethnic and class position.[45] The sexual division of labor, as manifested in this particular homework debate, has proved, as one student of British industrialization has put it, "central in structuring the poverty-reproduction-homework knot."[46] Mothers provided an available labor force for homework because of their unpaid labor. Clearly, homework as a type of labor that women performed for the economic well-being of their families helped to shape capitalist industrialization itself. Rather than considering homework a residue form of production, it needs to be seen as integral component of the many industries that structured their labor process around sending some time-consuming operations into the home to take advantage of cheap labor and reduce overhead.[47]

It was, in fact, the construction of motherhood that obscured this very process. If mothers were not workers, then waged labor at home became pin money, not central to the production of goods and services. If homeworkers were mothers, they could not be real workers because as mothers their time was too flexible. They merely supplemented a man's wages, so who could say that their work was necessary? Such reasoning led homework advocates, especially those who deployed anti-Communist rhetoric, to paint state regulation as an invasion of the privacy of the home. Ironically, however, they failed to note that paid labor, a public activity, had entered the social space they would save from the state.

Homework opponents, on the other hand, merely switched the terms of this equation. For them, the invader of the home became the factory or office rather than the state. But they too separated the home from the workplace, reproduction from production. The dilemma was that homework denied such dichotomy by both placing the two realms in the same space and by making production dependent on the conditions of reproduction.

This division of mother from worker had another consequence: Not only did it obscure the labors of women within the home, it denied the womanhood of those women who had to labor outside the home. Since women of color and working-class women of all races have predominated among those who could not rely on a man's wage to meet household needs, it was these women in particular who found themselves further denigrated by this social construction of motherhood.[48] Only certain groups of mothers became homeworkers: African-American women were least likely to be hired for homework; while immigrant women, including those from the Americas and Asia, were most likely.[49] That U.S. society has considered Black women to be primarily workers and not mothers helps to justify racial segmentation. That many immigrant groups keep their women within the family also reinforces the economic structures that insert such new arrivals into the labor market in ways that distinguish by race and ethnicity. As long as we deny that mothers are workers, even if they labor for wages and not just for the family, we maintain the basis for a public policy that sustains unequal power relations.

Notes

1. For an extended discussion of these points, see Eileen Boris, *Home to Work: Motherhood and the Politics of Industrial Homework in the United States* (New York: Cambridge University Press, 1993).

2. For this history, see Eileen Boris, "Regulating Industrial Homework: The Triumph of 'Sacred Motherhood,'" *Journal of American History* 71 (March 1985), pp. 745–763; Eileen Boris, "Homework Regulation and the Devolution of the Post-War Labor Standards Regime: Beyond Dichotomy," in Christopher Tomlins and Andrew King, eds., *Labor Law In America: Critical and Historical Perspectives* (Baltimore: Johns Hopkins University Press, 1992), pp. 260–282. On the Women's Bureau coalition after the war, Cynthia Harrison, *On Account of Sex: The Politics of Women's Issues, 1945–1968* (Berkeley: University of California Press, 1988), p. 9.

3. See Steve Rosswurm, "An Overview and Preliminary Assessment of the CIO's Expelled Unions," in Steve Rosswurm, ed., *The CIO's Left-Led Unions* (New Brunswick: Rutgers Univ. Press, 1992), pp. 1–17.

4. Analysis of this event is based on files still housed in the New York State Department of Labor, Brooklyn office. I would like to thank Hugh McDaid, head of the Sweatshop Taskforce, for providing access to these files. See, State of New York, Department of Labor, "Order No. 5," Box 8, folder 3, New York Consumers' League Papers, Labor-Management Documentation Center, Cornell University; "To: New York State Board of Standards & Appeals, From: . . ." pp. 1–4, folder, "Direct Mail: Briefs and Statements," NYDOL. On

legislative intervention, see Inter Office Memorandum, "To: Supervisors, From: George Ostrow, Re: Direct Mail Order, Date: August 17, 1953," and attached letters, file, "Homework: Direct Mail."

5. For this "work ethic for women," Joanne Meyerowitz, "Beyond 'The Feminine Mystique': The discourse on American Women, 1945–1950," p. 17, unpublished paper presented at the eighth Berkshire Conference on the History of Women, June 1990.

6. My strategy reflects a concern among feminist scholars to contextualize "the linguistic turn" associated with Joan Scott and others who would focus on language to elicit meaning. As Nancy Fraser has asked, "what sorts of conditions underpin the fact that some agents' discursive constructions have more cultural authority than others? What are the sources outside discourse of discursive dominance and subordination?" For that we must turn to "large structural and institutional" forces, fully aware that our understanding of them is mediated by language. See Fraser, Review of *Gender and History* and *Gender and the Politics of History*, in *NSWA Journal*, 2 (Summer 1990), p. 508.

7. No adequate history of these years exists. For overviews, see William Chafe, *Unfinished Journey* (New York: Oxford University Press, 1986) and George Lipschultz, *Class and Culture in Cold War America: "A Rainbow At Midnight"* (Holyoke: Bergen, 1982); for women and trade unions, Dorothy Sue Cobble, "Reassessing the 'Doldrum Years': Working Class Feminism in the 1940s," unpublished paper presented at the eighth Berkshire Conference on the History of Women, June 1990; for women reformers, Harrison, *On Account of Sex.*

8. U.S. Women's Bureau, *Changes in Women's Occupations, 1940–1950*, Bulletin No. 253 (Washington: GPO, 1954), pp. 2–9.

9. Hazel Kyrk, "Family Responsibilities of Earning Women," in U.S. Women's Bureau, *The American Woman—Her Changing Role as Worker, Homemaker, Citizen*, Bulletin No. 224 (Washington: GPO, 1948), p. 63. Kyrk, Professor of Home Economics and Economics at the University of Chicago, answered, in fact, that "no restrictions should be placed on their freedom to enter a gainful pursuit," and suggested the problems that occurred came from people living in nuclear families. She suggested that the married mother and wife who was hurt was the one with the least resources, forced by economic circumstances to labor. The woman was particularly burdened, Kyrk argued, if young children and heavy household responsibilities were present. Here women's rights and women's burdens as reasons for paid labor merged in a postwar pragmatic evaluation of the "problem."

10. U.S. Women's Bureau, *Handbook of Facts on Women Workers*, Bulletin No. 225 (Washington: GPO, 1948), pp. 1–12, 32–33; Janet M. Hooks, *Women's Occupations Through Seven Decades*, Bulletin No. 218 (Washington: GPO, 1951), p. 77; U.S. Women's Bureau, *"Older" Women as Office Workers*, Bulletin No. 248 (Washington: GPO, 1953), p. 57.

11. Joan Wallach Scott, "The Mechanization of Women's Work," *Scientific American* (September 1982), pp. 166–167; Margery Davies, *Women's Place Is At the Typewriter* (Philadelphia: Temple University Press, 1982); Cindy Sondik Aron, *Ladies and Gentlemen of the Civil Service: Middle-Class Workers in Victorian America* (New York: Oxford Univ. Press, 1987), pp. 86–91; U.S. Department of Labor, Bureau of Labor Statistics, "Proceedings of the Fourteenth Annual Convention of the Association of Governmental Labor Officals of the United States and Canada," *Bulletin*, No. 455 (Washington: GPO, 1927), p. 90; "Homework on Direct Mail Operations, New York State," State of New York Department of Labor, unpublished typescript, c. 1949. For another description of the direct mail industry as "factory industries," see "Memorandum for the Industrial Commissioner," August 1, 1949.

12. "General Background, 1/19/51," folder, "Homework: Direct Mail, Reports re Industry," typescript, pp. 13–15; "Homework on Direct Mail Operations," pp. 7–18; Press Release, "To Control Homework in Direct Mail Industry,"*NEWS*, July 18, 1950, Box 8, folder 3, New York Consumers' League Papers; "Memorandum for the Industrial Com-

missioner, Re: Application of Labor Law, Article 13, to 'Homeworkers' in the Direct Mail Industry," August 1, 1949, file "Legal"; George Ostrow to J. D. Wolf, July 2, 1952, "Re: Brief of Petitioners Before the New York State Board of Standards and Appeals," file "Homework, Direct Mail, Reports re Industry," pp. 2–4.

13. "Homework on Direct Mail Operations," pp. 23–7.

14. The actual numbers are: for homeworkers, 1,950; for inside typists, 1,810.

15. "Homework on Direct Mail Operations," pp. 31–51. Direct mail earnings were down from many other average hourly and weekly earnings among typists in New York City in the late 1940s. According to one study by the NYDOL, in 1947, women in factory offices earned $40.76 a week, compared to $59.10 for their male counterparts. From *Handbook of Facts on Women Workers*, p. 28. The lowest that class B typists earned from January to February 1948 was $.95 (women) and $1.02 (men) an hour. From U.S. Department of Labor, Bureau of Labor Statistics, *Salaries of Office Workers in Selected Large Cities*, Bulletin No. 943 (Washington: GPO, 1948), Table I, p. 29.

16. This figure does not necessarily represent the number of completed families; nor does it take into account the beginning of the baby boom. Given the age range of the women, it is possible that many had not yet completed their families.

17. Many may have been second or third generation Italian or Jewish, suggesting how the daughters and granddaughters of industrial homeworkers merely switched work process, not site of labor. Yet since ethnicity was not recorded in the Department's survey, and the original survey interviews have not survived, we can't be sure about this speculation. Homeworkers who wrote to the Department of Labor in the 1960s protesting a ban on collating did have Italian and Jewish surnames. See Boris, *Home to Work Sweated Motherhood*, ch. 10.

18. At home, 4% were age 55 or older; in the direct mail houses, 13% were age 50 or older.

19. "Homework on Direct Mail Operations," pp. 28–31, 18. Inter-office Memorandum. To: Mrs. Marconnier, From: D. Maier and E. Kadish, Subject: Data on Supply of Typists Available for Letter Shop Work, August 29, 1949, pp. 3–4, in "Homework: Direct Mail. Surveys and Complaints." For median age of clerical workers, *Changes in Women's Occupations, 1940–1950*, p. 5.

20. *Ibid.*, pp. 28–9. On the growth of New York City in these years, see Kenneth Jackson, *Crabgrass Frontier* (New York: Oxford University Press, 1985).

21. "Homework on Direct Mail Operations," p. 29.

22. *Ibid.*, p. 17.

23. For an analysis of the demand factor in homework, Hilary Silver, "The Demand for Homework: Evidence from the U.S. Census," in Eileen Boris and Cynthia R. Daniels, eds., *Homework: Historical and Contemporary Perspectives on Paid Labor at Home* (Urbana: University of Illinois Press, 1989), pp. 103–129.

24. Henry Hoke, "A Report on a Mess," reprint from *The Reporter of Direct Mail Advertising*, August 1950, in NYDOL files; copy memo from John J. Patafio, June 17, 1949; John Patafio to Hon. Lee B. Mailler, August 24, 1950. Significantly, Patafio argued as "a father and a small businessman" who saw the order destroying the business he hoped to hand over to his sons, veterans who had sacrificed for their country. See also, E. C. Walker to Emily Sims Marconnier, Director (division of Industrial Relations Women in Industry), October 12, 1950, which says that the letters "were originated by the Reporter of Direct Mail advertising who published the original information that reached the smaller people out in the sticks, like ourselves." See also, Emily Sims Marconnier to Hon. Samuel Faile, October 4, 1950, all in "Correspondence 50–55."

25. John D. Breton to Hon. Thomas E. Dewey, August 28, 1950; Christian Weyand of the True Church of Christ International to Hon. Charles E. Dewey [sic.], October 2, 1950; Gregory Greubel to His Excellency Thomas E. Dewey, August 29, 1950; Mrs. Agnes Lyons to dear Sir, September 1, 1950, all in "Correspondence 50–58."

26. For the most recent interpretation along this line, Elaine Tyler May, *Homeward Bound: American Families in the Cold War Era* (New York: Basic Books, 1988).

27. Meyerowitz, "Beyond 'The Feminine Mystique': The Discourse on American Women, 1945–1950."

28. R. De Pace, Manager, Elliott Addressing Machine Company to His Excellency, Thomas E. Dewey, August 21, 1950, in "Correspondence 50–58;" see, also, Henry Benisch to Hon. Anthony R. Saverese Jr., December 28, 1970. For the use of such privacy arguments linked to right to work, see Eileen Boris, "'A Man's Home Is His Castle': Tenement House Cigarmaking and the Judicial Imperative," in Ava Barton, ed., *Work Engendered: Toward a New History of American Labor* (Ithaca: Cornell University Press, 1991), pp. 114–141.

29. Robert R. Updegraff to Mr. Edward Corsi, September 21, 1950; (Miss) Frances Micalizzi to Hon. Thomas E. Dewey, with copies to Senator MacNeal Mitchell, Assemblywoman Maude Ten Eyck, and Commissioner Edward Corsi, no name, n.d., all in "Correspondence 50–58." See, also, Mrs. G. Vivian Hyland to Governor Thomas E. Dewey, Tenth, 1950; Assemblyman Samuel Faile to Hon. Edward Corsi, September 26, 1950; R.P. Wilhelm to Honorable Thomas E. Dewey, August 28, 1950.

30. (Mrs.) Robert B. Boothby to Governor Thomas E. Dewey, September 8, 1950; (Mrs.) Louisa Bidanset to Gov. Thos. B. Dewey, September 7, 1950, "Correspondence 50–58."

31. Testimony of Jack Arnoff, "Of Public Hearing on Industrial Homework in the Letter Shop Industry," May 24, 1949, p. 42.

32. Clarence M. Roach to My dear Governor, August 29, 1950; P.O. Johnson to the Honorable Irving Iyes, August 28, 1950, in "Correspondence 50–58."

33. Oliver Pilat, "Department of Labor," *New York Post Home News*, April 19, 1949, p. 38; May 2, 1949, p. 34; clippings in "Homework, Direct Mail: Publicity" and *ibid.*, May 25, 1949, n. p., in "Homework: Direct Mail, Procedure and Inter-Office Memo; " testimony of Miss Angus and Miss Kaye, in "Of Public Hearing on Industrial Homework in the Letter Shop Industry," May 24, 1949, pp. 28, 25, unpublished typescript, in file "Home Labor— Letter Shop Industry," NYDOL Library, Brooklyn.

34. *Ibid.*, testimony of Mr. Fixler, Mr. Greenspan, and Mr. Sobel, pp. 15, 10, 20–21. Greenspan quoted from his prepared statement, "Statement on Typing Homework, Submitted by Local 16, United Office and Professional Workers of America, C.I.O," p.2.

35. George Ostrow, Administrator, Homework Bureau, "Re: Brief of Petitioners Before the New York State Board of Standards and Appeals," July 2, 1952, pp. 9–10, "Homework: Direct Mail: Reports re Industry." Comment on typing stand by Mr. De Groodt in "Minutes of Public Hearing on Industrial Homework in the Direct Mail Industry," October 5, 1949, pp. 19-20.

36. Testimony of Haloise Moorehead, "Of Public Hearing on Industrial Homework in the Letter Shop Industry," pp. 26–27.

37. Testimony of A.J. Howard, Harry Stein, in *ibid.*, pp. 17, 33.

38. Testimony of Mr. Gilman, Mr. De Groodt, "Minutes of Public Hearing on Industrial Homework in the Direct Mail Industry," October 5, 1949, pp. 12–13, 4.

39. Testimony of De Groodt, *ibid.*, p. 17; testimony of Harry Ochshorn, "Of Public Hearing on Industrial Homework in the Letter Shop Industry," May 24, 1949, p. 13.

40. Testimony of Mr. Stein, *ibid.*, pp. 32–34; Testimony of Mr. De Groodt, "Minutes of Public hearing on Industrial Homework in the Direct Mail Industry, October 5, 1949, p. 5; Wendell F. Adams to The Honorable Thomas E. Dewey, November 24, 1950, p. 3, "Correspondence, 50–58."

41. Paul Kline to Mr. Edward Corsi, May 31, 1949, p. 2, in "1950–55: Briefs and Statements;" Brief for Appellant, "In the Matter of the Claim for Benefits Under Article 18 of the Labor Law made by Josephine F. Riley, Claimant," Appeal No. 18, 687–49, p. 13; "Minutes of Public Hearing," p. 8.

42. State of New York, Department of Labor, Unemployment Insurance Appeal Board, "Decision," Case No. 29,904–51, May 9, 1952, esp. pp. 7–8; see, also, Supreme Court,

Appellate Division, Third Judicial Department, Appeal Board Case No. 29,904–51, Decision Handed down March 11, 1953, file "Legal."

43. Daniel Arvan, the attorney for the direct Mail Master Contract Association, for one, expressed this concern. See, "Of Public Hearing on Industrial Homework in the Letter Shop Industry," p. 23. See also, Albert Gilman, "*Do You Want Homework Eliminated?*", December 8, 1949, in "Homework: Direct Mail: Briefs and Statements."

44. Wage and Hour and Public contracts Divisions, Division of Regulation and Research, Branch of Research and Statistics, "Employment of Homeworkers under the Fair Labor Standards Act," July 1959, pp. 2–5, 7–8, Department of Labor Library, Francis Perkins Building, Washington, D.C.; Milton Derber, "Industrial Homework: An Old Problem Lingers On," Lecture Series No. 17 (Institute of Labor and Industrial Relations, University of Illinois, Champaign, 1958), pp. 7, 10; Ethel Klein, *Gender Politics: From Consciousness to Mass Politics* (Cambridge: Harvard University Press, 1984), p. 39; Rochelle Gatlin, *American Women Since 1945* (Jackson: University of Mississippi Press, 1987), pp. 30–32.

45. Evelyn Nakano Glenn, "From Servitude to Service Work: Historical Continuities in the Racial Division of Paid Reproductive Labor," *Signs: Journal of Women in Culture and Society*, 18 (Autumn 1992), pp. 1–43.

46. Sonya Rose, *Limited Livelihoods: Gender and Class In Nineteenth-Century England* (Berkeley: Univ. of California press, 1992), p. 101.

47. For the working of the homework system, Boris, *Sweated Motherhood, passim.*

48. Eileen Boris, "The Power of Motherhood: Black and White Activist Women Redefine the 'Political,' " in Sonya Michel and Seth Koven, eds., *Mothers of a New World: Maternalist Politics and the Origins of Welfare States* (New York: Routledge, 1993); Evelyn Nakano Glenn, "Racial Ethnic Women's Labor: The Intersection of Race, Gender and Class Oppression," *Review of Radical Political Economics*, 17 (Fall 1985), pp. 86–108.

49. For who does homework today, see Robert E. Kraut, "Telecommuting: The Trade-Offs of Home Work," *Journal of Communication* 39 (Summer 1989), pp. 20–31; Marilyn Webb, "Sweatshops for One: The Rise in Industrial Homework," *Village Voice* (February 10–16, 1982), pp. 24, 27.

Chapter 9

FAMILY DAY CARE PROVIDERS: DILEMMAS OF DAILY PRACTICE

Margaret K. Nelson

INTRODUCTION

Since the early nineteenth century, motherhood has been constructed as an intensely private, full-time activity, for middle-class, white American women.[1] This construction presents itself as a stumbling block to women who need or choose to work outside the home. "Experts" warn about the negative consequences of nonmaternal care for very young children; these warnings intensify the guilt many women feel when they assume roles that interfere with a single-minded devotion to their children. Thus it is not surprising that many women seek a form of substitute care resembling that which some mothers used to, and most women were expected to, offer their own children. Family day care, defined as "nonresidential care provided in a private home other than the child's own," is a popular form of out-of-the-home care, especially for very young children.[2]

Discussions of child care arrangements usually focus on "working mothers" and their children. In this chapter, however, the angle of vision is turned toward the third party in these arrangements, the providers themselves.[3] Family day-care providers unavoidably straddle public-private boundaries because they usually care for their own children, while at the same time they take care of other mothers' children. They offer a public service that, although it has an ambiguous occupational identity (baby-sitter? child care worker?), is increasingly subject to state scrutiny.

As scholars have noted, the public-private dichotomy, though flawed as a description of reality, does have the function of isolating sets of appropriate norms.[4] People expect their private and public lives to make different claims and to offer different rewards. These differences are high-lighted with respect to the issue of care, and especially, the care of young children. In the *private* world, ideally, relationships are "nurturing, en-during . . . noncontingent [and] governed by feelings of morality."[5] Thus, according to the "domestic code," the cultural ideal of mothering assumes intense, exclusive bonds between the mother and her child, and it assumes a mother's willingness to respond to her child's emotional and physical needs, even when to do so is at the cost of her own well-being.[6] Yet, in this very privatized vision of caregiving, where children are often per-ceived as a parent's property, a mother's obligations are balanced by her prerogatives; mothers have leeway in defining the morality and discipline appropriate to their children's care. In the *public* world, relationships may remain "impersonal, competitive, contractual, and temporary."[7] Al-though in institutional settings, paid caregivers may engage in many of the same activities as mothers, they do so with different prerogatives, and they must accomplish their tasks without becoming overly attached to, or identified with, their clients.[8]

The norms defining private and public life are also gendered. As the feminist scholarship on caregiving argues, if care is the work a woman is compelled to do, it is also an essential component of her identity.[9] Since the emergence of industrial capitalism, when men and "work" moved into the public world, women were left in and given complete responsibility for the activities of the domestic domain. They were also identified with those tasks that, because they were now defined as "not work," were assumed to flow from innate nurturance. Women were thus assumed to have no independent rights or interests, but to subordinate their needs willingly to those dependent on them.[10] In contrast, men have been free to pursue (and, indeed, compelled to seek) a life in the public sphere that assumes they are acting as autonomous individuals, as in-dividuals with rights.[11]

The ambiguous location between private and public spheres, and their accompanying sets of expectations, is not unique to family day care. Women who do carework in public settings (for instance, teachers, nurses), women who do carework in other people's homes (for instance, domestic workers, home health aides), and women who do home-based work (for instance, industrial homework, telecommuting) all straddle public-private boundaries. But family day-care providers are positioned in a very particular way. While those who work in public settings fre-quently have to negotiate around institutional structures that impede the formation of bonds of attachment and the provision of personalized care, they often are "protected" by these very same institutional structures and by the norm of professional detachment.[12] Those who provide care in other people's homes might have fewer protections, but like those who work in public settings, they can achieve a physical (if not emotional) separation between their private lives and their paid employment. This separation is not possible for family day-care providers. And while those who incorporate productive relations into the private domain have to balance the simultaneous demands of paid and unpaid work, they do not engage in the *same* tasks in both sets of activities. This differentiation between family day-care providers and these other workers is not meant to imply that the latter straddle the fence without conflict; but it is to point to the fact that family day-care providers may face a distinctive set of dilemmas.

These dilemmas stand at the heart of this analysis. In what follows, I first describe the methods for this study. I then demonstrate that family day-care providers construct their work in a manner that draws from the nineteenth-century, middle-class ideal of mothering. I suggest that this style emerges from both the structural constraints of family day care and from experiential learning, and I demonstrate how, in drawing on their experiences of caregiving, family day-care providers acquire a distinctive body of practical knowledge that they seek to protect. I then explore more fully the dilemmas of actual practice.

First, as we will see, family day-care providers in this study choose to provide family day care in order to enact a "traditional," at-home, mothering ideal. In doing so, they inevitably offer a service in which they do not believe. That is, to the extent that they have chosen *not* to seek employment outside the home because they feel strongly that a mother should be available to, and fully engaged with, *her* own children, the family day-care provider offers to other people's children a service that she could not accept for her own. And, although she is acting from the position of a "traditional" mother—and seeking to preserve that ideal— she enables other women to alter and enlarge the meaning of "motherhood" to include both paid work outside the home and substitute child care for at least part of the day. By bringing other people's children into her domestic sphere, the family day-care provider transforms the meaning and enactment of motherhood in yet another way. Not only does she redefine the "traditional" mother as someone who can combine both productive and reproductive work in the home, but in doing so she inevitably compromises her ideal of good mothering.

A second kind of dilemma has to do with the family day-care provider's relationship to the work of caring for other people's children. Whereas members of some communities embrace a more collective responsibility for children, and incorporate a variety of kinds of relationships to young children,[13] within the world of white, working- and middle-class women in the U.S. from which most of the family day-care providers and their clients in this study are drawn, mothering is constructed not only as a private activity but as an exclusive one as well. In this context the formation of intense, emotional bonds with other people's children becomes problematic; these bonds have to be balanced with the awareness of limited authority, responsibility, and the inevitability of loss.

METHODS AND SAMPLE CHARACTERISTICS

Methods

In the summer of 1986 I mailed a questionnaire to each of the 463 registered day-care providers in the state of Vermont; responses were received from 225 providers (a response rate of forty-nine percent). The following summer I distributed questionnaires to 105 unregistered family day-care providers located through snowball sampling techniques.[14] The questionnaires covered a range of issues, including the number of years the women had been providing child care, reasons for opening a day-care home, attitudes towards child care, problems, and background information. During the summer of 1988 I also conducted a telephone survey of sixty-three registered and twelve unregistered providers no longer involved in family day care. Questions in this survey asked providers about their reasons for leaving family day care.

Over a two-year period, I conducted lengthy, semistructured interviews with thirty registered day-care providers (twenty-one of whom had also completed questionnaires) and forty unregistered day-care providers (ten of whom has also completed questionnaires). Questions in the interview dealt with a wide range of issues, including relationships with children and parents, the impact of the work on members of the provider's family, and sources of stress and satisfaction. I also conducted interviews in 1989 with sixteen women who had ceased providing family day care.

Sample Characteristics

The family day-care providers in this study were almost uniformly married women (eighty-six percent) with children of their own (ninety-six percent). Over half (fifty-six percent) of the women had at least one child of preschool age and therefore cared full-time for both their own and nonresident children. The women in the study ranged in age from twenty-one to seventy-one with a mean of 34.5. The number of years of involvement in the occupation ranged from recent initiates, who had been working for less than a year, to one woman who had been offering care for twenty-three years; the median number of years as a family day-care provider was three. Most (ninety-four percent) of the women had completed a high school education, and half of the women had some education beyond high school. The median household income for providers fell between twenty thousand dollars and twenty-five thousand dollars at a time when the median family income in the state for a married couple with a wife in the labor force and a child under the age of six was $21,137.[15] With one exception, all of the women who were interviewed were white.

Constructing the Role of Family Day-care Provider as Mothering

The family day-care providers in my study clearly construct their role in line with the white, middle-class cultural ideal of mothering. The women viewed the development of personal and intimate relationships as an essential component of family day care: seventy-five of the respondents agreed strongly with the statement "a family day-care provider should be like a mother to the children in her care." In discussing their feelings about the children the women use familial analogies: "They are my part-time kids"; "I'm trying to give the children a sense of family"; "I'm like a second mom"; "I think of them as extended members of my family"; "These guys are like my own kids"; "I'm offering closeness and security—my motherhood."

Moreover, most family day-care providers wanted to create for the children in their care the same environment they assume prevails in a home with a mother present. Eighty-one percent of the questionnaire respondents felt it was "very important" to provide "a homelike atmosphere." Interviews confirmed this approach: "I try to make the child comfortable here"; "I try to give them the experiences I gave to my own children"; "I want this to be a nurturing place"; "They should be at home here"; "I like this being just like a home." When I asked, "What do you do with the children," the analogy to a mother's care emerged again:

> I don't schedule the day. They do their thing and I do mine around whatever they are doing. . . . If the ironing's got to be done, the ironing gets done. If the laundry's got to be done—I don't do all of these things after they leave at night. I don't do a thing any different than I did what I was home with my own two. What's got to be done gets done.

Although most women do not find time to attend to much housework, some can and they see their actions as beneficial to the children: "They see you doing these things and it's just like mom."[16] The manner in which providers use these terms suggests that they believe their meanings are obvious, that everyone knows what kind of care a mother offers and what a home is. As providers talk they reveal the specific content of the mothering ideal with which they work.

High on the list of priorities is to keep the children safe and to attend to their everyday needs while they are in their care. Most of the family day-care providers, when asked to describe their style of child care or what they are trying to accomplish with the children, also mention discipline:

> I expect the child to respect me as a person and I, in return, respect them as an individual, their privacy. If they want to be left alone, fine. I try to encourage manners, politeness, sharing with other children, as well as playing together in a group. Just generally learning to respect other people's property.

But neither safety nor discipline necessitates constant interaction. The majority of family day-care providers is convinced that a home is a place where children should play, learn through playing, and can be left alone for periods of times to amuse themselves. While they may read to the children or bring out toys and equipment, most do not feel that instruction should be the core of a child's day; only twenty-four percent of the questionnaire respondents said that it was "very important" to offer children a structured or planned day; only thirty-nine percent indicated that they thought it was "very important" to include "educational activities" in the daily round of events.[17] In fact, a substantial number of the providers feel that too much emphasis on "ABCs" is inappropriate and unnecessary for young children: "I'm not one who feels [preschool education] is important." Providers do, however, stress other kinds of learning, particularly the development of social skills: fifty-three percent said they thought this was "very important." As one provider said, "you teach them everything they have to know about life." And another provider contrasted this kind of teaching with the emphasis on education, and drew a boundary between her responsibility and that of parents: "I don't spend a lot of time trying to teach the kids. I tell [the parents] that is their job. I teach them what life is about."

When women were asked questions about the concrete differences they perceived between the care they give and that offered to children in a day-care center, they were quite articulate and insistent: they responded that day-care centers neither encourage the "warmth, love, and intimacy" nor offer the "one-on-one" care of a family setting. Some providers suggested that because day-care centers, like schools, follow a schedule of activities, they do not allow for a free-flowing responsiveness to the individual child's needs and interests. Almost all of the women interviewed believed that a home is the preferable location for the daily care of young children.

Homelike care thus refers to the kind of activities that prevail; it also refers to the pacing of these activities and the attentiveness and affection that makes this pacing responsive to children's needs. It is an ideal that assumes a commonality among all homes and among all mothers. Family day-care providers know well that the children in their care come to them from very different backgrounds, from families with widely varying material resources and caregiving styles. In asserting a shared notion of homelike care, they deny that these differences are significant. They embrace instead some common core that they believe defines mothering, whether it is for their own or someone else's child.

CREATING AND DEFENDING THE PROVIDER'S STYLE

This construction of family day-care as mothering has roots in the structural constraints within which providers offer their services, and in the kind of prior experiences available to the women who do this work. As family day-care providers enact this ideal, they gain confidence in their abilities and develop an interest in defending their autonomy.

Structural Factors

By definition, family day-care providers remain at home, and merge paid and unpaid care in a single setting. This makes it difficult for the provider to distinguish between what she is doing for her *own* children and what she is doing for the children who come to her on a daily basis. There is, as well, a material underpinning to the emphasis on homelike care. A preschool pedagogy is expensive.[18] Although the providers spend weekends scouring garage sales for toys and equipment, they cannot afford to spend too much on these items. As one woman said, "I'm a *home* day care. I can only do so much with what I can afford. I can't buy luxurious things."

There is also a pragmatic underpinning to this kind of care. Most day-care centers and preschools divide children into single age groups (in order to lessen the variations in the kinds of demands to which they are called to respond), and tie parents to specified schedules (in order to reduce the frequency with which they are interrupted). Thus they are equipped to plan activities appropriate for a narrow range of children and to follow a schedule. Family day-care providers don't have these luxuries: "It's hard with the little ones [around] to sit down and work on our alphabet. I leave that up to the mother to do at home."

The isolation in which they work makes it difficult to go on field trips ("We go to the playground—but that is hard unless you have someone with you") or to maintain an energetic level of activity ("In a center, workers have a break and therefore children have a person with more gusto. I can't keep up that level"). The work surrounding meal preparation and cleaning takes time that might otherwise be devoted to interaction with the children. Because their work space is also their living space, they have obligations to make the day care "invisible" at the end of the day. They cannot totally rearrange the house to meet children's needs or leave unfinished activities in place.

As providers acknowledge these constraints, they often distinguish between their offerings and those in other forms of group care. Occasionally, as some of their comments suggest, they also differentiate between their care and that of mothers in a manner that curiously reverses the more usual division of labor between mothers and other caregivers. When they identify their homes as being the site in which children receive casual care and love, mothers, as well as teachers, are assigned responsibility for formal instruction.

Experiential Factors

If structure constrains and shapes the family day-care provider's style, a construction of the work as mothering also emerges from experience. Most family day-care providers draw on a distinctive set of experiences through which they believe they have acquired the skills necessary to perform competently the role they have defined.

Many providers, when asked how they learned to care for children, begin with a discussion of their own mothers' care for them. Providers also draw on their own early experiences of caring for young children. While conforming to the expectations of young girls, they had innumerable opportunities to develop caregiving skills. In answer to the question, "What kind of training have you had?" one woman said,

> Training? I was the oldest of eleven children—does that count? I have brothers and sisters at home right now that are like my own. I potty-trained them, I broke them of their bottle, I nurtured them, I gave them all the things that they needed. . . . I felt I was ready [to start caring for children]. I come from a big family—there was lots of us around.

Another woman, when asked whether she had ever cared for children before answered, "Just my whole life. My mother was sick when my younger sister was born and I baby-sat . . . from the time I was eight."

Most significantly, family day-care providers talk about learning from the experience of caring for their *own* children. As one woman said, "I've been told—and I feel—that [my own children] are great kids. . . . The way I raised them is what I do with the kids I baby-sit for . . . and [my children] are doing fine so far." Indeed, because they see the work as an extension of mothering, they believe they are prepared to handle the job without receiving formal training.[19] One woman laughed at a question about her qualifications:

A woman came the other day and she was asking, "What special training do you have in dealing with children?" And I said, "I'm the mother of six children, that's all the special training that I feel like I need." As far as taking a book that tells me how to deal with children . . . I don't want that. I don't believe in book-raising children.

As these comments suggest, for many providers there is no clear distinction between their current activities and their personal histories of more casual caregiving. They learned early that they were supposed to be nurturant, to be altruistic, to share their love and their homes with others.[20] In fact, some women could not answer the question of why they opened a family day-care home without reference to these earlier experiences; others could not even identify the moment at which they had begun to offer family day-care as such, because they started so informally.[21] And although when pushed to do so they locate their own ability to care for children in concrete experiences, so hidden is most of this kind of experiential learning that they believe that they are simply doing something that comes naturally to women. Thus both their commitment to caregiving, and their ability to do so effectively, are presented as apparently innate parts of being a woman and mother.[22] If they acknowledge that child care does not come easily to all women ("I don't think that everyone is cut out to do this"), they deny that it requires a cultivated set of skills. "I don't have any skills," said one woman. "Anyone who has been a mother can do this," added another.

Claiming Autonomy

Yet, no matter how casually they begin, or how adamantly they claim that they rely on "common sense" alone, as women persevere in the occupation they also acknowledge that they have acquired a distinct body of knowledge and a set of skills Sara Ruddick defines as "maternal thinking."[23] They mention learning to deal with crises and injuries; learning about developmental stages; and learning how to manage the complexities of relating to a wide range of ages. Some mention specific skills which ease the burden of their work: "I have gotten better at putting them to bed—I know that sounds funny but it could be difficult. I am also better at learning how long their attention span is." Some women say that they have become more flexible over time in response to their newfound ability to accurately assess children's moods: "I used to go with a routine and stick to that. Now I am looser than I used to be because I have learned how to be and to get the same thing accomplished while being looser." Many women speak about having become more patient. The definition of patience that one respondent (a provider for twenty-three years) gave me suggests that this aspect of the caregiver's experience is particularly complex:

> Patience is understanding the individuality of all of these children. . . . I could have another 181 [children] and each one of them would be different again. There's no two that need the same amount of loving or need the same amount of reprimanding. Each one needs a little extra something of some sort, which is fun finding with that individual. I think [that is part of the challenge].

Implicitly, then, providers recognize the value of experiential knowledge. They also become adamant about defending an individual style against those who would interfere with the manner in which they practice their work. Perhaps because family day-care providers conduct their work in isolation, they have reason to assume that they will have some autonomy. In fact, eighty-two percent of the questionnaire respondents agree with the statement, "I like [family day-care as a] job because it allows me to be my own boss"; seventy-nine percent agree with the statement, "I like my job because it allows me to be creative." And perhaps because they are raising their own children at the same time, they believe they should be able to make independent decisions about caregiving. But they also believe that they deserve independence. A claim for autonomy based on confidence in personal judgment emerges clearly, for example, when unregistered providers explain why they choose not to comply with specific state regulations, such as those that limit them to a specified number of children: "I just don't see what the big deal is. I just feel if you can handle it then it's up to you. . . . I've done it for seven years now. I just figure if I don't take on any more [children] than I can handle, I'm fine." Although providers understand why parents might seek the assurance of regulation, they proclaim their rights:

> I didn't want to have to hang a paper towel rack in my bathroom because they're not allowed to use towels. I just don't want to rearrange my whole house. My house is clean and its neat and its childproof. . . . I didn't want the regulations. That's not really fair, because if I had to send my child to child care I would probably want someone who's registered. . . . With all the child abuse that goes on, I think [registration] is appropriate. Yet that's touchy because it is still your house . . . you're talking about, or your family and you don't want to change your whole life style for it.

DILEMMAS OF ACTUAL PRACTICE

Two kinds of dilemmas face family day-care providers: the first concerns their inadvertent (indeed, reluctant) redefinition of mothering; the second revolves around the tensions of mothering other people's children.

Redefining Mothering

Offering a Service in Which They Do Not Believe

While the family day-care provider's style has its roots in both structure and experience, the *motivation* to do this work is based in a desire to care for her own children while earning a living. The women in this study defined themselves as mothers who are committed to mothering as their primary role.[24] Even those women who had worked previously as paid caregivers in an institutional setting did not offer these experiences (or an interest in building on the knowledge they had gained there) as an explanation for why they began to provide care at home. They said simply that they wanted to be home while their children were growing up.

At a time when increasing numbers of women work outside the home and leave their children in the care of others, the ferocity of this commitment is somewhat surprising. Several factors can help explain why these women are so insistent about this traditional model of child care. First, a high proportion of the providers experienced extensive family breakdown as children. These women explicitly linked their dreams for their children with the goal of avoiding the pain that characterized their own lives. Second, a precarious economic situation creates its own uncertainty. The poorer women in this study spoke about the significance of a parent's vigilance as a means to protect children from the "troubles" which afflicted them or their peers. Among some of these women a distrust of public institutions and the norms embedded there gave an additional reason for keeping their children "close to home and in the care of people who share parental values."[25]

Third, some of the family day care providers had formerly worked outside the home, and although they offered a variety of reasons for leaving wage labor, they said *first* that they could not bear the thought of having someone else rear the children:

I took three months off after I had [my daughter]. I never really thought that I would ever not work. . . . It was just about a year to the date after I went back to work that I decided, well, I really don't want to work any more, because I felt that I really needed to stay home—because of Alice. I wanted her to have a nice family life and I wanted her to have a mom and dad that knew her. . . . [I had] a real good person taking care of her . . . so I never had a second thought about leaving her as far as the sitter was concerned. But when I left her I felt kind of empty almost, and I couldn't wait to get done with work.

Some of these women are so embedded in their current choice they "forget" they ever led a different life: One woman, for example, told me her son had not done well in child care during the year she was employed outside the home, and then later in the interview she insisted she had never had anyone else care for her child.

Finally, and perhaps most significantly, an involvement in family day care feeds back on and reinforces one's original commitment. A provider finds confirmation of the importance of staying home with her *own* children in her observations of children who are separated from their parents all day, and in her assessment of what these children are missing. One of their major criticisms of women who leave their children with them is that these women are inconsistent and inadequate disciplinarians. They also believe that the children who are with them lack the sense of attachment to their parents and the daily experience of receiving love. This also is a reason for staying home with their own, and another pole around which good mothering revolves. "What is good care?" I asked one woman. She answered, "Most of the time it is just making sure that they are taken care of and showing the love they *should be getting at home* (emphasis added)."

Paradoxically, then, not only are family day-care providers attempting to offer the kind of care they do not think it is possible for anybody except a "real" mother to offer (and which they do not trust anybody but themselves to give to their own children), but they facilitate the movement of other women into the labor force even though they fervently believe these women should remain at home. On a daily basis, family day-care providers experience the unresolved dilemma of working hard to do well at something they do not value themselves:

> The bottom line is, I feel every mother at every expense should stay home with their child. . . . I always felt in the back of my mind, why don't they stay home with their children. . . . I can't understand why it was more important for them to shuffle papers. . . . And I still haven't figured it out.
>
> I was offering a service that I didn't really believe was in the child's best interest. I think young children should be home with their parents. It was hard for me too to be providing that service when I don't think that's what's best for the kids.

Compromising Their Own Mothering

Family day-care providers thus allow other women to be mothers in a manner they personally find unacceptable. Even more troubling, perhaps, is the fact that, as they care for their own children at the same time and in the same place that they care for others, they believe they alter the content and meaning of their *own* mothering.

We have noted that family day-care providers "choose" this occupation because they want to stay home and be mothers. But the family day-care provider must respond to the demands of the domestic domain while she responds to the demands of her paid work. This integration is not without costs.

Because the decision to embark on family day care is so firmly entrenched in a notion of its benefits for their children, providers have difficulty discussing problems. When they are asked how their children have responded to family day care, they generally begin with a positive statement about its consequences. Only reluctantly do they acknowledge a gap between actual and anticipated effects. We can hear this in how one woman's response to the question, "How do your children feel about your work?" was gradually qualified: "Oh, they love it. Well, It doesn't bother them too much. Occasionally they might get a little bit jealous." Providers not only have to acknowledge this gap, but they sometimes have to redefine "good" parenting.

The provider's ideal of good mothering for young children has been defined above. They believe strongly in opportunities for free play, consistent discipline, and intense affection; they believe in "being there" for their children. But they are only partially able to enact this ideal. The presence of other children limits the extent to which a woman is available to her own children; the presence of other children also highlights the nature of the different and intense dynamic between a mother and her own child.

Many providers say that one or more of their children are threatened by the intrusion of other children into the private domain. They also acknowledge that they have to put up with a range of distressing behavior patterns. Because acknowledgment of these negative effects is extremely painful for a provider who has defined her role as being the "good" or even "perfect" mother, she may be quick to minimize or deny them. She may suggest that the problems are the incidental results of a temporary situation: The new baby she is caring for is making it harder for her toddler who now feels displaced; her son is missing a particular day-care friend who recently left. One woman, for example, said that her daughter was having a hard time because "the other ones are all younger and they don't talk as well so she doesn't have anyone to socialize with." She quickly added, "But she's getting a lot better."[26] The women also assert that the problems are easily balanced by the benefits. They say that their children learn how to share, that they have companions to play with on a daily basis, and that they become more independent.[27]

But they cannot always write off the negative aspects. If they say their children grow from sharing, they also say their children never have the option of *not* sharing:

I found that my children have to share everything. They have to share their toys, they have to share their mother, they have to share their rooms—even their beds at times. I kind of feel . . . guilty about that at times. So that is my problem. That is me thinking that way.

And they acknowledge that, as a result, a child may even be less generous than s/he would be otherwise: "I think Emily is more giving than Jonah because he's always had to share his toys and whatever with everyone [whereas she had five years alone.] I think Emily's less selfish than Jonah is."

Finally, they admit that although they are home, they have little time to spend in focused interaction with their own children and little time to attend to their children's particular needs. These needs—and the way they are jeopardized—vary with the age of the child. Women with pre-school children speak about "shortchanging" them, about children "losing out" or being "lost in the shuffle" because they are raised among so many others:

> I felt guilty because Peter was part of so many kids. I don't ever think I necessarily put him first. I remember feeling guilty that I was shortchanging Peter. He was just part of the gang.
>
> It feels like [my daughter's] losing out [from my doing day care]. But I wanted to be home. It's a hard decision to make. I mean, if you have to work—I mean most people have to work. I wanted to be home but I wanted to be with my kids.
>
> [M]y children get lost in the shuffle. That's what bothered me sometimes. You try to be fair to all of them. You don't give your child special priority.

Women with older children, who remain home at this stage in their lives in part because they want to be there at the end of the school day, acknowledge that they are unable to give the special attention they believe their children want and deserve.[28]

> We had a problem in the beginning when my kids got home and they wanted to tell me about their day and [the other children] wanted to tell me too because I was the first person they saw when they got off the bus. And it was like she's my mother, not yours, and it was real hard in that respect.

They mention other problems as well. The inability to participate in school activities is an issue for some women who recognize the irony in the fact that although they are home *for* their own children, they cannot do all that a good mother should:

> That's been my biggest disappointment this year, not being able to go to my daughter's school when I wanted to. Yet here I was at home and I still couldn't leave.

Moreover, they know that a home geared to activities for small children can be a source of irritation to an older child who resents having her or his room used for naps, and finding favorite toys broken. If the providers invent practical solutions to these problems (a bedroom off-limits; toys kept on high shelves) they cannot entirely erase the pain they feel in having to redefine good mothering in more limited terms than those motivating their involvement in the occupation.

Providers have even more difficulty talking about a set of issues that touch on the distinctive nature of the relationship between a mother and her own child. As will be discussed below, most providers are unwilling to say they treat their own children any differently from the way they treat other people's children. In fact they take considerable pride in being fair—in giving equal treats, equal hugs, equal praise, and equal punishment—and they contrast themselves with other providers who do not act this way. But the presence of other children highlights the fact that they believe that there *is* a different relationship between themselves and their own children; the presence of other children may also exacerbate this relationship.

Only reluctantly, and with probing, do providers admit that not only do they feel differently about their own children ("Of course, I would be lying if I said I didn't love mine more") but that they find themselves locked into different patterns of interaction. The first acknowledgment comes in the form of suggesting that other children act better for them than they do for their own parents, and that their *own* children are the most difficult to handle.

> Other people's children are not as demanding. When you tell your children "no" they always ask fifty times more. When I tell other people's children "no" they don't ask again. . . . They are more obedient than your own.
> You know, your own kids don't seem to mind you as well as someone else's kids. . . . No child pushes me as much as my own.

When asked how they respond to these different behavior patterns, providers admit to a kind of reaction that threatens both their ideal of consistent discipline *and* their ideal of equal treatment.

> Sometimes I'm easier on [my middle child] and sometimes I'm harder on her and I know it and I get mad at myself. When I'm easier I don't feel so bad until she starts getting bratty. And then I say, "Darn it, it's your own fault." All these toys here are my kids' toys and Emma has to share. . . . I don't handle [sharing of toys] the same way every time and that's a problem. Sometimes I'll let Emma have her own way around it and . . . that's when I feel like I'm giving in to Emma. And then the times when I'm hard on her she might do something wrong and so will the other kids and she'll get

in more trouble than they would. My attitude is sometimes, well you know better, you live with me. . . . So I hate myself for being that way.

But if providers can readily document these different interactions, they are reluctant to *explain* them. When asked to discuss why it was they thought that their own children were more difficult, providers invariably began by saying they didn't know. They then hinted at a possible truth: "I don't know . . . your own children, maybe they're a little more secure in you so they can test you more"; "I don't know why that is. They feel more secure maybe with their own parents? I don't know. They let their inner feelings out? They let their inner selves really show?"

Providers whose own children are no longer part of the day-care group allow themselves to understand these dynamics more fully. Retrospectively, they admit that they were harder on their own children because they cared so much about the outcomes of child rearing ("I expected my own to be perfect"). But a provider who still has young children in her child care group cannot easily acknowledge the extent to which identification with her own child locks her into a special kind of relationship, made visible by the difference from her feelings about other children, and exacerbated by her own different, and occasionally inconsistent, reactions.

Whether or not they actually say they leave for these reasons, after the fact, former providers allow themselves to speak openly about the strains they denied while still engaged in the occupation.[29]

I always wondered if I really benefitted my kids by taking care of other people's kids at home because it was a lot more of my time, and my patience was more worn out by the end of the day than it would have been if I had just had my own.

Mothering Other's Children

Family day-care providers seem to accept the role of substitute mother for their paid caregiving, and they experience that activity much as mothers do. As they give the children the security of a home, five days a week, for eight or nine hours each day, sometimes over a period of several years, family day-care providers "learn to love" the children. Seventy-seven percent of the questionnaire respondents agreed with the statement, "I get emotionally involved with the children in my care." And they speak about both the rewards and satisfactions, and the problems and discontents of their work in terms similar to those of mothers.[30]

The conflation of the mother role with the provider role was so complete that when I asked, "Do you feel differently about your own children and the other children in your care?" the answer I almost uniformly received was, "I treat them all the same." Tellingly, in emphasizing external behavior (the way the children are treated) the providers avoided answering the question about the way they *felt* about the children. It is a form of denial that their feelings for their own children differed from their feelings for their clients.[31] Having dismissed professional caregiving, the provider embraces mothering. Having done so, she cannot easily speak about the manner in which she deviates from this ideal.

But a contradiction is present. Mothering is the most desirable style for a family day-care provider, but it is a style she must adopt incompletely.[32] Among white, working- and middle-class women, motherhood confers the exclusive privileges of claiming, molding, and keeping; neither these women nor their clients believe that other people's children can be claimed, molded, and kept. To think that one can do so with other people's children creates a situation where one can only be disappointed. And this style of motherhood denies a financial calculus and limits, yet a day-care provider who refuses reimbursement or fails to establish limits to the care she gives invites exploitation. The family day-care provider cannot answer a question about feeling directly, because there is no direct way to describe how one maintains an ideal by deviating from it. We can hear this confusion when providers use a "but" to describe their feelings: "I love these children *but* they're not my own"; "I enjoy caring for children *but* it is a job for me."

The Limits of Responsibility

One of the most disturbing aspects of mothering is the realization that the capacity to protect one's child is limited. A mother cannot watch every move or inoculate her child against every hurt. A mother has to rely on the hope that she has equipped her children to deal with life's vagaries. For day-care providers the limits of protection are narrowed. The day-care provider can ensure a loving and safe environment for specified hours; she cannot ensure that the child is being adequately clothed, fed, and nurtured during the hours that the child is with his or her parents. Children go home at the end of the day, and the parents may or may not properly attend to the cough or diarrhea. Children leave for good after a couple of years and the parents may or may not complete the job of teaching them to share or to have good manners.

Limited Authority

Competent and successful caring for children relies on certain skills. While providers may denigrate their abilities, they can also recognize that they have acquired knowledge about children in general, as well as intimate knowledge about the individual children who come to them. Moreover, because the family day-care provider is dealing with many children at once, discipline and the imposition of routines are not just matters of individual style, but practical necessities. All children have to nap at the same time, eat the same food, and follow the same rules.

The women find satisfaction in exercising their skills, but they are often thwarted in their attempts to do so. Feminist analysis has uncovered the many ways in which a mother's confidence is challenged by the authority of male experts.[33] Family day-care providers, perhaps, experience even more "interruptions." Parental supervision, state requirements, public oversight, and occasionally, the scrutiny of a husband all influence child care style.

Parents give explicit instructions pertaining to the care of their own children. These instructions can undermine a provider's confidence; they can also serve to remind the provider that her authority is limited: "[I don't like it when] they're saying, well, I'm still in charge even though I'm not here, therefore I'm going to tell her like I would tell a teenage baby-sitter the rules." In addition, state regulations constrain their ability to freely define appropriate care, and public oversight creates a climate of distrust about possible mistreatment of children.[34] As one woman said, "You don't yell out the back door to the children because someone might hear you." The provision of day care overlaps with family life in time as well as space. A day-care provider's husband might indicate resentment about the wear and tear accompanying home-based child care; he might also try to control it in certain ways, such as suggesting that the provider discipline children in prescribed ways, that the provider not continue to care for particular children, or, in extreme cases, that she cease doing the work altogether.

These intrusions undermine the provider's authority. When providers speak about wanting to ensure the safety of the children, there is an edge of anxiety about whether they can afford to allow the child to take the kind of risks a mother might: "I worry more about somebody else's child." Providers also say they try to put off questions about sex and religion, recognizing these as "private" matters best handled in the family: "I suggest they talk to their mother about that."

The most concrete manifestation of this difference shows up with respect to the issue of punishment.[35] Most providers believe that it is wrong—and even cruel—to spank someone else's child, even though many of them find it an appropriate disciplinary technique for their own children. The concern also shows up at the other end of the spectrum. Some providers worry about showing too much physical affection:[36]

Now it's really child abuse this and child abuse that. I'm afraid to get too close. I can still hug them and stuff. But still, in the back of my mind I

don't want anyone accusing me. . . . You think about it, what do you classify
as child abuse or sexual abuse or verb‹ abuse?

Thus, although providers say that they do with others what they do
with their own children and treat them like their own, probing suggests
that this "common sense" response is modulated by the consciousness
that the child is not her own.

Loss

The most painful difference between mothering one's own child and
mothering another's child is the inevitability of loss. These relationships
are contingent: a parent can withdraw a child at any moment the parent
decides that a different situation is preferable. Even when the situation
is working well, these relationships are temporary. They are bounded
daily by the return of the mother, and bounded ultimately by the child's
maturation.

In some ways the most painful losses are those that are initiated by a
parent out of dissatisfaction. These losses threaten the provider's self-
confidence as well as her relationship to a child. Providers speak about
these losses with a special anguish:

> One day [the mother] called me up and said she wasn't going to bring him
> back because she didn't think he was happy here. And that really bothered
> me and I asked, "Why don't you think he's happy here? What do you want
> me to do?" And she said, "It's nothing to do with you. I just don't think
> he is happy here. He doesn't want to go." . . . I was upset because I thought
> I did something wrong. I thought I had let his crying bother me too
> much. . . . I started to wonder whether I should be taking care of other
> people's kids.

But the more expected losses are anguishing as well, and tears come to
a provider's eyes when describing how loss interrupts relationships of
love: "I lost one to kindergarten and some going closer to home. It's very
hard. You feel like you're losing a part of you." When these losses are
anticipated, a provider can do some of the work of grieving in advance.
This might help them deal with the actual moment of parting; it cannot
alleviate the pain altogether.

The link between loss and affection is demonstrated in the frequency
with which providers, when asked about their feelings about children,
spontaneously speak about losing them: "I love these children. I feel
terrible when I lose one." This constant awareness of loss makes becoming
too attached to the children a risky proposition.

Financial Constraints

There is another reality as well. Family day-care providers do this work, in part, because they need the money. If they become too attached to the children in their care, that is, if they identify too strongly with the model of mothering, they can neither ask for money at the end of the week nor impose restrictions on the hours of care they provide. Almost every provider could remember a time when she let concern for a child draw her into making a decision which was not in her interest:

> I had one parent that owed me money when she left. . . . It was as much my fault as it was hers because I just let it go on and on for six months. But she was in the process of a divorce. It was really affecting the child that I had. I just could not put that child through one more trauma of having to go to a new sitter on top of everything else he was going through. He was three years old and I could just see what this divorce was doing to this little boy. . . . It was really my fault. I could have given him up. I just couldn't because I wouldn't put him through not knowing where he was going to go.

Detached Attachment

Providers do not explicitly acknowledge that the care they offer is different from mothering. Yet the emotional component of that care, what I call the feeling rule of "detached attachment," is characterized by some limits drawn around the caregivers' emotional engagement with the children.[37]

Providers frequently referred to this detachment they have created and the emotional labor in maintaining it: "I reserve something, knowing that they're not mine"; I hold back a little"; "I don't want to get too attached." Almost every provider could talk about one child to whom she had become overly attached. Almost every provider spoke about not letting this happen again:

> I won't take one on from six months and watch it grow up like that again if I've got any feeling that they're going to be taken away from me. . . . I felt that I was doing a good job and I enjoyed [the child] just as much as [the parents] did, watching it grow up and being a part of its life. Maybe I did get too attached."

Quite frequently they draw on an image of a "real" mother to deflect the child's attachment, to remind the child that his or her loyalties must rest elsewhere. One woman, who often took care of a child overnight, said that while the mother was away she would talk about "Mommy" to the child and repeat constantly that "Mommy is coming back."[38] Another provider more bluntly said, "I tell them they have to be nice to Mommy."

Family day-care providers feel strongly that to do otherwise would be wrong for the child, that it is an integral part of their job to sustain the mother-child bond:

> I know Sarah really likes me. I know she does. I can tell. And I like Sarah. She's a nice little girl. But her mother has to be there for her. . . . I can't give what Sarah needs. I can give her the attention. I can care for her. I can make her feel good about herself. But I'm not her mother. You want to give the child what he [sic] needs without giving so much that you are interfering with the way he or she feels about his own parents.

At the same time the provider is also clearly protecting herself. The provider needs this image of the mother as much, if not more than the child, as a reminder of her own limited role. The failure to keep this image alive can have devastating emotional consequences, as one woman suggests:[39]

> With my nieces I'd have to stop and say to myself, "you're not their mother." For an example, the older one . . . had long hair and she wanted her hair cut. She wanted me to cut her hair. And I said, "Are you sure you want your hair cut?" And she said, "Oh, I'm sure I want it cut." And I said, "All right, after your bath tonight I'll cut your hair." And I did it and I never thought about it. And I put the kid to bed and I was upset all night. I said, I don't believe I cut her hair without asking her mother. . . . All night I just tossed and turned. . . . I just agonized all night long about how I could do that *without even thinking of the mother.* Those girls were becoming more and more my own.

The genuine struggle involved in recreating the mother-child bond for the child, and in reasserting it as more significant than her own feelings, is clear evidence that while providers hold it as an ideal, as they become central in a child's life and allow a child to become central in their own, they actually create the conditions for its subversion.

But if providers settle on a form of detachment out of necessity—so that they can accept interference in their caregiving, so that they don't get hurt by loss, so that they don't make decisions that are not in their best interests—it is clear that this resolution is partial at best. Detached attachment has to be recreated daily; it is difficult to sustain emotionally; and it may even, on occasion, conflict with their ability to offer good care. One provider who had left the occupation for center-based care explained at length how caregiving in this new setting freed her from this struggle, and thus enabled her to offer better care:

> I think that's part of what was making me burned out. I really felt that was where some of it was, from letting myself become too attached to the chil-

dren. You have to keep a little bit of distance. Because, I think the fact that I had them here all the time they became . . . so much a part of my family that made it kind of crazy. . . . I haven't distanced myself from any of the children [at the center] but I don't have the hours with them. I think that makes a difference. . . In a three hour span you can't get as close. And you always know that there's somebody else that can take over there whereas [at home] there wasn't. I was their sole person for support, authority, love, or whatever. I think [at the center] I always know there's somebody else who can step in and take over and do the same job that I'm doing, and that makes a difference. You don't have to pull on yourself as much because you're not the be-all and end-all. . . . I think in ways it makes me feel freer to be able to communicate with [the children] and be with them. . . . I don't have to feel I'm the only person who's going to get through to them.

CONCLUSION

Family day-care illustrates in a particular form the current fragility and fluidity of public-private boundaries. Family day-care providers are motivated by a desire to remain in the domestic domain, to serve a "traditional" role as mothers; they have to take on paid work because of changing economic realities. In the nineteenth century, "the permeable boundaries for women between unpaid and paid labor allowed nursing to pass back and forth when necessary";[40] the same is true of child care today. Family day-care providers move, if not effortlessly, repeatedly between unpaid care of their own children and a combination of unpaid care of their own and paid (and publicly supervised) care of other children while remaining in the domestic domain.

Ironically, family day-care providers who define themselves as "traditional mothers," facilitate a redefinition of mothering as a central activity of what it means to be a woman. They also bear some of the burdens of this process. One burden is the contradiction of offering a service in which they don't really believe. Another is the necessity of redefining their own mothering to make it congenial with the reality of the ongoing demands of their paid work. From a different perspective, they have to resolve the tensions between "public" and "private" caregiving in a work situation that is marked by innumerable intrusions, and in a world where children are defined as private property. In short, in caring for the children of working mothers, and in caring for their own at the same time, almost against their will, they allow both their own and other women's mothering to be "extended to incorporate some kind of working experiences."[41] And they incorporate a communal element into child rearing, while seeking to enact a more privatized version of this care.

If these changes are "against their will," they are not *only* resisted.

Because they are struggling to sustain a traditional life-style, and often, the accompanying gendered division of labor, many family day-care providers might be viewed as being aligned with a conservative political stance.[42] But this is not the whole picture. The work of family day care is also grounded in, and experienced as, a deep commitment to meeting the needs of children for stable and loving care; as providers enact their role, they recognize that such care does not depend on a biolgoical relationship with—on being the real mother of—a child. They, too, on numerous occasions, benefit from the nurturance they offer; they find great rewards in watching and fostering growth. And' they believe that good caregiving is grounded in the experience of gaining intimate knowledge of the individual child. In each of these understandings—the commitment to children, the recognition of the rewards of "mothering," an appreciation of the experiential basis for caregiving—they stand on ground shared by at least some feminists, as well as at least some members of the political right. Moreover, in forging ties with children and with the parents of those children, and in meeting the needs of members of their own families, family day-care providers acknowledge the centrality of affective ties in their own lives. They act on the basis of an implicit (and sometimes explicit) understanding of community, of our fundamental interconnectedness and interdependence. In these commitments too, they transcend political boundaries.

At the same time, unlike those who only look backward to an idealized past, to a vision of community in which women—and women alone—"naturally" chose to serve others (and thereby sacrificed their own needs), the political ideology of family day-care providers is transmuted as a result of their daily activities. Perhaps because they bear some of the burdens of the current social transformation, they are compelled to acknowledge these changes. They know their own families cannot get by without two incomes; they acknowledge the same is true for most of their clients. They know there is no going back.

If they remain at home and enact a traditional gender role, they transform that home and those roles. Out of necessity, they ask their sons, as well as their daughters, to help with domestic tasks; in caring for the children of others as well, they learn to respect individual differences and require behaviors that transcend gender. Whether it is because they have less of a personal investment in the children—or because of their own increased understanding of these matters—they find themselves responding open-mindedly to a boy who plays with dolls, a girl who plays with trucks. In any case, at a practical level they have to make do—each member of the child care group has to learn to get along with and play with others, to wear whatever clothes, and play with whatever toys, are at hand. Moreover, the work of family day care brings women into contact with a wide range of others, some of whom share their class position and social outlook, some of whom do not. They have to learn to find a new basis for understanding, to be open to views and attitudes which challenge their own.

From the base of their own experience, providers move towards a recognition of the need for autonomy in their own lives, and an understanding of this need that is closer to a feminist vision of adult roles for women than it is to the belief in individualism touted by the Right. As Susan Cohen and Mary Fainsod Katzenstein argue,[43]

> Individualism, for the Right, is encouraged by the family even as it must be, in another sense, sacrificed to the family. The Right maintains that the family is uniquely qualified to instill norms of independence and freedom in its young. Yet the exercise of this individualism is to happen outside, not within, the family. Within the family, community supersedes individuality. The choices men and women make inside the family are to be curtailed by the parameters of biology and tradition. Outside the family, however, individualism may flourish—but an individualism (feminist critics charge) that embraces only men.

But providers learn they cannot sacrifice their own individualism and autonomy, and still be effective social actors who meet their own and their families' needs, at the same time as they meet the needs of the women and children who are their clients. Over time they have to develop—and learn to trust and value—their own caregiving styles, even as these emerge from a complex mix of experience, practical necessity and compromise. In the process of negotiation with parents, husbands, and state officials, they often find themselves developing new communication skills, and acquiring the self-esteem to surmount their own socialization; they fight for and defend their own interests as they seek solutions to dilemmas they face.

In their daily lives, then, at a narrow level, providers seek to balance the norms of the public world and those of the private domain. At a deeper level, they are struggling to find a balance between autonomy and community. Because our society charges women with the burden of community, while granting men the privileges of autonomy; and because the necessary structural support for achieving this balance for members of *both* sexes is sorely lacking, family day-care providers often "fail." But their stories are clear demonstrations of the truism that, if caregivers are going to meet their own needs as well as those of care recipients, they must find that balance. Ensuring this basis for caregiving is, perhaps, one of the biggest challenges facing our society today.

Notes

1. For historical analyses of the emergence of the ideology of domesticity and womanhood see Barbara Welter, "The Cult of True Womanhood: 1820–1860," *American Quar-*

terly (Summer, 1966), pp. 151–171; Gerda Lerner, "The Lady and the Mill Girl: Changes in the Status of Women in the Age of Jackson," *American Midcontinent Studies Journal* (10, 1969), pp. 5–15; Carl Degler, *At Odds: Women and the American Family from the Revolution to the Present* (New York: Oxford University Press, 1980). For a good review of how motherhood has been constructed—and how it has been critiqued by feminists—see Evelyn Nakano Glenn, "Gender and the Family," pp. 348–381 in Beth B. Hess and Myra Marx Ferree, eds., *Analyzing Gender: Handbook of Social Science Research* (Newbury Park, CA: Sage Publications, 1987).

2. Steven Fosburg, *Family Day Care in the United States: Summary of Findings*, vol. I (Washington, D.C.: U.S. Government Printing Office, U.S. Department of Health and Human Services, 1981), p. 1. For a recent accounting of the frequency with which different kinds of child care arrangement are used, see Sandra L. Hofferth et al., *National Child Care Survey, 1990* (Washington, D.C.: The Urban Institute Press, 1991). This study separates "family day care" and care by relatives in a home other than the child's. It is difficult, therefore, to know the extent to which the latter category (of relative care) involves women such as the ones I am describing in this study. In 1990, 18.6 percent of children under age five with employed mothers were in family day care; and an additional 11.3 percent of these children were being cared for by relatives in a home other than their own. In contrast, 26.5 percent of these children were cared for in a child care center.

3. In this chapter I assume that all family day-care providers are women. Although there are a handful of men engaged in this activity in Vermont, none were included in this study. In fact, family day care is so dominated by women that the summary report of the national day-care home study does not discuss gender at all. See, Fosburg, *Family Day Care in the United States.*

4. For useful discussions of this issue, see Rayna Rapp, "Family and Class in Contemporary America: Notes Toward an Understanding of Ideology," in Barrie Thorne and Marilyn Yalom, eds., *Rethinking the Family: Some Feminist Questions* (New York: Longman, 1982), pp. 168–187; Barrie Thorne, "Feminist Rethinking of the Family: An Overview," in Thorne and Yalom, *Rethinking the Family*, pp. 1–24.

5. Thorne, "Feminist Rethinking of the Family," p. 18.

6. In spite of much recent talk about "parenting," the burden for a child's well-being still rests on mothers. See Susan Rae Peterson, "Against 'Parenting,' " in Joyce Trebilcot, ed., *Mothering: Essays in Feminist Theory* (Totowa, N.J.: Rowman & Allanheld, 1984), pp. 62–69; and Janet Farrell Smith, "Parenting and Property," in Trebilcot, *Mothering*, pp. 199–212.

7. Thorne, "Feminist Rethinking of the Family," p. 18.

8. Sara Freedman, "To Love and to Work: The Ghettoization of Women's Labor in the Home and the School," Unpublished paper, 1987; Jeff Hearn, "Patriarchy, Professionalisation, and the Semi-Professions," in Clare Ungerson, ed., *Women and Social Policy: A Reader* (London: MacMillan, 1985); Carole E. Joffe, *Friendly Intruders: Childcare Professionals and Family Life* (Berkeley: University of California Press, 1977); Sara Lawrence Lightfoot, "Family-School Interactions: The Cultural Image of Mothers and Teachers," *Signs* 3 (2)(1977); Sara Lawrence Lightfoot, *Worlds Apart: Relationships Between Families and Schools* (New York: Basic Books, 1978); Sandra Schiff, *Mother Care/Other Care* (New York: Basic Books, 1984).

9. See, for example, the essays in Emily K. Abel and Margaret K. Nelson, eds., *Circles of Care: Work and Identity in Women's Lives* (Albany: State University of New York Press, 1990); and the essays in Janet Finch and Dulcie Groves, eds., *A Labour of Love: Women, Work and Caring* (London: Routledge and Kegan Paul, 1983).

10. Even when women followed the domestic tasks into the public world (as nurses, teachers, social workers), they were caught in a dilemma: "forced to act as if altruism (assumed to be the basis for caring) and autonomy (assumed to be the basis for rights) are separate ways of being, even human characteristics distributed along gender lines." Susan

M. Reverby, "The Duty or Right to Care: Nursing in Historical Perspective," in Abel and Nelson, *Circles of Care*, pp. 132–149). Their activities there are frequently judged by standards, such as warmth, intimacy, and friendliness, that were formerly applied only to services in the private domain; see Arlie Russell Hochschild, *The Managed Heart: The Commercialization of Human Feeling* (Berkeley: The University of California Press, 1983).

11. Autonomy is the linchpin of a (male) professional model of caregiving in the public domain; professional caregivers adopt a norm of detachment that systematically precludes an identification with clients, and, arguably, the possibility of intense caring about them.

12. Emily K. Abel and Margaret K. Nelson, "Circles of Care: An Introductory Essay," pp. 4–34, in Abel and Nelson, *Circles of Care*.

13. Patricia Hill Collins argues that within African-American communities, the relationships between women and their (biological) children are often less exclusive, and that many different women may have an active role in ensuring the well-being of children:

> In African-American communities, fluid and changing boundaries often distinguish biological mothers from other women who care for children. Biological mothers, or bloodmothers, are expected to care for their children. But African and African-American communities have also recognized that vesting one person with full responsibility for mothering a child may not be wise or possible. As a result, othermothers—women who assist bloodmothers by sharing mothering responsibilities—traditionally have been central to the institution of Black motherhood.
> (Patricia Hill Collins, *Black Feminist Thought: Knowledge, Consciousness and the Politics of Empowerment* (Boston, Unwin Hyman, 1990), p. 119.

14. In the course of distributing questionnaires to unregistered providers, I picked up an additional ten registered providers, bringing the total for that group to 235. The organization of family day care in Vermont offers three legal alternatives. Licensing is required of providers with more than six full-time nonresident children. Because almost all licensed day care occurs in formal centers rather than in private homes, no licensed providers are included in this analysis. Registration is required of those who offer care to children from more than two different families, and may legally include six full-time children of preschool age, and four part-time school-age children. Women caring for (any number of) children from no more than two different families may remain unregistered. Those who care for more than this number and fail to register constitute the "illegal" population of family day-care providers. Vermont, Department of Social and Rehabilitation Services, *Journal for Family Day Care Homes*, (Montpelier, Vermont: Division of Licensing and Registration, 1985). A 1985 study of child care in Vermont estimated that approximately seventy-five percent of all children under the age of six with parents in the labor force were in (legal or illegal) unregulated care. See Amy Davenport, *The Economics of Child Care* (Montpelier, Vermont: The Governor's Commission on the Status of Women's Childcare Task Force, 1985).

15. U.S. Bureau of the Census, *1980 Census: Vermont* (Washington, D.C.: Government Printing Office, 1980). The median household income among the comparable group of family day-care providers (i.e., married with a child under the age of six) fell between twenty-five thousand dollars and thirty thousand dollars.

16. This inclusion of housework into the daily routine is another way in which family day-care providers are distinguished from caregivers in public settings.

17. See also Elaine Enarson, "Experts and Caregivers: Perspectives on Underground Childcare," in Abel and Nelson, *Circles of Care*; Jean Marzollo, "Child-Care Workers Speak Up," *Parents' Magazine* 62 (April 1987).

18. Basil Bernstein, "Class Pedagogies: Visible and Invisible," in Jerome Karabel and A.H. Halsey, eds., *Power and Ideology in Education* (New York: Oxford University Press, 1977), pp. 513–534.

19. Even those who had undergone extensive training to become nurses or teachers, when asked what skills they drew on, mentioned motherhood before their occupation.

20. When parents choose a family day-care provider because "she is a mother" or because "she grew up in a large family," they rely on just this kind of learning; this learning is also assumed by a public policy structured around the willingness of women to provide this kind of informal care. (Ironically, this policy simultaneously assumes that these lessons have taken root *and* attempts to regulate providers—just in case.)

21. While these patterns of continuity describe some women, there is a "deviant" group who operate family day-care homes in an explicit way as part of a career. Again, the career is child care. But they are formally trained workers who choose family day care because it offers desired working conditions.

22. For a very similar discussion of experiential learning and how it is "naturalized," see Marjorie DeVault, *Feeding the Family: The Social Organization of Caring as Gendered Work* (Chicago: University of Chicago Press, 1991), especially p. 119.

23. Sara Ruddick, "Maternal Thinking," in Trebilcot, *Mothering*, pp. 213–230.

24. A good characterization of this kind of woman can be found in Kristin Luker, *Abortion and the Politics of Motherhood* (Berkeley: University of California Press, 1984). Family day care as an extension of mothering is presented differently, though equally concretely, for a substantial minority of the women who see in the provision of child care a way to further satisfy a thwarted maternal impulse. Women who could not afford a larger family, women who could not (physically) bear more children, women who longed for a daughter and had only sons (or vice versa), and women whose grown children have left them pining over an empty nest, all located their motivation in an as-yet-unfulfilled need to mother.

25. Lillian B. Rubin, *Worlds of Pain: Life in the Working-Class Family* (New York: Basic Books, 1976), p. 87.

26. Interestingly, although no provider acknowledged this, it is possible that offering family day care gives the provider a mechanisms for discounting and remaining unconcerned about even serious behavioral problems. To the extent that the provider can unclaim that these problems are the result of the presence of day care, she has to acknowledge that day care has had a cost. On the other hand, she does not have to acknowledge that there are ways in which her own children have deep-seated or serious developmental problems of their own.

27. Curiously, although these conditions characterized the lives of many of the family day-care providers (and, they suggest, prepared them for their current role), they do not want their children to have these same kinds of experiences: their reproduction of the social relations of class is reluctant and inadvertent.

28. Several husbands added comments indicating that they too believed that their own children were being neglected at these times:

> I wish my kids could explain some of their feelings because sometimes I think some of their days are just difficult. It's like when Jimmy went to kindergarten last year and he'd come just at the time when Erica was serving lunch and he'd come in with all these neat things and Erica just did not have the time to sit down [with him]. I think that's one thing my children are missing out sometimes.

> I think it's tough on our boys when they come home from school and there's a house full and they don't get the attention they were used to before.

> The disappointment they felt must have been expressed to their wives.

29. On the turnover survey, providers were significantly less likely to express agreement with the statement, "My children have adjusted easily to sharing me with others," than they had two years earlier when they responded to the original questionnaire.

30. For research on mother's attitudes toward their role, see Mary Georgina Boulton,

On Being a Mother: A Study of Women with Pre-School Children (London: Tavistock, 1983); see, also, the essays in Jean F. O'Barr, Deborah Pope and Mary Wyer, eds., *Ties That Bind: Essays on Mothering and Patriarchy* (Chicago and London: The University of Chicago Press, 1990).

31. Alternatively, this answer might be taken as an indication of the difficulty of separating treatment and feeling. Caregiving involves instrumental tasks and emotions. We care for someone because we care about them; when we care about someone we take care of their needs. Yet if it were just this difficulty, we might find that mothers could not separate the tasks and the emotions. However, most mothers can separate the two easily (e.g., I love my child but I hate changing diapers, getting up in the middle of the night, and losing contact with the adult world).

32. As noted above, in communities where mothering has a more collective aspect, this contradiction might not occur. See Collins, *Black Feminist Thought.*

33. Barbara Ehrenrich and Deidre English, *For Her Own Good: 150 Years of the Experts' Advice to Women* (New York: Doubleday, 1979); Alison Jagger, *Feminist Politics and Human Nature* (Totowa, N.J.: Rowman and Allanheld, 1983).

34. The rules for registration of Vermont's Department of Social and Rehabilitation Services determine the number of children that can be cared for within the home by a family day-care provider, and the kind of discipline that can be used. The registration process opens the provider to public scrutiny, and limits her ability to take in and care for children as she sees fit. See Vermont, Department of Social and Rehabilitation Services.

35. I distinguish here between the broad kind of discipline which is central to the provider's notion of what she is offering to children, and the specific methods of punishment for misbehavior that are employed. For public debates about the use of corporal punishment in day-care settings in Vermont, see *Burlington Free Press,* "Parents Still Have Control of Day-Care Discipline," Editorial (May 20, 1983), p. 12a; "Spanking in Day-Care Centers: Parents Should Make Decision," Opinions Page (February 15, 1984) p. 8a; "Snelling Puts Pen to Spanking Ban," (April 16, 1984) p. 6b; David Karvelas, "Day Care Spanking Opposed," *Burlington Free Press* (May 12, 1983) p. 1b.

36. Vermont, Department of Social and Rehabilitation Services. For interesting discussions of the issue of child abuse and how it can divide caregivers, see Susan Contratto, "Child Abuse and the Politics of Care," *Journal of Education* 168 (3)(1986), pp. 70–79; Linda Gordon, "Child Abuse, Gender and the Myth of Family Independence: A Historical Critique," *Child Welfare* 64 (3)(May June 1985), pp. 213–224. For recent reports of sexual abuse in day-care settings, see David Finkelhor and Linda Meyer Williams with Nanci Burns, *Nursery Crimes: Sexual Abuse in Day Care* (Newbury Park: Sage Publications, 1988).

37. For discussions of the concept of "feeling rules," see Arlie Russell Hochschild, "The Sociology of Feelings and Emotion: Selected Possibilities," in Marcia Millman and Rosabeth Moss Kanter, eds., *Another Voice: Feminist Perspectives on Social Life and Social Science* (Garden City, N.Y.: Anchor/Doubleday, 1975); and A. Hochschild, *The Managed Heart.*

38. These reminders are not just to offer necessary reassurance to the child during a potentially traumatic separation; they serve the provider's interest in not allowing the child to become too attached.

39. By inserting the mother into the relationship, and thus implicitly drawing a distinction between what she provides and what a mother offers, the day-care provider is also recreating a notion of mothering as something that exists only between a mother and her child. This kind of relationship she reserves for her *own* children. Thus mothering is not cheapened (which paradoxically it would be if it involved a monetary fee) by being confused with something different.

40. Susan M. Reverby, "The Duty or the Right to Care: Nursing and Womanhood in Historical Perspective," in Emily K. Abel and Margaret K. Nelson, eds., *Circles of Love: Work and Identity in Women's Lives* (Albany: State University of New York Press, 1990), 132–150.

41. Chiara Saraceno, "Shifts in Public and Private Boundaries: Women as Mothers and Service Workers in Italian Daycare," *Feminist Studies* 10 (1)(1984), p. 27.

42. As I wrote this chapter, the Republicans were trying to reassert their claim to represent "traditional family values."

43. Susan Cohen and Mary Fainsod Katzenstein, "The War Over the Family Is Not Over the Family," in Stanford M. Dornbusch and Myra H. Strober, eds., *Feminism, Children, and the New Families* (New York: The Guilford Press, 1988), p. 44.

Chapter 10

WORKING AT MOTHERHOOD: CHICANA AND MEXICAN IMMIGRANT MOTHERS AND EMPLOYMENT[1]

Denise A. Segura

In North American society, women are expected to bear and assume primary responsibility for raising their children. This socially constructed form of motherhood encourages women to stay at home during their children's early or formative years, and asserts activities that take married mothers out of the home (for instance, paid employment) are less important or "secondary" to their domestic duties.[2] Motherhood as a social construction rests on the ideological position that women's biological abilities to bear and suckle children are "natural," and therefore fundamental to women's "fulfillment." This position, however, fails to appreciate that motherhood is a culturally formed structure whose meanings can vary and are subject to change.

Despite the ideological impetus to mother at home, over half of all women with children work for wages.[3] The growing incongruence between social ideology and individual behaviors has prompted some researchers to suggest that traditional gender role expectations are changing (for example, greater acceptance of women working outside the home).[4] The profuse literature on the "ambivalence" and "guilt" employed mothers often feel when they work outside the home, however, reminds us that changes in expectations are neither absolute nor uncontested.

Some analysts argue that the ambivalence felt by many employed mothers stems from their discomfort in deviating from a socially constructed "idealized mother," who stays home to care for her family.[5] This image of motherhood, popularized in the media, schoolbooks, and public policy, implies that the family and the economy constitute two separate spheres, private and public. Dubois and Ruiz argue, however, that the notion of a private-public dichotomy largely rests on the experiences of white, leisured women, and lacks immediate relevance to less privileged women (for instance, immigrant women, women of color), who have historically been important economic actors both inside and outside the home.[6] The view that the relationship between motherhood and employment varies by class, race, and/or culture raises several important questions. Do the ideology of motherhood and the "ambivalence" of employed mothers depicted within American sociology and feminist scholarship pertain to women of Mexican descent in the United States? Among these women, what is the relation between the ideological constructions of motherhood and employment? Is motherhood mutually exclusive from employment among Mexican-heritage women from different social locations?

In this chapter I explore these questions using qualitative data gathered from thirty women of Mexican descent in the United States—both native-born Chicanas (including two Mexico-born women raised since preschool years in the U.S.) and resident immigrant Mexicanas.[7] I illustrate that notions of motherhood for Chicanas and Mexicanas are embedded in different ideological constructs operating within two systems of patriarchy. Contrary to the expectations of acculturation models, I find that Mexicanas frame motherhood in ways that foster a more consistent labor market presence than do Chicanas. I argue that this distinction—typically bypassed in the sociological literature on motherhood, women and work, or Chicano Studies—is rooted in their dissimilar social locations—that is, the "social spaces" they engage within the social structure created by the intersection of class, race, gender, and culture.[8]

I propose that Mexicanas, raised in a world where economic and household work often merged, do not dichotomize social life into public and private spheres, but appear to view employment as one workable domain of motherhood. Hence, the more recent the time of emigration, the less ambivalence Mexicanas express regarding employment. Chicanas, on the other hand, raised in a society that celebrates the expressive functions of the family and obscures its productive economic functions, express higher adherence to the ideology of stay-at-home motherhood, and correspondingly more ambivalence toward full-time employment—even when they work.

These differences between Mexicanas and Chicanas challenge current research on Mexican-origin women that treats them as a single analytic category (for instance, "Hispanic") as well as research on contemporary views of motherhood that fails to appreciate diversity among women. My examination of the intersection of motherhood and employment among Mexican immigrant women also reinforces emerging research focusing on women's own economic and social motivations to emigrate to the U.S. (rather than the behest of husbands and/or fathers).[9]

My analysis begins with a brief review of relevant research on the relationship between motherhood and employment. Then I explore this relationship in greater detail, using in-depth interview data. I conclude by discussing the need to recast current conceptualizations of the dilemma between motherhood and employment to reflect women's different social locations.

THEORETICAL CONCERNS

The theoretical concerns that inform this research on Chicana/Mexicana employment integrate feminist analyses of the hegemonic power of patriarchy over work and motherhood with a critique of rational choice models and other models that overemphasize modernity and acculturation. In much of the literature on women and work, familial roles tend to be portrayed as important constraints on both women's labor market entry and mobility. Differences among women related to immigrant status, however, challenge this view.

Within rational choice models, motherhood represents a prominent social force behind women's job decisions. Becker and Polachek, for example, argue that women's "preference" to mother is maximized in jobs that exact fewer penalties for interrupted employment, such as part-time, seasonal, or clerical work.[10] According to this view, women's pursuit of their rational self-interest reinforces their occupational segregation within low-paying jobs (for example, clerical work) and underrepresentation in higher-paying, male-dominated jobs that typically require significant employer investments (for example, specialized training). Employers may be reluctant to "invest" in or train women workers who, they perceive, may leave a job at any time for familial reasons.[11] This perspective views motherhood as a major impediment to employment and mobility. But it fails to consider that the organization of production has developed in ways that make motherhood an impediment. Many feminist scholars view this particular development as consistent with the hegemonic power of patriarchy.

Distinct from rational choice models, feminist scholarship directs attention away from individual preferences to consider how patriarchy (male domination/female subordination) shapes the organization of production resulting in the economic, political, and social subordination of women to men.[12] While many economists fail to consider the power of ideological constructs such as "family" and "motherhood" in shaping behavior among women, employers, and the organization of production itself, many feminist scholars focus on these power dynamics.

Within feminist analyses, motherhood as an ideology obscures and legitimizes women's social subordination because it conceals particular interests within the rubric of a universal prerogative (reproduction). The social construction of motherhood serves the interest of capital by providing essential childbearing, child care, and housework at a minimal cost to the state, and sustains women as a potential reservoir of labor power, or a "reserve army of labor."[13] The strength of the ideology of motherhood is such that women continue to try to reconcile the "competing urgencies"[14] of motherhood and employment despite the lack of supportive structures at work or within the family.

Because employers view women as mothers (or future mothers), they encounter discrimination in job entry and advancement.[15] Because women are viewed as mothers, they also work a "second shift" at home.[16] The conflict between market work and family work has caused considerable ambivalence within women. Berg, for example, notes that one of the dominant themes in analyzing women and work is the "guilt" of employed mothers based on "espousing something different" from their own mothers.[17]

The notion Berg describes of "conflict" or "guilt" rests on several suppositions. The first assumption is that motherhood is a unilaterally oppressive state; the second, that employed mothers feel guilt; and the third, that today's employed mothers do not have working mothers (which partially explains their "guilt feelings"). Inasmuch as large numbers of working-class, immigrant, and racial ethnic women have long traditions of working in the formal and informal economic sectors, such assumptions are suspect.

Research on women of Mexican descent and employment indicates their labor force participation is lower than that of other women when they have young children.[18] Moreover, Chicanas and Mexicanas are occupationally segregated in the lowest-paying of female-dominated jobs.[19] Explanations for their unique employment situation range from analyses of labor market structures and employer discrimination[20] to deficient individual characteristics (for instance, education, job skills)[21] and cultural differences.[22]

Analyses of Chicana/Mexicana employment that utilize a cultural framework typically explain the women's lower labor force participation, higher fertility, lower levels of education, and higher levels of unemployment as part of an ethnic or cultural tradition.[23] That is, as this line of argument goes, Chicano/Mexican culture emphasizes a strong allegiance to an idealized form of motherhood and a patriarchal ideology that frowns upon working wives and mothers and does not encourage girls to pursue higher education or employment options. These attitudes are supposed to vary by generation, with immigrant women (from Mexico) holding the most conservative attitudes.[24]

There are two major flaws in the research on Chicana/Mexicana employment, however. First, inconsistency in distinguishing between native-born and resident immigrant women characterizes much of this literature. Second, overreliance on linear acculturation persists. Both procedures imply either that Chicanas and Mexicanas are very similar, or that they lie on a sort of "cultural continuum," with Mexican immigrants at one end holding more conservative behaviors and attitudes grounded in traditional (often rural) Mexican culture, and U.S.-born Chicanos holding an amalgamation of cultural traditions from Mexico and the United States.[25] In terms of motherhood and employment, therefore, Mexicanas should have more "traditional" ideas about motherhood than U.S.-born Chicanas. Since the traditional ideology of motherhood typically refers to women staying home to "mother" children rather than going outside the home to work, Mexicanas theoretically should not be as willing to work as Chicanas or North American women in general—unless there is severe economic need. This formulation, while logical, reflects an underlying emphasis on modernity—or the view that "traditional" Mexican culture lags behind North American culture in developing behaviors and attitudes conducive to participating fully in modern society.[26] Inasmuch as conventional North American views of motherhood typically idealize labor market exit to care for children, embracing this prototype may be more conducive to maintaining patriarchal privilege (female economic subordination to men) than facilitating economic progress generally. In this sense, conceptualizations of motherhood that affirm its economic character may be better accommodating to women's market participation in the U.S.

The following section discusses the distinct views of motherhood articulated by Chicanas and Mexicanas and their impact on employment attitudes and behaviors. In contrast to the notion that exposure to North American values enhances women's incentives to work, proportionately more Chicanas than Mexicanas express ambivalence toward paid employment when they have children at home. I analyze these differences among a selected sample of clerical, service, and operative workers.

METHOD AND SAMPLE

This paper is based on in-depth interviews with thirty Mexican origin women—thirteen Chicanas and seventeen Mexicanas—who had participated in the 1978 to 79 or 1980 to 81 cohorts of an adult education and employment training program in the greater San Francisco Bay Area.[27] All thirty respondents had been involved in a conjugal relationship (either legal marriage or informal cohabitation with a male partner) at some point in their lives before I interviewed them in 1985, and had at least one child under eighteen years of age. At the time of their interviews, six

Chicanas and fourteen Mexicanas were married; seven Chicanas and three Mexicanas were single parents.

On the average, the married Chicanas have 1.2 children at home; the Mexicanas report 3.5 children. Both Chicana and Mexicana single mothers average 1.6 children. The children of the Chicanas tend to be preschool age or in elementary school. The children of the Mexicanas exhibit a greater age range (from infant to late adolescence), reflecting their earlier marriages and slightly older average age.

With respect to other relevant characteristics, all but two Mexicanas and five Chicanas had either a high school diploma or its equivalent (GED). The average age was 27.4 years for the Chicanas; and thirty-three years for the Mexicanas.[28] Upon leaving the employment training program, all the women secured employment. At the time of their interviews, about half of the Chicanas (n = 7); and three-fourths of the Mexicanas were employed (n = 12). Only two out of the seven (twenty-eight percent) employed Chicanas worked full-time (thirty-five or more hours per week) whereas nine out of the twelve (seventy-five percent) employed Mexicanas worked full-time. Most of the Chicanas found clerical or service jobs (for example, teacher assistants); most of the Mexicanas labored in operative jobs or in the service sector (for example, hotel maids), with a small minority employed as clerical workers.

I gathered in-depth life and work histories from the women to ascertain:

(1) What factors motivated them to enter, exit, and stay employed in their specific occupations;
(2) whether familial roles or ideology influenced their employment consistency; and
(3) whether other barriers limited their job attachment and mobility.

My examination of the relationship between motherhood and employment forms part of a larger study of labor market stratification and occupational mobility among Chicana and Mexican immigrant women.[29]

MOTHERHOOD AND EMPLOYMENT

Nearly all of the respondents, both Chicana and Mexicana, employed and nonemployed, speak of motherhood as their most important social role. They differ sharply in their employment behaviors and views regarding the relationship between motherhood and market work. Women fall into four major groups. The first group consists of five *Involuntary Nonemployed Mothers* who are not employed but care full-time for their children. All of these women want to be employed at least part time. They either cannot secure the job they want and/or they feel pressured to be at home mothering full-time.

The second group consists of six *Voluntary Nonemployed Mothers* who are not employed but remain out of the labor force by *choice*. They feel committed to staying at home to care for preschool and/or elementary school age children.

The third category, *Ambivalent Employed Mothers*, includes eleven employed women. They have either preschool or elementary school age children. Women in this group believe that employment interferes with motherhood, and feel "guilty" when they work outside the home. Despite these feelings, they are employed at least part-time.

The fourth group, *Nonambivalent Employed Mothers* includes eight employed women. What distinguishes these women from the previous group is their view that employment and motherhood seem compatible social dynamics irrespective of the age of their children. All eight women are Mexicanas. Some of these women believe employment could be problematic, however, *if* a family member could not care for their children or be at home for the children when they arrived from school.

Chicanas tend to fall in the second and third categories, whereas Mexicanas predominate in the first and fourth groups. Three reasons emerged as critical in explaining this difference:

1. the economic situations of their families;
2. labor market structure (four-fifths of the nonemployed Mexicanas were involuntarily unemployed); and
3. women's conceptualizations of motherhood, in particular, their expressed *need* to mother.

Age of the women and number of children did not fall into any discernible pattern, therefore I did not engage them in depth within my analysis.

First, I consider the situation of the *Voluntary Nonemployed Mothers*, including three married Chicanas, one single-parent Mexicana and one single-parent Chicana. All but one woman exited the labor market involuntarily (for reasons such as layoffs or disability). All five women remain out of the labor force by choice. Among them, the expressed need to mother appears strong—overriding all other concerns. They view motherhood as mutually exclusive from employment. Lydia, a married Chicana with a small toddler, articulates this perspective:

Right now, since we've had the baby, I feel, well he [her husband] feels the same way, that I want to spend this time with her and watch her grow up.

See, because when I was small my grandmother raised me so I felt this *loss* [her emphasis] when my grandmother died. And I've never gotten that *real love*, that mother love from my mother. We have a friendship, but we don't have that "motherly love." I want my daughter to know that I'm here, especially at her age, it's very important for them to know that when they cry that mama's there. Even if it's not a painful cry, it's still important for them to know that mommy's there. She's my number one—she's all my attention . . . so working-wise, it's up to [her husband] right now.

Susana, a Chicana single parent with a five-year-old child said:

I'm the type of person that has always wanted to have a family. I think it was more like I didn't have a family-type home when I was growing up. I didn't have a mother and a father and the kids all together in the same household all happy. I didn't have that. And that's what I want more than anything! I want to be different from my mother, who has worked hard and is successful in her job. I don't want to be successful in the same way.

Lydia, Susana, and the other voluntarily unemployed Chicanas adamantly assert that motherhood requires staying home with their children. Susana said: "A good mother is there for her children all the time when they are little and when they come home from school." All the Chicanas in this category believe that motherhood means staying home with children—even if it means going on welfare (AFDC). This finding is similar to other accounts of working-class women.[30]

The sense shared among this group of women that motherhood and employment are irreconcilable, especially when children are of preschool age, is related to their social locations. A small minority of the Chicanas had been raised by nonemployed mothers (n = 3). They feel they should stay at home with their children as long as it's economically feasible. Most of the Chicanas, however, resemble Lydia and Susana, who had been raised by employed mothers. Although these women recognize that their mothers had worked out of economic need, they believe they did not receive sufficient love and care from their mothers. Throughout their interviews, this group of Chicanas expressed hostility and resentment against their employed mothers for leaving them with other caretakers. These feelings contribute to their decisions to stay at home with their children, and/or their sense of "guilt" when they are employed. Their hostility and guilt defies psychoanalytic theories that speculate that the cycle of gender construction locking women into "exclusive mothering" roles can be broken if the primary caretaker (the mother) undertakes more diverse roles.[31] Rather, Chicanas appear to value current conceptionalizations of motherhood that prioritize the expressive work of the mother as distinct from her economic activities.

This group of Chicanas seems to be pursuing the social construction of motherhood that is idealized within their ethnic community, their churches, and society at large.[32] Among Chicanos and Mexicanos the image of *la madre* as self-sacrificing and holy is a powerful standard against which women often compare themselves.[33] The Chicana informants also seem to accept the notion that women's primary duty is to provide for the emotional welfare of the children, and that economic activities which take them outside the home are secondary. Women's desire to enact the socially constructed motherhood ideal was further strengthened by their conviction that many of their current problems (for instance, low levels of education, feelings of inadequacy, single parenthood) are related to growing up in families that did not conform to the stay-at-home mother/father-as-provider configuration. Their evaluation of the close relationship between motherhood and economic or emotional well-being of offspring parallels popular emphasis on the primacy of individual efforts and the family environment to emotional vigor and achievement (Parsons and Bales 1955; Bradley and Caldwell 1984; Caspi and Elder 1988; Parcel and Menaghan 1990).[34]

Informants in this group speak to a complex dimension of mothering and gender construction in the Chicano/Mexicano communities. These women reject their employed mothers' organization of family life. As children, most had been cared for by other family members, and now feel closer to their grandmothers or other female relatives than to their own biological mothers. This causes them considerable pain—pain they want to spare their own children. Many, like Susana, do not want to be "successful" in the tradition of their own employed mothers. Insofar as "success" means leaving their children with other caretakers, it contradicts their conceptualization of motherhood. Rather, they frame "success" in more affective terms: having children who are happy and doing well in school. This does not suggest that Chicanas disagree with the notion that having a good job or a lucrative career denotes "success." They simply feel that successful careers could and should be deferred until their children are older (for instance, in the upper grades of elementary school) and doing well academically and emotionally.

Only one married Mexicana, Belen, articulated views similar to those of the Chicanas. Belen left the labor market in 1979 to give birth and care for her newborn child. It is important to note that she has a gainfully employed husband who does not believe mothers should work outside the home. Belen, who has two children and was expecting a third when I interviewed her, said:

> I wanted to work or go back to school after having my first son, but my husband didn't want me to. He said, "no one can take care of your child the way you can." He did not want me to work. And I did not feel right

having someone else care for my son. So I decided to wait until my children were older.

Belens' words underscore an important dynamic that impacted on both Mexicana and Chicana conceptualizations of motherhood: spousal employment and private patriarchy. Specifically, husbands working in full-time, year-round jobs with earnings greater than those of their wives, tended to pressure women to mother full-time. Women who succumb to this pressure become economically dependent on their husbands and reaffirm male authority in the organization of the family. These particular women tend to consider motherhood and employment in similar ways. This suggests that the form the social construction of motherhood takes involves women's economic relationship to men as well as length of time in the U.S.

Four Mexicanas and one Chicana were involuntarily nonemployed. They had been laid off from their jobs or were on temporary disability leave. Three women (two Mexicanas/one Chicana) were seeking employment; the other two were in the last stages of pregnancy but intended to look for a job as soon as possible after their child's birth. All five women reported feeling "good" about being home with their children, but wanted to rejoin the labor force as soon as possible. Ideologically these women view motherhood and employment as reconcilable social dynamics. As Isabel, an unemployed production worker, married with eight children, said:

> I believe that women always work more. We who are mothers work to maintain the family by working outside, but also inside the house caring for the children.

Isabel voiced a sentiment held by all of the informants—that women work hard at motherhood. Since emigrating to the U.S. about a decade ago, Isabel had been employed nearly continuously, with only short leaves for childbearing. Isabel and nearly all of the Mexicanas described growing up in environments where women, men, and children were important economic actors. In this regard they are similar to the *Nonambivalent Employed Mothers*—all of whom are also Mexicanas. They tended not to dichotomize social life in the same way as the *Voluntary Nonemployed Chicanas* and *Ambivalent Employed* informants.

Although all of the Chicanas believe that staying home best fulfills their mother roles, slightly fewer than half actually stay out of the labor market to care for their young children. The rest of the Chicanas are employed and struggling to reconcile motherhood with employment. I refer to these women as *Ambivalent Employed Mothers*. They express guilt about working and assert they *would not work* if they did not have to for economic reasons. Seven of these women are Chicanas; four are Mexicanas.

To try and alleviate their guilt and help meet their families' economic goals, most of the Chicanas work in part-time jobs. This option permits them to be home when their children arrive from school. Despite this, they feel guilty and unhappy about working. As Jenny, a married Chicana with two children, ages two and four, who is employed part-time, said:

> Sure, I feel guilty. I *should* [her emphasis] be with them [her children] while they're little. He [her husband] really feels that I should be with my kids all the time. And it's true.

Despite their guilt, most of the women in this group remain employed because their jobs offer them the means to provide for family economic betterment—a goal that transcends staying home with their children. However, women's utilization of economic rationales for working sometimes served as a smoke screen for individualistic desires to "do something outside the home" and to establish a degree of autonomy. Several women, for example, stated that they enjoyed having their "own money." When I asked these women to elaborate, they typically retreated to a familistic stance. That is, much of *her* money is used *for the family* (for example, child care, family presents, clothing). When money is used *for the woman* (make-up, going out with the girls) it is often justified as necessary for her emotional well-being, which in turn helps her to be a good wife and mother.

The Mexicana mothers who are employed express their ambivalence somewhat differently from the Chicanas. One Mexicana works full-time; the other three are employed part-time. Angela, a Mexicana married with one child and employed full-time as a seamstress, told me with glistening eyes:

> Always I have had to work. I had to leave my son with the baby-sitter since he was six months old. It was difficult. Each baby-sitter has their own way of caring for children which isn't like yours. I know the baby-sitter wouldn't give him the food I left. He always had on dirty diapers and was starving when I would pick him up. But there wasn't any other recourse. I had to work. I would just clean him and feed him when I got home.

Angela's "guilt" stemmed from her inability to find good, affordable child care. Unlike most of the Mexicanas, who had extensive family networks, Angela and her husband had few relatives to rely on in the U.S. Unlike the Chicana informants, Angela did not want to exit the labor market to care for her child. Her desire is reinforced by economic need; her husband is irregularly employed.[35] For the other three Mexicanas in this group, guilt as an employed mother appears to have developed with stable spousal employment. That is, the idea of feeling guilty about full-time employment emerged *after* husbands became employed in secure, well-paying jobs and "reminded" them of the importance of stay-at-home, full-time motherhood. Lourdes, who was married with eight children and working as a part-time hotel maid said:

> I was offered a job at a —— factory, working from eleven at night to seven in the morning. But I had a baby and so I wasn't able to work. I would have liked to take the job because it paid $8.25 an hour. I couldn't though, because of my baby. And my husband didn't want me to work at night. He said, "If we both work at night, who will take care of the children? So I didn't take the job.

To thwart potential guilt over full-time employment and to ease marital tension (if she had taken this job she would have earned more money than her husband), Lourdes declined this high-paying job. When her child turned two, she opted to work part-time as a hotel maid. Lourdes, and the other Mexicanas employed part-time, told me that they *would* work full-time *if* their husbands supported their preferences. Mexicanas' ambivalence, then, is related to unease about their children's child care situations, as well as to anger at being held accountable to a narrow construction of motherhood enforced by their husbands.

All *Ambivalent Employed Mothers* report worrying about their children while at work. While this does not necessarily impair their job performance, it adds another psychological or emotional burden on their shoulders. This burden affects their ability to work full-time (overtime is especially problematic) or seek the means (especially schooling) to advance in their jobs.

Women seem particularly troubled when they have to work on weekends. This robs them of precious family time. As Elena, a Chicana single parent with two children, ages nine and three, who works part-time as a hotel maid, said:

> Yes, I work on weekends. And my kids, you know how kids are—they don't like it. And it's hard. But I hope to find a job soon where the schedule is fixed and I won't have to work on weekends—because that time should be for my kids.

There is a clear sense among the women I interviewed that a boundary between *time for the family* and *market time* should exist. During times when this boundary folds, women experience both internal conflict (within the woman herself) and external conflict (among family members). They regard jobs that overlap on family time with disfavor and unhappiness. When economic reasons compel women to work during what they view as family time, they usually try to find as quickly as possible a different job that allows them to better meet their mother roles.

Interestingly, the Chicanas appear less flexible in reconciling the boundaries of family time and market time than the Mexicanas. That is, Chicanas overwhelmingly "choose" part-time employment to limit the amount of spillover time from employment on motherhood and family activities. Mexicanas, on the other hand, overwhelmingly work full time (n = 9) and attempt to do both familial caretaking and market work as completely as possible.

This leads us to consider the fourth category I call *Nonambivalent Employed Mothers.* This category consists of Mexicana immigrants, both married and single-parent (six and two women, respectively). Mexicanas in this group do not describe motherhood as a *need* requiring a separate sphere for optimal realization. Rather, they refer to motherhood as one function of womanhood compatible with employment insofar as employment allows them to provide for their family's economic subsistence or betterment. As Pilar, a married Mexicana with four children, employed full-time as a line supervisor in a factory, said: "I work to help my children. That's what a mother should do." This group of Mexicanas does not express *guilt* over leaving their children in the care of others so much as *regret* over the limited amount of time they could spend with them. As Norma, a Mexicana full-time clerical worker, who is married with two children ages three and five, said:

> I don't feel guilty for leaving my children because if I didn't work they might not have the things they have now.... Perhaps if I had to stay at home I would feel guilty and frustrated. I'm not the type that can stay home twenty-four hours a day. I don't think that would help my children any because I would feel pressured at being cooped up [*encerrada*] at home. And that way I wouldn't have the same desire to play with my daughters. But now, with the time we have together, we do things that we want to, like run in the park, because there's so little time.

All of the Mexicanas in this group articulate views similar to Norma's. Their greater comfort with the demands of market and family work emanates from their social locations. All of the Mexicanas come from poor or working-class families, where motherhood embraced both economic and affective features. Their activities were not viewed as equal to those of men, however, and ideologically women saw themselves as *helping* the family rather than *providing* for it.

Few Mexicanas reported that their mothers were wage-laborers (n = 3), but rather, described a range of economic activities they remembered women doing "for the family."[36] Mexicanas from rural villages (n = 7) recounted how their mothers had worked on the land and made assorted products or food to sell in local marketplaces. Mexicanas from urban areas (n = 5) also discussed how their mothers had been economically active. Whether rural or urban, Mexicanas averred that their mothers had taught them to "help" the family as soon as possible. As Norma said:

> My mother said: "it's one thing for a woman to lie around the house but it's a different thing for the work that needs to be done. As the saying goes, work is never done; the work does you in [*el trabajo acaba con uno; uno nunca acaba con el trabajo*].

Lourdes and two other Mexicanas cleaned houses with their mothers after school. Other mothers sold clothes to neighbors, cooked and sold food, or did assorted services for pay (for example, giving penicillin shots to neighbors). The Mexicanas do not view these activities as "separate" or less important than the emotional nurturing of children and family. Rather, they appreciate both the economic and the expressive as important facets of motherhood.

Although the Mexicanas had been raised in worlds where women were important economic actors, this did not signify gender equality. On the contrary, male privilege, or patriarchy, characterizes the organization of the family, the economy, and the polity in both rural and urban Mexican society.[37] In the present study, Mexicanas indicated that men wielded greater authority in the family, the community and the state than women. Mexicanas also tended to uphold male privilege in the family by viewing both domestic work and women's employment as "less important" than the work done by men. As Adela, a married Mexicana with four children, said: "Men are much stronger and do much more difficult work than women." Mexicanas also tended to defer to husbands as the "head" of the family—a position they told me was both "natural" and "holy."[38]

WORKING AT MOTHERHOOD

The differences presented here between the Chicanas and Mexicanas regarding motherhood and employment stem from their distinct social locations. Raised in rural or working-class families in Mexico, the Mexicanas described childhoods where they and their mothers actively contributed to the economic subsistence of their families by planting crops, harvesting, selling homemade goods, and cleaning houses. Their situations resonate with what some researchers term a family economy, where all family members work at productive tasks differentiated mainly by age and sex.[39] In this type of structure, there is less distinction between economic life and domestic life. Motherhood in this context is both economic and expressive, embracing both employment as well as childrearing.

The family economy the Mexicanas experienced differs from the family organization that characterizes most of the Chicanas' childhoods. The Chicanas come from a world that idealizes a male wage earner as the main economic "provider," with women primarily as consumers, and only secondarily as economic actors.[40] Women in this context are mothers first, wage earners second. Families that challenge this structure are often discredited, or perceived as dysfunctional and the source of many social problems.[41] The ambivalence Chicanas recurrently voice stems from their belief in what Kanter calls "the myth of separate worlds."[42] They seek to realize the popular notion or stereotype that family is a separate structure—a haven in a heartless world. Their attachment to this ideal is underscored by a harsh critique of their own employed mothers and themselves *when* they work full-time. Motherhood framed within this context appears irreconcilable with employment.

There are other facets to the differences between Chicanas and Mexicanas. The Mexicanas, as immigrant women, came to the United States with a vision of improving the life chances of their families and themselves. This finding intersects with research on "selective immigration." That is, that Mexican immigrants tend to possess higher levels of education than the national average in Mexico, and a wide range of behavioral characteristics (for instance, high achievement orientation) conducive to success in the U.S.[43]

The Mexicanas emigrated hoping to work—hence their high attachment to employment, even in physically demanding, often demeaning jobs. Mexican and Chicano husbands support their wives' desires to work *so long as* this employment does not challenge the patriarchal structure of the family. In other words, so long as the Mexicanas: (1) articulate high attachment to motherhood *and* family caretaker roles, (2) frame their employment in terms of family economic goals, and (3) do not ask men to do equal amounts of housework or childcare, they encounter little resistance from husbands or other male family members.

When Mexican and Chicano husbands secure good jobs, however, they begin pressuring wives to quit working or to work only part-time. In this way, Mexican and Chicano men actively pursue continuity of their superordinate position within the family. This suggests that the way motherhood is conceptualized in both the Mexican and Chicano communities, particularly with respect to employment, is wedded to male privilege, or patriarchy. Ironically then, Mexicanas' sense of employment's continuity with motherhood enhances their job attachment but does not challenge a patriarchal family structure or ethos.

Similarly, Chicanas' preference for an idealized form of motherhood does not challenge male privilege in their community. Their desire to stay at home to mother exercised a particularly strong influence on the employment behavior of single-parent Chicanas and women with husbands employed in relatively good jobs. This preference reflects an adherence both to an idealized, middle-class life-style that glorifies women's domestic roles, as well as to maintenance of a patriarchal family order. Chicanas feel they should stay at home to try and provide their children with the mothering they believe children should have—mothering that many of them had not experienced. Chicanas also feel compelled by husbands and the larger community to maintain the status of men as "good providers." Men earning wages adequate to provide for their families' needs usually urged their wives to leave the labor market. While the concept of the good provider continues to be highly valued in our society, it also serves as a rationale that upholds male privilege ideologically and materially, and reinforces the myth of separate spheres that emanates from the organization of the family and the economy.

CONCLUSION

By illustrating how Chicanas and Mexicanas differ in their conceptualizations and organization of the motherhood and employment nexus, this study demonstrates how motherhood is a culturally formed structure with various meanings and subtexts. The vitality of these differences among a group who share a common historical origin and many cultural attributes underscores the need for frameworks that analyze diversity among all groups of women. Most essential to such an undertaking is a critique of the privileging of the "separate spheres" concept in analyses of women and work.

The present study provides additional coherence to recent contentions that the private-public dichotomy lacks immediate relevance to less privileged women (for instance, Chicana and Mexican immigrant women). In the process of illustrating how Chicanas and Mexicanas organized the interplay between motherhood and employment, it became clear that a more useful way of understanding this intersection might be to problematize motherhood itself. Considering motherhood from the vantage point of women's diverse social locations revealed considerable heterogeneity in how one might speak of it. For example, motherhood has an economic component for both groups of women, but it is most strongly expressed by Mexicana immigrants. The flavor of the expressive, however, flows easily across both groups of women, and for the Mexicanas embraces the economic. What this suggests is that the dichotomy of the separate spheres lacks relevance to Chicanas and Mexicanas, and other women whose social origins make economic work necessary for survival.

This leads us to consider the relative place and function of the ideology of motherhood prevalent in our society. Motherhood constructed to privilege the woman who stays at home serves a myriad of functions. It pushes women to dichotomize their lives rather than develop a sense of fluidity across roles, responsibilities, and preferences. Idealized, stay-at-home motherhood eludes most American women with children. As an ideology, however, it tells them what "should be," rendering them failures *as women* when they enter the labor market. Hence the feelings of ambivalence that characterized employed mother's lives for the most part—except those who had not yet internalized these standards. The present research provided examples of such women, along with the understanding that other women from different social locations may demonstrate distinct ways of organizing the motherhood-employment nexus as well.

Feminist analyses of women and work emphasize the role of patriarchy to maintain male privilege and domination economically and ideologically. It is important to recognize that male privilege is not experienced equally by all men, and that patriarchy itself can be expressed in different ways. The present study found that notions of motherhood among Mexicanas and Chicanas are embedded in different ideological constructs operating within two systems of patriarchy. For Mexicanas, patriarchy takes the form of a corporate family model, with all members contributing to the common good. For Chicanas, the patriarchal structure centers more closely around a public-private dichotomy that idealizes men as economic providers, and women primarily as caretakers-consumers.

The finding that women from more "traditional" backgrounds (such as rural Mexico) are likely to approach full-time employment with less ambivalence than more "American" women (such as the Chicanas) rebuts linear acculturation models that assume a negative relationship between ideologies (such as motherhood) constructed within "traditional" Mexican society, and employment. It also complements findings on the negative relationship between greater length of time in the U.S. and high aspirations among Mexicans.[44] This suggests that employment problems (for example, underemployment, unemployment) are related less to "traditional" cultural configurations than to labor market structure and employment policies. Understanding the intersections between employment policy, social ideology, and private need is a necessary step toward expanding possibilities for women in our society.

Notes

1. This article is a revised version of "Ambivalence or Continuity?: Motherhood and Employment among Chicanas and Mexican Immigrant Women," *AZTLAN, International Journal of Chicano Studies Research* (1992). I would like to thank Maxine Baca Zinn, Evelyn Nakano Glenn, Arlie Hochschild, Beatriz Pesquera, and Vicki Ruiz for their constructive feedback and criticism of earlier drafts of this paper. A special thanks goes to Jon

Cruz for his assistance in titling this paper. Any remaining errors or inconsistencies are my own responsibility. This research was supported in part by a 1986–87 University of California President's Postdoctoral Fellowship.

2. Betsy Wearing, *The Ideology of Motherhood, A Study of Sydney Suburban Mothers* (Sydney: George Allen and Unwin, 1984); Barbara J. Berg, *The Crisis of the Working Mother, Resolving the Conflict Between Family and Work* (New York: Summit Books, 1986); Nancy Folbre "The Pauperization of Motherhood: Patriarchy and Public Policy in the United States," *Review of Radical Political Economics* 16 (1984). The view that mothers should not work outside the home typically pertains to married women. Current state welfare policies (e.g., Aid to Families with Dependent Children [AFDC], workfare) indicate that single, unmarried mothers belong in the labor force, not at home caring for their children full-time. See Naomi Gerstel and Harriet Engel Gross, "Introduction," in N. Gerstel and H. E. Gross, eds., *Families and Work* (Philadelphia: Temple University Press, 1987), pp. 1–12; Deborah K. Zinn and Rosemary C. Sarri, Turning Back the Clock on Public Welfare," in *Signs: Journal of Women in Culture and Society* 10 (1984), pp. 355–370; Nancy Folbre "The Pauperization of Motherhood; Nancy A. Naples, "A Socialist Feminist Analysis of the Family Support Act of 1988," AFFILIA 6 (1991), pp. 23–38.

3. Allyson Sherman Grossman, "More than Half of All Children Have Working Mothers," Special Labor Force Reports—Summaries, *Monthly Labor Review* (February, 1982), pp. 41–43; Howard Hayghe, "Working Mothers Reach Record Number in 1984," *Monthly Labor Review* 107 (December, 1984), pp. 31–34; U.S. Bureau of The Census "Fertility of American Women: June 1990," *Current Population Report*, Series P-20, No. 454, (Washington D.C.: United States Government Printing Office, 1991). In June 1990, over half (53.1 percent) of women between the ages of 18–44 who had had a child in the last year were in the labor force. This proportion varied by race: 54.9 percent of white women, 46.9 percent of Black women, and 44.4 percent of Latinas were in the labor force. See U.S. Bureau of the Census (1991), p. 5.

4. Simon and Landis report that a 1986 Gallup Poll indicates that support for married women to work outside the home is considerably greater than 1938 levels: 76 percent of women and 78 percent of men approve (1989: 270). Comparable 1938 levels are 25 percent and 19 percent, respectively of women and men. The 1985 Roper Poll finds the American public adhering to the view that a husband's career supersedes that of his wife: 72 percent of women and 62 percent of men agree that a wife should quit her job and relocate if her husband is offered a good job in another city (189: 272). In the reverse situation, 20 percent of women and 22 percent of men believe a husband should quit his job and relocate with his wife (1989: 272). Simon and Landis conclude: "The Women's Movement has not radicalized the American woman: she is still prepared to put marriage and children ahead of her career and to allow her husband's status to determine the family's position in society" (1989: 269). Rita J. Simon and Jean M. Landis, "Women's and Men's Attitudes About a Woman's Place and Role," *Public Opinion Quarterly* (1989), 53: 265–276.

5. Arlie Hochschild with Anne Machung, *The Second Shift, Working Parents and the Revolution at Home* (New York: Viking Penguin Books, 1989); Kathleen Gerson, *Hard Choices* (Berkeley, California: University of California Press, 1985); Barbara J. Berg, *The Crisis of the Working Mother, Resolving the Conflict Between Family and Work* (New York: Summit Books, 1986). The concept of "separate spheres" is approached in a variety of ways and often critiqued. See Michele Barrett, *Women's Oppression Today, Problems in Marxist Feminist Analysis* (London, Verso Press, 1980); Nona Glazer "Servants to capital: Unpaid domestic labor and paid work," *Review of Radical Economics* 16 (1984), pp. 61–87. Zaretsky contends that distinct family and market spheres arose with the development of industrial capitalism: "men and women came to see the family as separate from the economy, and personal life as a separate sphere of life divorced from the larger economy." See Eli Zaretsky, *Capitalism, The Family and Personal Life* (New York: Harper Colophon Books, 1976), p. 78. This stance is substantially different from that of early radical feminist approaches,

including Firestone, who argued that the separation antedates history. See Shulamith Firestone, *The Dialectic of Sex* (New York: Bantam Books, 1970). Other scholars assert that the relations of production and reproduction are intertwined and virtually inseparable. See Heidi Hartmann, "Capitalism, Patriarchy and Job Segregation by Sex," in Martha Blaxall and Barbara Reagan, eds., *Women and the Work Place* (Chicago, Illinois: University of Chicago Press, 1976), pp. 137–169.

6. Hood argues that the "ideal" of stay-at-home motherhood and male provider has historically been an unrealistic standard for families outside the middle and upper classes. She points out that early surveys of urban workers indicate between 40% and 50% of all families supplemented their income with the earnings of wives and children. See Jane C. Hood, "The Provider Role: Its Meaning and Measurement," *Journal of Marriage and the Family* 48 (May, 1986), pp. 349–359.

7. It should be noted that native-born status is not an essential requirement for the ethnic label, "Chicana/o." There are numerous identifiers used by people of Mexican descent, including: Chicana/o, Mexican, Mexican-American, Mexicana/o, Latina/o, and Hispanic. Often people of Mexican descent use two or three of the above labels, depending on the social situation (e.g., "Mexican-American" in the family or "Chicana/o" at school). See John A. Garcia, "Yo Soy Mexicano . . . : Self-identity and Sociodemographic Correlates," *Social Science Quarterly 62* (March, 1981), pp. 88–98; Susan E. Keefe and Amado M. Padilla, *Chicano Ethnicity* (Albuquerque, NM: University of New Mexico Press, 1987). My designation of study informants as either "Chicana" or "Mexicana" represents an analytic separation that facilitates demonstrating the heterogeneity among this group.

8. Patricia Zavella, "Reflections on Diversity among Chicanos," *Frontiers* 2 (1991), p. 75.

9. See Rosalia Solorzano-Torres, "Female Mexican Immigrants in San Diego County," in V. L. Ruiz and S. Tiano, eds., *Women on the U.S.-Mexico Border: Responses to Change* (Boston: Allen and Unwin, 1987), pp. 41–59; Reynaldo Baca and Bryan Dexter, "Mexican Women, Migration and Sex Roles," *Migration Today 13* (1985), pp. 14–18; Sylvia Guendelman and Auristela Perez-Itriago, "Double Lives: The Changing Role of Women in Seasonal Migration," *Women's Studies* 13 (1987), pp. 249–271.

10. Gary S. Becker, "Human Capital, Effort, and the Sexual Division of Labor," *Journal of Labor Economics* 3 (1985 Supplement), pp. S33–S58; Gary S. Becker, *A Treatise on the Family* (Cambridge, MA: Harvard University Press, 1981); Solomon W. Polachek, "Occupational Self-Selection: A Human Capital Approach to Sex Differences in Occupational Structure," *Review of Economics and Statistics* 63 (1981), pp. 60–69; S. Polachek "Occupational Segregation Among Women: Theory, Evidence, and a Prognosis" in C. B. Lloyd, E. S. Andrews and C. L. Gilroy, eds., *Women in the Labor Market* (New York: Columbia University Press, 1981), pp. 137–157; S. Polachek, "Discontinuous Labor Force Participation and Its Effect on Women's Market Earnings," in C. Lloyd, ed., *Sex Discrimination and the Division of Labor* (New York: Columbia University Press, 1975), pp. 90–122. Becker's classic treatise, *Human Capital*, uses the following example borrowed from G. Stigler, "The Economics of Information," *Journal of Political Economy* (June 1961): "Women spend less time in the labor force than men and, therefore, have less incentive to invest in market skills; tourists spend little time in any one area and have less incentive than residents of the area to invest in knowledge of specific consumption activities." See Gary S. Becker, *Human Capital* (Chicago: University of Chicago Press, 1975), p. 74.

11. Some institutional economists argue that "statistical discrimination" is one critical labor market dynamic that often impedes women and minorities. See Kenneth Arrow, "Economic Dimensions of Occupational Segregation: Comment I," *Signs: Journal of Women in Culture and Society* 1 (1987), pp. 233–237; Edmund Phelps, "The Statistical Theory of Racism and Sexism," in A. H. Amsden, ed., *The Economics of Women and Work* (New York: St. Martin's Press, 1980), pp. 206–210. This perspective suggests that prospective employers often lack detailed information about individual applicants and

therefore utilize statistical averages and normative views of the relevant group(s) to which the applicant belongs in their hiring decisions (e.g., college-educated men tend to be successful and committed employees; all women are potential mothers; or women tend to exit the labor force for childbearing).

Bielby and Baron pose an important critique to the underlying rationale of statistical discrimination. They argue that utilizing perceptions of group differences between the sexes is "neither as rational nor as efficient as the economists believe." That is, utilizing stereotypical notions of "men's work" and "women's work" is often costly to employers and therefore irrational. This suggests that sex segregation is imbedded in organizational policies which reflect and reinforce "belief systems that are also rather inert." See William T. Bielby and James N. Baron, "Undoing Discrimination: Job Integration and Comparable Worth," in C. Bose and G. Spitze, eds., *Ingredients for Women's Employment Policy* (New York: State University of New York Press, 1987), p. 216, pp. 221–222.

12. Annette Kuhn, "Structure of Patriarchy and Capital in the Family," in A. Kuhn and Annemarie Wolfe, eds., *Feminism and Materialism: Women and Modes of Production* (London: Routledge and Kegan Paul, 1978); Heidi Hartmann, "Capitalism, Patriarchy, and Job Segregation by Sex," in Martha Blaxall and Barbara Reagan, eds., *Women and the Work Place* (Chicago, Illinois: University of Chicago Press, 1976), pp. 137–169; H. Hartmann, "The Family as the Locus of Gender, Class, and Political Struggle: The Example of Housework," *Signs: Journal of Women in Culture and Society* 6 (1981), pp. 366–394; Michele Barrett *Women's Oppression Today, Problems in Marxist Feminist Analysis* (London: Verso Press, 1980).

13. Lourdes Beneria and Martha Roldan, *The Crossroads of Class and Gender, Industrial Homework, Subcontracting, and Household Dynamics in Mexico City* (Chicago: The University of Chicago Press, 1987); L. Beneria and Gita Sen, "Accumulation, Reproduction, and Women's Role in Economic Development: Boserup Revisited," in E. Leacock and H. I. Safa, eds., *Women's Work: Development and Division of Labor by Gender* (Massachusetts: Bergin and Garvey Publishers, 1986), pp. 141–157; Dorothy Smith, "Women's Inequality and the Family," in N. Gerstel and H. E. Gross, eds., *Families and Work* (Philadelphia: Temple University Press, 1987), pp. 23–54.

14. This phrase was coined by Arlie R. Hochschild and quoted in Lillian B. Rubin, *Intimate Strangers, Men and Women Together* (New York: Harper and Row, 1983).

15. Rosabeth Moss Kanter, *Men and Women in the Corporation* (New York: Basic Books, 1977). Bielby and Baron note: "employers expect certain behaviors from women (e.g., high turnover) and therefore assign them to routine tasks and dead-end jobs. Women respond by exhibiting the very behavior employers expect, thereby reinforcing the stereotype." Bielby and Baron, "Undoing Discrimination: Job Integration and Comparable Worth," p.221.

16. Arlie Hochschild with Anne Machung, *The Second Shift, Working Parents and the Revolution of Home* (New York: Viking Penguin Books, 1989).

17. Barbara J. Berg, *The Crisis of the Working Mother, Resolving the Conflict Between Family and Work* (New York: Summit Books, 1986), p. 42.

18. Howard Hayghe, "Working Mothers Reach Record Number in 1984," *Monthly Labor Review* 107 (December, 1984), pp. 31–34; U.S. Bureau of the Census, "Fertility of American Women: June 1990" in Current Population Report, Series P-20, No. 454 (Washington D.C.: United States Government Printing Office, 1991); U.S. Bureau of Census Report, "Fertility of American Women: June 1986" in Current Population Report, Series P-20, No. 421 (Washington D.C.: United States Printing Press). In June 1986 (the year closest to the year I interviewed the respondents where I found relevant data), 49.8 percent of all women with newborn children were in the labor force. Women demonstrated differences in this behavior: 49.7 percent of white women, 51.1 percent of Black women, and 40.6 percent of Latinas with newborn children were in the labor force. See U.S. Bureau of the Census "Fertility of American Women: June 1986" (1987), p. 5.

19. Bonnie Thornton Dill, Lynn Weber Cannon, and Reeve Vanneman, "Pay Equity: An Issue of Race, Ethnicity and Sex" (Washington D.C.: National Commission on Pay Equity, February, 1987); Julianne Malveaux and Phyllis Wallace, "Minority Women in the Workplace," in K. S. Koziara, M. Moskow, and L. Dewey Tanner, eds., *Women and Work: Industrial Relations Research Association Research Volume* (Washington D.C.: Bureau of National Affairs, 1987), pp. 265–298; Vicki L. Ruiz, "'And Miles to go. . . .': Mexican Women and Work, 1930–1985" in L. Schlissel, V. L. Ruiz, and J. Monk, eds., *Western Women, Their Land, Their Lives* (Albuquerque: University of New Mexico Press, 1988), pp. 117–136.

20. Mario Barrera, *Race and Class in the Southwest: A Theory of Racial Inequality* (Notre Dame, IN: University of Notre Dame Press, 1979); Tomas Almaguer, "Class, Race, and Chicano Oppression," in *Socialist Revolution* 5 (1975), pp. 71–99; Denise Segura, "Labor Market Stratification: The Chicana Experience," *Berkeley Journal of Sociology* 29 (1984), pp. 57–91.

21. Marta Tienda and P. Guhleman, "The Occupational Position of Employed Hispanic Women," in G. J Borjas and M. Tienda, eds., *Hispanics in the U.S. Economy* (New York: Academic Press, 1985), pp. 243–273.

22. Edgar J. Kranau, Vicki Green, and Gloria Valencia-Weber, "Acculturation and the Hispanic Woman: Attitudes Towards Women, Sex-Role Attribution, Sex-Role Behavior, and Demographics," *Hispanic Journal of Behavioral Sciences* 4 (1982), pp. 21–40; Alfredo Mirande and Evangelina Enriquez, *La Chicana, The Mexican American Woman* (Chicago: The University of Chicago Press, 1979).

23. Kranau, Green, and Valencia-Weber, "Acculturation and the Hispanic Woman," pp. 21–40; Alfredo Mirande, *The Chicano Experience: An Alternative Perspective* (Notre Dame: University of Notre Dame Press, 1985).

24. Vilma Ortiz and Rosemary Santana Cooney, "Sex-Role Attitudes and Labor Force Participation among Young Hispanic Females and Non-Hispanic White Females," *Social Science Quarterly* 65 (June, 1984), pp. 392–400.

25. Susan E. Keefe and Amado M. Padilla, *Chicano Ethnicity* (Albuquerque, NM: University of New Mexico Press, 1987); Richard H. Mendoza, "Acculturation and Sociocultural Variability," in J. L. Martinez Jr. and R. H. Mendoza, eds., *Chicano Psychology*, Second Edition (New York: Academic Press, 1984), pp. 61–75.

26. Maxine Baca Zinn, "Mexican-American Women in the Social Sciences," *Signs: Journal of Women in Culture and Society* 8 (1982), pp. 259–272. M. Baca Zinn, "Employment and Education of Mexican-American Women: The Interplay of Modernity and Ethnicity in Eight Families," *Harvard Educational Review* 50 (February 1980), pp. 47–62. M. Baca Zinn, "Chicano Family Research: Conceptual Distortions and Alternative Directions," *Journal of Ethnic Studies* 7 (1979) pp. 59–71.

27. For additional information on the methods and sample selection, I refer the reader to Denise A. Segura, "Chicanas and Mexican Immigrant Women in the Labor Market: A Study of Occupational Mobility and Stratification," unpublished Ph.D. dissertation, Department of Sociology, University of California, Berkeley (1986).

28. The ages of the Chicanas range from 23 to 42 years. The Mexicanas reported ages from 24 to 45. The age profile indicates that most of the women were in peak childbearing years.

29. Denise A. Segura, "Chicanas and Mexican Immigrant Women in the Labor Market."

30. For an example, see Betsy Wearing, *The Ideology of Motherhood, A Study of Sydney Suburban Mothers* (Sydney: George Allen and Unwin, 1984).

31. For an example, see Nancy Chodorow, *The Reproduction of Mothering* (Berkeley: University of California Press, 1979).

32. Manuel Ramirez III and Alfredo Castaneda, *Cultural Democracy, Bicognitive Development, and Education* (New York: Academic Press, 1974); Robert F. Peck and Rogelio Diaz-Guerrero, "Two Core-Culture Patterns and the Diffusion of Values Across Their Bor-

ders," *International Journal of Psychology* 2 (1967), pp. 272–282; Javier I. Escobat and E. T. Randolph, "The Hispanic and Social Networks," in R. M. Becerra, M. Karno, and J. I. Escobar, eds., *Mental Health and Hispanic Americans: Clinical Perspectives* (New York: Grune and Stratton, 1982).

33. Alfredo Mirande and Evangelina Enriquez, *La Chicana, The Mexican American Woman* (Chicago: The University of Chicago Press, 1979); Margarita Melville, "Introduction" and "Matrascence" in M. B. Melville, ed., *Twice a Minority: Mexican American Women* (St. Louis: The C.V. Mosby Co., 1980), pp. 1–16; Gloria Anzaldua, *Borderlands, La Frontera: The New Mestiza* (San Francisco: Spinsters/Aunt Lute Book Co., 1987); Linda C. Fox, "Obedience and Rebellion: Re-Vision of Chicana Myths of Motherhood," *Women's Studies Quarterly* (Winter, 1983), pp. 20–22.

34. Talcott Parsons and Robert Bales, *Family, Socialization, and Interaction Processes* (New York: Free Press, 1955); Robert H. Bradley and Bettye M. Caldwell, "The Relation of Infants' Home Environments to Achievement Test Performance in First Grade: A Follow-up Study," *Child Development* 55 (1984), pp. 803–809; Toby L. Parcel and Elizabeth G. Menaghan, "Maternal Working Conditions and Child Verbal Facility: Studying the Intergenerational Transmission of Inequality from Mothers to Young Children," *Social Psychology Quarterly* 53 (1990), pp. 132–147; Avshalom Caspi and Glen H. Elder, "Emergent Family Patterns: The Intergenerational Construction of Problem Behavior and Relationships," in R. Hinde and J. Stevenson Hinde, eds., *Understanding Family Dynamics* (New York: Oxford University Press, 1988).

35. For a full discussion of the interplay between economic goals and economic status of the respondents and their employment decisions, I refer the reader to Denise Segura, "The Interplay of Familism and Patriarchy on Employment among Chicana and Mexican Immigrant Women," in the *Renato Rosaldo Lecture Series Monograph* 5 (Tucson, AZ: The University of Arizona, Center for Mexican American Studies, 1989), pp. 35–53.

36. Two of the Mexicanas reported that their mothers had died while they were toddlers and therefore were unable to discuss their economic roles.

37. Patricia M. Fernandez-Kelly, "Mexican Border Industrialization, Female Labor-Force Participation and Migration," in J. Nash and M. P. Fernandez-Kelly, eds., *Women, Men, and the International Division of Labor* (Albany: State University of New York Press, 1983), pp. 205–223; Sylvia Guendelman and Auristela Perez-Itriago, "Double Lives: The Changing Role of Women in Seasonal Migration," *Women's Studies* 13 (1987), pp. 249–271; Reynaldo Baca and Dexter Bryan, "Mexican Women, Migration and Sex Roles," *Migration Today* 13 (1985), pp. 14–18.

38. Research indicates religious involvement plays an important role in gender beliefs. See Ross K. Baker, Laurily K. Epstein, and Rodney O. Forth, "Matters of Life and Death: Social, Political, Religious Correlates of Attitudes on Abortion," *American Politics Quarterly* 9 (1981), pp. 89–102; Charles E. Peek and Sharon Brown, "Sex Prejudice among White Protestants: Like or Unlike Ethnic Prejudice?" *Social Forces* 59 (1980), pp. 169–185. Of particular interest for the present study is that involvement in fundamentalist Christian churches is positively related to adherence to traditional gender role ideology. See Clyde Wilcox and Elizabeth Adell Cook, "Evangelical Women and Feminism: Some Additional Evidence," *Women and Politics* 9 (1989), pp. 27–49; Clyde Wilcox, "Religious Attitudes and Anti-Feminism: An Analysis of the Ohio Moral Majority," *Women and Politics* 48 (1987), pp. 1041–1051. Half of the Mexicanas (and all but two Chicanas) adhered to the Roman Catholic religion; half belonged to various fundamentalist Christian churches (e.g., Assembly of God). Two Chicanas belonged to other Protestant denominations. I noticed that the women who belonged to the Assembly of God tended to both work full-time in the labor market and voice the strongest convictions of male authority in the family. During their interviews many of the women brought out the Bible and showed me the biblical passages that authorized husbands to "rule" the family. Catholic women also voiced traditional beliefs regarding family structure but did not invoke God.

39. Frances Rothstein, "Women and Men in the Family Economy: An Analysis of the Relations Between the Sexes in Three Peasant Communities," *Anthropological Quarterly* 56 (1983), pp. 10–23. Ruth Schwartz Cowan, "Women's Work, Housework, and History: The Historical Roots of Inequality in Work-Force Participation," in N. Gerstel and H. E. Gross, eds., *Families and Work* (Philadelphia: Temple University, 1987), pp. 164–177. Louise A. Tilly and Joan W. Scott, *Women, Work, and Family* (New York: Holt, Rinehart, and Winston, 1978).

40. Jessie Bernard, "The Rise and Fall of the Good Provider Role," *American Psychologist* 36 (1981), pp. 1–12; J. Bernard, *The Future of Motherhood* (New York: Penguin Books, 1974); Jane C. Hood, "The Provider Role: Its Meaning and Measurement," *Journal of Marriage and the Family* 48 (May, 1986), pp. 349–359.

41. Lorraine O. Walker and Mary Ann Best, "Well-Being of Mothers with Infant Children: A Preliminary Comparison of Employed Women and Homemakers," *Women and Health* 17 (1991), pp. 71–88; William J. Doherty and Richard H. Needle, "Psychological Adjustment and Substance Use Among Adolescents Before and After a Parental Divorce," *Child Development* 62 (1991), pp. 328–337; Eugene E. Clark and William Ramsey, "The Importance of Family and Network of Other Relationships in Children's Success in School," *International Journal of Sociology of the Family* 20 (1990), pp. 237–254.

42. Rosabeth Moss Kanter, *Men and Women of the Corporation* (New York: Basic Books, 1977).

43. John M. Chavez and Raymond Buriel, "Reinforcing Children's Effort: A Comparison of Immigrant, Native-Born Mexican American and Euro-American Mothers," *Hispanic Journal of Behavioral Sciences* 8 (1986), pp. 127–142. Raymond Buriel, "Integration with Traditional Mexican-American Culture and Sociocultural Adjustment" in J. L. Martinez, Jr. and R. H. Mendoza, eds., *Chicano Psychology*, Second Edition (New York: Academic Press, 1984), pp. 95–130; Leo R. Chavez, "Households, Migration and Labor Market Participation: The Adaptation of Mexicans to Life in the United States," *Urban Anthropology* 14 (1985), pp. 301–346.

44. Raymond Buriel, "Integration with Traditional Mexican-American Culture and Sociocultural Adjustment," in J. L. Martinez, Jr. and R. H. Mendoza, eds., *Chicano Psychology*, Second Edition (New York: Academic Press, 1984), pp. 95–130. In their analysis of differences in educational goals among Mexican-Americans, Buriel and his associates found that: "third generation Mexican Americans felt less capable of fulfilling their educational objectives." See Raymond Buriel, Silverio Caldaza, and Richard Vasquez, "The Relationship of Traditional Mexican American Culture to Adjustment and Delinquency among Three Generations of Mexican American Adolescents," *Hispanic Journal of Behavioral Sciences* 4 (1982), p. 50. Similar findings were reported by Nielsen and Fernandez: "we find that students whose families have been in the U.S. longer have *lower* [their emphasis] aspirations than recent immigrants." See Francois Nielsen and Roberto M. Fernandez, *Hispanic Students in American High Schools: Background Characteristics and Achievement* (Washington D.C.: United States Government Printing Office, 1981), p. 76.

In their analysis of Hispanic employment, Bean and his associates reported an unexpected finding—that English-proficient Mexican women exhibit a greater "constraining influence of fertility" on their employment vis-à-vis Spanish-speaking women. They speculate that more acculturated Mexican women may have "a greater desire for children of higher quality," and therefore "be more likely to devote time to the informal socialization and education of young children." They wonder "why this should hold true for English-speaking but not Spanish-speaking women." See Frank D. Bean, C. Gray Swicegood, and Allan G. King, "Role Incompatibility and the Relationship Between Fertility and Labor Supply Among Hispanic Women" in G. J. Borjas and M. Tienda, eds., *Hispanics in the U.S. Economy* (New York: Academic Press, 1985), p. 241.

Part IV ————————————————————————

THE POLITICS OF MOTHERING: THE DIALECTICS OF STRUGGLE AND AGENCY

Chapter 11

MOTHERING UNDER SLAVERY IN THE ANTEBELLUM SOUTH

Stephanie J. Shaw

Mothering under slavery was truly contested terrain. The process of mothering in the antebellum South serves as one of many useful case studies for examining social constructions of mothering from a variety of viewpoints. Questions related to single parenting, women's working outside the home, surrogacy, and reproductive rights have historical antecedents in the political economy of slavery. While aspects of this essay reflect consideration of many of these questions, the focus is on the mothering of enslaved children by women who sought to define the process for themselves while living in a system where others claimed control of the process outright.

Because the successful operation of a political economy of slavery depended on the effective management of both productive labor (physical labor related to the production of ordinary goods and services) and reproductive labor (all the tasks related to the generation of and maintenance of human life), it was not possible for any aspect of slave life, including mothering, to develop entirely under the control of and based on the desires of those who were enslaved. But perhaps more significantly, because mothering, as philosopher Sara Ruddick suggests, involves the protection and preservation of life, the fostering of emotional and intellectual development, and the preparation of a child for his or her expected social roles, slave owners and enslaved women participated in the processes of mothering in ways that often, ironically, reinforced each others' interests.[1]

While slaveholders and the women they enslaved often necessarily acted in these ways, historian Lawrence W. Levine provides a poignant example suggesting that their views were sometimes in opposition. He writes of a New Orleans freedman who remarked: "I was once whipped,

... because I said to my misses, 'my mother sent me.' We were not allowed to call our mammies 'mother'. It made it come too near the way of the white folks."[2] The freedman's interpretation was that slaveholders would go to violent extremes to protect what they perceived as white culture. Perhaps also embedded in his remark is a suggestion about the extent to which the alleged ownership of human chattel brought with it a construction of mothering that, from the slaveholders' point of view, defied both biological matters of fact and contemporary social traditions. Neither the slaveholders nor the women they claimed to own, however, had complete control over the process.

The history of antebellum slavery is fraught with paradoxes. In the first instance, slaveholders had routinely to demonstrate their power or control over those who were enslaved; yet absolute rigidity would only reveal the slaveholders' tenuous grip. Slaveholders had to provide some food, clothing, and shelter to those they claimed to own, because a semblance of dependency was critical to maintaining the system. But they could not provide too much because they also wanted to turn as handsome a profit as possible. And, at a time when slavery had been abolished in the rest of the Western world, slaveholders had to argue that the system was a benevolent one with one purpose—the protection and support of a class of people not competent to provide for themselves. Yet all the while, slaveholders had to count on those very slaves they claimed paternalistically to protect to use wit and skills to provide the many services and necessities they demanded for themselves. These contradictions, and the ways in which both slaveholders and the women they enslaved supported them, are especially apparent in the processes by which all those involved sustained the lives of children born into the system.

Anna Bishop, born a slave in 1849 in Alabama, remembered during her old age that "All de women on Lady Liza's place had to go to de fiel' ev'y day an' dem what had suckerlin' babies could com in 'bout nine o'clock in the mawnin' an' when de bell ring at twelve an' suckerlin' 'em."[3] The women were not relieved of their productive responsibilities simply because they had children, but because of the productive consequence of their reproductive labor, adjustments had to be made. Enhancing the survival of those newborns would eventually add to the labor force, because those children would be in the field, too, before the age of ten pulling up weeds, carrying buckets of water back and forth to the field hands, or otherwise employed in some productive capacity, and thus contributing to the system.[4] Consequently, allowing the women to leave the fields to nurse not only enhanced the survival of the children, but also relieved the owners of the obligation to provide extra food for the infants and to place more women in the nursery (losing their labor elsewhere) in order to feed the babies. Nursing mothers fulfilled the job requirement and in so doing gained some relief from the demands on them for physical labor. Some women, no doubt, also saw these feedings not as another work assignment, but as an opportunity to bond with and to nurture their children. Thus, the women fulfilled both their own interest in mothering and the owner's interest in their productive and reproductive responsibilities.[5]

Though many former slaves remembered their owners as compassionate people who showed special concern for women, infants, the elderly, and families, most available documentation is of a nature that makes it difficult to draw out slave owners' compassion and separate it from their business interests.[6] In an especially clear example, Virginian Robert Snead expressed concerns to his wife, Octavia, about the health of one slave child:

> You should be more than cautious, and especially with the children and Effia; Effia is often complaining with her throat and it may go hard with her. I should dislike for you to lose her as she is handy about sewing and our family is getting so large it would be a great loss on[?] her.[7]

Most examples, however, are more ambiguous. Slave owners, for example, regularly supplemented the diet of pregnant and nursing women by giving them extra food. In some instances, doing so was an act of generosity, but such acts also helped to protect the economic investments in human chattel while also allowing enslaved women to provide better for the nourishment of their children.[8]

Enslaved women, however, did not always depend on slaveholders to provide the means for sustaining the children's lives. While seemingly acting within the various restrictions of their owners' mandates, some women's efforts to preserve the lives of their children, to nurture them, and to encourage their development are legendary. Linda Brent explained their successes in terms of "determined will" and "mother love." When she was about to be separated from her children for the first time, upon determining that no one could or would help her, she concluded:

> I had a woman's pride, and a mother's love for my children; and I resolved that out of the darkness of this hour a brighter dawn should rise for them. My master had power and law on his side; I had a determined will. There is might in each.[9]

Brent's and other slave women's testimonies contradict slave owners' regular portrayal of the system as a benevolent one in which slaveholders provided for those unable to provide for themselves.

Enslaved women regularly demonstrated their ability to provide a higher standard of life for their children than their owners were willing to provide. Rose, whose family name is not known, was separated from her mother when she was a child in Virginia, but partly because she was not a great distance from her mother and because they both remained in the same white family, her mother regularly sent money and fruit with the white family members, who visited back and forth.[10] Many slaves maintained small gardens in order to supplement their own and their children's diets. And while hunting and fishing are regularly characterized as a part of male slave efforts to support their families, Addie Vinson, born in the 1840s, remembered his mother performing these duties. She fished for her family at night after working all day at her other required tasks. "Many's de time," he recalled, "i'se seed my mammy come back from Barbers Crick wid a string of fish draggin' from her shoulders down to de ground." Moreover, his mother did not take the four days after Christmas as holidays, as did most of the adults in the slave community; instead, she used the four days to weave and wash for white people who lived in the area, and with the meager pay was able to provide materially for her children beyond that which their owner provided.[11]

The ability of slaves to earn money, buy fruit, plant a garden, or catch a fish made some difference in the lives of their children. But if those opportunities were not present, and often that was indeed the case, all was not lost, at least not for ingenious and daring slaves. Especially willful, courageous, clever, and perhaps lucky ones succeeded at "taking" some of what they needed to sustain themselves and their families. Georgia house servant Charlotte Raines accomplished the feat by wearing a flour sack tied around her waist under her skirts, into which she dropped so much food on a day-to-day basis that it bumped her knees when she walked. Alice Marshall, a Virginia woman who was nearly grown when the Civil War ended, also remembered her mother appropriating food for the children.

> I tell you, honey, mistiss Sally had a plenty, but we ain' fared de bes' by no means. She ain' never give us 'nough to eat; so my mother had to git food de bes' way she could. I 'member one way special. When de preacher come to mistiss' for Sunday morning breakfast, de white folks all git together an' have prayers. Den' tis my mother tek basket, go in de smoke house, git all de meat she want. When de preacher der, mistiss ain' bother 'bout nothin'. Minds you, we ain' 'lowed to ever put our foot inside de meat house. Ole mistress kept de floor covered wid sawdus' an' dat smoothed off even. An' she better not find nary track in dat sawdus'. Anyhow my mother gwan in der, but she ain' never fergit to rub out her tracks. We got meat an' my mother ain' got caught neither.[12]

From the point of view of slave owners, clothing for young children was as unnecessary a luxury as meat. They were, after all, nonproductive beings and would not begin to pay for their upkeep (through work) until they were about ten years old. Slave owners at first allocated children two shirts a year—a lightweight one for the warm seasons and a heavier one for the winter. Boys and girls wore this pullover, sliplike shirt and received no other clothing from their owners until they were nearly teen-agers. Delia Garlick, who was separated during her childhood from her mother, never even owned an undershirt until just before the birth of her first child. She possessed but a "shimmy an' a slip for a dress . . . made out of de cheapes' cloth that could be bought." Frederick Douglass and other male slaves recalled receiving their first pairs of pants as historic events. And sometimes even the cold weather of winter had little effect on this practice unless other slaves undertook the task of providing additional clothing for the children.[13]

Former Alabama slave, Sara Murphy, born in the early 1850s, noted that the mothers of enslaved children where she lived regularly wove long underwear from cotton for the children. Linda Brent's grandmother provided her with most of her clothing during her childhood and adolescence, giving her an alternative to the linsey-woolsey dress that she received every winter as her clothing ration, which, incidentally, marked her as a slave. Brent's grandmother also bought her a new pair of shoes one winter, but Mrs. Flint, her young mistress's mother, took them because they squeaked, and it disturbed her. Slaveholders rarely allocated shoes to slave children before they were capable of performing productive labor. But even when the children were fortunate enough to have leather shoes, they were usually very crude items, and special care had to be taken of them if they were to protect the children's feet, which often went without socks. Horace Muse, who was nearly thirty-two years old at the end of the Civil War, remembered that:

> no matter what tasks mother got to do, fo' she go to bed she clean dem shoes an' grease em' wid tallow grease. Git stiff as a board in cold weather, an' lessen you grease 'em dey burn your feet an' freeze 'em too.[14]

Where enslaved women and men provided necessary food and clothing for their children, slave owners did not have to worry about deficiencies. This regular demonstration of resourcefulness proved the fallacy of slave owners' claims that the institution served a necessary and benevolent purpose. In the owners' views, those whom they enslaved were not capable of caring for themselves. But women's interest in their children, and their ability to raise them to some extent by their own standards, regularly gave lie to the slaveholders' claims. These women's efforts, however, also simultaneously supported the owners' interest and made it possible for owners to continue to neglect the needs of these women and children whom they claimed to own.

Those who mothered slave children on a day-to-day basis recognized that nutritional and material neglect endangered the health of their children, who might or might not have the sense to come in out of the cold if they were playing outdoors. And when they did come in this did not necessarily guarantee warmth and comfort, because allocated housing was often shabby, at best. Beyond recreation, too, slave children had work responsibilities that required them to be out-of-doors sometimes, and little could be done to change that. Fannie Berry's owner once sent her five miles during a storm to get liquor for him. As Berry ran in the rain, trying to make it home, she finally stopped to take off her shirt and put it over her head. Had she had on anything else, her action might have served the purpose for which she intended it, but instead, she quite possibly only made herself even more vulnerable to the weather by this act. Her mother, however, recognizing all the dangers facing her child traveling alone, in the storm, half-dressed, came to meet her and brought another wrap to keep her warm and dry. After Berry got home, "Sallie an' June, ol' gals," rubbed her down with warm grease until she felt warm. Her owner's wife gave her a stiff drink of whiskey. And then she went to bed.[15]

While slave owners' interest in maintaining their property led them to provide most of the basic necessities, those committed to mothering slave children invariably provided more. For Linda Brent, it meant a dress made of something other than so-called "negro cloth." Or it meant being handed food for breakfast or dinner as she passed her grandmother's gate on her way to complete errands for her owner.[16] For Sally Murphy, Everett Ingram, and many others who endured slavery as children, it meant withstanding the doses of turpentine, castor oil, or teas made from Jerusalem oak and other ingredients their elders prepared for them in an effort to protect their health. And few children grew up without wearing bags of asafetida around their necks, which mothers believed prevented illness.[17]

There is much evidence to suggest enslaved women's interest in mothering their children, but often women's efforts were brutally conditioned by the structure of the larger political economy, and by the slaveholders who worked to sustain it. Scholars, for example, have presented substantial evidence to prove the persistence of the nuclear slave family, traditionally defined, but tradition had little to do with how those families survived intact. At a time when femininity was defined by motherhood and mothering in the larger society, slave owners frequently did not allow slave women to mother their children. The women's productive labor was often viewed as much more valuable to their owners than the reproductive labor involved in rearing a child who, as yet, had no value. As a consequence, new patterns of childcare emerged, with a variety of people mothering slave children. Historian Deborah Gray White demonstrates the importance of an existing network among enslaved women that helped to facilitate adequate childcare.[18] When slave owners chose the ones to perform these tasks, they usually called upon people whose own productive capacities had significantly diminished but who could still perform the (presumably) less physically demanding tasks of mothering.

All children where Phoebe Faucette lived were cared for by "some old man or some old woman." Georgia Baker, born in the 1840s in Georgia, was cared for by her grandfather, about whom she said "all he done was to sit by the fire all day with a switch in his hand and tend the children whilst their mammies was at work." Allen Sims, who was probably not yet ten years old at the end of the Civil War, recalled that "Aunt Mandy, what was too old to work, looked atter all de little nigger chilluns, whilst dey mammy's working. . . . " An elderly man slave named Payne had to move every time his daughter was relocated in order to care for her children. And though this arrangement might have served this family's interest well, the slave owners' feminization of this man's work role was mostly a matter of expediency. The daughter would take care of herself, the master's work, and her father. And he would take care of her children while she was engaged in other work. The slave owner did not have to care for anyone. Callie William's mother kept slave children in a small cabin with homemade cradles while the other women worked in the fields. The mothers returned from the fields to feed their nursing infants twice a day. And while both the nurse and the mother shared some time with the children, both were limited in what they could do, for in this case the mothers had to return to the fields, and the nurse usually had other tasks to perform as well.[19]

The assignment of extra tasks seems to have been common in the case of women nurses. Williams's mother had to spin two to four cards of cotton while she watched the children. Tennessee planter Benjamin Bedford's nurse tended the children in addition to her main duties as a laundress and cook. Bedford advised his overseer that:

> the negro woman who cooks and washes when not engaged in that business [is] to churn, work butter, work in the garden, make up negro clothing or attend to little negroes or such needful employment about the yard that is necessary and proper because it does not consume all her time to cook and wash.

Many of those who cared for slave children had other major work responsibilities, because slave owners rarely considered child care an activity requiring all of the nurse's time.[20]

Particularly in cases where those assigned to care for children had many other responsibilities, there was a great chance the children would not receive close attention; they might even unavoidably be neglected. While Mandy McCulough Cosby's recollection about slavery, "de way de chillun rol roun' in the big nurses room," could indicate that the children enjoyed a carefree and unhibiting environment, for example, it could also suggest the lack of attention they received. McCullough, born in the 1830s, witnessed these events as an adult, and her memory of what might have been haphazard child care was not all that different from the memory of slightly younger George Womble, who characterized meal time in the nursery. The horrible scene involved children eating with animals from a trough, a popular method of feeding where there were a lot of children. The children gathered around the trough were not allowed to hit the animals, and they ate with their hands up to the sides of their heads so that the dogs and pigs could not lick them in the face as they ate. While this form of feeding might not have been typical for most slave children, it probably inspired many mothers to devise alternatives to the child care arranged by their owners. They knew that the nursery was not necessarily the best place for their small children.[21]

One alternative involved requiring older children to care for the younger ones. Sylvia Witherspoon's mother left Sylvia in charge of her siblings when she (the mother) had to report to the fields. "She would tie the smalles' baby on my back so's I could play wid out no inconvenience," Witherspoon recalled. Joseph Holmes' mother had eight children, and she made each one of them responsible for another. Holmes remarked: "we was raised in pairs. I had a sister who come along wid me, an' iffen I jumped in the river she done it too. An' iffen I go th'ough a briar patch, her[e] she come along too." Mary Smith's mother left her in charge of her younger siblings. Smith, who reported being only seven years old at the time of surrender, was but a child herself. In order to help her with her large responsibilities, she noted that her mother would "pin a piece of fat back [meat] on my dres' before she went to de fiel' and when de baby cry I tek him up and let 'em suck 'em."[22]

We can never know precisely why these child care responsibilities often went to other children. No doubt, in some instances, these children and their mothers were owned by people who did not have a nursery where older men and women took care of those too young to work and to take care of themselves. It is likely that in some instances these individual women and their children were the only slaves on the site. But perhaps some mothers had the ability to choose not to leave their children in nurseries where they were available. And considering that a well-instructed child could provide some personal attention to the child being cared for, while a nurse, assigned by the owner to care for numerous children and also to attend to other work details, could not, such a decision was not necessarily irresponsible. And, moreover, if mothers were not able or allowed to care for their children, those siblings could also help to reinforce family bonds in a system where slaveholders often ignored them.

In any case, under some circumstances, either none of these alternatives were available or they simply were not acceptable, and slave women took their children to the fields with them, though doing so represented no small amount of danger. During the early nineteenth century, women on Saint Simons Island carried their infants with them to the field in baskets they carried on their heads. According to Julia Rush, a former slave, Oliver Bell's mother was a plow hand, but she took him to the field with her every morning and sat him under a post oak tree, where he usually remained until she called or went for him. "Dat tree was my nurse," Bell recalled. Sara Colquitt, who was born in the 1830s, took her two children with her to the field as well; she tied the youngest to a tree limb (perhaps making a swing, in effect) to keep him or her away from bugs on the ground. And Roxy Pitts, born in 1855, whose mother succeeded in escaping from her owner, was taken to the field along with her younger sister by her father, who "kep' a bottle of sweeten water in he shirt to keep [it] warm to gib de baby when it cry."[23] To a large degree, it was simply not possible for those who were enslaved to determine totally for themselves the method by which or the extent to which their children would be cared for. But as some of the above examples suggest, the extent to which these children were nurtured (or the extent to which they could be) depended not only on their owners' whims and resources, but on the women's need, willingness, and ability to improvise as well.

It is possible, however, to overestimate the ability of enslaved women to work the system to their own advantage. The work requirements that slaveholders and overseers imposed on them and their children often made it impossible for mothers to carry out or even to improvise this personal maternal work. Women of childbearing age were in their prime as productive laborers, and neither the biological fact of motherhood, nor the traditional gendered construction of mothering applied to them as far as slaveholders were concerned. Maternal work under this system was not simply a social responsibility left to the interests and abilities of mothers; it was a work assignment that utilized the labor of men, women who were not the biological mothers, and children. Children were fortunate when these workers saw their responsibilities as more than a work assignment and sought to fulfill the broader responsibilities of mothering. But the fact is that the recollections of some freed men and women growing up in the system suggest that not all slave children experienced the benefits of mothering.

Enslaved adults often worked from sunup to sundown at one task, and after that, they attended to weaving, spinning, shucking corn, mending tools, and other indoor work assignments. And as Cordellia Thomas said, "come day, go day, no matter what happen, growin' chillun had to be in bed at deir reg'lar time."[24] Former Georgia slave Will Sheets noted that the most he ever saw of his mother was when she came to the cabin at night and "den, us chilluns was too sleepy to talk. Soon as us et, us drapped down on a pallet and went fast asleep." More to the point, and indicating both adult and childhood work responsibilities, Tom Singleton remembered that the adults "were too busy to talk in de daytime, and at night us wuz so wiped out from hard work (us) just went to sleep early and never talked." Mandy McCullough, reared in Alabama, recalled that children who did not yet have work responsibilities played all day, ate their supper at the trough in the yard, and "some of dem jes' fall ovah on de groun' asleep, and is picked up, and put on dey pallet in de big chillen's room." During the work week, at least, these children were, by necessity, mothered by others or not at all.[25]

Perhaps the most difficult aspect of slavery for mothers came with the breakup of families because of sale or hiring out. Under these circumstances, sometimes the best that they could do was to ask and hope that someone else would care for their children. Mingo White, probably born in the 1840s, moved to Alabama with his family when he was four or five years old. He was:

> jes' a li'l thang; tooked away from my mammy an' pappy jes' when I needed 'em mos'. The only caren' that I had ever knowed anything 'bout was give to me by a frien' of my pappy. His name was John (W)hite. My pappy tol' him to take care of me for him. John was a fiddler 'n many a night I woke up to find myse'f 'sleep 'twix his legs whilst he was playin' for a dance for de white folks.

Laura Clark, only a few years younger than White, was one in a group of children sold from their North Carolina home to an Alabaman. The new owner either bought or hired elder slaves Julie Powell and Henry to care for them during the trip by wagon to the deep South. "Wa'n't none of dem ten chillin no kin to me," Clark recalled, "and he never brout my mammy so I had to leave her behine. I recollect mammy said to ond [aunt] Julie, 'take keer my baby chile . . . and iffen I never sees her no mo' raise her for God." Clarks' referral to Julie as aunt should be read not simply as the traditional respect that slaves showed for elders by giving them kinship titles, but also to indicate that there developed a bond between them based on a caring, familial relationship.[26]

In spite of the extensive efforts of all those who mothered slave children, the overall conditions of slavery were often not conducive to preserving the lives of slave children. While infant mortality rates generally declined over the decades, some mothers experienced death rates among their children that were as high just before the demise of slavery as they were at the end of the eighteenth century. Slaveholders sought solutions to protect their investments, which were not only a source of their wealth, of course, but a source of their political power and social status as well.

One London businessman who owned slaves in the United States wrote to his correspondent, probably a relative who was acting as his overseer:

> I am grieved to hear of the mortality among the negro children, and am very much afraid there is not proper care taken of them. You tell me there were ten born last year, and but one of them is living, and that [one] but three days old. . . . [I]s there no method to be fallen on to prevent it; suppose something by way of [illegible] was given to such of them as raise their children and to wenches that took care of them in the lying in aft(?) the children were brought you [illegible] to make them more careful and attentive.

More than fifty years later, Nicholas Edmunds recorded the following vital statistics for his slave woman, Harriot: She gave birth to Washington on August 28, 1851, and he died on November 14, 1851. Dolly was born on March 4, 1853, and died on August 31, 1853. Luke, born on March 20, 1854, died on September 17, 1854. Sally, born on April 5, 1857, died six months later. A son, not named, was born on August 25, 1860 and died four days later. And Albert was born on November 1, 1861 and died nine months later (on August 10, 1862). Four of Harriet's children were listed with no death dates (b. 1850, 1855, 1858, and 1859) and therefore quite possibly lived to be set free. Still, five of ten children did not see the first anniversary of their births, one made it only to his first birth anniversary.[27]

Notwithstanding all the possible "natural" factors contributing to high infant mortality rates in the eighteenth century and isolated problems in the nineteenth, the letter from the British slaveholder cited above suggests other considerations. He proposes that enslaved women could be induced to take better care of the infants, and raises a question about the extent to which adults deliberately contributed to the deaths of their children. Undoubtedly, many women made choices not to preserve the lives of slave children. And in these instances the evidence of contested terrain is vivid.

A Fairfax County, Virginia, court convicted Ally, the slave of George Miller, for "exposing (her child) as causing its death" in 1835. A Buckingham County Court convicted Polley of murdering her child in 1818. Kesiah allegedly killed her infant daughter on April 13, 1834. The courts sentenced all of the women to hang.[28] Between the 1840s and the 1860s, William Massie, the prominent Virginia planter and diarist, regularly noted his suspicions regarding the deaths of slave children on his plantation. In one instance he noted that Gabriel, the sixteen-month-old child of Lizzie "was murdered right out by his mother's neglect and barbarous cruelty." At another point he wrote that Rhoda's fourteen-month-old son "was neglected . . . by its mother and died like a dog." And about Lucy's children, Romulus and Remus, born in 1844, Massie wrote that Remus died of neglect, and "Romulus died by waste caused by the natural neglect of his infamous mother."[29]

The accounts of alleged infanticide cases may, of course, be suspect in light of more recent medical discoveries that indicate the importance of their contexts. Poor nutrition, low birth weights, poor pre- and postnatal care, and even genetic disposition quite possibly caused some or all of these infants to fall victim to Sudden Infant Death Syndrome (SIDS).[30] When Mississippi farmer T. S. Jones wrote to a relative in Tennessee in 1852 about his slave woman, Milly, who had recently "overlaid" her child, he noted that this incident made "three out of four children [that] she has killed in that way in eight years. This last one was a fine, likely, healthy child about seven months old." Milly could have, in her exhaustion, unknowingly "overlaid" her children. She might even have deliberately killed them. The only thing certain is that children who succumb to SIDS are likely to have siblings who suffer the same fate. And, consequently, Milly might simply have been destined to suffer the loss of her children.[31]

Still, there are many irrefutable examples of infanticide. Amey, slave of John Grisham from King and Queen County, Virginia, killed her two infant children, Isbell and Harrison, on April 13, 1799. She cut their throats with an ax. Sixteen years later, Jenny (Powhatan County, Virginia) killed her three children. And Hannah, a Granville County, North Carolina, slave, killed her child Soloman. One witness at her trial testified that after Hannah cut her child's throat, she attempted to slit her own, and upon failing, asked Bob, another slave, to "put her away."[32]

On occasion, slave women threatened infanticide in an attempt to affect an owner's behavior. One often-cited example involves a woman who successfully prevented her owner from selling her away from her child as punishment for some offense. Upon hearing that she could not take her child with her, the woman raised the infant into the air by its feet, threatening to smash its head into the ground rather than to leave it behind. She fully understood her master's value system and his proprietary interest in her child, and she used that understanding to ensure the maintenance of her values and to take the child with her. Though the latter example is an important one to the contrary, one must also acknowledge the possibility that some of these women suffered from postpartum depression and acted as a result of some psychological trauma beyond their control.[33]

Certainly there remain many questions as to the extent to which slave mothers killed their children. Undoubtedly some did, and many did not. Where they did, infanticide sometimes represented a powerful example of women's opposition to this form of sexual and economic exploitation. But these examples could also reflect that the women possessed such a reverence for humanity and a level of self-determination that they simply decided to prevent a child, whose life they felt responsible for, from growing up in a system in which their owners demonstrated little respect for either.[34] Vincent Harding provides a chilling example of this, in which a husband and wife "shut up in a slave baracoon and doomed to the southern market . . . did by mutual agreement send the souls of their children to Heaven rather than have them descend to the hell of slavery." Both parents killed themselves after killing their children.[35]

Several scholars have noted the records of Southern physicians who remarked on the high rate of abortion among slave women. (No doubt some spontaneous abortions or miscarriages were included here.) One physician said planters believed "that the Blacks are possessed of a secret by which they destroy the fetus at an early stage of gestation." Another noted with some surprise that "whole families of women . . . fail to have any children." One planter claimed to have discovered that "the slaves had concocted a medicine with which they were able to terminate their unwanted pregnancies." And another said he had "an older female slave (who) had discovered a remedy for pregnancies and had been instrumental in all . . . the abortions on his place."[36]

Women's decisions to have abortions might represent a political act of defiance if they determined that they would not give birth to children in a system that allowed no consistent recognition of them as those children's mothers. That is, after some analyses of their situations, they could have decided not to have children, because those children would belong to slave owners, not to themselves. The famous successful runaway, Ellen Craft, at least, at first refused to marry because "marriage meant children—children who would belong to Robert Collins" rather than to her and her husband. But Ellen Craft's ability to decide, while enslaved, not to marry and not to conceive might represent an unusual case. Rather, what is most evident is that many women did not have a choice. Many were "married up" against their will. And whether "married" or not, many were raped.[37] Still, even when slave women had abortions, refused to conceive, or committed infanticide in order to protect children from a lifetime of slavery, they often did so in the interest of mothering. And even when they made such decisions without considering the child's future, they made mothering decisions—decisions not to mother.

Probably, most slave women allowed children they conceived to be born, to live, and to grow up in the slave system. And just as these adults often provided children with more food and clothing than their owners allowed, they also attempted to nurture the youngsters and to minimize their encounters with the most brutal aspects of the system. In a rare slave letter, which exemplifies one woman's attempt to prepare a future for her grandchildren and great-grandchild, Nancy Venture Woods presented a most convincing case to her owner.

Dear Master   I will now inform you about my little family   six grand-children and one great grand child and I am now a great grandmother Virgin is the eldest   Nancy the next who has now become a mother William Brutus Venten Jane & George is the names of the children that I have taken care of—Virgin desires to be put to a trade and I think it would be the best for him   a tailor or shoe maker would suit him best in consequence of a hurt he has had in his ancle which he still feels at times   I had rather keep the rest if agreeable to you to assist me in supporting the small ones but I feel willing that you should do by them as you please as for my own part I am a good deal afflicted with the rhe[u]matic pains and I hope Daer M[as]ter if I should be the longest liver you will remember your old servant for I wish to end my days in this place   if I was to be carried from her[e] now it seems that I could not be satisfied   I also wish to keep the children as long as I live except such as you think best to put to a trade

  you will please write to mr. guion concerning the putting of Virgin to a trade and he will see to the business.[38]

Woods' finely crafted letter carefully combined a good amount of ex-pectation, deference, and humility in a clever attempt to remain in the city of Raleigh, North Carolina, rather than to return to the plantation in New Bern, to keep these children with her, to place the eldest of them at a particular kind of work—skilled work—and to place any others, that she might not keep with her, in a trade. She probably began her letter informing her owner of the expansion of her family to affect the way in which he would receive her requests. That is, her letter first made the point that her owner's property had increased because of her. And in every instance where she acknowledged his authority in the matter, she also reminded him of why her desires should prevail. Though Woods' letter is a rare document, her intention to create a particular kind of future for the children was probably not uncommon among enslaved women; it represents a hallmark of mothering. But examples of women's attempts to prepare a specific kind of future for their children are difficult to come by. It is much easier to show how parents and others attempted to prepare children for the actual future that awaited them, which in most cases involved living within the slaveholders' reach and almost always included the possibility of being separated from the family unit.[39]

Parents began very early to discipline children in ways that would be important for their survival as they matured, and as their contact with owners and overseers increased. The process began during childhood and in the "nursery," where lessons could be taught clearly but gently. Aunt Mandy, who took care of Allen Sims and numerous other children while their mothers worked in the fields and elsewhere, would "pop" him and the others with a brush when they did not obey her. But Sims added, "she fuss more dan she whipt." It was important for the children not only to respect the authority of their Black elders, but also to learn to respect authority figures in general if they were to survive under the supervision of slaveholders and overseers. Reflecting the importance of such lessons, one woman recalled being beaten during her childhood by her owner for not calling a nine-month-old white child "miss." Theodore Fontaine Stewarts' mother, a cook, beat her children if she caught them stealing anything from the kitchen where she worked. In doing so, she was instilling in them a moral code that prohibited random theft, and was discouraging them from participating in acts that would bring severe punishment if they were caught by whites. Simultaneously, she was protecting her job, which probably allowed her to provide for her children—with leftover food and cast-off clothing—in a manner better than she could have if she had been forced to go to the field to work because of problems her children had created.[40]

Martha Showvley's mother made concerted efforts to teach her children not to meddle in the affairs of others. The importance of such a lesson is illustrated by the death of a Richmond County, Georgia, slave woman whose owner beat her to death after hearing a child's innocent conversation. The woman had given birth to twins one day and on the next day was ordered to scrub the floors of her owner's home. After she fainted while working, her mistress had a slave take her to her cabin and another one finish the scrubbing. The mistress's husband was satisfied that the work was done when he returned, but a slave child innocently told him what had happened in his absence. The owner mercilessly beat the woman because, he said, she was lazy and deceitful, and she died the same day while still tied to the whipping post. Teaching children to hear and not repeat, to see and not disclose, was critical to controlling the conditions of their survival, and to survival itself, because many of the goings-on in the slave quarters would not have been acceptable to the owners.[41]

Probably most important, in terms of their preparation for future roles, slave children were taught to work and to work well. From birth, the futures of these children were geared toward work, and it was the job of their parents and other adults to see that they were able to fulfill that responsibility. But as much as it was the job of adult slaves to socialize children to their roles as workers, the adults' commitments to mothering also motivated them to psychologically prepare the children for this work. The adults provided with their strict disciplinary measures some protection for the children because, as historian Eugene Genovese observes, "parents knew that soon enough the indulgence [of slave owners] would give way to the whip. Better they instill elementary habits and discipline in their children early and according to their own measure."[42]

Jennie Kendricks' mother probably took her oldest daughters with her to the spring to wash at night, not simply to have their help and their company but to teach them how to wash, and to convey to them that, being girls, that is what they would eventually have to do, even after working all day at something else. Ferebe Rogers said she virtually "come up twix the plow handles" because her mother took her to the fields and began to teach her how to plow when she was quite young. Will Sheets learned from an older slave woman named Mandy to drive cattle to and from the pasture. And Mary Smith's mother provided Smith, when she was only seven years old, with her first lessons in chopping cotton. Many children learned to spin thread from their mothers who were weavers. And Charlie Dink, when he was seven or eight years old, walked the rows in the field with his mother "totin' cawn for her to drap." By this process, he not only began to learn to work, but also relieved his mother of concerns about his care while she worked.[43]

Because the work roles slave children faced very early came under the direct supervision of sometimes sadistic owners and overseers, teaching children to work hard and well was, quite possibly, the best way in which their parents could protect them—short of running away with them. By the time many of these children were five years old, they were assigned to fanning flies away from slave owners or their visitors.[44] At a very young age many children began to carry food to the fields and water to both the house and the fields from nearby wells and springs.[45] Between the ages of five and ten, they set and waited on tables in the big house, threaded needles, spun thread, picked up cow chips, swept yards, and performed a variety of other work details.[46] Doing these tasks diligently and effectively could save them from severe punishment.

Mollie Mitchell, born around 1845, went to work hoeing in the field at the age of seven, but she got whipped often because she could not "keep in the row." Tom Singleton, born in 1838, had occasional childhood whims that caused him to neglect his work role, and received his only beating as a child because he got involved in a marble game after his mistress had sent him to get thread. Easter Jones, a dishwasher in her owner's house, had to remove the dishes from scalding water, but she knew, even as a youngster, that "if I drap it dey whip me. Dey whip you so hard your back bleed. . . ." One ex-slave woman claimed to have had bones broken as a child on more than one occasion by her mistress, who beat her with a fire iron for not waking up quickly enough to see to the crying white infant to whom she was supposed to attend. And Delia Garlic's mistress ran a hot iron down Delia's arm and hand after she accidently hurt the white child to whom she attended.[47]

Those who mothered slave children had good reason, then, to work hard at preparing the children for their eventual work assignments. These children would too soon be caught between the labor requirements inherent in the system and their own natural inclinations and abilities as children. Thus it is not surprising that Emmaline Kilpatrick vividly remembered Black children growing up faster than white children did.

Jasper Battle noted that slave children grew so fast that most of those assigned to nursing "warn't no older dan de white chillun dey tuk keer of." He also claimed that slave children "12 or 14 years old [in] dem days was big as a white child 17 or 18 years old." Battle was around 21 years old upon emancipation and therefore not only spoke from personal experience but also from years of observation.[48] Clearly, Battle was equating responsibility with age and size, because slave owners subjected the children they owned to an accelerated passage from childhood to adulthood. Very early in the children's lives, owners began to characterize them as "grown" or "most grown," thereby justifying putting them to work at a young age. The children's parents and others who mothered them could do little to alter this reality. And so they reared their children in a way that would better prepare them for it.

The exigencies of day-to-day life, in fact, necessarily resulted in a type of mothering that often reinforced the oppressive system of which it was a part. As women provided food, clothing, and shelter for children beyond that provided by slave owners, they helped to fortify the system. And as they taught those children to work in fields, in kitchens, at sewing and spinning machines, they prepared the children for a future of work and possibly a future as slaves. When they devised alternative child care arrangements that allowed them to keep up their work in the fields, the big houses, or on some property other than that of their owners, the slaveholders' proprietary interest in these children was further protected at no additional expense to themselves.

But mothering under slavery was not always a matter of women's indirect and unavoidable support of the system. Where women engaged, directly and indirectly, in abortions and infanticide, they picked away at one of the bases of the system's life itself—reproduction. And even as they performed mothering tasks that reinforced the system of slavery, they also chipped away at institutional assumptions about dependency (cultural, material, and political) and thereby helped to prepare their children for freedom.

They did this in part by transmitting a set of values and traditions to the children that reinforced a kind of self-sufficiency, community culture, and group identity that could help to sustain them within and beyond their enslavement. When mothers left their older children in charge of younger ones, they not only answered their child care problems, but they also provided the children with important lessons in assuming responsibility for one another. When women taught children to address other Black people not related to them by blood as "aunt," "uncle," and "granny," they taught children that "family" had a basis not only in kinship but in community as well.[49] When members of the slave community devised the means or took advantage of opportunities to supplement their allotted rations of food, clothing, or shelter, they demonstrated their ability to care for themselves despite persistent portrayals of them as perpetual dependents. And ultimately, while the teaching of children to work effectively prepared those children for work as slaves, it also prepared them for freedom. More profoundly than slaveholders could have predicted, the efforts of enslaved women who mothered children in the antebellum south simultaneously served the interests of both slaveholders and slaves.

Notes

Comments provided by John B. Boles, John C. Burnham, Evelyn Nakano Glenn, and Pat Washington were especially helpful in this revision of the original conference paper.

This paper, primarily concerning North Carolina, Virginia, Texas, Georgia, and Alabama, is part of a larger study in progress on slave women. The larger study has been supported by an Ohio State University Seed Grant, a North Carolina Society Archie K. Davis Fellowship, a Mellon teaching fellowship at Rice University, a grant from the Virginia Historical Society, and a fellowship at the Virginia Foundation for the Humanities and Public Policy.

1. See Sara Ruddick, *Maternal Thinking: Toward a Politics of Peace* (Boston, MA: Beacon Press, 1989).
2. Lawrence W. Levine, *Black Culture and Black Consciousness: Afro-American Folk Thought From Slavery to Freedom* (Oxford: Oxford University Press, 1977), p. 139.
3. George P. Rawick, ed., *The American Slave: A Composite Autobiography*, vol. 6 (Westport, CT: Greenwood Publishing Company, 1973), p. 36. References from these volumes will be cited hereafter thusly: Rawick, Alabama, 6:36.
4. See Rawick, Alabama, 6:181, in which Adeline (last name unknown) recalled: "I was jes' a li'l gal den. I was jes' big 'nuff to tote water to de fiel' to de folks wukking and to min' de gaps in the fence to keep de cattle out when dey was gatherin' de crops." Ella Grandberry couldn't remember having time to play as a child. She said "ever since I kin 'member I had a water bucket on my arm totin' water to de han's. Iffen I wan't doin' dat, I was choppin' cotton." Bishop, at the age of six or seven, was at work helping to tend to the women workers' babies and going back and forth to the field to call those who were needed for feedings. Hanna Johnson became a nurse at the age of ten, and Caroline Hunter began polishing silver and setting the tables of the big house at the age of five. Before Hunter was ten, she was put in the field to work all day. See Rawick, Alabama, 6:157; Georgia, part 3, 13:47, 58; Georgia, part 4, 13:183; Charles L. Perdue, Jr., Thomas E. Barden, and Robert K. Phillips, eds., *Weevils in the Wheat: Interviews with Virginia Ex-Slaves* (Bloomington, IN: Indiana University Press, 1980), pp. 158–159.
5. This, of course, is not to say that all women wanted to nurture their children. In fact, later discussions will show that some did not. But for those who did want to, nursing the children provided one of the few opportunities during the day to do so.
6. For examples of evidence of owner sensitivity, see Alfred Moore to William Augustus Blount, September 22, 1835, box 193.21, f. 6, J. G. Blount papers, North Carolina State Library and Archives, Raleigh, NC. This letter concerns a Louisiana slave owner's efforts to buy the children of two adult slaves whom he already owned. In Horatio J. Eden, biographical sketch, Tennessee State Library and Archives, Nashville, TN, Eden, a former slave, speaks kindly of his former owners. And see Rebecca J. McLeod to J. S. Beers, September 1, 1862, box 2, f. 25, Rosenberg Library, Galveston, TX. In this letter, McLeod expressed interest in seeing that her slaves who were hired out were fed and clothed properly, that one girl not be separated from her mother who was going blind, and that none of them

be sold to settle any debts that her husband, recently deceased, might have owed. (McCleod's interests could also have been purely economical.) And see R. A. Adams to Mrs. Jno. W. Gilliam, January 29, 1855, box 2, f. 1850–1855, Slave Trade Papers, Alderman Library Archives, University of Virginia, Charlottesville, VA. This document indicates that Adams was also in the process of settling her husband's estate. She had hired out all of the slaves, most of them with their families intact. It is also clear in this letter, however that an elderly woman had not been placed, and Adams had apparently made no attempts to keep her with any of the other families. Because of the woman's age, Adams simply assumed that it would be impossible to place her.

7. Robert Winn Snead to Octavia Snead, November 17, 1861, (verifax copy), Robert Snead papers, Virginia Historical Society, Richmond, VA. (Cited hereafter as VHS.)

8. For an example of one slave owner's habit of providing more food to such women, see "Negro Account Books: Items given Negroes, 1817–1835," Massie Family papers, University of Texas-Austin, Barker Texas History Center. (Cited hereafter as UT-BTHC.)

9. Linda Brent (pseud., Harriet Jacobs), *Incidents in the Life of a Slave Girl*, L. Maria Child, ed., Intro. by Walter Teller (1861, San Diego, CA: Harcourt, Brace, Jovanovich, 1973), p. 87.

10. Lizzie Bain to "sister," January 26, 1857, William T. Bain papers, Perkins Library Archives, Duke University, Durham, NC. The William Deveraux family papers located at UT-BTHC provide much detail about the maintenance of family connections among slaves through their owners and their owners' family. The Deveraux family, over the generations, lived in Georgia, Alabama, Louisiana, and Texas, and over the years the slave families were divided among various members of the white family. But the correspondence among the whites show attempts of the slaves to maintain contact with their own multigenerational, interstate family.

11. Rawick, Georgia, part 4, 13:102, 108. And for other examples of men and women's efforts to supplement the family diet, see Rawick, Georgia, part 3, 13:81–82, 156; part 4, 120.

12. Rawick, Georgia, part 3, 13:191; Perdue, et al., *Weevils*, pp. 201–202. Many former slaves distinguished between "taking" from the master and "stealing" from other slaves. In this regard, see George P. Rawick, *From Sundown To Sunup: The Making of the Black Community* (Westport, CT: Greenwood Publishing Company, 1972), p. 69; Eugene D. Genovese, *Roll, Jordan, Roll: The World The Slaves Made* (New York, NY: Vintage Books, 1976), pp. 602–603. And see May Satterfield's discussion of her mother's conversations with her after emancipation. Satterfield related, "She tell me dat 'po' nigger had to steal back dar in slav'y eben to git 'nuf t' eat. White fo'ks so mean didn't eben want niger t' eat. Do nothin' but work day and night. Done heard her say she been in de field 'long side de fence many day and' git creasy (cress) an' poke sallet an' bile it 'dout a speck o' greese an' give it to us chillum 'cause de rashon de white fo'ks lounce [allowance] out fo' de week done give out. . . . She say dey eben had to steal apples an' stuff lak dat as much as dey was on de place." Satterfield apparently believed the slaves were stealing. Having been reared after freedom came, she had a code of ethics that defined taking something not belonging to one as stealing unequivocally. Still, she sympathized with her mother and other slaves and in fact went on to explain that slave owners forced slaves to learn to steal. See Perdue, et al., *Weevils*, pp. 244–245.

13. Rawick, Alabama, 6:131; Georgia, part 1, 12:108; part 3, 13:150, 239; part 4, 13:103; Jasper Battle remembered that slave children wore "dresses" until they were about five years old, at which time boys got shirts. And Ed McCree remembered that they "wore shirts that looked lak nightgowns. You jus' pulled one of dem slips over your haid and went on' cause you was done dressed for the whole week, day and night." See Rawick, Georgia, part 1, 12:65; part 3, 13:60. It should be noted here that slave mistresses often made these basic clothes for the children. Sewing for the entire "household" was often one of the "plantation mistresses' " many duties.

14. Rawick, Alabama, 6:294–95; Brent, *Incidents*, 17–18; Purdue, et al., *Weevils*, 217.

15. Perdue, et al., *Weevils*, 32.

16. Brent, *Incidents*, 9.

17. See for examples, Rawick, Alabama, 6: 216, 295; Georgia, part 3, 13:19, 129.

18. Deborah Gray White, *Ar'n't I a Woman: Female Slaves in the Plantation South* (New York: W. W. Norton, Co., 1985).

19. Rawick, Georgia, part 1, 12:40; part 4, 13:183, 13:259; Alabama, 6:343, 426; Thomas Webber, *Deep Like the Rivers* (New York, 1978), p. 174; Stacey K. Close, "The Role and Status of the Elderly Male Slave in the Plantation South," (M.A. thesis, Ohio State University, 1990), p. 6; Leslie Owens, *This Species of Property: Slave Life and Culture in the Old South* (Oxford: Oxford University Press, 1976), p. 203.

20. Benjamin Bedford to Julian Bedford, July 31, 1854, Benjamin W. Bedford letterbook, b. 1, f. 2, Tennessee State Library and Archives, Nashville, TN. And see Bedford's contract and instructions to his overseer on a Mississippi plantation, dated September 7, 1858. On the farm where Henry Wright lived in Georgia, the old woman who cared for the children also cared for the ill and did the cooking. See Rawick, Georgia, part 4, 13:198–99.

21. Rawick, Alabama, 6: 90; Georgia, 4, 13: 186–87.

22. Rawick, Georgia, part 3, 13:287; Alabama 6:192, 429. For other examples of why mothers might not want their children to be kept at the nursery, even if their owners had provided one, see Georgia, part 4, 13: 206–07, in which Dink Walton Young described the nursery in such a way that it sounds like an animal pen.

23. Rawick, Alabama, 6:27–32, 87, 316; Georgia, part 3, 13:229. Rush was born in 1828 and was probably one of the oldest living ex-slaves in the country at the time of the WPA interviews. And as noted in the text, she lived on Saint Simons Island. It is possible that these women were following an African tradition. Certainly this was one of the places where Africanisms survived the longest. Also, see Richard Oxford's interview in Rawick, Georgia, part 3, 13:150, in which he notes, and it is either an exaggeration or evidence of a faulty memory, "women in dem days could pick five hundred pounds of cotton a day wid a child in a sack on dere backs." Men rarely picked five hundred pounds of cotton a day, and men generally outpicked women. But the point here is that some women performed field work while carrying their children.

24. Rawick, Georgia, part 4, 13:19.

25. Ibid., part 3, 13:265, 237; Alabama, 6:90.

26. Rawick, Alabama, 6:72, 413–18. On the granting of kinship titles, see Herbert G. Gutman, *The Black Family in Slavery and Freedom, 1750–1925*, (New York, NY: Vintage Books, 1977), pp. 220–29; White, *Ar'n't I a Woman*, p. 133.

27. Letter dated October 3, 1787, Edward Telfair papers, Perkins Library Archives, Duke University; Daybook of Nicholas Edmunds, Edmunds Family papers, box 3, section 7, p. 13, 23, VHS.

28. See *Commonwealth v. Ally, property of George Millan*, Fairfax County Court, February 18, 1835, b. 1969; *Commonwealth v. Kesiah, property of Henry L. Carter*, Henricho County Court, 5 May 1834, b. 1969; *Commonwealth v. Lucy, slave of Judith F??e*, Richmond Hustings Court, 16 September 1852, b. 1970; and *Commonwealth v. Lucy, slave of Thomas Batton*, Lewis County Court of Oyer and Terminer, 4 November 1819, b. 1968, APAR-VSLA. For some detailed analyses of these and other Virginia cases involving slaves, see Philip J. Schwarz, *Twice Condemned: Slaves and the Criminal Laws of Virginia, 1705–1865* (Baton Rouge, LA: Louisiana Southern University Press, 1988).

29. William Masie Account Books, February 27, 1844, p. 24; June 27, 1856, p. 35; February 7, 1861, p. 51; photocopy, VSLA. Liz, Rhoda, and Lucy are listed in Massie's 1862 Negro Account Books for having received certain clothes. Lizzie is listed as a house servant. In his "1862 List of Children to be Clothed," Liz is listed as having three children, and Rhoda is listed with three. See 1862 Negro Account Books, Massie Family Papers, UT-BTHC.

30. See Tod Savitt, *Medicine and Slavery: The Diseases and Health Care of Blacks in Antebellum Virginia* (Urbana, IL, 1978) and "Smothering and Overlaying of Virginia Slave Children; A Suggested Explanation," *Bulletin of the History of Medicine* 49 (Fall 1975), pp. 400–404. And for a discussion of the so-called suffocation of slave infants, see Michael P. Johnson, "Smothered Slave Infants; Were Slave Mothers at Fault?" *Journal of Southern History* 47 (November 1981), pp. 493–520. I have used the term "infanticide" throughout, though some of these children were beyond the stage of infancy.

31. See T. S. Jones to John Jones, June 21, 1852, T. S. Jones Family Correspondence, Special Collections, Vanderbilt University Library, Nashville, TN.

32. *Commonwealth v. Amey, property of John Gresham*, King and Queen County Court of Oyer and Terminer, 13 May 1799, b. 1966 and *Commonwealth v. Jenny, property of Peter Stratton*, Powhatan County Court of Oyer and Terminer, 7 September 1815, b. 1967, APAR-VSLA; testimony of T. B. Barnet, n.d., Granville County Slave Records, NCSA.

33. Gerda Lerner, *Black Women in White America: A Documentary History* (New York, NY: Vintage Books, 1978), p. 38. It is important to note, however, that social-science scholarship on postpartum depression has gone far beyond hormonal imbalance explanations. Some of these explanations that might be relevant in the case of slave women include "unresolved conflicts" regarding motherhood and mothering, physical exhaustion, and the trauma of childbirth itself. Brief discussions of this are included in Mary-Joan Gerson, Judith L. Alpert, and Mary Sue Richardson, "Mothering: The View From Psychological Research," *Signs* 9 (Spring 1984), pp. 434–453; Ann Oakley, "A Case of Maternity: Paradigms of Women as Maternity Cases," *Signs* 4 (Summer 1979), pp. 607–631.

34. Indeed, while the women were often charged with murder, a real issue in these legal proceedings was their crimes against property. That is, they had destroyed their masters' property.

35. Vincent Harding, "Religion and Resistance among Antebellum Negroes, 1800–1860," in August Meier and Elliot Rudwick, eds., *The Origins of Black Americans*, vol. 5 of *The Making of Black America* (New York, NY: Atheneum, 1969), p. 190.

36. Quotes on the evidence of abortion are in Darlene C. Hine, "Female Slave Resistance: The Economics of Sex," *The Western Journal of Black Studies* 3 (Summer 1979), pp. 124–126; White, *Ar'n't I a Woman*, pp. 84–89.

37. Dorothy Sterling, *Black Foremothers: Three Lives* (Old Westbury, NY: The Feminist Press, 1979), p. 11. Deborah Gray White, in *Ar'n't I A Woman*, provides examples of women being forced to marry and/or have sex with men chosen by their owners; of their refusing to have children by "husbands" forced on them by their owners; and of one woman killing her child because her mistress regularly beat the child. See pp. 85–88, 102–03.

38. Nancy Venture Woods to John Haywood, February 1825, box 19, f. 112, Ernest Haywood papers, Southern History Collection, University of North Carolina, Chapel Hill, NC.

39. It is entirely possible that Woods' daughter, the mother of most of these children, was not there because she was at her "prime" in terms of her productive labor capacity. Nancy Woods, however, was evidently past her prime when she was assigned to care for these youngsters when they were unable to care for themselves. By this process, their owner still benefitted from Woods' labor and was simultaneously relieved of caring for her and the children. This example is very similar to the one involving the elderly man, Payne, on p. 10.

40. Rawick, Georgia, part 4, 13:302–03; Alabama, 6: 358, 343.

41. Perdue, et al., *Weevils*, pp. 264–65; Rawick, Georgia, 4, 13:296–97.

42. Genovese, *Roll, Jordan, Roll*, pp. 510–511.

43. Rawick, Georgia, part 3, 13: 2, 17, 80, 104, 140, 214, 218, 237; part 4, 13:16, 120.

44. Ibid., Georgia, part 3, 13:88, 147; part 4, 13:101.

45. Ibid., Georgia, part 3, 13:47, 58, 72, 201, 237; part 4, 13:195.

46. Ibid., Georgia, part 1, 12: 114; part 3, 13: 71, 116, 133, 149; part 4, 13: 16, 195;

Alabama, 5:176, 181, 321, 429; Heloise M. Foreman, Lulu M. Wilson interview transcript, UT-BTHC, 2.

47. Rawick, Georgia, part 3, 13:133, 269; part 4, 13: 315, Alabama, 6:130.

48. Rawick, Georgia, part 1, 12:64.

49. Even more profoundly, the religious practices, folktales, and folk songs passed on by men and women, and the gang labor system of work itself, daily encouraged the formation of a collective consciousness that not only enhanced survival while enslaved, but also after emancipation. See, especially, Levine, *Black Culture and Black Consciousness*.

Chapter 12

UNDOCUMENTED LATINAS: THE NEW "EMPLOYABLE MOTHERS"

Grace Chang

The nomination of Zoe Baird for U.S. Attorney General in 1993 forced a confession that provoked a public uproar: Baird admitted to employing two undocumented Peruvian immigrants, as a baby-sitter and a driver, in clear violation of current immigration law prohibiting the hiring of "illegal" aliens. Responses to Baird's disclosure indicate her "crime" is a pervasive phenomenon.[1] Deborah Sontag reported in the *New York Times* that two-career, middle-class families employing so-called illegal immigrants to do child care and domestic work is so common that employment agencies routinely recommend undocumented immigrants to their clients. As the director of one Manhattan nanny agency said, "It's just a reality of life that without the illegal girls, there wouldn't be any nannies, and the mommies would have to stay home and mind their own kids."[2] Another agency's director said bluntly, "It all comes down to money . . . the reason that people hire immigrants without papers is that they're looking to save. If they want legal, they can get it, but it costs."[3] According to a survey of eighteen New York agencies, "illegal" workers earned as little as 175 dollars a week and "legal" workers as much as six hundred dollars.[4]

Thus the uproar surrounding Zoe Baird was not so much a response to the discovery that some people flouted the law by employing undocumented workers. This was hardly news. Rather, the public outcry was a reflection of resentment that this practice was so easily accessible to the more privileged classes while others, that is, working-class, "working" mothers, struggled to find any child care. As one critic of Baird commented, "I don't think it's fair. I raised my kids while I was working. I worked days. My husband worked nights at the post office. Our in-laws filled in when they had to."[5] Another woman pointed out "Average working mothers don't make nearly what she makes, and yet we are obligated to follow the law."[6]

What was conspicuously absent from most of the commentary on the Baird controversy was concern for the plight of the undocumented workers themselves. Ironically, two other news stories involving immigrant women working in private households appeared in a California newspaper at the same time Zoe Baird's situation was making headlines across the nation; yet these stories did not receive comparable attention. The first of these involved Claudia Garate, who immigrated from Chile at the age of nineteen in order to take a job as an au pair for a professional couple. Ms. Garate testified before the state Labor Commissioner in Sonoma County that she slept on the floor and worked on call twenty-four hours a day, seven days a week as a maid, baby-sitter, cook and gardener for fifty dollars a month. Garate's employers held on to her visa and passport, and withheld her pay for thirteen months, claiming they would deposit it in a bank account for her. The second case involved Maria de Jesus Ramos Hernandez, who left her three children in Mexico to work as a housekeeper in California. Once here, her employer repeatedly raped her, telling her that he had paid her way here and would have her jailed if she did not submit to him.[7]

Evidence indicates that while Garate's and Hernandez's cases may have been extreme, abuses of undocumented women working in private households were not uncommon. Lina Avidan, program director for the San Francisco-based Coalition for Immigrant and Refugee Rights and Services (CIRRS), said "I have clients who work ... seven days a week, doing child care from 6 a.m. to 10 p.m. [for] $200 a month. Clearly, they are working in the homes of the wealthy and they're not even getting minimum wage."[8] Spokeswomen for Mujeres Unidas y Activas, a San Francisco-based advocacy group for Latina immigrants, said they had heard countless reports from Latinas working as domestics who endure conditions approaching slavery or indentured servitude.[9] These statements were echoed by undocumented household workers in New York. For example, Dorothea Grant, a Jamaican woman who received a green card after working as a nanny for seven years, explained why American-born workers rarely apply for nanny jobs; "These days, most Americans see it as some kind of slavery."[10] Others reported that because their employers agreed to sponsor them for legal residency they felt like indentured servants in the interim, sometimes waiting up to ten years. One woman from Guyana who had applied for residency six years before was working on call round the clock as a housekeeper for her sponsoring family.[11]

Taken together, these accounts indicate that middle-class households often make exploitative use of immigrant women to do child care and domestic work. They also suggest that the advances of many middle-class, white women in the work force have been largely predicated on the exploitation of poor, immigrant women. While middle- and upper-class women entrust their children and homes to undocumented immigrant women, the immigrant women often must leave their own children in order to work. Some leave their children with family in their home countries, hoping to earn enough to return or send money back to them.[12] Thus, middle- and upper-class women are readily able to find "affordable" care for their children at the expense of poor immigrant women and their children. The employment of undocumented women in dead-end, low-wage, temporary service jobs—often under exploitative conditions—makes it possible for middle- and upper-class women to pursue salaried jobs, and not have to contend with the "second shift" when they come home.[13]

A predictable outgrowth of the Baird controversy has been the proposal that the existing law, the Immigration Reform and Control Act (IRCA) of 1986, be changed so that household employers are exempted from the prohibition against hiring "illegal" immigrants, or that household workers are given special visas.[14] If the law were changed to meet this "popular demand," it would only serve to perpetuate—and authorize by law—the exploitation of thousands of undocumented immigrants. Certainly there is much historical precedent for government-sanctioned exploitation of immigrants as cheap laborers in the U.S. For example, in response to the wartime demands of Southwestern agricultural employers for laborers, the Bracero Program was instituted in 1942, allowing for the importation of millions of Mexicans as temporary workers. These workers were bound to fixed low wages, and obliged to stay on certain farms until they were to be returned to Mexico at the end of their contractual periods.[15] Following this model, agribusiness lobbyists succeeded in getting provisions for agricultural "guest workers" written into IRCA, enabling growers to continue to draw on immigrants as a superexploitable labor pool. The current proposals raise the specter of a counterpart to these agricultural "guest workers" in private household work: "disposable nannies" who may be dumped once babies become older or newer immigrants can be found who are willing to work for even lower wages.

In this paper, I attempt to demonstrate that the Immigration and Naturalization Service (INS), through its execution of IRCA, has continued the historical role of the state in using government policies to maintain women of color as a superexploitable, low-wage labor force. This paper builds on socialist feminist theory proposing that the welfare state mediates the conflicting demands for female home and market labor by subsidizing some women to remain home in order to reproduce and maintain the labor force, while channeling others into low-wage work.[16] An historical example is the use of "employable mother" rules by many states from the 1940s through 1960s to deny Black mothers ADC/AFDC benefits, thereby coercing them to perform agricultural and domestic work. In implementing current immigration policy, the INS has continued this pattern. The INS's execution of IRCA, denying legalization to undocumented women whose citizen children have received public assistance, maintains these women in the secondary labor force, in private household work or institutional service work.[17]

In the first section of the paper, I review the Immigration Reform and Control Act of 1986, with particular attention to those provisions affecting undocumented women with dependents. Here I examine how public perceptions of immigrant women as welfare drainers may have influenced the law's creation and implementation. In the next section I present the case of *Zambrano v. Immigration and Naturalization Service*, in which a formal charge was made that the INS's implementation of IRCA discriminated against women by not making legalization available to them on an equal basis with men. I argue further that this discrimination was deliberate, with the intent of maintaining these women in the secondary labor force. In the final section, I review the historical precedent for the use of government policy to regulate the labor of women of color, that is, the "employable mother" rules. The parallel between IRCA and the "employable mother" rules illustrates how women of color and immigrant women have been denied access to adequate means of providing for their children—thus rendering them "available" for, indeed unable to refuse, low-wage work.

THE IMMIGRATION REFORM AND CONTROL ACT OF 1986: A COMPROMISE

The IRCA emerged in 1986 after nearly a decade of debate in Congress and in the public domain about what impact immigration, particularly "illegal" immigration, had on the U.S. economy. The Act had two main objectives that were possibly contradictory: to stem the tide of illegal immigration, and to provide rights and the chance to legalize their status to those undocumented immigrants who had already lived and/or worked in the country. Unable to reconcile these conflicting impulses, Congress incorporated a number of provisions into the law as concessions to various interest groups. First, to discourage illegal immigration, the law established employer sanctions against those who knowingly employed "illegal" immigrants. Second, to provide rights and protections to undocumented persons, the amnesty program offered those who could prove they had lived in the country "illegally" since at least 1982 the chance to apply for temporary resident status. Finally, in response to the concerns of growers about how the law might affect the availability of agricultural labor, Congress created three special classes of those who could enter the country or gain residency as agricultural workers.[18]

Some of the most heated debate surrounding IRCA centered around the issue of whether immigrants contribute to or deplete the public coffers. This debate led lawmakers to include in IRCA two provisions, the public charge exclusion and the five-year bar, governing whether those perceived as potentially welfare-dependent should be able to gain residency, and what entitlements "legalized persons" should be allowed to receive. Before examining these provisions more closely, it will be useful to look at some of the dimensions of this debate, in order to understand the political context in which these provisions were formulated and implemented. In the past, most public views and scholarly discussions on the "costs and benefits" of immigrants have emphasized the charge that male migrant laborers steal jobs from "native" workers. In the last decade, however, this concern has been drowned out by cries that immigrants impose a heavy welfare burden on "natives." A 1986 CBS/*New York Times* poll found that forty-seven percent of Americans believed that "most immigrants wind up on welfare."[19] In a review of studies on the economic impacts of immigration to the U.S., Annie Nakao reported for the *San Francisco Examiner*, "What is generally accepted is that immigrants do not take jobs from natives. . . . "[20] The abundance of studies examining how immigrants affect the U.S. economy disagree on many points, but most recent works seem to agree that Americans should be more worried about protecting public revenues than their jobs.[21]

Thus, a new twist in anti-immigrant rhetoric has emerged, with a focus on immigrants as economic welfare burdens. For example, Governor Pete Wilson deployed this rhetoric in marketing his proposals for slashing social service funds in California's 1992 budget. In his administration's report "The Growing Taxpayer Squeeze," Wilson called immigrants "tax receivers" and identified the "rising foreign immigrant population" as a major cause of growing tax expenditures for welfare, Medi-cal and public schools.[22] The new emphasis on the alleged depletion of public revenues by immigrants signals an implicit shift in the main target of anti-immigrant attacks. Men as job stealers are no longer seen as the "immigrant problem." Instead, immigrant women as idle, welfare-dependent mothers and inordinate breeders of dependents are seen as the great menace. Thus, a legislative analyst on Governor Wilson's staff reported that Latinas have an AFDC dependency rate twenty-three percent higher than the rate for all other women.[23] Such "findings" are almost always coupled with statements about higher birth rates among immigrant women, and the threat they pose to controlling population growth.[24]

Perhaps this new strategy, identifying immigrant women (and particularly Latinas) as the major threat to American public resources, reflects a growing awareness of changes that have occurred in the composition and nature of Mexican migration to the U.S. in the last two decades. Wayne Cornelius, of the Center for U.S.-Mexican Studies, reports that, beginning in the 1970s and through the 1980s, there was a shift in Mexican migration from that dominated by "lone male" (single or unaccompanied by dependents), seasonally-employed, and highly mobile, migrant laborers to a "de facto" permanent Mexican immigrant population including more women, children and entire families.[25] The change consists of more migration by whole families, more family reunification, and more migration by single women.[26] Cornelius explains that Mexico's crisis has driven more women to migrate to the United States, where there is "an abundance of new employment opportunities for which women are the preferred labor source," including child care, cleaning and laundry work.[27]

Cornelius's analysis of U.S. Census Bureau (1988) data suggests that, as a result of this expanded female migration, females may now represent the majority of "settled" undocumented Mexican immigrants.[28] In her study of undocumented Mexican immigrant communities, Pierette Hondagneu reports that it is the women who advocate and mobilize families toward permanent settlement in the U.S. Thus, she theorizes, U.S. xenophobia has come to focus on women because they are perceived as the leaders of this threatening demographic shift.[29]

Heightened awareness of these new demographics contributed to hysteria about protecting public revenues and guarding against the growth of a population of welfare dependents. These concerns undoubtedly influenced the inclusion of two provisions of IRCA, the public charge exclusion and the five-year bar, to restrict aliens' access to social services and public benefits. Clearly, these restrictions were formulated with the goal of limiting welfare expenditures. In executing IRCA, the INS went even further, utilizing an interpretation of the law that effectively denied amnesty to those seen as potential welfare abusers, that is, undocumented women with children. The following is a review of how these provisions were originally formulated, in order to illustrate how INS's interpretation of the law was more restrictive than intended by Congress.

The Five-Year Bar from Federal Assistance

The amnesty program represented a recognition, at least on the part of some lawmakers, that for years thousands of undocumented aliens had lived in the United States, worked, and contributed to the American economy without ever enjoying the rights of those recognized as full, "legitimate" members of the society.[30] Of course not all lawmakers had such generous intentions in mind in formulating IRCA. Many were more concerned with protecting public resources for "native" Americans than protecting the rights of the undocumented. The perception of immigrants as welfare burdens fueled fears that the amnesty program would create a tremendous, immediate strain on social service funds.[31] In direct response to these concerns, Congress included in IRCA a provision barring legalization applicants from most federal assistance programs, including AFDC, food stamps, and certain forms of Medicaid. The bar period extends for five years from the time the alien applies for temporary residency.[32]

The Public Charge Ground of Exclusion and the Special Rule

In addition to the five-year bar, a provision of immigration law dating back to 1882 was retained in IRCA to guard against the expected welfare drain by newly legalized aliens. This provision, excluding those "likely to become a public charge," is used to identify those who might be unable to support themselves because of some physical or mental limitation.[33] Prior to IRCA, all aliens applying for an immigrant visa were subject to a test to determine whether they were likely to be able to earn a living in the future. This "traditional test" is still used to assess whether alien heads of households can support themselves and their dependents.

This test considers factors such as the applicant's age, health, past and current income, education, and job skills. Past receipt of public benefits is considered a significant but not determinative factor. The traditional test gives applicants one way of overcoming the public charge ground of exclusion, even if they have received public benefits, if they can show that they are currently employed or able to provide for themselves and their families.[34]

Under IRCA, Congress established a "special rule" providing a second test for legalization applicants unable to pass the traditional test.[35] This test examines the alien's recent past, and requires the applicant to have a history of employment that demonstrates self-support without receipt of public cash assistance.[36] This history of employment need not be continuous, thus allowing for periods of unemployment and seasonal or migrant labor.[37] Congressional testimony indicates that Congress created the "special rule" with the intent of liberalizing the public charge standard or providing a second means of overcoming this standard.[38] Specifically, it was made with the recognition that many of the undocumented are "working poor," unlikely to become dependent on public benefits despite their low incomes.[39]

The amnesty, five-year bar, and public charge provisions of IRCA were formulated in the face of a wide spectrum of views on what rights and benefits should be extended to legalized immigrants. IRCA represented an uneasy compromise of these views, and the task of implementing IRCA was left to the discretion of the INS. In executing IRCA, the INS has applied more restrictive interpretations of the law. For example, Congress intended to open eligibility for legalization to large numbers of people, including those with low incomes, with the "special rule."[40] But the INS did not utilize the "special rule" properly, and instead implemented its own interpretations of the law, which were not consistent with Congress's liberalizing intent. The result of this practice was that many undocumented women who have received public assistance for their children were denied amnesty.

THE CASE OF *ZAMBRANO V. IMMIGRATION AND NATURALIZATION SERVICE*

The INS's implementation of IRCA, particularly its application of the law to undocumented women, is being challenged in the case of *Zambrano v. INS*. The class action suit was filed in the Ninth Circuit in April of 1988 on behalf of a group of plaintiffs who are mostly women with dependents, and the class that they represent.[41] The complaint against the INS, filed by California Rural Legal Assistance (CRLA), the National Immigration Law Center and San Mateo County Legal Aid, co-counsel for the plaintiffs, made two claims: that INS's practices contradicted the congressional intent of IRCA, and that these practices discriminated against and imposed extreme hardship on undocumented women with children.[42] The declarations of two of the plaintiffs, Marta Zambrano and Maria C., illustrate how the INS's execution of the amnesty and public charge provision of IRCA adversely affected undocumented women with children, and obstructed their chances of obtaining better working and living conditions.[43]

Marta Zambrano, whose name the case assumed, was a Mexican citizen who had lived continuously in the U.S. since 1979. Marta had four U.S. citizen children, ages eight, six, four and three at the time of her declaration in 1988. Between 1979 and 1983 she worked in a factory, picked cauliflowers, and did many kinds of work in the fields, even while she had two small children. She only began receiving AFDC for her children in 1983, when she became pregnant with her third child and her common-law husband left her because she refused to have an abortion.[44]

Marta first heard about the amnesty program in 1986 on the radio and through friends. She went to a program at her church for information and was told that she could not receive AFDC for her children if she wanted to legalize. She also heard on the radio and from her friends that people who received welfare were not eligible for legalization. Convinced that she would not qualify, Ms. Zambrano did not pursue an amnesty application. Only at the urging of an attorney did she file her application on May 4, 1988, the latest possible date. In June of 1988 she was interviewed by the INS and informed that her application was denied because her children had received AFDC.[45]

Marta received AFDC for her U.S. citizen children because their natural fathers contributed no support to the family. Since 1986, Marta had sought work, but was refused in many instances because she did not have work authorization, which she could only obtain through legalization. Potential employers turned Marta away for work in the fields and in dishwashing and housecleaning. Even when Marta obtained part-time work, she did not earn enough money to cover living expenses and child care.[46]

Anna R was less fortunate than Marta Zambrano, in that she never even applied for amnesty. She was a citizen of El Salvador and had lived in California since 1981. She had four children, two of whom were U.S. citizens. Shortly after IRCA was passed, Anna began preparing to apply for amnesty by gathering necessary documents. In January of 1988, Anna was abandoned by the father of her children. At that time she was unable to find full-time employment without work authorization, and applied for AFDC for her U.S. citizen children. She also began working as a housekeeper, one day per week for three different employers. She earned about four hundred dollars per month and received no support from her children's father.[47]

Anna heard from the radio, television, and her relatives that receipt of welfare would disqualify her from legalization. Thus she did not apply before the May 4, 1988 deadline, as she had intended to since 1986. Had she been informed that the receipt of AFDC by her U.S. citizen children should not disqualify her from legalization, she would have applied and should otherwise have been eligible.[48]

The other plaintiffs reported similar circumstances and obstacles to legalization. Each of the women had children, some or all of whom were U.S. citizens. Those who received AFDC payments had received them only for U.S. citizen children, who were fully entitled to these benefits. Most of the women had some work history and, if unemployed at the time of applying for amnesty, would presumably return to the work force when their family circumstances and child care needs allowed. Some were employed at the time, but their incomes were insufficient to provide for them and their dependents without supplementary AFDC benefits. One received SSI payments on behalf of her child, who had cerebral palsy.[49]

These women represent an entire class of people adversely affected by the improper INS practices. The plaintiffs contended that they are among the many thousands of undocumented persons Congress intended to offer an opportunity to legalize.[50] Yet they have been impeded from obtaining legal status and its benefits (such as work authorization) either through outright denial by the INS or because they were discouraged from applying based on information about the INS's improper practices. The complaint against the INS presented two claims, only the first of which has been addressed by the Court.

First Claim: The INS Has Violated IRCA

The complaint filed against the INS in April of 1988 alleged that the INS's policies and procedures were "in contradiction of the plain meaning of IRCA and Congressional intent."[51] The INS applied its own "Proof of Financial Responsibility" (PFR) regulations, which the plaintiffs maintained were more restrictive than intended in the liberalized standards created under IRCA.[52] The PFR regulations attributed public benefits received by an amnesty applicant's dependents to the applicant. As revealed in the declarations of the plaintiffs, this included AFDC received by U.S. citizen children, who were fully entitled to these benefits. The INS's use of these regulations resulted in the denial of amnesty to applicants who should otherwise have been eligible under IRCA's liberalized standards, such as the "special rule."[53]

The U.S. District Court for the Eastern District of California addressed the first claim in the *Zambrano* case, although a final decision still had not been rendered as of March 1993 (the time of writing). On July 31, 1989, after a thorough review of the INS regulations, the IRCA statute and the legislative history surrounding its passage, Judge Edward Garcia issued a partial summary judgment and a permanent injunction on the INS regulations. The INS was ordered to reopen the cases of those who had been adversely affected by the regulations. This included two classes of people: (1) those who filed applications on time but were denied as "likely to become a public charge" under the invalidated regulations; and (2) those who were eligible for legalization but had not applied because they were discouraged by information about the INS's prior practices.[54] The INS was ordered to accept amnesty applications until December 31, 1989 for this second class of people.[55]

The INS appealed the July 1989 decision on a number of grounds.[56] The INS first appealed it in the Ninth Circuit Court of Appeals.[57] In February of 1992, the Court ruled against the INS, and the INS subsequently filed a writ of *certiorari* to the U.S. Supreme Court in November of 1992.[58] If the Supreme Court does take up the case, it could remand it to the lower courts to decide the remaining issues, such as the second claim made against the INS.

Second Claim: The INS's Regulations Discriminate on the Basis of Sex

A second claim made against the INS which has not been addressed yet is the charge that the INS regulations are discriminatory on the basis of sex, and thus violate the equal protection clause.[59] The complaint asserted that the effect of the INS's regulations and procedures was that "legalization under IRCA [was] not made available or [was] made available on an unequal basis [with men] to substantial numbers of women."[60] Certainly, the declarations of the plaintiffs indicate that the INS's practices resulted in the wrongful denial of amnesty to many women whose children received AFDC or other benefits. Moreover, it has been estimated that, in California alone, at least four thousand potential women applicants chose not to apply for amnesty because they were discouraged by information about INS's regulations.[61]

Diane Bessette, who acted as a legalization counselor for Catholic Community Services in Sacramento, calls attention to a third group of women for whom the INS regulations have posed inhumane choices. These women have managed to qualify for temporary resident status but must again overcome the INS's public charge exclusion practices when they apply for permanent residency.[62] They must choose between continuing to receive public assistance for their dependents or losing this means of support in order to complete the legalization process.[63] Bessette points out that because many single women with children cannot survive without the assistance, many will be forced to forego adjusting to permanent residency.[64] In other words, these women face a double bind: without legal status and its concomitant work authorization, they cannot find employment at adequate wages. Without adequate wages, they must provide for their children by some means, but they sacrifice the chance to gain legal status for themselves if they receive aid for their children as supplements to these wages.

One woman who made a declaration in the *Zambrano* case revealed that she became homeless because she gave up public assistance to apply for amnesty.[65] Others who "choose" illegal status or are denied amnesty will most likely suffer unemployment or employment in exploitative circumstances because they lack work authorization.[66] Rather than bringing these women "out of the shadows," the law has served to condemn them and their children to an underclass. Perhaps one of the gravest consequences of the INS regulations has been to maintain this underclass and to perpetuate the racial feminization of poverty among undocumented immigrants.

A number of recent studies indicate that undocumented persons, particularly women, have become or remain part of an underclass despite the generous potentials of the amnesty program. This is manifested in two ways: first, undocumented women have been confined to employment in the secondary sector and often remain in highly exploitative work conditions for fear of losing their chances to legalize.[67] Second, these women earn incomes far below the poverty level; yet they underutilize public assistance and social services to which they or their children are fully entitled, again fearing that they will jeopardize their legalization applications by such use.[68] Moreover, these studies indicate that the INS has contributed to both of these patterns by its improper practices and its failure to publicize the proper regulations regarding amnesty and the public charge exclusion.[69] It should be noted that two of the studies cited here were conducted after the August 1988 order in *Zambrano* had already placed a temporary injunction on the improper INS regulations. Yet the responses of those surveyed indicate that widespread fear and misinformation persists about how use of public assistance would affect their amnesty applications. The evidence clearly refutes the myth of undocumented Latinas as nonworking welfare dependents, or public resource depletors. Instead, it suggests that the INS's practices have locked countless undocumented women and their dependents into an underclass, without access to legal recourse for workplace abuses or relief from poverty that legalization might afford them. Certainly at the very least, the evidence supports the second claim made in *Zambrano v. INS*, that the INS has "acted knowing and intending that the direct effect of their actions is to exclude or burden substantial numbers of women."[70]

For several reasons, the plaintiffs' attorneys have not yet pursued this second claim in the proceedings thus far. Earlier, they attempted to show that a large percentage of those persons who have been denied under the improper regulations are single women with children, but the INS refused to comply with discovery orders which would allow plaintiffs to compile statistics demonstrating this pattern.[71] Stephen Rosenbaum of CRLA, co-counsel for the plaintiffs, commented that sexual discrimination is extremely difficult to prove, and certainly the INS's noncompliance with the discovery orders has contributed to this difficulty. Furthermore, Rosenbaum commented that they have not pursued this claim because the argument of statutory violations by the INS, made in the first claim, was deemed stronger.[72]

Nevertheless, the evidence clearly suggests that INS's practices discriminate largely against women. In fact, one could argue that the second claim could be expanded to charge that the INS's actions constitute not only sexual but racial discrimination as well. Moreover, I would argue that through these actions the INS has performed its historical role in regulating the labor of immigrant women for local business interests in manufacturing and agriculture, and for middle-class households seeking child care and domestic workers.[73] Thus, it might be established that the INS indeed acted "knowing and intending" that the effects of its practices would be to exclude many women so they would need to seek or remain in low-wage employment. It will be useful here to examine the historical precedent of using welfare policy to regulate the labor of women of color.

THE HISTORICAL PRECEDENT FOR THE INS'S
ACTIONS: THE USES OF WELFARE POLICY IN
REGULATING WOMEN OF COLOR'S LABOR

In *Regulating the Poor: The Functions of Public Welfare,* Frances Fox Piven and Richard Cloward argue that poverty policy and practice have historically been coupled with labor practice to accommodate local employers' demands for low-wage labor. That is, poverty policy has been designed and implemented to serve two basic functions: first, in times of economic contraction, welfare can be expanded in order to quell or prevent civil unrest by unemployed masses. Or, second, in times of relative economic and political stability, welfare can be contracted to expel people from the rolls, thus ensuring their availability to perform low-wage labor according to local needs. Piven and Cloward aptly describe this second function as "enforcing" low-wage work for impoverished people considered to be "able-bodied," regardless of age or sex.[74]

Socialist feminist Mimi Abramovitz refines Piven and Cloward's thesis with regards to women in her book, *Regulating the Lives of Women.* Abramovitz proposes that the welfare state mediates the conflicting demands of patriarchal capitalism for women to provide two functions: (1) to remain in the home in order to reproduce and maintain the labor force; and (2) to do traditionally "female" low-wage work in the paid labor force. Abramovitz argues that the state resolves this conflict by encouraging and subsidizing some women to remain at home and nurture the current and future work force, while forcing others into low-wage work.[75] This division is achieved through poverty policies or practices which are predicated on racist assumptions that some women (that is, white women) are fit to be mothers and homemakers and thus "deserve" subsidies allowing them to remain in the home. Other women (that is, women of color and immigrant women) are deemed "unfit" nurturers—indeed, are thought to be undesirable reproducers—and thus are viewed as better suited to fulfill the demands for certain kinds of market labor.

I suggest that we need to reformulate this theory to account for phenomena such as undocumented women employed in child care and domestic work, in which women of color are simultaneously engaged in low-wage work and in paid reproductive labor for families other than their own. Sociologist Evelyn Nakano Glenn has recently postulated her model of the racial division of reproductive labor, which is helpful in explaining such phenomena.[76] Glenn argues that women of color have historically relieved privileged white women of much of the burden of reproductive labor by performing both private household and institutional service work. Moreover, she argues, women of color's performance of reproductive labor for others frees dominant-group women to pursue leisure or employment, thus making possible the privilege and "liberation" of white women.[77]

Drawing on Glenn's model, I propose that in some cases the state channels women of color into service work in order to "support" or completely assume the reproductive functions of privileged white women. The state thereby captures the labor of subordinate-group women for dominant-group women, benefitting middle-class households (both women and their partners in traditional nuclear families) and capital. The interests of each of these parties is served through the transferral of the burden of reproductive labor from white women to subordinate women—by ameliorating or eliminating conflicts over housework, thus helping to preserve the traditional nuclear family, or allowing middle- and upper-class women to contribute significantly to two-income families.

In the following section, I will trace how welfare policy has been applied differentially towards white women and women of color in order to enforce different kinds of labor for each group of women. This will allow us to analyze how the state has mediated the tension between the demand for women's reproductive labor and women's low-wage labor in the paid work force, both historically and in the contemporary period.

The Uses of Welfare Policy in Regulating the Labor of White Women and Women of Color

The Mothers' Pension program, the first program of public assistance to dependent children, was created to support women at home as the proper guardians of their children and "stable" home life necessary to cultivate good citizens.[78] The founders of the Mothers' Pension program never claimed that this good home life was to be extended to all women and children; nor were all women thought to be able to maintain good homes for children. The creators envisioned limiting this support to a privileged group of mothers. The White House Conference convened in 1909 to outline the program produced two principles: first, a select group of families would be removed from the class of paupers and from the stringent provisions of the Poor Law. Second, the state would provide assistance to enable these women to keep their children in their own homes rather than in institutions in order to nurture them into productive citizens. In return, these mothers were to demonstrate that they were proper and competent custodians of their children and that they could maintain "suitable homes" for them.[79]

This second principle was the basis for the "suitable homes" rules that were retained in many states throughout the operation of the Mothers' Pension program and its successors. In her classic study, *Aid to Dependent Children*, Winifred Bell argues that this rule became a convenient means by which welfare officials could identify Black mothers of "illegitimate" children as "unfit" and "undeserving" of aid.[80] The available statistics suggest that the operative definitions of "fit" and "deserving" implied white and widowed.[81] Moreover, Bell suggests that receipt of a Mothers' Pension grant was thought to bestow prestige upon these mothers, to "set them apart from the totality of mothers" as those who were expected to "achieve the ideal of devoted, selfless, and competent motherhood."[82]

In reality, the Mothers' Pension grants did not provide sufficient support to enable these chosen few to devote themselves solely to their child rearing duties. The program requirements presented contradictory obligations, defining "worthy" women as those who did not leave their children yet still managed to earn as much as possible.[83] Some states limited the amount of time a "worthy" mother could leave the home to three days a week. Many women resolved this dilemma by taking in laundry, thus simultaneously earning money and the status of "worthiness."[84]

The stated rationale behind the Aid to Dependent Children (ADC) program, established under the 1935 Social Security Act, seemed to remove this contradiction, asserting that mothers should be relieved of the double burden of wage earning and caring for children. The Committee on Economic Security published a report in 1935 stating that the ADC program was designed "to release from the wage-earning role the person whose natural function is to give her children the physical and affectionate guardianship necessary not alone to keep them from falling into social misfortune, but more affirmatively to make them citizens capable of contributing to society."[85] Thus, with the inception of the ADC program, federal policy proposed that the first obligation of women with children should be to nurture children into productive citizens, and that this maternal mission should not be hindered by work in the paid labor force.

Sylvia Law argues that between 1935 and 1968, federal policy embodied the principle that women with children were unemployable.[86] Under Federal ADC/AFDC guidelines in effect from 1939 to 1969, "Considerations Regarding Employment of Mothers' advised against exerting pressure on mothers which might lead them to neglect their maternal or homemaking duties:

> The time available for domestic responsibilities is limited for an employed mother. She must either neglect her home or make inroads on her physical resources. The resulting nerve strain may affect her contribution to industry as well as to the well-being of her family. . . . The role of the public assistance agencies is, by assistance and other services, to help the mother arrive at a decision that will best meet her own needs and those of her children.[87]

In most cases, however, the interests of local employers competed with the needs of mother and child and, for certain groups of women, the ideal of state-supported, full-time mothering was sacrificed to the demands of capitalism. Officially, federal policy "discouraged" states from using public assistance to coerce mothers to work outside the home. For example, the Handbook of Public Assistance Administration advised: "The Bureau of Public Assistance recommends against any policy of denying or withdrawing aid to dependent children as a method of bringing pressure upon women with young children to accept employment. . . ."[88] Nevertheless, individual caseworkers and local state agencies exercised wide discretion over the administration of grants and have used a variety of mechanisms to deny women of color this protection against coercion into the work force.

In many states and localities, ADC and AFDC administrative rules contained explicit wagework requirements for mothers but they were applied selectively to poor women of color while preserving the option of full-time mothering for others.[89] Often these rules functioned as a pretext for expelling or denying women of color access to welfare, thus forcing them to seek work in the marginal labor market. For example, Louisiana adopted the first "employable mother" rule in 1943, requiring all AFDC families with children seven years or older to be denied assistance if the mother was presumed "employable" in the fields. Undoubtedly the rule was directed at nonwhite mothers, since this seasonal labor was almost exclusively performed by nonwhites.[90]

The statements of caseworkers suggest that racist assumptions often influenced them to view Black mothers as particularly well suited for employment, and these views guided their eligibility determinations. These assumptions included the beliefs that Black mothers had always worked in the past, that appropriate employment opportunities were more abundant for Black women, and that child care needs did not pose a problem for these mothers—ostensibly because the children were cared for by extended family members. Or, perhaps more to the point, because caseworkers did not believe it necessary to maintain the same standards of proper home life and maternal care for Black children. One Louisiana caseworker unabashedly expressed these assumptions about the unique employability of Black mothers:[91]

> [The] Negro mother has always worked in the past. The grandmother was there to look after the children. Now the mother has quit work. She stays at home and sits on the porch and rocks. Nobody wants to make the children suffer. What they want is for the mother to get out and work.

A colleague of this caseworker replied:

> What the people who make these criticisms are chiefly interested in is cheaper servants. It makes no difference to them one way or the other what

happens to Negro children. They are not interested in whether the mother has someone to leave the children with or not. What they want is to get a cook at $5 a week as they used to.

One can only infer from such statements that caseworkers recognized (though perhaps did not accept uncritically) the function of their agencies in accommodating local demands for cheap labor. As the remarks of one observer indicate, the attitude that the "employable Negro mother" could and should be coerced to remain in agricultural or domestic work often translated into the practice of denying Black families public assistance:[92]

The number of Negro cases is few due to the unanimous feeling on the part of the staff and board that there are more work opportunities for Negro women and to their intense desire not to interfere with local labor condi- tions. . . . There is hesitancy on the part of lay boards to advance too rapidly over the thinking of their own communities, which see no reason why the employable Negro mother should not continue her usually sketchy seasonal labor or indefinite domestic service rather than receive a public assistance grant.

Thus, both explicit administrative measures such as the suitable home and employable mother rules, and the more covert attitudes of some caseworkers making eligibility determinations, operated to bar or expel women of color from the rolls, to extract them from their homes and deliver them to local employers for domestic or agricultural work. The widespread use of these rules and the prevalence of these attitudes from the 1940s through the 1960s need to be viewed in their historical context: after World War II, vigorous efforts were made to encourage white, mid- dle-class women to return to the home as guardians of their children and domesticity. Simultaneously, efforts were made to direct Black women back to these same homes as domestic workers.[93] The overall result was to create altogether separate standards and conditions under which women of color and white women had to mother, relegating each group to particular functions within the system of patriarchal capitalism, and thus reinforcing race- and class-based divisions between women.

In the late 1960s, a series of legal challenges to restrictive welfare reg- ulations succeeded in overturning some of the mechanisms which had been used to perpetuate these differential standards. Among these was a challenge to the Georgia employable mother rule in a class action suit, *Anderson v. Burson* (1968), filed on behalf of a group of AFDC mothers. The Georgia rule, enacted in 1952, permitted welfare officials to deny aid to mothers with children over one year of age on the assumption that the women were employable if suitable work was available.[94] "Suitable" meant employment at any wage, and the rule prohibited county welfare departments from supplementing that wage, even if it was lower than the welfare grant levels. Moreover, the rule authorized county welfare officials to deny all new applications and to close all existing cases of mothers deemed employable during "periods of full employment," that is, during cotton-picking season.[95]

The plaintiffs in *Anderson v. Burson* argued that the rule had been used much more frequently to keep Black women off the rolls than white women, thus violating the equal protection provisions under the Fourteenth Amendment of the U.S. Constitution. On April 5, 1968, a three-judge federal court in Atlanta struck down certain portions of the Georgia "employable mother" rule, validating the charge that it violated equal protection standards.[96] The Court argued that the practice of denying supplementary benefits to mothers who were employed for less money than they would receive on welfare contradicted the purpose of the AFDC program. The plaintiffs also requested the right to refute the assumption that they could obtain work merely because a welfare official claimed that they were employable.[97] The Court struck down a provision requiring the applicant to demonstrate that suitable employment was not available.[98]

The relevance of this case to the *Zambrano* case should be clear. In many ways, the INS regulations were implemented to produce much the same results as the "employable mother" rules. First, the improper INS regulations were used more frequently to discourage Latina mothers from using AFDC or other public benefits and to discourage these women from receiving benefits in the future, even after they were legalized. Second, as has already been argued, the INS practices contradicted the purpose of the "special rule" under IRCA, to expand access to legalization and its benefits to the undocumented working poor. Finally, it seems that INS officials assumed that these mothers had adequate means of supporting their children through employment while at the same time ensuring that, without legalization and the accompanying work authorization, these women could not acquire jobs providing a decent wage. Yet if they attempted to supplement their inadequate wages with AFDC, they eliminated their chances of gaining legal status themselves and the possibility of better providing for their families in the future.

The regulation of undocumented Latina mothers under IRCA closely resembles the regulation of Black mothers under the "employable mother" rules. In each case the notion of nonwhite mothers as employable exists alongside prevailing dominant culture's views that a mother's employment outside the home harms her children's development. For each group of women, their construction as those who can and should work outside the home rationalizes the practice of denying support to them as mothers. This denial of aid forces these women to forego full-time mothering and to seek or remain in marginal work, for which they are seen as better suited. The parallel suggests that the notion of nonwhite mothers as uniquely employable has never been eradicated but, rather, has been enforced through a variety of government policies and practices.

CONCLUSION

Some feminists have proposed that subsidies to women with children should be expanded in the recognition that full-time mothering is work and should be properly rewarded. Wendy Sarvasy, for example, has called for us to recapture some of the original principles behind the Mothers' Pension program: that mothers be seen as civil servants and provided with pensions as compensation for their services in nurturing future citizens.[99] Such proposals repeat the original flaw of the Mothers' Pension program: limiting support to an elite group of women by defining "deserving" mothers as full-time mothers, while few women actually find full-time mothering viable. Under the current racial division of reproductive labor, some women cannot stay at home with their own children while they mother other people's children and keep other people's homes. Ironically, the assumption of these reproductive functions by women of color and immigrant women for white middle-class or professional women allows the latter group *not* to choose full-time mothering, opting for careers and other pursuits which may be more rewarding economically or personally. Thus, proposals to reward full-time mothering offer nothing to most women of color, for whom this occupation is rarely an option.

Furthermore, women of color may not view full-time mothering as the ideal. Historically, women of color have had to work, even while raising small children, either to supplement inadequate wages garnered by their men, or to provide for families in the absence of male providers. In response, communities of color have often constructed alternatives to dominant society's model of the family in which men are providers and women primarily dependents and consumers. For example, Carol Stack and Linda Burton report that male, female, old, and young members of low-income African-American families negotiated shared caretaking responsibilities, enabling women to earn wages during early childbearing years.[100] Similarly, the Mexicana mothers in Denise Segura's study viewed employment as compatible with mothering, as it enabled them to contribute toward the collective good of the family.[101]

Thus, proposals to reform the welfare system through revaluing the work of full-time mothering fail to address the needs of women of color and further marginalize them in their struggles to provide for their families. A more radical proposition—and one which might begin to address the plight of women of color who are poor working mothers—would be to recognize and reward women for the services they provide through both their productive and reproductive labors. In the case of the Latina mothers in *Zambrano*, this would necessitate a demystification of these women as welfare-dependents, and a recognition that they are working mothers, often heads of household or at least significant providers for their families. More importantly, such a demystification might compel the state to recognize the many ways in which these women benefit American capital and society at large—through paid (but grossly undercompensated) productive labor, through reproductive labor for others, and through the reproductive functions they perform within their own families. The fact that they too, in raising their own children, provide a service in nurturing future adult citizens should not be obscured by public ignorance casting their children as somehow less worthy.

In return for all of these contributions, these women should at least be afforded access to citizenship.[102] This would mean that they would not jeopardize their chances to gain legal status in seeking public assistance, including AFDC, for their children, many of whom are American citizens by birth and therefore fully entitled to these benefits. The professed goal of AFDC is to give temporary support to poor mothers so that ultimately they may be able to provide for their families through wage earning. If this is indeed the objective of AFDC, then denying amnesty to undocumented women who have received aid for their children contradicts this purpose by undermining these women's abilities to increase their employment options and earning powers. As we have seen, government policies have been utilized to handicap rather than support undocumented mothers. These practices facilitate U.S. employers' ability to extract cheap labor from these women and at the same time allow the state to evade responsibility for the welfare of citizen children. Undocumented women have been forced to choose between aid for their children or the possibility to gain legal status. Those who "choose" aid for their children condemn themselves to remain in an underclass, unrecognized as "productive citizens," yet functioning as perhaps the ultimate servants of our society.

Notes

I would like to thank Evelyn Nakano Glenn and Linda Rennie Forcey for their encouragement throughout this project and help in developing this paper. I owe special thanks to Stephen Rosenbaum for sharing his expertise on the *Zambrano* case and making thoughtful comments on earlier drafts. I am also grateful to Arlene Keizer, Jose Novoa and Jiannbin Shiao for their comments. This paper would not have been possible without generous contributions of time by my husband, Chad Zucker, and brother, Philip Chang, who read drafts, made suggestions and, most importantly, cared for my children while I wrote. I am also indebted to a number of women who were "othermothers" to my children during this project: Alana Althouse, Dora Pulido, Anna Pusina, Tsegeweini Teclealfa, and my mother, Janet Chang.

1. The *San Francisco Chronicle* reported that, although no precise figures exist, "experts believe a large percentage of the estimated 3 million undocumented workers now residing in the United States are employed in child-care and domestic work." "Hiring of Aliens is a Widespread Practice," *San Francisco Chronicle* (January 15, 1993), p. A6.

2. Deborah Sontag, "Increasingly, Two-Career Family Means Illegal Immigrant Help," *New York Times* (January 24, 1993), p.A-1.

3. Ibid., p. A-13.

4. Ibid.

5. Felicity Barringer, "What Many Say About Baird: What She Did Wasn't Right," *New York Times* (January 22, 1993), p. A1.

6. Ibid., p. A10.

7. Carla Marinucci, "Immigrant Abuse: 'Slavery—pure and simple,' " *San Francisco Examiner* January 10, 1993, pp. A-1, A-8.

8. Carla Marinucci, pp. A1, A8. A 1991 CIRRS survey of Chinese, Filipina and Latina undocumented women in the San Francisco Bay area revealed that the majority (58%) of the employed undocumented Latinas surveyed held jobs in housecleaning and in-home care of children or the elderly, while the remainder worked in service jobs or factories. They were usually earning between $250 and $500 per month. Forty percent of these women were supporting between one and three people on these wages, while 38% were supporting between four and six. The CIRRS survey also confirmed that undocumented women suffer many forms of worker exploitation, including not being paid for work, being paid lower wages than documented coworkers, and sexual harassment. Chris Hogeland and Karen Rosen, "Dreams Lost, Dreams Found: Undocumented Women in the Land of Opportunity," (San Francisco: Coalition for Immigrant and Refugee Rights and Services, Immigrant Women's Task Force, 1991), pp. 10–11.

9. Carla Marinucci, "Silence Shields Abuse of Immigrant Women," *San Francisco Examiner* January 11, 1993, pp. A-1, A-10.

10. Sontag, p. A13.

11. Ibid.

12. The CIRRS report suggested that the availability of "underground" service jobs for women in housecleaning, child care, and the garment industry encourages women to migrate alone or without families. As one respondent, Rosa, explained: "I am very worried because we left the children with my parents who are very old. We have not been able to send money home as planned because everything costs so much here." Hogeland and Rosen, p. 5.

13. This is not to imply that all middle-class women have immigrant women workers at their disposal, or that all private household employers exploit their employees. My point here is that there is a group (i.e. middle-class households) whose interests are served by ensuring the availability of poor immigrant women to perform household service work at low wages.

14. Several proposals for a visa for "home care workers" (i.e., domestic workers, child care workers, and home health aides) emerged in response to the Zoe Baird affair. For example, the American Immigration Lawyers Association (AILA) proposed the creation of a new category of "home care workers" visa, similar to the H2-A temporary agricultural visa. (See Note 15.) Under this plan, a household employer would identify a job position, swear by affidavit that s/he could not find a qualified U.S. citizen or resident to fill the position, and petition to hire a foreign-born person, who would gain temporary legal status on the first day of the job. Interview with Warren Leiden, Executive Director of AILA, Washington, D.C., March 22, 1993.

The Coalition for Immigrant and Refugee Rights and Services (CIRRS) have suggested a different approach, requiring the Department of Labor to determine that there is a shortage of domestic workers. An applicant would qualify by demonstrating that she has worked in the " home care" industry for a certain period of time, and by stating her intention to continue in this work for some time. Interview with Lina Avidan, Program Director of CIRRS, San Francisco, California, March 15, 1993.

15. Hundreds of thousands of Mexicans were imported each year between 1942 and the program's official termination in 1964. Braceros were to be returned to Mexico at the end of their contractual periods. Although the program was seen as a temporary measure, it has contributed to a number of persistent trends. Scholars now view it as having been a major stimulus for illegal Mexican migration to the U.S. during and subsequent to the program. Furthermore, it set a precedent for other programs of its type, "establishing a type of worker who was clearly set off as a Mexican national only temporarily in the United States." Mario Barrera, *Race and Class in the Southwest: A Theory of Racial Inequality* (Notre Dame: University of Notre Dame Press, 1979), pp. 116–122. For example, the temporary H–2A agricultural worker or "guest worker" programs extended under IRCA of 1986 preserved or institutionalized the Bracero Program. See also Note 18 and Kitty Calavita, Inside the State—The Bracero Program, Immigration, and the INS (New York: Routledge, 1992).

16. See Mimi Abramovitz, *Regulating the Lives of Women: The Social Functions of Public Welfare from Colonial Times to the Present* (Boston: South End Press, 1989).

17. Under the INS's interpretation of the public charge provisions of the law, the receipt of public assistance disqualifies an alien from adjusting immigration status at two stages: first when applying for temporary residency, and again when applying for permanent residency. In addition, under the five-year bar, an alien applying for legalization is prohibited from receiving most forms of public assistance from the time he or she applies for temporary residency to the time he or she gains permanent residency. These provisions are discussed in greater detail later in this chapter.

18. Undocumented workers who worked for ninety days in agriculture between May of 1985 and May of 1986 could gain temporary legal resident status as "special agricultural workers" (SAWs). If the SAW pool dropped below sufficient numbers, additional workers could be admitted as Replenishment Agricultural Workers (RAWs). Finally, the category of nonimmigrant, temporary, agricultural workers (H–2As) was maintained so that growers could obtain laborers if they were unable to find legal resident or citizen workers. Those entering under this type of visa are presumed to be here temporarily, and not intending to remain. Immigration Reform Task Force, "Report from the States on the State Legalization Impact Assistance Grant Program," (Washington, D.C.: American Public Welfare Association, May 1989), pp. 1, 28–30. See also Leonard Dinnerstein and David M. Reimers, *Ethnic Americans* (New York: Harper & Row Publishers, 1988), pp. 103–106 for an overview of IRCA and its origins.

19. CBS/*New York Times* poll, July 14, 1986, cited in Julian Simon, *The Economic Consequences of Immigration* (Cambridge: Basil Blackwell, Inc., 1989), p. 105.

20. Annie Nakao, "Assessing the Cost of Immigration," *San Francisco Examiner* (December 1, 1991), pp. B–1, B–3.

21. The perception that immigrants drain the public coffers through heavy reliance on welfare persists despite much evidence to the contrary. It is my contention that the "problem" of immigrant welfare dependency is a myth. I have addressed this issue extensively in my paper, "Immigrants and Entitlements: Do They Get What They Deserve?" in which I argue that studies produced by sources ranging from the most conservative to liberal agree that immigrants contribute more to public revenues than they receive. For example, Julian Simon says in his study, *The Economic Consequences of Immigration*, that "illegal" immigrants provide the greatest economic pluses because they use practically no "welfare services," while about three quarters pay Social Security and income taxes. Simon, p. 125.

22. Terri Lobdell and Lewis Butler, "Tending Our Future Together," *California Perspectives*, (November, 1991) pp. 31–41; and California Department of Finance, "California's Growing Taxpayer Squeeze," *California Perspectives* (November, 1991), p. 4. See also Rob-

ert Gunnison and Greg Lucas, "Wilson Blames Fiscal Woes on State Migration Trend," *San Francisco Chronicle* (November 14, 1991), p. A–4.

23. Nakao, p. B–3.

24. See, for example, Nakao. Ibid.

25. Wayne Cornelius, "From Sojourners to Settlers: The Changing Profile of Mexican Migration to the U.S.," (San Diego: Center for U.S.-Mexican Studies, University of California, San Diego, August 15, 1990), p. 17; published in Jorge Bustamante, Raul Hinojosa, and Clark Reynolds, eds., *U.S.-Mexico Relations: Labor Market Interdependence* (Stanford, CA: Stanford University Press, 1991).

26. Ibid., 18.

27. Cornelius says there has been rapid expansion in jobs for which undocumented Mexican women are the "preferred" labor source. In the San Francisco Bay area, there is a "booming market" for these women in child care, house and office cleaning and laundry work. In the border cities of San Diego and El Paso, Texas, domestic work has become institutionalized as the exclusive work of undocumented female immigrants. Also, Mexican immigrant women still dominate the garment firms, semiconductor manufacturing firms, fruit and vegetable canneries, and packing houses of California. Cornelius, pp. 19–20.

28. Ibid., 17.

29. Pierrette M. Hondagneu, "Gender and the Politics of Mexican Undocumented Immigrant Settlement," Ph.D. Dissertation, University of California (1990), p. 249.

30. In a Report of the House Judiciary Committee, the plight of the undocumented was aptly described: "These people live in fear, afraid to seek help when their rights are violated, when they are victimized by criminals, employers or landlords or when they become ill. . . . " House of Representatives Report No. 682 (I), 99th Congress, 2nd Session (1986), cited in *California Rural Legal Assistance (CRLA) v. Legal Services Corporation (LSC)*, No. 89–16734., D.C. No. CV–89–1850–SAW, Opinion (October 26, 1990), 13299. The remarks of one congressman, a Representative Smith, suggest that some lawmakers hoped to bring relief to the undocumented through IRCA: "We will be bringing people out of a shadow economy, people will be paying taxes, people will be coming out into the sunshine, there will not be the abuse of workers, employers will not be able to provide poor-quality jobs for people, they will not be able to oppress people." Congressional Record H10596–7 (Daily Edition October 15, 1986), cited in *CRLA v. LSC*, 13299.

31. A Senate Judiciary Committee report states: "The Committee notes the concern expressed by state and local governments regarding the potential fiscal impact arising from participation in public assistance programs by the legalized population. This concern is related to the experience . . . with refugee populations, whose dependence on special Federal entitlement programs has reached 70% in the past year, thereby thwarting the primary intent of the . . . program, which is to encourage economic self-sufficiency among refugees." Report of the Committee on the Judiciary on S. 2222, Senate Report No. 485, 97th Congress, 2nd Session, (Washington, D.C.: Government Printing Office, June 1982), p. 49.

32. Charles Wheeler, "Alien Eligibility for Public Benefits," Immigrants' Rights Manual of the National Immigration Law Center (September, 1990), pp. 11–45.

33. Charles Wheeler and Beth Zacovic, "The Public Charge Ground of Exclusion for Legalization Applicants," *Interpreter Releases*, 64, No. 35 (September 14, 1987), p. 1046.

34. Wheeler, pp. 11–48.

35. Wheeler and Zacovic, p. 1047.

36. 8 USC Section 1255a(d)(B)(iii). "Public cash assistance" includes only those programs which provide monetary assistance, not in-kind benefits such as food stamps or medical services. Wheeler, pp. 11–49.

37. Wheeler, pp. 11–49.

38. Wheeler & Zacovic, p. 1047.

39. Ibid. A 1985 study by the Migrant Health Care Project estimated that 30–40% of undocumented persons had incomes below the federal poverty level guidelines, although

more than 90% of these men and 64% of these women were employed. (L. Chavez and R. Rumbaut, et al., *The Politics of Migrant Health Care* (San Diego: University of California, August 1985). Thus, a large proportion of legalization applicants might be viewed as potential public charges, solely on the basis of their low incomes. With the "special rule," Congress tried to prevent the use of income as the sole criterion for determining the excludability or admissibility of applicants such as these.

40.   Wheeler & Zacovic, p. 1047.

41.   The Ninth Circuit includes Arizona, California, Nevada, Oregon, Washington, Idaho, Montana, Alaska, Hawaii, Guam, and the Mariana Islands.

42.   Second Amended Complaint, *Zambrano v. INS*, Civ. No. S–88–455 EJG/EM (E.D. Cal. Aug. 26, 1988), pp. 18–19. Subsequent to August of 1988, the National Immigration Law Center and San Mateo County Legal Aid withdrew from the case and the Mexican American Legal Defense and Education foundation (MALDEF) joined CRLA as cocounsel.

43.   The only named male plaintiff was himself temporarily disabled by kidney failure, and received County General Assistance while undergoing treatment and therapy for his disability.

44.   Second Amended Complaint, pp. 3–5.

45.   Ibid.

46.   Ibid.

47.   Ibid., pp. 10–11.

48.   Ibid.

49.   Ibid., pp. 3–11.

50.   Ibid., p. 2.

51.   Ibid., p. 2.

52.   Ibid., p. 18.

53.   Ibid., p. 19.

54.   Order Granting Plaintiffs' Motions for Partial Summary Judgment, Permanent Injunction and Redefinition of Class, *Zambrano v. INS*,Civ., No. S–88–455 EJG/EM (E.D. Cal. July 31, 1989), pp. 8–19.

55.   Ibid., p. 19.

56.   First, the INS has challenged the order to review the cases of those class two members who applied for amnesty under the extended deadline. Second, the INS has contended that the courts do not have jurisdiction over this matter, arguing that the plaintiffs should be required to exhaust the administrative remedies before gaining judicial review. This jurisdictional issue has been raised by the INS in the *Zambrano* case as well as a number of other cases involving the legalization program (e.g. *Ayuda v. Thornburgh, Catholic Social Services v. Barr, LULAC v. INS, Perales v. Thornburgh*). Third, the INS has contended that plaintiffs' counsel should not have access to the names of the class one members. This information was conveyed to me in interviews with Susan Drake, Attorney at Law, National Immigration Law Center, October 1990, and with Stephen Rosenbaum, Attorney at Law, California Rural Legal Assistance, November 25, 1991.

57.   *Zambrano v.INS* 972 F2d 1122 (9th Cir. 1992).

58.   Petition for *certiorari* pending, *INS v. Zambrano* 92–849, 61 U.S.L.W. 3404 (1992).

59.   Second Amended Complaint, p. 19.

60.   Ibid.

61.   Declaration of Beth Zacovic, Legal Aid Attorney, at 2, *Zambrano v. INS* Civ. No. S–88–455 EJGEM (E.D. Cal. May 17, 1988). Ms. Zacovic obtained these statistics in an interview with a legislative analyst for Los Angeles County in April 1988; cited in Bessette, p. 301. Diane Bessette, "Getting Left Behind: The Impact of the 1986 Immigration Reform and Control Act Amnesty Program on Single Women With Children," *Hastings International and Comparative Law Review*, 13, No. 2 (Winter 1990), p. 300.

62.   Thus,there are two ways in which receipt of public assistance can be a disqualifying factor in an application for legal residency. First, under the public charge provisions, receipt

of public assistance either prior to applying for temporary residency or prior to applying for permanent residency, may be counted against an applicant. Second, under the five-year bar, a legalization applicant must not receive certain public benefits after applying for temporary residency in order to maintain his or her application in good standing.

63. Bessette, p. 303.

64. Ibid.

65. Declaration of Mavis Anderson, cited in Bessette, p. 304.

66. Ibid., p. 302.

67. The CIRRS survey revealed that undocumented women suffer many forms of worker exploitation, including not being paid for work, being paid lower wages than documented coworkers, and sexual harassment. In 1991, the U.S. Labor Department investigated abuses in the garment industry, such as runaway shops and shops which don't pay employees for months at a time. The Department estimated that 337 employees were owed $87,330 by eighteen El Paso garment industry employers. The study reported that these abuses were prevalent in the industry because its workers, mostly poor Latinas in the process of applying for legal residency, are too frightened of deportation to complain. Spokespersons for the International Ladies Garment Worker's Union in New York, and a group called La Mujer Obrera ("the Working Woman") in Texas emphasized that the abuses are related specifically to women's pending amnesty applications. Women who are applying for amnesty continue working for employers who pay late or not at all because they fear their employers will rescind the certification of steady employment necessary to complete their applications. (Belkin, 1990)

68. The first study, conducted in 1989 by the Comprehensive Adult Student Assessment System (CASAS), found that newly legalized persons used services and benefits at very low rates, "probably lower than for the [California] population as a whole." Two factors need to be considered to see how the improper INS regulations may have affected these rates: (1) the family profiles of the respondents and (2) the proper IRCA regulations regarding amnesty applicants' rights to public assistance and services. Of those who participated in the survey, approximately 43% of the families had at least one child born in the U.S. This implies that for almost half of the survey participants, at least one family member should not have been restricted by his or her immigration status, by IRCA's five-year bar, or by public charge concerns. AFDC, the program which raised complications most often in the *Zambrano* case, is restricted by the five-year bar for legalization applicants and is a cash assistance program. Therefore it is only available to the citizen children of newly legalized persons, but receipt of these benefits should only be attributed to the children themselves, not their parents. Yet fewer than one percent (0.9%) of pre-1982 families reported receiving AFDC benefits at the time of the survey.

CASAS tried to uncover reasons for these low usage rates with one question in the survey, asking: "Within the last five years, have you ever needed assistance but been reluctant to apply for it for any reason? If yes, why?" 87% of the respondents said they had not needed or had never been reluctant to apply for assistance. Given the level of confusion about the public charge provision, one can speculate that some of these respondents simply may not have wished to reveal having ever needed assistance. The second largest group of respondents (8%) reported that they had needed assistance but feared jeopardizing their amnesty applications. California Health and Welfare Agency, "A Survey of Newly Legalized Persons in California," (Sand Diego, California: Comprehensive Adult Student Assessment System, 1989), pp. 7-3 through 7-12. See also the reports of the Immigration Reform Task Force, pp. 10-11; and Hogeland and Rosen, 19.

69. The INS has failed to publicize accurate information about the amended regulations, even after the improper regulations were permanently enjoined under the 1989 order. The INS claims that it issued "clarification memos" in 1987 and 1988, but the Court rejected these claims, pointing out that they were never disseminated to the public. (Order, pp. 5-6.)

70. Second Amended Complaint, 19.

71. Diane Bessette, "Getting Left Behind: The Impact of the 1986 Immigration Reform and Control Act Amnesty Program on Single Women With Children," *Hastings International and Comparative Law Review*, 13, No. 2 (Winter 1990), p. 300.

72. Interview with Stephen Rosenbaum, Attorney at Law, California Rural Legal Assistance, November 25, 1991.

73. In this paper, I draw on socialist feminist theory, which proposes that the state regulates the labor of women through welfare policy. Internal colonialist theory proposes that the state regulates the labor of immigrants through immigration policy. This is achieved through immigration policies which allow for the importation or "recruitment" of foreign labor, and policies which deny these laborers the rights of citizens, thus rendering them more easily exploitable. For more extensive discussion of this topic, see Mario Barrera, *Race and Class in the Southwest*, especially pp. 116–122. See also supra, Note 15.

74. Frances Piven and Richard Cloward, *Regulating the Poor: The Functions of Public Welfare* (New York: Random House, Inc., 1971, pp. 123–131.

75. Abramovitz, *Regulating the Lives of Women*, pp. 313–318.

76. Evelyn Nakano Glenn defines reproductive labor to include: "activities such as purchasing household goods, preparing and serving food, laundering and repairing clothing, maintaining furnishings and appliances, socializing children, providing care and emotional support for adults, and maintaining kin and community ties." Evelyn Nakano Glenn, "From Servitude to Service Work: Historical Continuities in the Racial Division of Paid Reproductive Labor," *Signs*, 18, No. 1 (Autumn 1992).

77. Ibid.

78. "Home life is the highest and finest product of civilization. It is the great molding force of mind and or character. . . . Children of parents of worthy character, suffering from temporary misfortune and children of reasonably efficient and deserving mothers who are without the support of the normal breadwinner, should, as a rule, be kept with their parents, such aid being given as may be necessary to maintain suitable homes for the rearing of the children. . . . " Proceedings of the conference on the Care of Dependent Children, Washington, D.C., January 25, 26, 1909, p. 9, cited in Roy Lubove, *The Struggle for Social Security 1900–1935* (Cambridge, Massachusetts: Harvard University Press, 1968), p. 98.

79. Winifred Bell, *Aid to Dependent Children* (New York: Columbia University Press, 1965), p. 5.

80. Ibid., pp. 93–110, 111–123.

81. Ibid., p. 9.

82. Ibid., p. 13.

83. Sylvia A. Law, "Women, Work, Welfare and the Preservation of Patriarchy," *University of Pennsylvania Law Review* 131, No. 6, (1983), p. 1258.

84. Bell, pp. 3–19; cited in Law, p. 1257.

85. Abramowitz, p.314.

86. Law, p.1254.

87. Ibid., p. 1257.

88. U.S. Department of Health, Education and Welfare's Handbook of Public Assistance Administration, 1943; cited in Law, p. 1257.

89. As discussed previously, the "suitable home" rules, instituted ostensibly to monitor the moral fitness of mothers, enabled welfare officials to rationalize limiting the coverage of Black and "illegitimate" children. (Bell, p. 181) Thus they had much the same effect as the "employable mother" rules, necessitating that the women denied assistance for their children seek low-wage work. Abramovitz argues that these rules were used specifically to pressure Black women back into domestic work after World War II, when they tried to avoid returning to this work after being released from wartime employment. (Abramovitz, p. 326)

90. Piven and Cloward, p. 134.

91. Bell, p. 64.

92. Bell, pp. 34–5, quoting a review of a Southern field supervisor's report; citing Mary S. Larabee, "Unmarried Parenthood Under the Social Security Act," *Proceedings of the National Conference of Social Work, 1939* (New York: Columbia University Press, 1939), p. 449.

93. Abramovitz, p. 326.

94. Piven and Cloward, pp. 134–135.

95. Piven and Cloward, pp. 134–5.

96. The judgment stated that the provisions prohibiting supplementation of wages " . . . violated equal protection as imposing discrimination bearing no reasonable relation to financial needs or discriminating on [the] basis of source of income." [*Anderson v. Burson,* 300 F. Supp. 401 (1968), 401.] Thus, the decision did not address the charge that the discrimination was racially based, as the plaintiffs suggested.

97. Piven & Cloward, p. 308.

98. *Anderson v. Burson,* 300 F. Supp. 401 (1968), 403.

99. Wendy Sarvasy, "Reagan and Low-Income Mothers: A Feminist Recasting of the Debate," in M.K Brown, eds., *Remaking the Welfare State: Retrenchment and Social Policy in America and Europe* (Philadelphia: Temple University Press, 1988), pp. 253–276, especially 269. See also: Roy Lubove, p. 102 and Susan Tiffin, *In Whose Best Interest? Child Welfare Reform in the Progressive Era* (Westport, Conn: Greenwood Press, 1982), p. 125.

100. Carol Stack and Linda Burton, "Kinscripts: Reflections on Family, Generation, and Culture," in E. Nakano Glenn, G. Chang, and L. Rennie Forcey, eds., *Mothering: Ideology, Experience, and Agency* (New York: Routledge, 1993).

101. Denise Segura, "Working at Motherhood: Chicana and Mexican Immigrant Mothers and Employment," in E. Nakano Glenn, G. Chang, and L. Rennie Forcey, eds., *Mothering: Ideology, Experience, and Agency* (New York: Routledge, 1993).

102. Of course, access to citizenship and to public benefits is not all that is required to improve conditions for these women. The typical wage for the work undocumented women are concentrated in, such as child care, is not an adequate family wage, even with supplementation by public assistance. Thus, in addition to the opportunity to gain legal status, fair wages and worker benefits and protections should be extended to undocumented women, particularly private household workers, whose employers are difficult to monitor.

Chapter 13

RACE AND "VALUE": BLACK AND WHITE ILLEGITIMATE BABIES, 1945–1965

Rickie Solinger

There are two histories of single pregnancy in the post-World War II era, one for Black women and one for white. But for girls and women of both races, being single and pregnant has revealed that, either publicly or privately, their fertility can become a weapon used by others to keep such females vulnerable, defenseless, dependent and, without male protection, in danger. One aspect of single pregnancy that sharply and powerfully illustrates both the common vulnerability of unwed mothers and the racially distinct treatment they have received is the question of what an unmarried girl or woman can or will do with her illegitimate child.

Throughout my study of unwed pregnancy in the pre-*Roe v. Wade* era,[1] racially distinct ideas about the "value" of the illegitimate baby surface again and again as central to an unmarried mother's fate. In short, after World War II, the white bastard child was no longer the child nobody wanted. The Black illegitimate baby became the child white politicians and taxpayers loved to hate. The central argument of this essay is that the "value" of illegitimate babies has been quite different in different historical eras, and that in the United States during the mid-twentieth century, the emergence of racially specific attitudes toward illegitimate babies, including ideas about what to do with them, fundamentally shaped the experiences of single mothers.

Social, cultural, and economic imperatives converged in the postwar era in such a way as to sanction very narrow and rigid, but different, options for Black and white unwed mothers, no matter what their personal preferences. Black single mothers were expected to keep their babies, as most unwed mothers, Black and white, had done throughout the history of the United States. Unmarried white mothers, for the first time in this country's history, were urged to put their babies up for adoption. These racially specific prescriptions exacerbated racism and racial antagonism in postwar America, and have influenced the politics of female fertility into our own time.

During the Progressive era of the late nineteenth and early twentieth centuries up through the 1930s, social commentators and social service professionals typically considered an illegitimate baby a "child of sin," the product of a mentally deficient mother.[2] As such, this child was tainted and undesirable. The girl or woman, Black or white, who gave birth to it was expected by family, by the community, and by the state to bring it up. Commentators assumed that others rarely wanted a child who stood to inherit the sinful character—the mental and moral weaknesses—of its parent. Before World War II, state laws and institutional regulations supported this mandate, not so much because there were others vying for the babies, but so as to ensure that the mothers would not abandon the infants. State legislators in Minnesota and elsewhere required mothers seeking care in maternity homes to breast-feed their babies for three months and more, long enough to establish unseverable bonds between infant and mother.[3]

Prewar experts stressed that the biology of illegitimacy stamped the baby permanently with marks of mental and moral deficiency, and affirmed that moral conditions were embedded in and revealed by these biological events.[4] Likewise, the unwed mother's pregnancy both revealed her innate biological and moral shortcomings, and condemned her, through the illicit conception and birth, to carry the permanent stain of biological and moral ruin. The biological experience she underwent was tied to her moral status in a fixed, direct, and inexorable relationship. Equally important, her motherhood was immutable. While the deficiencies, the stain, and her ruination violated her biological integrity, as well as her social and moral standing in the community, the unwed mother's maternal relation to the child was not compromised. That was also fixed directly and inexorably by the biological facts of conception and birth.

These attitudes reflected, in part, the importance of bridal virginity and marital conception in mainstream American culture. They also reflected early twentieth-century ideas among moral and medical authorities regarding the strong link between physical, mental, and moral degeneracy and the degeneracy of sex. Until the 1940s, illegitimacy usually carried one meaning; cultural, racial, or psychological determinants which admitted group or individual variability were not sought to explain its occurrence. In this prewar period, social, religious, and educational leaders rarely called for the rehabilitation of unwed mothers or suggested that there were steps they could take to restore their marriageability and their place in the community. What was lost could not be regained; what was acquired could not be cast off. Consequently, most unwed mothers did not have choices to make in that era about the disposition of the bastard child.

WHITE UNWED MOTHERS AND THEIR BABIES: THE POSTWAR ADOPTION MANDATE

After the war, state-imposed breast-feeding regulations and institutional policies asserting the immutability of the white unwed mother's relationship to her illegitimate baby became harder to sustain in the face of a complex and changing set of social conditions. First, the demographic facts of single pregnancy were changing. White birth control and abortion remained illegal and hard to obtain. More girls and women were participating in nonmarital, heterosexual intercourse; thus more of them became pregnant and carried babies to term.[5] As nonmarital sex and pregnancy became more common (and then very common during the later postwar period), it became increasingly difficult to sequester, punish, and insist on the permanent ruination of ever larger numbers of girls and women. This was particularly the case since many of these single pregnant females were members of the growing proportion of the population that considered itself middle class. As a result, it became increasingly difficult for parents and the new service professionals, themselves members of the middle class, to sanction treating "our daughters" as permanently ruined.

In addition, a strain of postwar optimism emerged that rejected the view that the individual, white, unwed mother was at the mercy of harmful environmental or other forces having the power to determine her fate. The modern expert offered the alternative claim that illegitimacy reflected an emotional and psychological, not environmental or biological disorder. It was, in general, a symptom of individual, treatable neuroses. Reliance on the psychological explanation redeemed both American society and the individual female. Moreover, by moving the governing imperative from the body (biology) to the mind (psychology), all of the fixed relationships previously defining white illegitimacy became mutable, indeterminate, even deniable.

Psychological explanations transformed the white unwed mother from a genetically tainted unfortunate into a maladjusted woman who could be cured. While there was no solvent that could remove the biological stain of illegitimacy, the neuroses that fostered illegitimacy could respond to treatment. The white out-of-wedlock child, therefore, was no longer a flawed by-product of innate immorality and low intelligence.[6] The child's innocence was restored and its adoptability established. At the same time, psychologists argued that white unwed mothers, despite their deviant behavior, could be rehabilitated, and that a successful cure rested in large measure on the relinquishment of the child.[7] The white unwed mother no longer had an immutable relationship to her baby.

In postwar America, the social conditions of motherhood, along with notions about the psychological status of the unwed mother, became more important than biology in defining white motherhood. Specifically, for the first time, it took more than a baby to make a white girl or woman into a mother. Without a preceding marriage, a white female could not achieve true motherhood. Leontine Young, the prominent authority on social casework theory in the area of unwed mothers, cautioned in 1954, "The caseworker has to clarify for herself the differences between the feelings of the normal [married] woman for her baby and the fantasy use of the child by the neurotic unmarried mother."[8] Accepting these new imperatives, social authorities insisted on the centrality of the male to female adult roles, thereby offsetting postwar concerns that women were aggressively undermining male prerogatives in the United States. Experts explained that the unwed mother who came to terms with the baby's existence, symbolically or concretely, and relinquished the child, enhanced her ability to "function [in the future] as a healthy wife and mother."[9]

Release from the biological imperative represented a major reform in the treatment of the many white unwed mothers who desperately desired a way out of trouble, a way to undo their life-changing mistake. The rising rate and numbers of white single pregnancy, particularly among unmarried, middle-class women, would have created an ever larger number of ruined girls and women if unwed mothers continued to have no option but to keep their illegitimate children. In a postwar society that increasingly privileged couples, marriage, children, families, and conformity, this prospect would not have been a happy one. The option of placing an illegitimate child for adoption became, in a sense, an unplanned but fortuitous safety valve for thousands of white girls and women who became unwed mothers but—thanks to the sanctioning of adoption—could go on to become properly married wives and mothers soon thereafter.

This arrangement could only work if there was a sizable population of white couples who wanted to adopt infants, and who didn't mind if the babies had been born to unwed mothers. In the postwar period, this condition was met in part because the postwar family imperative put new pressures on infertile couples who in the past would have remained childless. A social scientist in the mid-1950s referred to illegitimate babies as "the silver lining in a dark cloud":

> Over one in ten of all marriages are involuntarily childless. Since most of these couples desire to adopt a baby, illegitimacy is a blessing to [them]. Curiously, from their standpoint there are not enough illegitimate births

because most of these couples must wait one or two or three years in order to adopt a baby, and some are never able to have one because there is not enough for all who want them.[10]

In the early 1950s a leading social work theorist, using what was becoming a popular metaphor, worried about "the tendency growing out of the demand for babies to regard unmarried mothers as breeding machines . . . [by people intent] upon securing babies for quick adoptions."[11]

Through adoption, then, the unwed mother could put the mistake— both the baby *qua* baby, and the proof of nonmarital sexual experience— behind her. Her parents were not stuck with a ruined daughter and a bastard grandchild for life. And the baby could be brought up in a normative family, by a couple prejudged to possess all the attributes and resources necessary for successful parenthood.

Some unmarried pregnant girls considered abortion the best way to efface their mistake, but the possibility in the mid-1950s of getting a safe, legal, hospital abortion was slim, in fact, slimmer than it had been in the prewar decades. If a girl or woman knew about hospital abortions, she might appeal to a hospital abortion committee, a (male) panel of the director of obstetrics/gynecology, and the chiefs of medicine, surgery, neuropsychiatry and pediatrics. In hospitals, including Mt. Sinai in New York, which set up an abortion committee in 1952, the panel of doctors met once a week and considered cases of women who could bring letters from two specialists diagnosing them as psychologically impaired and unfit to be mothers.[12]

By the early 1950s, doctors claimed that new procedures and medications had eliminated the need for almost all medically indicated abortions.[13] That left only psychiatric grounds, which might have seemed promising for girls and women desperate not to have a child.[14] After all, psychiatric explanations were in vogue, and white unwed mothers were categorically diagnosed as deeply neurotic, or worse. There was, however, a catch. These abortion committees had been set up to begin with because their very existence was meant to reduce requests for "therapeutic" abortions, which they did.[15] It was, in fact, a matter of pride and competition among hospitals to have the highest ratio of births to abortions on record.[16] But even though psychiatric illness was the only remaining acceptable basis for request, many doctors did not believe in these grounds. A professor of obstetrics in a large university hospital said, "We haven't done a therapeutic abortion for psychiatric reasons in ten years. . . . We don't recognize psychiatric indications."[17] So an unwed pregnant girl or woman could be diagnosed and certified as disturbed, probably at considerable cost, but she couldn't convince the panel that she was sick enough. The committee may have, in fact, agreed with the outside specialists that the abortion petitioner was psychotic, but the panel often claimed the problem was temporary, with sanity recoverable upon delivery.[18]

The doctors were apparently not concerned with questions about when life begins. They were very concerned with what they took to be their responsibility to protect and preserve the links between femininity, maternity, and marriage. One doctor spoke for many of his colleagues when he complained of the "clever, scheming women, simply trying to hoodwink the psychiatrist and obstetrician" in their appeals for permission for abortions.[19] The mere request, in fact, was taken, according to another doctor, "as proof [of the petitioner's] inability and failure to live through the destiny of being a woman."[20] If such permission were granted, one claimed, the woman "will become an unpleasant person to live with and possibly lose her glamour as a wife. She will gradually lose conviction in playing a female role."[21] An angry committee member, refusing to grant permission to one woman, asserted, "Now that she has had her fun, she wants us to launder her dirty underwear. From my standpoint, she can sweat this one out."[22]

For many doctors, however, condemning the petitioner to sweat it out was not sufficient punishment. In the mid-1950s, in Maryland, a doctor would almost never agree to perform a therapeutic abortion unless he sterilized the woman at the same time.[23] The records of a large, Midwestern, general hospital showed that between 1941 and 1950, seventy-five percent of the abortions performed there were accompanied by sterilization.[24] The bottom line was that, if you were single and pregnant (and without rich or influential parents who might, for example, make a significant philanthropic gesture to the hospital), your chances with the abortion committee were pretty bleak. Thousands of unhappily pregnant women each year got illegal abortions, but for thousands of others, financially, morally, or otherwise unable to arrange for the operation, adoption seemed their only choice.

Service agencies, however, found the task of implementing the adoption mandate complicated. Many who worked with white unwed mothers in maternity homes, adoption agencies, or public welfare offices in this period had to braid unmatched strands into a coherent plan. Agency workers were deeply uneasy about separating babies from the one individual who until recently had been historically and culturally designated as best suited, no matter what her marital status, to care for her own baby. In addition, the community response to out-of-wedlock pregnancy and maternity in the United States had historically been punitive.[25] Keeping mother and child together was simultaneously in the child's best interest and the earned wages of sin for the unwed mother. Until the postwar era, most social workers had trained and practiced in this tradition.[26]

After World War II, social workers struggled to discard the two most basic assumptions that had previously guided their work with white unwed mothers. These girls and women were no longer considered the best mothers for their babies. And they would no longer be expected to pay for their illicit sexual experience and illegitimate pregnancy by living as ruined women and outcast mothers of bastard children. Social workers were now to offer them a plan which would protect them from lasting stigma and rehabilitate them for normative female roles. The psychological literature supporting definitions of unwed mothers as not-mothers, the interest of many white couples in obtaining newborn babies, and postwar concepts of family helped social workers accept new ideas about the disposition of illegitimate white babies.

After the war, in all parts of the country, public agencies, national service organizations, and maternity homes allocated the resources and developed techniques for separating mother and child. Services became increasingly so streamlined that in many maternity homes, such as the Florence Crittenton Home in Houston, "Babies [went] directly from the hospital to children's [adoption] agencies."[27] Indeed, public and private agencies were functioning in an environment in which the separation of single mother and child was becoming the norm. In Minnesota, for example, in 1925 there were two hundred such separations; in 1949, one thousand; between 1949 and 1955, approximately seventeen hundred each year. Nationally, by 1955, ninety thousand babies born out of wedlock were being placed for adoption, an eighty percent increase since 1944.[28]

To meet the demand and to justify their own existence, agencies and individual operators not infrequently resorted to questionable tactics, including selling babies for profit. When the federal government undertook to investigate widespread coercive and profit-oriented adoption practices in the United States in the 1950s, the task was assigned to Senator Estes Kefauver's Subcommittee to Investigate Juvenile Delinquency. This committee was charged with redressing the problem of adoption for profit and assuring the "suitability of the home" for adoptable children, a criterion which could not, by definition, be met in homes headed by unmarried mothers.[29] While illegitimate pregnancy and babies had, in the past, been a private matter handled by family members, perhaps assisted by charity workers, by mid-century, these issues had become public concerns and public business.

The Kefauver committee and the organizations and individuals it investigated defined white unmarried mothers out of their motherhood. If not by law, then *de facto*, they were not parents. This judgment was in line with and supported various forms of state control over single, pregnant girls and women, and those who might become pregnant, including, of course, the state's formal and informal proscriptions against birth control for unmarried girls and women, its denial of access to safe, legal abortion, and its tolerance in many places of unsafe, illegal abortions. The state determined what types of agencies and individuals an unmarried mother could deal with in planning for her child, and either strongly suggested or legislated which ones were "morally wrong." These state prerogatives allowed some agencies and individuals to abuse and exploit childbearing, single, white women.

A very articulate, eighteen-year-old, unmarried mother from Minnesota wrote to her governor in August, 1950, illustrating how some public agencies took direct action to separate white babies from their mothers, even against the mother's will. She said that a welfare worker in her city told her she could not keep her baby, "that the baby should be brought up by both a mother and a father." Having gotten no satisfaction, she wrote in frustration and anger to President Truman:

> With tears in my eyes and sorrow in my heart I'm trying to defend the rights and privileges which every citizen in the United States is supposed to enjoy under our Constitution [but are] denied me and my baby.... The Welfare Department refuses to give me my baby without sufficient cause or explanation.... I have never done any wrong and just because I had a baby under such circumstances the welfare agency has no right to condemn me and to demand my child be placed [for adoption].[30]

A year earlier, a young man living in Sterling, Colorado wrote to the Children's Bureau about a similar case. In this situation, a young man and a young deaf woman had conceived a baby out of wedlock, but planned to marry. When the man went to the Denver Welfare Department for assistance a few days before the baby was born, he found that the baby had already been targeted for adoption.

This case, in particular, demonstrates a couple of key assumptions underlying the behavior of some agency workers in matters of out-of-wedlock adoptions. The young mother was deaf. As a handicapped person and an unmarried girl, her maternity, as well as her child, was considered illegitimate, and could be rightfully terminated by the authorities. Physically defective women had curtailed rights as mothers, just as physically defective illegitimate babies had diminished opportunities to join the middle class. This case also suggests the very important notion that white babies were so valuable because in postwar America, they were born not only untainted but also *unclassed*. A poor, "white trash" teenager could have a white baby in Appalachia; it could be adopted by an upper-middle-class couple in Westport, Connecticut, and the baby would, in that transaction, become upper-middle-class also.

Finally, this case illustrates that agency workers believed that a successful separation often depended on an early and very quick transaction. This was noticed by contemporaries, including the authors of a state-certified report on adoption in Cook County, Illinois that warned about the problems that arose when "mothers come into court service division to sign a consent either on the day they are released from the hospital, or shortly thereafter [and] are physically and emotionally upset to the extent that they are not capable of making rational decisions."[31]

Courts also facilitated adoption abuse. A chief probation officer in the Richmond County, Alabama, Juvenile Court spent a great deal of her time finding and "freeing" white babies for adoption, using her position to legitimize these activities. One unwed mother told of her encounter with the officer, a Miss Hamilton. She said:

> Several hours after delivery [Miss Hamilton] informed me that my baby had been born dead. She told me that if I signed a paper she had, no one, my family or friends, would know about the situation, and that everything would be cleared up easily. She described the paper as being a consent authorizing the burial of the child. . . . I signed the paper without really looking at it, as I was in a very distressed and confused condition at the time.

This young woman went on to say that, "Two years later I was shocked to receive in the mail adoption papers from the Welfare Department in California since I was under the impression that the child was deceased."[32]

Illegalities and abuse existed in some mainstream institutions, but a great many of the worst abuses were committed by individual baby brokers—lawyers, doctors and nonprofessionals cashing in on the misfortune of unwed mothers. In postwar, consumerist America, institutions promoted services and attitudes to protect the out-of-wedlock child from market-driven deals, and to see that it was well placed. On the other hand, these same institutions were themselves behaving in market-oriented ways as they promoted a specific, socially beneficial product: the two-parent/two-plus child family. This double message justified the baby brokers' commoditylike treatment of unwed mothers and their babies. Charlton G. Blair, a lawyer who handled between thirty and sixty adoptions a year in the late 1950s, justified his operation by denying he ever "paid one red cent" to a prospective mother of an illegitimate child to persuade her to part with the baby. But in suggesting why the adopting parents were willing to pay up to fifteen hundred dollars for a child, which included the lawyer's seven hundred fifty-dollar fee, Blair defined his sense of the transaction very clearly: "If they're willing to pay three thousand dollars for an automobile these days, I don't see why they can't pay this much for a child."[33] A baby broker in Texarkana, Texas boasted to an employee that she had sold 993 illegitimate babies throughout the United States and that she wanted to make it one thousand before she died.[34]

A case which dramatically captures the plight of poor, white, unwed mothers was presented at the Kefauver hearings by Mary Grice, an investigative reporter for the *Wichita Beacon*. Grice testified about a woman, "Mrs. T.," who had been in the adoption business since 1951 or 1952. "Mrs. T." warehoused unwed, pregnant girls in the basement of her home. "She would have them on cots for prospective adoptive parents [who] would come in and she would take them downstairs, and she would point to the girls and say, 'Point out the girl that you want to be the mother of your child.' " Grice's investigation revealed that "Mrs. T." kept on average seven unmarried mothers in her basement at a time, and that she would oversee a number of the deliveries herself in the basement. According to Grice, between one hundred and fifty and one hundred and sixty-four adoptions each year of this sort were taking place in Sedgwick County, Kansas. "Mrs. T." often collaborated with Grace Schauner, a Wichita abortionist. Unmarried pregnant girls and women would first see Schauner, and if they decided not to have an abortion, they would be referred to "Mrs. T." who would "care for them and sell their infants after birth."[35]

"Mrs. T's" girls were the ones whose class, gender, and race combined to render them most vulnerable. Because they were poor, they did not have the information or other resources to resist baby-market operators. Because they were female (specifically, white females), their socially mandated shame precluded self-protection and motherhood. Because they were white, their babies had value. This combination of poverty, race and gender—in a context which defined white unwed mothers as not-mothers, and defined their babies as valuable—put some white, unwed mothers in a position of extreme vulnerability.

Again, there is no question that for many white unwed mothers, the opportunity to place their babies independently meant that they could get exactly what they needed when they needed it: money to live on, shelter, medical care, and assurances about the placement of the baby, all with no questions asked. These girls and women were often spared the delays, the layers of authority, the invasions of privacy, the permanent black mark engraved in the files of the welfare department, and they were spared the pressure to reveal the father's name, all of which characterized the bureaucratic agency approach.[36] Their experience demonstrated how difficult it was for institutions to perform simultaneously as agents of social control and as sources of humanitarian assistance for the needy and vulnerable.

The stories of unwed mothers abused by the baby market reveal how class, gender, and (white) race together created the possibilities to use these girls and women for profit. Cultural constructions of female sexuality and maternity in the postwar decades, and the sanctions against sexual and maternal nonconformity, sent unwed mothers with few resources into the anonymous marketplace which offered, simultaneously, protection and danger.

An intruder in the courtroom in Miami, Florida, where a section of the Kefauver hearings was held in November, 1955, expressed the frustration of some girls and women who felt they had lost control over the disposition of their illegitimate children. This woman stood up, unbidden, and lectured the men before her in a loud voice. She said,

> Excuse me. I am not leaving no court. . . . You have to carry these children nine months and then you have them taken away by the Catholic Charities, and then they throw you out and drag you all over the street. . . . I'm no drunk, I'm no whore. . . . I gave birth to two children and had them taken away from me. I don't sleep nights thinking about my children. What do you people care? Don't take my picture. You people have no feelings at all. That man [a judge testifying that there are plenty of services available for unwed mothers] is sitting there and lying—lying. These people just take other people's children away from them. All that he has said is a lie. My baby was born . . . and I haven't seen it since. . . . How would you like it? Year after year you have to go to the people . . . and ask them why you can't have your children.[37]

Clark Vincent, a sociologist who closely followed the treatment of white, unwed mothers in this era, offered the following vision of a world in the near future where the state would have unrestrained authority to determine who is a mother.

> If the demand for adoptable infants continues to exceed the supply; if more definitive research . . . substantiates that the majority of unwed mothers who keep their children lack the potential for "good motherhood"; and if there continues to be an emphasis through laws and courts on the "rights of the child" superseding the "rights of the parents"; then it is quite probable that in the near future unwed mothers will be "punished" by having their children taken away from them at birth. Such a policy would not be enacted nor labeled overtly as "punishment." Rather it would be implemented under such pressures and labels as "scientific finding," "the best interests of the child," "rehabilitation goals for the unwed mother," and the "stability of the family and society."[38]

THE BLACK UNWED MOTHER AND HER CHILD: A TAXPAYERS' ISSUE

In postwar America, there was only one public intention for white, unwed mothers and their babies: separate them. Toward Black, single mothers and their babies, however, there were three broadly different public attitudes.[39] One attitude, often held by middle-of-the-road politicians, social service administrators, and practitioners, maintained that Blacks had babies out of wedlock because they were Negro, because they were ex-Africans and ex-slaves, irresponsible and immoral, but baby-loving. According to this attitude, the state and its institutions and agencies could essentially ignore breeding patterns, since Blacks would take care of their children themselves. And if Blacks did not, they were responsible for their own mess. Adopting Daniel Moynihan's famous phrase from this period, I call this public attitude toward Black illegitimacy *benign neglect*.

A second response to Black mothers and babies was *punitive*. The conservative, racist politicians who championed this position argued simply that the mothers were bad and should be punished. The babies were expendable because they were expensive and undesirable as citizens. Public policies could and should be used to punish Black unmarried mothers and their children in the form of legislation enabling states to cut them off from welfare benefits, and to sterilize or incarcerate "illegitimate mothers."[40]

I label the third way of seeing this group *benevolent reformist*. Employees at the United States Children's Bureau and many in the social work community who took this position maintained that Black girls and women who had children out of wedlock were just like whites who did the same. Both groups of females were equally disturbed and equally in need of help, particularly in need of social casework. Regarding the baby, benevolent reformers held that Black, unwed mothers should be accorded every opportunity to place the infant for adoption, just like whites.

Despite these different attitudes toward Black women and their babies, proponents of all three shared a great deal. First, they shared the belief that the Black, illegitimate baby was the product of pathology. This was the case whether it was a pathology grounded in race, as it was for the benign neglecters and the punishers, or in gender, as it was for the benevolent reformers. Second, all commentators agreed that the baby's existence justified a negative moral judgment about the mother and the mother-and-baby dyad. The Black illegitimate infant was proof of its mother's moral incapacities; its illegitimacy suggested its own probable tendencies toward depravity. Because of the eager market for white babies, this group was cleared of the charge of inherited moral taint, while Black babies were not. Indeed, proponents of each of the three perspectives agreed that the unwed, Black mother must, in almost every case, keep her baby. Where they differed was in explaining why this was so. The different answers reflected different strains of racism and carried quite different implications for public policies and practices regarding the Black, unmarried mother and her child.

The benign neglecters began to articulate their position at about the same time that the psychologists provided new explanations for white, single pregnancy. In tandem, these developments set Black and white, unwed mothers in different universes of cause and effect. According to these "experts," Black and white single mothers were different from each other in several ways. When Black, single girls and women had intercourse, it was a sexual, not a psychological act, and Black mothers had "natural affection" for their children, whatever their birth status. The white, unwed mother had only neurotic feelings for her out-of-wedlock child. The "unrestrained sexuality" of Black women, and their capacity to love the resulting illegitimate children, were perceived as inbred traits, and unchangeable parts of Black culture.

Thus, by becoming mothers, even unwed mothers, Black women were simply doing what came naturally. There was no reason for social service workers or policymakers to interfere. It was also important in this regard that the operative concept of "culture" excised considerations of environment. Environment was not a primary factor in shaping female sexual behavior or the mother's relationship to her illegitimate baby. These were determined by "culture," an essentially biological construct. Therefore, since professionals could only have an impact on the immediate situation—and could not penetrate or rearrange Black "culture," it was doubly futile to consider interfering. The absence of services for these women and their children was justified in this way. Issues regarding Blacks and adoption were quickly dismissed by those who counselled neglect. Agencies claimed that Blacks didn't want to part with their babies, and, just as important, Black couples didn't want to adopt children.[41]

White policymakers and service providers often pointed to the Black grandmothers—willing, able, loving, and present—to justify their contentions that the Black family would take care of its own, and that no additional services were necessary. Yet when grandmothers rendered such service, policymakers labelled them "matriarchs" and blamed them for "faulty personality growth and for maladaptive functioning in children."[42] The mother was similarly placed in a double bind. She was denied services because she was black, an alleged cultural rather than a racial distinction, and then she was held responsible for the personal and social consequences.[43] The social service system was, in this way, excused from responsibility or obligation to Black, unwed mothers.

The punishers, both Southern Dixiecrats and Northern racists, drew in part on the "cultural" argument to target both the unwed mother and her baby. They held that Black culture was inherited, and that the baby would likely be as great a social liability as its mother. Moreover, they claimed that for a poor, Black woman to have a baby was an act of selfishness, as well as of pathology, and deserved punishment.[44] Once the public came to believe that Black illegitimacy was not an innocuous social fact, but carried a direct and heavy cost to white taxpayers, many whites sanctioned their political representatives to target Black, unwed mothers and their babies for attack.[45]

The willingness to attack was expressed, in part, by a special set of tropes which drew on the language and concepts of the marketplace. The "value" assigned to the illegitimate child-as-commodity became useful in classifying the violation of the Black, unwed mother in a consumer society. Repeatedly, Black, unmarried mothers were construed as "women whose business is having illegitimate children."[46] This illicit "occupation" was portrayed as violating basic consumerist principles, including good value in exchange for a good price, for a product which, in general, benefits society. Black, unmarried mothers, in contrast, were said to offer bad value (Black babies) at a high price (taxpayer-supported welfare grants) to the detriment of society, demographically and economically. The behavior of these women—most of whom did not receive Aid to Dependent Children grants for their illegitimate children[47]—was construed as meeting only the consumerist principle that everything can, potentially, be a commodity. These women were accused of treating their reproductive capacities and their children as commodities, with assigned monetary values. From this perspective, Black, unmarried mothers were portrayed as "economic women," making calculated decisions for personal, financial gain.[48]

The precise economic principle most grossly violated by these women was, according to many, that they got something (ADC) for nothing (another Black baby); they were cheating the public with a bad sell. The fact that it was, overwhelmingly, a buyers' market for Black babies "proved" the valuelessness of these children, despite their expense to the taxpaying public.[49] White babies entered a healthy sellers' market, with up to ten couples competing for every one adoptable infant.[50]

Spokespeople for this point of view believed that Black, unmarried mothers should pay dearly for the bad bargain they foisted on society, especially on white taxpayers. But many felt that rather than paying for their sins, Black women were being paid, by ADC grants, an exchange which encouraged additional sexual and fiscal irresponsibility.[51] Thus, society was justified in punishing Black, unwed mothers. In addition, the Black, unmarried woman, allegedly willing to trade on her reproductive function, willing to use her body and her child so cheaply, earned the state's equal willingness to regard her childbearing capacity cheaply, and take it away, for example, by sterilization legislation.

The ironic truth was that ADC benefits were such inadequate support (and employment and child care opportunities so meager or nonexistent) that government policies had the effect of causing, not responding to, the economic calculations a woman made that might lead to pregnancy. The average welfare payment per child, per month, was $27.29 with monthly averages less than half that amount in most Southern states.[52] The following encounter illustrates the relationship between illegitimacy and economics, from one woman's point of view.

> When the case analyst visited the family, the little girl came in with a new dress and shoes. The mother explained that it was the last day of school and the child had begged for new clothes like the other children had. She got them, but the mother's comment was, "I hope that dress does not cause me another baby."[53]

This mother's economic and sexual calculations were rooted in poverty and maternal concern, not in some desire to multiply inadequate stipends through additional pregnancies.

In Florida, the assumptions of welfare officials and legislators concerning the "business" intentions of Black, unwed mothers received a jolt in the early 1960s, when mothers withdrew from the ADC program rather than risk having their children taken away from them and sent, for example, to the homes of married relatives, under the state's "suitable home" law. This law aimed to punish illegitimate mothers who "persisted" in having babies, while saving taxpayers' money by reducing welfare rolls. "At least some [social workers] anticipated that among Negro families, the 'extended family pattern' would ease the pain of separation and rarely generate resistance to placement. But as one mother said, 'People give away puppies and kittens, but they don't give away their children.' "[54] In the face of the persistence of a slave owners' mentality among Florida's welfare professionals and politicians, and the commodization of children this view supported, Black women demonstrated their adherence to a value system which placed their children and their bodies outside of the economic nexus, as far as the government and the welfare system were concerned.[55]

The public's interest in casting Black, unwed mothers and their babies as consumer violators was reflected in opinion polls that suggested the American public wanted to withhold federal support, or food money, from illegitimate, Black babies.[56] Among dissenters were people who believed it was wrong "to deny food to children because of the sins of the parents."[57] Both groups, however, fell into a trap set by conservative politicians who found it politically profitable to associate Black illegitimacy in their constituent's minds with the rising costs of public welfare grants. The Aid to Dependent Children caseload increased in the postwar period for many reasons, including the basic increase in numbers of children and families, and the increase in households headed by women because of divorce, separation, desertion, *and* illegitimacy. Between 1953 and 1959, the number of families headed by women rose 12.8 percent, while the number of families rose only 8.3 percent.[58] While white sentiment was being whipped up to support punitive measures against Black "subsidized immorality,"[59] only about sixteen percent of nonwhite, unwed mothers were receiving ADC grants.[60] Adoption, which was not an option for most Blacks, was the most important factor in removing white children from would-be ADC families. Of unwed, white mothers who kept their children, thirty percent, or nearly twice as large a percentage as Blacks, were receiving Aid to Dependent Children grants in 1959.[61] Yet in the minds of large segments of the white public, Black, unwed mothers were being paid, in welfare coin, to have children. The "suitable home" laws which were originally designed, it was claimed, to protect the interests of children, were not instrumental in stopping those payments. The children in question represented low value to politicians leading the attacks on welfare costs. These were politicians who had no qualms about using Black, illegitimate children as pawns in their attempt to squash Black "disobedience" via morals charges.[62]

Led by Annie Lee Davis, a Black social worker at the United States Children's Bureau, many members of the social work community worked unceasingly to convert benign neglecters and punishers into benevolent reformers. Davis was a committed integrationist. She was dedicated to convincing the white social service establishment that Black, unmarried mothers needed and deserved the same services as their white counterparts. In 1948, Davis addressed this message to her colleagues: "Within minority groups, unmarried mothers suffer guilt and shame as in the majority group." She added, "I know there are those who will challenge this statement," but, she insisted, "In the process of adopting the cultural traits of the dominant group in America all groups are striving to be American."[63]

Davis insisted white public officials and social workers be brought to believe that Black, unwed mothers were psychologically and morally the equals of whites. Only then would Blacks be eligible for the best available services. Ironically, Davis believed that a key element of proof was to establish that Blacks were as interested in adoptive placements for their illegitimate babies as whites were urged to be. Her task was to convince her colleagues that lack of alternative options alone created the custom and the necessity that Blacks kept their illegitimate children.

Benevolent reformers typically took the position that it was unacceptable and potentially racist to assume that Blacks did not want every opportunity that whites had, including adoption. But it was extremely difficult for the reformers to suggest that some Black, single mothers wanted their children, and others did not. It was not simply unwed mothers and their babies at issue, it was the race. For the reformers, constructing an equivalency between Black and white unmarried mothers was the most promising and practical route to social services and social justice.

But even if a Black, single mother did consider placing her child for adoption, she knew that the likelihood that the agency would expeditiously approve a couple as adoptive parents was slim.[64] While a white, unwed mother could expect a rapid placement, the Black one knew that her child would be forced, in part because of agency practices, to spend months in foster homes or institutions before placement, if that was ever achieved. For example, adoption agencies frequently rejected Blacks who applied for babies, claiming they did not meet the agency's standards for adoptive parents. They also neglected to work with schools and hospitals in contact with Black, unwed mothers to improve referral services between these institutions and the agencies, because they feared recruiting Black babies when there might not be homes for them. In these ways the organizations that reformers depended on to provide services for Black, unwed mothers equal to those for whites, and to make it more possible for society to perceive these Blacks in the same way as they saw whites, did not hold up their end. The reformers had their integrationist vision, but the institutions of society would not cooperate, even when some Black, unwed mothers did.

In fact, the evidence from postwar Black communities suggests that the Black, unwed mother accepted responsibility for her baby as a matter of course,[65] even when she was sorry to have gotten pregnant.[66] A study in the mid-1960s cautioned the social work profession: "Social work wisdom is that Negroes keep because there is no place to give the baby up, but the study showed . . . that Negroes did not favor adoption, opportunities or their absence notwithstanding." Findings showed that the issue of disposition of the child was the only one that consistently yielded a difference between Black and white respondents, no matter whether they were the unwed mother, her parents, or professional staff. In fact, the Blacks revealed their determination to keep mother and child together and the whites their determination to effect separation, "no matter how [the investigator] varied the content of the questions."[67]

In the same period in Cincinnati, several researchers captured the comments of the mothers themselves. Some girls and women focused on the needs of the baby. One typical respondent claimed, "An innocent child should not be denied his mother's love." Joyce Ladner's subjects in another Midwestern city considered the illegitimate baby as "a child who had the right to be cared for and reared in the community of his parents without stigmatization."[68] Others in the Cincinnati study focused on the strength of their own needs, "I'd grieve myself to death if I let my baby go." A few predicted they would have had nervous breakdowns if they hadn't been allowed to keep their babies. A representative outlook drew on the sanctified status of motherhood: "The Lord suffered for you to have a baby. He will suffer for you to get food for the baby." Still others expressed themselves in forward-looking, practical terms, "You were less apt to have regrets if you kept the baby than if you let him go."[69]

For many Black, unwed mothers, the reasons to keep a baby were simply grounded in an immutable moral code of maternal responsibility. A young, Black woman said, "Giving a child away is not the sort of thing a good person would do"; and a teenager asserted, "My parents wouldn't let me give up the baby for adoption."[70] Two Black women in Philadelphia subscribed to this morality. One said:

> I sure don't think much of giving babies up for adoption. The mother mightn't be able to give it the finest and best in the world, but she could find a way like I did. My mother had thirteen heads and it was during the Depression. . . . *She* didn't give us away.

The other commented, "If you have a child, bring it up. Take the responsibility. Hard or easy, it's yours."[71]

The central question for all of these Black, single mothers was how good a mother you were, not whether you were legally married.[72] The overriding stimulus in structuring the personal decisions of these girls and women was a "powerful drive toward family unity, even if the family is not the socially approved one of father, mother and children."[73] In a study of thirty poor, single, Black mothers, only two told the investigators that they would advise another woman in their situation to give the baby up, and both cited difficulties with the welfare office as their reason.[74] The author of the study referred to the "vehemence" of most Black, single mothers about their decision to keep the child.[75]

Helen Harris Perlman, recognizing the negative attitudes of social workers toward girls and women who failed to relinquish illegitimate babies, counselled her colleagues in the 1960s, "Even if more opportunities for adoption of Negro babies become possible, there is a strong probability that most Negro mothers—indeed, most unwed mothers—will want to keep their babies."[76]

CONCLUSION

A research team in North Carolina investigating illegitimacy concluded in the early 1960s that one major difference between white and Black unwed mothers was that the white girl generally felt that a "new maturity" had come with the experience of conceiving out of wedlock. The team claimed that this was not true for the Black subjects, and explained: "The white subculture demands learning from experience," so the white unwed mother must learn her lesson. The white girl "has probably been encouraged to look within herself for the reasons for her mistake because the white subculture stresses individual responsibility for error."[77]

These observations capture a great deal of the intentionality underlying the white culture's treatment of unwed mothers under the adoption mandate. For these girls and women, the "lesson" was twofold: no baby without a husband; and no one is to blame but yourself. Learning the lesson meant stepping on the road to maturity and womanhood. The illegitimate child was an encumbrance or an obstacle to following this route. The ability to relinquish was constructed as the first, most crucial step in the right direction.

Joyce Ladner, in her study of Black women in the 1960s, dealt with the same issue—the relationship between illegitimacy and maturity. She suggested a strikingly different finding:

> The adolescent Black girl who became pregnant out of wedlock changed her self-conception from one who was approaching maturity to one who had attained the status of womanhood. . . . Mothers were quick to say that their daughters had become grown, that they have "done as much as I have done."[78]

The road to maturity for Black, unwed mothers was unmediated. Maturity accompanied maternity, the baby's legal status notwithstanding.

Both Black and white women in the postwar era were subject to a definition of maturity that depended on motherhood. The most pervasive, public assumption about Black and white unwed mothers, however, was that their nonmarital childbearing did not constitute maternity in the culturally sanctioned sense. The treatment of these girls and women reinforced the notion that legitimation of sexuality and maternity were the province of the state and the community, and were not the rights of individual girls and women. In the case of white, unwed mothers, the community (including the mother herself, and her family) with government support, was encouraged to efface episodes of illicit sex and maternity. Outside of marriage neither the sex nor the resulting child had "reality" in the community or in the mother's life. They became simply momentary mental aberrations. In the case of Black, unwed mothers, sexuality was brute biology and childbearing its hideous result. The state, with the support of public institutions, could deface the Black, single mother's dignity, diminish her resources, threaten her right to keep her child, and even threaten her reproductive capacity.

In both cases, the policies and practices which structured the meanings of race and gender, sexuality, and motherhood for unwed mothers were tied to social issues—such as the postwar adoption market for white babies, and the white, taxpaying public's hostile identification of ADC as a program to support Black, unwed mothers and their unwanted babies—which used single, pregnant women as resources and scapegoats.

In the immediate pre-*Roe v. Wade* era, the uses of race combined with the uses of gender, sexuality, and maternity in ways that dealt Black and white unwed mothers quite different hands. According to social and cultural intentions for the white, unwed mother and her baby, relinquishment of the baby was meant to place all scent of taint behind them and thus restore good value to both. The Black, unwed mother and her child, triply devalued, had all their troubles before them.

Notes

1. This essay is taken from a larger study, *"Wake Up Little Susie": Single Pregnancy and Race in the Pre-*Roe v. Wade *Era* (New York: Routledge, 1992).
2. See, for example, Charlotte Lowe, "Intelligence and Social Background of the Unmarried Mother," *Mental Hygiene* 4 (October, 1927), pp. 783–794; and Henry C. Schumacher, M.D., "The Unmarried Mother: A Socio-Psychiatric Viewpoint," *Mental Hygiene* 4 (October, 1927), pp. 775–782.
3. Maryland passed such a law in 1919 and Wisconsin in 1922. It was claimed that these laws would reduce high infant mortality rates, although they were never shown to do so. Maternity home residents were targeted since this group was considered most likely, in its search for secrecy, to abandon its babies. See Elza Virginia Dahlgren, "Attitudes of a Group of Unmarried Mothers Toward the Minnesota Three Months Nursing Regulation and Its Application," M.A. thesis, University of Minnesota, 1940.
4. See, for example, Percy Kammerer, *The Unmarried Mother* (Boston: Little, Brown & Co., 1918) and Schumacher, "The Unmarried Mother."
5. Even though many studies published in this era claimed that rates of illicit coition were not rising in the postwar era, the fact that the illegitimacy rates and illegal abortion rates were higher than ever suggests otherwise. See, for example, Alfred C. Kinsey, Wardell B. Pomeroy, Clyde E. Martin, and Paul H. Gebhard, *Sexual Behavior in the Human Female* (Philadelphia: W. B. Saunders Company, 1953), chap. 8. Also see Phillips Cutright, "Illegitimacy in the United States: 1920–1968," in Charles F. Westoff and Robert Parke, Jr., eds., *Demographic and Social Aspects of Population Growth* (Washington, D.C.: Commission on Population Growth and the American Future), p. 384.
6. See Viviana A. Zelizer, *Pricing the Priceless Child: The Changing Social Value of Children* (New York: Basic Books, 1985) for an interesting discussion of related issues.
7. See, for example, Mary Lynch Crockett, "An Examination of Services to the Unmarried Mother in Relation to Age at Adoption Placement of the Baby," *Casework Papers, 1960* (New York: Columbia University Press, 1960), pp. 75–85.
8. Leontine Young, *Out of Wedlock* (New York: McGraw Hill, 1954), p. 216.
9. Janice P. Montague, "Acceptance or Denial—The Therapeutic Uses of the Mother/Baby Relationship," paper presented at the Florence Crittenton Association of America Northeast Conference, 1964.
10. Winston Ehrmann, "Illegitimacy in Florida II: Social and Psychological Aspects of Illegitimacy," *Eugenics Quarterly* 3 (December, 1956), p. 227.
11. Leontine Young, "Is Money Our Trouble?" paper presented at the National Conference on Social Work, 1953.
12. Mary Calderone, ed., *Abortion in the United States* (New York: Harper and Brothers, 1958), pp. 92–93, 139; Alan Guttmacher, "Therapeutic Abortion: The Doctor's Dilemma," *Journal of Mt. Sinai Hospital* 21 (1954), p. 111; Lewis Savel, "Adjudication of Therapeutic Abortion and Sterilization," in Edmund W. Overstreet, ed., *Therapeutic Abortion and Sterilization* (New York: Harper and Row, 1964), pp. 14–21.
13. Calderone, ed., *Abortion in the United States*, pp. 86–88.
14. See, for example, J.G. Moore and J.H. Randall, "Trends in Therapeutic Abortion: A Review of 137 Cases," *American Journal of Obstetrics and Gynecology* 63 (1952), p. 34.

15. Harry A. Pearce and Harold A. Ott, "Hospital Control of Sterilization and Therapeutic Abortion," *American Journal of Obstetrics and Gynecology* 60 (1950), p. 297; James M. Ingram, H.S.B. Treloar, G. Phillips Thomas, and Edward B. Rood, "Interruption of Pregnancy for Psychiatric Indications—A Suggested Method of Control, *Obstetrics and Gynecology* 29 (1967), pp. 251–55.

16. See, for example, Charles C. Dahlberg, "Abortion," in Ralph Slovenko, ed., *Sexual Behavior and the Law* (Springfield, IL.: Charles Thomas, 1965), p. 384.

17. Arthur Mandy, "Reflections of a Gynecologist," in Harold Rosen, ed., *Therapeutic Abortion* (New York: The Julian Press, 1954), p. 291.

18. Gregory Zillboorg, "The Clinical Issues of Postpartum Psychopathology Reactions," *American Journal of Obstetrics and Gynecology* 73 (1957), p. 305; Roy J. Heffernon and William Lynch, "What Is The Status of Therapeutic Abortion in Modern Obstetrics?" *American Journal of Obstetrics and Gynecology* 66 (1953), p. 337.

19. Nicholson J. Eastman, "Obstetric Forward," in Rosen, *Therapeutic Abortion,* p. xx.

20. Theodore Lidz, "Reflections of a Psychiatrist," in Rosen, *Therapeutic Abortion,* p. 279.

21. Flanders Dunbar, "Abortion and the Abortion Habit," in Rosen, *Therapeutic Abortion,* p. 27.

22. Mandy, "Reflections," p. 289.

23. Manfred Guttmacher, "The Legal Status of Therapeutic Abortion," in Rosen, *Therapeutic Abortion,* p. 183. Also see Nanette Davis, *From Crime to Choice: The Transformation of Abortion in America* (Westport CT.: Greenwood Press, 1985), p. 73; Johan W. Eliot, Robert E. Hall, J. Robert Willson, and Carolyn Hauser, "The Obstetrician's View," in Robert E. Hall, ed., *Abortion in a Changing World,* Vol. 1 (New York: Columbia University Press, 1970), p. 93; Kenneth R. Niswander, "Medical Abortion Practice in the United States," in David T. Smith, ed., *Abortion and the Law* (Cleveland: The Press of Case Western Reserve University, 1967), p. 57.

24. David C. Wilson, "The Abortion Problem in the General Hospital," in Rosen, *Therapeutic Abortion,* pp. 190–1. Also see Myra Loth and H. Hesseltine, "Therapeutic Abortion at the Chicago Lying-In Hospital," *American Journal of Obstetrics and Gynecology* 72 (1956), pp. 304–311, which reported that 69.4% of their sample were sterilized along with abortion. Also relevant are Keith P. Russell, "Changing Indications for Therapeutic Abortion: Twenty Years Experience at Los Angeles County Hospital," *Journal of the American Medical Association* (January 10, 1953), pp. 108–111, which reported an abortion-sterilization rate of 75.6%; and Lewis E. Savel, "Adjudication of Therapeutic Abortion and Sterilization," *Clinical Obstetrics and Gynecology* 7 (1964), pp. 14–21.

25. See, for example, Michael W. Sedlak, "Young Women and the City: Adolescent Deviance and the Transformation of Educational Policy, 1870–1960," *History of Education Quarterly* 23 (1983), pp. 1–28.

26. See Lillian Ripple, "Social Work Standards of Unmarried Parenthood as Affected by Contemporary Treatment Formulations," Ph.D. Dissertation, University of Chicago, 1953.

27. *Directory of Maternity Homes* (Cleveland: National Association of Services for Unmarried Parents, 1960).

28. U.S. Congress, Senate Judiciary Committee, Subcommittee to Investigate Juvenile Delinquency, Interstate Adoption Practices, July 15–16, 1955, 84th Congress, 1st sess. (Washington, D.C.: Government Printing Office, 1955), p. 200.

29. U.S. Congress, Senate Judiciary Committee, Subcommittee to Investigate Juvenile Delinquency, Commercial Child Adoption Practices, May 16, 1956, 84th Congress, 2nd sess. (Washington, D.C.: Government Printing Office, 1956), p. 6.

30. Duluth, Minnesota to Governor Luther Youngdahl, August 2, 1950, and to President Truman, August 14, 1950 Box 457, File 7-4-3-3-4, Record Group 102, National Archives.

31. U.S. Congress, Commercial Child Adoption Practices, May 16, 1956, p. 86.

32. Ibid., p. 120.

33. *New York Times* (July 10, 1958).

34. U.S. Congress, Senate Committee on the Judiciary, Subcommittee to Investigate Juvenile Delinquency in the United States, 84th Congress, 2nd sess., Unpublished Hearing, May 11, 1956.

35. U.S. Congress, Senate Judiciary Committee, *Hearings Before the Subcommittee to Investigate Juvenile Delinquency, Interstate Adoption Practices*, Miami, Florida, November 14–15, 1955, 84th Congress, 1st sess. (Washington, D.C.: Government Printing Office, 1956), p. 54–56.

36. U.S. Congress, Interstate Adoption Practices, July 15–16, 1955, p. 206.

37. U.S. Congress, Interstate Adoption Practices, Miami, Florida, November 14–15, 1955, p. 245.

38. Clark Vincent, "Unwed Mothers and the Adoption Market: Psychological and Familial Factors," *Journal of Marriage and Family Living* 22 (May 1960), p. 118.

39. See Solinger, *"Wake Up Little Susie"* chap. 7 for a fuller discussion of these three public perspectives.

40. See Winifred Bell, *Aid to Dependent Children* (New York: Columbia University Press, 1965); and Julius Paul, "The Return of Punitive Sterilization Proposals," *Law and Society Review* 3 (August, 1968), pp. 77–106.

41. See, for example, Andrew Billingsley and Jeanne Giovannoni, *Children of the Storm* (New York: Harcourt, Brace and Jovanovich, Inc., 1972), p. 142.

42. Patricia Garland, "Illegitimacy—A Special Minority-Group Problem in Urban Areas," *Child Welfare* 45 (February 1966), p. 84.

43. Ibid.

44. See, for example, the editorial, "It Merits Discussion," Richmond News Leader, March 22, 1957.

45. During the period considered here, Black women in the South were among the first in the United States to receive publicly subsidized birth control, sterilization, and abortion services. See Thomas Shapiro, *Population Control Politics: Women, Sterilization and Reproductive Choice* (Philadelphia: Temple University Press, 1985); Gerald C. Wright, "Racism and the Availability of Family Planning Services in the United States," *Social Forces* 56 (June, 1978), pp. 1087–1098; and Martha C. Ward, *Poor Women, Powerful Men: America's Great Experiment in Family Planning* (Boulder: Westview Press, 1986).

46. See, for example, the *New York Times*, August 28, 1960, which quotes Louisiana Governor Jimmie H. Davis justifying the recent state legislation targeting "those who make it their business to produce illegitimate children."

47. See *Illegitimacy and Its Impact on the Aid to Dependent Children Program*, Bureau of Public Assistance, Social Security Administration, U.S. Department of Health, Education and Welfare (Washington, D.C.: Government Printing Office, 1960).

48. The *Atlanta Constitution*, January 25, 1951. The *Constitution* reported that the Georgia State Welfare Director, making an argument for denying Aid to Dependent Children grants to mothers with more than one illegitimate child, noted that "Seventy percent of all mothers with more than one illegitimate children are Negro.... Some of them, finding themselves tied down to one child are not adverse to adding others as a business proposition." A Philadelphia judge recommended in 1958 that mothers of three or more illegitimate children be jailed [because it is] apparent that childbearing has become a business venture to collect relief benefits." *New York Times*, March 4, 1958.

49. "A Study of Negro Adoptions," *Child Welfare* 38 (February, 1959), p. 33, quoting David Fanshel, *A Study in Negro Adoptions* (New York: Child Welfare League of America, 1957): "In moving from white to Negro adoptions we are moving from what economists would call a 'seller's market' ... to a 'buyer's market.'"

50. See, for example, Lydia Hylton, "Trends in Adoption," *Child Welfare* 44 (February, 1966), pp. 377–386. Hylton cites the figures of 182 white applicants for every 100 white

infants in the mid-1960s, although higher ratios were obtained earlier in the period of this study. In 1960, a government report claimed that in some communities, there were ten suitable applicants for every white infant, *Illegitimacy and Its Impact*, p. 28.

51. One of a number of readers responding irately to a *New York Times'* editorial in support of giving welfare grants to unmarried mothers, wrote to the *Times*, "As for your great concern for those careless women who make a career of illicit pregnancy, they should either bear the expense or be put where they can no longer indulge in their weaknesses." *New York Times*, July 7, 1961.

52. *New York Times*, August 9, 1959. In late 1958, average monthly family grants in the ADC program were $99.83 nationally, but in the South, ranged between $27.09 in Alabama and $67.73 in Texas. Bell, *Aid to Dependent Children*, p. 224.

53. Hazel McCalley, "The Community Looks at Illegitimacy," Florence Crittenton Association of America Papers, Box 3, folder: FCAA Annual 11th, 1960–61, Social Welfare History Archives, University of Minnesota (hereafter cited as SWHA). See *Facts, Fallacies and the Future—A Study of the ADC Program of Cook County, Illinois* (New York: Greenleigh Associates, 1960), p. 29, for a prominent, contemporary discussion concerning how small welfare grants to single mothers were directly responsible for increasing these women's financial and social dependence on men.

54. "Suitable Home Law," (Jacksonville: Florida Department of Public Welfare, 1962), pp. 25–26; quoted in Bell, *Aid to Dependent Children*, p. 132.

55. An excellent study of Black, single mothers' strategies in this era is Renee M. Berg, "A Study of a Group of Unmarried Mothers Receiving ADC," Doctor of Social Work dissertation, University of Pennsylvania School of Social Work, 1962.

56. A Gallup Poll conducted in 1960 found that only "one in ten [respondents] favored giving aid to further children born to unwed parents who have already produced an out of wedlock child." *St. Louis Post Dispatch*, August 8, 1961.

57. *Milwaukee Journal*, August 9, 1961.

58. *Illegitimacy and Its Impact*, p. 30.

59. *Buffalo Currier Express*, December 5, 1957.

60. *Illegitimacy and Its Impact*, p. 36.

61. Ibid.

62. See "The Current Attack on ADC in Louisiana," September 16, 1960, Florence Crittenton Association of America Papers, Box 3, folder: National Urban League, New York City, SWHA.

63. Annie Lee Davis, "Attitudes Toward Minority Groups: Their Effect on Services for Unmarried Mothers," paper presented at the National Conference on Social Work, 1948.

64. See Seaton W. Manning, "The Changing Negro Family: Implications for the Adoption of Children," *Child Welfare* 43 (November 1964), pp. 480–485; Elizabeth Herzog and Rose Bernstein, "Why So Few Negro Adoptions?" *Children* 12 (January–February 1965), p. 14–15; Billingsley and Giovannoni, *Children of the Storm*; Fanshel, *A Study in Negro Adoption*; Trudy Bradley, "An Exploration of Caseworkers' Perceptions of Adoptive Applicants," *Child Welfare* 45 (October, 1962), p. 433–443.

65. Elizabeth Tuttle, "Serving the Unmarried Mother Who Keeps Her Child," *Social Welfare* 43 (October, 1962), p. 418.

66. See *Facts, Fallacies and Future*, pp. 19–20; 552 out of 619 mothers of illegitimate children in this study did not want another child but reported that they had no information about how to prevent conception.

67. Deborah Shapiro, "Attitudes, Values and Unmarried Motherhood," in *Unmarried Parenthood: Clues to Agency and Community Action* (New York: National Council on Illegitimacy, 1967), p. 60.

68. Joyce Ladner, *Tomorrow's Tomorrow: The Black Woman* (New York: Doubleday and Co., 1971), pp. 2, 8.

69. Ellery Reed and Ruth Latimer, *A Study of Unmarried Mothers Who Kept Their Babies* (Cincinnati: Social Welfare Research, Inc., 1963), p. 72.

70. Shapiro, "Attitudes, Values," p. 61.

71. Renee Berg, "Utilizing the Strengths of Unwed Mothers in the AFDC Program," *Child Welfare* 43 (July 1964), p. 337.

72. Ibid.

73. Berg, "A Study of a Group of Unwed Mothers Receiving ADC," p. 96.

74. Ibid., p. 93.

75. Ibid., p. 95.

76. Helen Harris Perlman, "Observations on Services and Research," in *Unmarried Parenthood: Clues to Agency and Community Action* (New York: National Council on Illegitimacy, 1967), p. 41.

77. Charles Bowerman, Donald Irish, and Hallowell Pope, *Unwed Motherhood: Personal and Social Consequences* (Chapel Hill: University of North Carolina, 1966), p. 261.

78. Ladner, *Tomorrow's Tomorrow*, pp. 214–215.

Chapter 14

BIOLOGY AND COMMUNITY: THE DUALITY OF JEWISH MOTHERING IN EAST LONDON, 1880-1939

Susan L. Tananbaum

INTRODUCTION

Responding in part to anti-Semitism, but largely to economic privation, some two-and-a-half million Jews left Eastern Europe between 1880 and 1939. Most settled in North America, but a significant minority, about 250,000, made their homes in England, including nearly one hundred thousand working-class girls and women. England's Jewish population, as a result of both this immigration and birth-rate increase, grew from about sixty thousand in 1880 to some three hundred fifty thousand on the eve of World War II.[1]

The Jewish community the immigrants joined placed tremendous emphasis on family life, and had strong ethnic and religious ties and a high marriage rate.[2] Most of the immigrants settled in the East End of London, where the women spent their days immersed in mothering, thus influencing nearly every sphere of their children's lives. As Jewish immigrants created new communities, however, a variety of patterns of mothering, of child rearing, and interfamilial relationships and expectations emerged. Some took shape from traditions in the old country, and others had their genesis in London, New York, and the other great immigrant cities.

Part of mothers' many-faceted responsibilities was to guide working-class girls to Jewish adulthood in London's turn-of-the-century ghettos. Formative influences for these new patterns included not only the biological mother, relatives, close friends, and neighbors, but also the native-born, established, and largely middle-class, Jewish community. What can be called communal mothering took place through voluntary, Jewish-sponsored, social service programs, care committees attached to local schools, girls' clubs and settlements, apprenticeships, and rescue organizations. In all these programs, middle-class, Jewish women sought to anglicize immigrant girls and their mothers by moving them into less crowded housing and occupations, training them to be good citizens, and exposing them to English culture, athletics, and religious practice.

Often the biological and communal mothers shared hopes and aspirations. Identifying their differences is important, however, because it indicates areas of tension among generations and classes, and highlights varying forms of ethnic identity. It raises questions about how the Jewish community kept these girls respectable and Jewish, yet anglicized; how they tailored gendered socialization efforts for girls and women; and how they viewed the immigrant mothers who tended to resist assimilation.

To a very great degree, Jewish mothers fulfilled the image, perhaps overly so, of caring mothers who stayed at home with their children. Mothers were the protectors and enablers, particularly for husbands and sons. "We each lived in our own world, except for my mother who lived in all our worlds," noted Bernard Kops in his memoir. "But each of our worlds was held together by our home in Stepney Green." In an incident that would ring true for many, Kops described one of the very few nights his mother went out. When he had been injured by a falling sewing machine, his sister, Essie, had Bernard rushed to the hospital. His mother, upon her return, declared " 'The one time I go out and look what happens! I'm never going out again.' . . . She just stayed with her family, watching and worrying."[3]

Consciously or not, communal mothers also appropriated much of the stereotyped maternal metaphor. Motivated by genuine concern, some communal mothers established infant welfare clinics, mothers' clubs, and home visitation programs. Wherever they could influence immigrant mothers, they did. Where they could not, they focused on the next generation. In tandem with efforts of board and voluntary schools, and alongside a natural process of anglicization, communal mothers helped shape England's newest residents.

Thanks to rich sources, one can learn a great deal about communal mothering. There is much less material from the perspective of immigrant women, and there is no one area of mothers' attitudes to which the historian can refer to build a precise picture of Jewish mothers' conception of their roles, or of the relationships between them and their daughters. Impressionistic data, memoirs, interviews, some survey material, the contemporary press, and scattered testimony in parliamentary documents, however, do enable one to gain an understanding of different constructs of mothering, and thus offer an understanding of some of the values and lessons biological and communal mothers passed on to young women. Also helpful is evidence of the different expectations mothers harbored for their sons.

The sources are more abundant for analyzing the parenting role of the Jewish community; what it sought to inculcate, as well as which methods of mothering it hoped would filter back to foreign-born mothers. These different constructions reflect the complex web of class biases, as well as the established community's prescriptive and ideal versions of mothering, as opposed to descriptive realities and economic necessities.[4]

BIOLOGICAL MOTHERING

Biological mothers provided the most typical and extensive mothering; these women bore and raised their children, and taught their daughters, in particular, a wide range of practical skills and values. Members of London's established, middle-class, Jewish community created the second model. These "social betters" had arrived in England some fifty to seventy years earlier, though some had ties to Jewish migrants who returned to England during the period known as "the Resettlement" of Cromwellian England.[5]

Parents from both the immigrant and established groups tended to regard the birth of a girl as a mixed blessing. While female children could help out at home, they also represented a financial burden, especially in the days of compulsory dowries.[6] Girls' weddings meant an expenditure not required for sons. Daughters earned much less than their brothers and remained more dependent upon their parents longer than sons. Yet, as one contemporary writer suggested, Jewish parents spoiled their daughters; though such a practice, he hastened to add, did not mean "any undue degree of freedom is accorded them."[7]

Convention dictated that mothers heavily influenced their daughters as they grew up, allowing them to acculturate to English society, while at the same time preparing them to bear and rear the next generation of Jewish children. We have very little direct evidence about this process, however. Frequently immigrant women did not speak English, rarely worked outside their homes, and usually remained anonymous in historical records. Furthermore, mothering for the foreign-born could involve a role reversal, because girls and young women spoke English, attended schools, and knew something of English culture, whereas many of their mothers did not.[8]

Mothering roles kept women in a separate sphere from men for much of their lives. Husbands and fathers often travelled to England ahead of the rest of the family, often leaving mothers behind with several children.[9]

In the novel *A Family of Shopkeepers,* for example, Jacob Samuels left his wife Ada, not long after marrying, to establish a home in England. Ada, already caring for one small child, was pregnant with another. While living in her husband's small, Eastern European town of Prozhnie, she earned a little money from crocheting. She travelled to London just before delivering a daughter, and very soon after began taking up the sewing aprons for money.[10]

Both men and women among the immigrants en route to England faced unscrupulous ticket agents or thieves, but some of the women also experienced sexual harassment, or became the targets of white slavers during their travel. The Jewish Association for the Protection of Girls and Women (JAPGW) was extremely concerned with the large number of young women travelling alone. They were "unprotected," the Association noted, and "ignorant of the language and customs of this country and, worse still, ignorant of the dangers awaiting them at the port."[11]

Once in England, girls received less education than boys; their schooling emphasized domestic training and highly circumscribed, work-related skills.[12] Most Jewish women expected to work full time, but for a limited period only *outside* their homes. The vast majority married and left the factories and workshops after the birth of their children. Such child care responsibilities made a woman's experience unique, especially in the way motherhood brought young women into contact with a variety of communal organizations staffed by middle-class, Jewish women, whether school officials, social workers, or settlement house leaders.

Lessons from mothers to daughters included the teaching of domestic duties, the passing on of religious traditions, and some training in economic survival skills. Mothers' lives were difficult ones, as exemplified by Ada Samuels, who ran the family store in the novel *A Family of Shopkeepers.* All day she scurried back and forth from the kitchen to the store, now nursing a son, then preparing dinner, and always trying to keep up with the mending, while Jacob, her husband, worked at a stall in the market. Proud of her wifely skills, Ada always prepared tasty, three-course meals, but felt her efforts unappreciated. When her husband and daughter, as was their custom, read the newspaper through dinner, "Ada said to the world in general, 'Nobody sees what they eat, nobody knows what taste it has.'"[13] Hard work characterized working-class and immigrant mothers' lives. As one East Ender recalled:

> I think women, particularly working-class women, carried the brunt of the household, ... because they were generally responsible for handling all the money. They were the ones who paid the rent and worried when there was *no* rent. ... Although the men worked very long hours, in bad conditions, in many ways I think they never suffered the same stress as women.

The household domain did offer an arena of some power for women, but constant childbearing and money worries meant an essentially sacrificial role.[14]

From a young age, girls began to learn how to sacrifice. Their brothers, for example, had greater economic freedom. Parents expected daughters to turn over their pay, contributing to a girl's dependence, and preventing her from making financial choices. Often, mothers restricted daughters' social activities. In an interview, one women described her mother's refusal to allow her and her sister "to parade all down Whitechapel [Street] looking for young men."[15]

COMMUNAL MOTHERING

Many of the native-born, English Jews engaged in communal mothering concluded that their coreligionists required various forms of educational and charitable assistance, and they generally found a receptive audience when visiting the immigrant women. As one visitor noted, "the ladies are pleased to recognise the civility with which they are received by the poor in their homes."[16] Communal mothers entered the lives of immigrants through membership on visiting committees of social service organizations such as the Jewish Board of Guardians for the Relief of the Jewish Poor (known as the Board or the JBG), as volunteers in infant welfare clinics and settlement houses, or, less directly, through the Union of Jewish Women (UJW).

The efforts of the volunteers reflected their concern with anti-semitism, Judaism's requirement of caring for the less fortunate, feelings of ethnic solidarity, and appreciation of the commonality of experiences among women of different classes. A number of specific goals stand out. Professional and volunteer workers wanted first and foremost to anglicize the foreigners. They did so by offering a variety of activities and advice through which they could establish moral standards, and monitor girls' behavior. Social reformers also promoted occupational diversification, self-help, and housewifery skills.

A certain ambivalence characterized the response of middle-class, Jewish women to their poorer sisters. Jewish tradition led them to offer generous charitable assistance, but concern about growing anti-semitism also spurred them to develop a multifaceted program to acculturate the immigrants as rapidly as possible.[17] These established, English Jews offered advice, and sought to influence immigrant behavior patterns in such areas as care committees, girls' clubs, day nurseries, happy evenings, maternal and child welfare clinics, and employment advisory services.

A variety of assumptions informed the efforts directed toward immigrant children: children were more malleable than their parents; mothers formed the crucial link to home life; and the working class required training. While committed to Judaism, established Jews, therefore, worked diligently to introduce English ways, standards of cleanliness, decorous religious worship, and occupational diversity to immigrants. They discouraged overcrowding, sweated industries, Yiddish, and traditional forms of Jewish education. This anglicization campaign, peaking in the interwar years, found its most effective locus in the schools. Jewish leaders praised English schools and the excellent training they provided; in the words of one rabbi:

> With . . [the immigrants'] children the process of assimilation is little short of marvelous in its rapidity and completeness. A couple of years spent in one of the Jewish Free Schools or in a Board School suffices to convert them into children who not only speak but think English.[18]

Basil Henriques, warden of the Oxford and St. George's Jewish Settlement, believed, however, that anglicization required even greater commitment from Jewish communal leaders. While dismissing many of the anti-alienists' charges against immigrant Jews, Henriques argued that "the real problem lies in the aloofness on the part of the Jew, in his non-assimilation." To some degree, the warden believed, language and religious differences explained the immigrants' reluctance to mix with Gentiles. But he also felt that the Anglo-Jewish community had taken only halfhearted measures "to counteract this trend." He was particularly critical of the Federation of Synagogues, an Orthodox, and largely immigrant, umbrella organization, "who appoint as leaders to their many Synagogues men who are even more foreign than the congregations themselves." Nor did the native-born community, in Henriques' opinion, provide adequate support for clubs that tried "to counteract this aloofness," and far too few Jewish social workers served in immigrant neighborhoods.

> The alien Jews [Henriques declared] . . . have their own newspapers, they speak their own language, they patronize their own shops. Many of them have been in this country as long as twenty years, and still cannot properly speak, let alone write, the language. They are ignorant of English customs, and of English habits, and the whole general outlook of their fellow-countrymen.[19]

Henriques accepted a suggestion in *The Times* that only English Jews, who themselves had assimilated successfully, could offer aliens the necessary education.[20] Such encouragements and reproaches led many in the Jewish community to take up a mothering role.

MOTHERING AND WORK

In recent years, there has been a good deal of debate over the extent and nature of women's work. Among Jewish women, the debate extends to their mothers' lives in Eastern Europe. There are two largely idealized versions: in the first, traditional images of Jewish women often place them at the center of the family's economic survival.[21] Eastern European mothers were said to have provided the sole support for their families while the menfolk spent their lives immersed in holy literature. Respected Jewish historians such as Simon Dubnow helped to promote this view.[22] No doubt the picture accurately reflected the lives of some Jewish families. Full-time study, however, was always an elite pursuit, and only those of comfortable means or exceptional talent enjoyed this life-style.

In the second, quite different but still idealized, version, Jewish women worked prior to marriage, and not thereafter. In that vein, a Jewish unionist claimed that "in a Jewish family the husband is the sole bread-winner. A Jewish married woman is seldom found in a factory or workshop. . . . As soon as a Jewish girl gets married she quits the shop."[23] Testimony from the Interdepartmental Committee on Physical Deterioration supports this view. Charles Booth, for example, attributed the taller heights of Jewish children "to the fact that the Jewish mothers do not work." Husbands, he testified, expected their wives to take care of their homes, and not to assist with earning.[24]

Closer to reality than either of these idealizations was a different picture: Jewish mothering *regularly* included work beyond that of the household after marriage and the arrival of children, typically inside the home, but outside if necessary. Numerous sources indicate that women did continue to work after marriage, whether by offering child care services, assisting their husbands, caring for boarders, cooking lunches, or taking in sewing and laundry.[25] Rarely did anyone record these forms of labor and economic contributions to the family, and never in any systematic fashion. Women, while confined to the home and committed to family, interspersed paid work, typically piecework, with other domestic chores. Many daughters later failed to perceive such activities as work, and had only vague memories of their mothers having provided some of the family's income. In many homes, in fact, integrating paying work into home life was so common that it was seen as merely part of the wife's duties. While the exact figures are unobtainable, it is clear that Jewish social convention did not frown on all forms of female employment, and even viewed women's work as an activity that enabled their husbands to honor God. This was surely an influential message to daughters and to sons.

Works by Rickie Burman and Susan Glenn explore Jewish women's contributions to their families, and attempt to locate the roots of those patterns in the immigrants' Eastern European experiences. Burman's research on Jewish immigrant women in Manchester, England shows that women who functioned as the sole breadwinner in the family typically supported husbands who pursued scholarly activities. Yet "other evidence," notes Burman, "can be cited to show that in some households both men and women were economically active." In numerous descriptions of East European Jewish women, in fact, "the wife's economic role was perceived as subsidiary to that of her husband."[26]

Making use of folk songs, poems, and memoirs, Glenn builds a rich description of women's work in New York City. Describing the garment industry, she finds that some fifty thousand Jewish women worked in the needle trades.[27] Glenn logically contends that these figures underestimate the actual numbers of women workers. Census-takers failed to count some women who worked in their homes, or to detect others who, wary of government officials, intentionally evaded the enumerators.

Clara Collet, in her study of foreign employment in England, described her visits to tailoring workshops where she found few married women and children. She writes that:

> evidence, ... derived from actual visits to workshops supports the conclusions drawn from the experiences of Jewish organizations to the effect that the competition of married Jewesses in the labour market ... is so slight as to be negligible. ... We need only pay attention to the unmarried women and girls together with a few deserted wives.[28]

She found only 2.5 percent of the Jewish women workers to be married, compared with approximately eight percent of non-Jewish women. The same pattern appeared in cap-making and waterproofing establishments.[29]

> Very rarely was a middle-aged Jewess to be seen in any one of these workshops; the few non-Jewish workers in them, ... seemed in nearly every case older than the majority of the Jewesses, very few of whom looked over twenty-three years of age. The small number of Jewish girls who seemed under sixteen years of age, was also remarkable.[30]

Unfortunately, however, arriving at a realistic estimate of women's labor force participation, whether married or not, is very difficult. Government statistics tend to be highly suspect, and often seriously underestimated the extent of wage labor among women, particularly those who were married.[31]

Establishment, Anglo-Jewish, communal leaders did not encourage married women to work, or even to supplement men's wages. A clear sense of a mother's obligation to family pervades the advice so freely given to women and their daughters by communal mothers. The native-born community, and particularly the JBG, encouraged mothers to remain at home in order to care for their children.[32] "Sending women with young families out to work, except in special cases," argued communal leader Hannah Hyam, "I am very much opposed to; it is the cause of ruin of many young lives."[33] Hyam had no objection to such women earning a few shillings a week by undertaking machining, needlework, or some other task *at home.* Such work would keep poor relief from inducing pauperization. As Hyam put it, "the home will be kept together [and] the children cared for by their natural guardian . . . [and the mother] will have every inducement to practice habits of industry."[34] The JBG preferred to support widowed mothers who needed to work, rather than risk forcing possible neglect on those with children. A mother's role was to remain at home, "to look after her rooms, and prepare proper food for the little ones."[35] Most Jewish girls consequently grew up in homes with their mothers nearly always present.

Nevertheless, statistical data from both Eastern Europe and England indicate that a small though significant number of married women joined their single daughters in workshops, factories, and stores. Many women do recall their mothers going out to work at some point during their childhood. Pearl Osen, for example, reported that her mother "was in the workshop constantly." Helen Goldstein described her mother yelling at the girls who worked for her in a millinery shop in Stamford Hill, one of the better immigrant areas.[36]

Some mothers' work, particularly if it was outside of the home, left an indelible mark on their daughters. Sara Oppenheim, who was born in February of 1924 and grew up in the East End, recounted that her mother, who had come to England at the turn of the century, worked her whole life. Oppenheim acknowledged the significance of her mother's work experience:

> It's a very interesting thing, I reflect on it a great deal, because I think that although it was adversity that forced my mother out, in fact it was because she went out to work that her horizons were widened. That she actually became very much a woman of the world. And independent.

Oppenheim also remembers that her mother, while working until seven or seven-thirty in the evening in a workshop, managed to keep an immaculate home with beautiful tablecloths and embroidered doilies on the table.[37] Clearly, then, both those Jewish immigrant mothers who worked outside the home, and those who worked in the home, offered spoken and unspoken messages of self-reliance and strength to their daughters.

The low wages paid to men and the availability of various forms of labor for women suggest that women's contributions to the family economy were essential to the survival of many, and possibly most, Jewish families. The regularity of male employment and wages varied by occupation and location, and thus affected women's need to work accordingly.[38] Few working-class men earned enough money to support a growing family on their incomes alone.[39] Yet the high marriage rates among Jewish women, child rearing duties, the paucity of day nurseries, and the formidable tasks of housekeeping made it difficult for women to work outside the home.[40] Thus, only work that was an extension of domestic chores, or thought to be useful and "proper" for mothers and single women, gained the support of established Jewry, and seemingly, found acceptance among immigrant mothers and many of their daughters.

Clearly, the vast majority of married women's wages derived from home-based labor. Sara Mashluck's mother embroidered collars and cuffs until Sara was eleven, and then took a fruit stand, and later a fruit and vegetable stall in the market.[41] The predominance of small workshops in London's garment industry, and the nature of London's economic structure encouraged the extensive use of homeworkers.[42] *The Lancet,* for example, described a fully employed man's wages in Liverpool as insufficient for basic needs; many could find full-time work for no more than seven months per year. Such conditions regularly forced a man's wife and family to work. Often tailors had little to do at the beginning of the work week, only to have employers "rush" them at the end of the week. A homeworker and her children, working for mere pennies, would often be called upon to help her husband "at his bench, [so that the employers could] . . . 'sweat' profit out of them."[43] Workshops were small, business irregular, and the homeworkers used neither space nor electricity, and could be hired and let go at will. In the 1880s, when social reformers began investigating the conditions of such labor, they found that a typical work week could be sixty to seventy hours long and still not yield a living wage.[44]

Lack of training and heavy domestic responsibilities forced women to accept the unskilled labor available to them. Rarely skilled, homeworkers received particularly small compensation, worked solely at the will of the employer, and were too isolated to become involved in unions. Employers generally paid homeworkers by piece-rates, and the sewing machine, which was mass produced by 1861, probably encouraged more such work by adding to the tasks that could be performed at home. Homeworkers could buy a machine on an installment plan; companies such as Singer would then collect the weekly fee.[45]

The leaders of the Jewish community were well aware of the tenuous nature of the unskilled garment trades. Communal mothering therefore made a significant effort to diversify the immigrants' occupations. Despite a lack of interest on the part of Jewish girls and their mothers, the JBG and the JAPGW campaigned in favor of domestic service for single girls.[46] Most Jewish families, however, did not want their daughters to work in Christian homes, and few, in contrast to other working-class girls, left home prior to marriage.[47] The Board and the JAPGW however, believed that service kept idle girls from evil. The JAPGW concluded that the financial difficulties of the Domestic Training Home for Girls, a school for training domestic servants, came about because women and girls had other options and domestic service was falling generally into disrepute.[48] The Union of Jewish Women, an umbrella organization of women's groups, offered regular encouragement to young women to enter nursing and domestic service, and helped to place particularly well-qualified governesses.[49] The 1904 annual report of the UJW indicates the Union was satisfied enough with having convinced four factory girls and tailoresses to enter service.[50] Such lessons, it asserted, enabled girls to help out at home, eased mothers' burdens, and prepared girls for their "real" jobs— as wives and mothers.

Families did not always appreciate the intervention of religious and social service organizations. The UJW described the time-consuming case of one poor man whose death left two daughters destitute. The girls were too old to enter the Norwood Orphanage; so the UJW began raising funds to place the younger one at the London Training Home to be prepared for domestic service. Nonetheless, reported the Union, "when, after much trouble we had nearly all the amount required, the relatives decided to take charge of both girls themselves."[51]

LESSONS FOR DAUGHTERS

While some did realize that they were poor, and that their mothers worked hard for the family, many daughters did not perceive the precariousness of their family's financial situation. Mothers tried very hard to protect their daughters from that reality. Girls, however, did not remain children for long; most left school by age fourteen, entered factories and workshops, and began working twelve to fourteen hours per day. Economic circumstances and parental pressure forced many girls to enter the labor market before their brothers. Some mothers could accept that their daughters, having only limited education, would enter low-skilled work. Their brothers could make better use of additional education, or vocational training, if the girls made the necessary sacrifices.

Nettie Adler, daughter of a chief rabbi, spoke at the founding conference of the UJW. She noted that parents displayed very little originality in the choice of occupations for their daughters, "seldom consult[ing] the individual taste of a girl when choosing a trade for her." Furthermore, said Mrs. Adler, "the girl, unaware of any other outlet for her energies, seldom thinks of resisting her parents' wishes by endeavouring to obtain employment under better conditions."[52]

Despite the fact that many women and girls came to London or New

York with hopes of continuing their education, most acquiesced to family demands, contributing whatever they could earn.[53] While mothers may have appreciated their daughters' thirst for knowledge, the average parent in a working-class home in London's East End found it hard to defer a daughter's income until the school leaving age of fourteen. Some girls and women did continue their education at night school, or through the settlement houses, but many were too exhausted from work or bound by household duties. Clearly most mothers had neither the time nor money to allow their daughters to remain in school, much less pursue careers that required extensive training. Sacrifice for their sons seemed to make more sense, as they would support the next generation.[54]

Communal mothering, on the other hand, led to the development of a range of programs for girls, including clubs, a domestic training home, and apprenticeships. Such efforts opened up new opportunities and a wider cultural world.[55] Leaders of Anglo-Jewry favored apprenticeships as an alternative to "dead-end" trades, and expressed pleasure when increasing numbers of girls and boys sought them. The Industrial Committee of the JBG thought it not "chimerical . . . that, if properly supported, the operations of the Industrial Committee . . . may in time completely revolutionize the occupations and circumstances of the Jewish poor."[56] Immigrant parents, however, resisted efforts by the Board to place Jewish girls in a wider and more skilled range of occupations, much to the frustration of the Industrial Committee.[57]

The JBG also sponsored a workroom which, in 1881, employed an average of fifty-seven women, and had goals that went well beyond mere economic self-sufficiency. The Industrial Committee of the Board hoped to:

> [C]ontinue the noble work of the Jewish Schools by teaching girls various handicrafts, while they are yet too young to enter regular employment, thus enabling them to earn their own livelihood, and to become moral and industrious members of society.[58]

In 1881, for example, twenty-one girls completed their apprenticeship in the workrooms, and were proclaimed "now fully competent to earn their own living." The Board hired a teacher who offered "embroidery of gold, silver, worsted and silk," hoping that many girls would find this more lucrative than plain needlework.[59] The organizers of the workroom viewed their efforts as definitely "remedial."[60] Girls employed there,

> while removed from the temptations surrounding them in the East-end workshops, . . . [would] be educated in those habits of cleanliness, order and discipline which are still sadly wanting among the poor of our community.[61]

The apprenticeship program continued to grow during the early years of the century; by 1902 the Industrial Committee had 719 apprentices, but only forty-three were girls. While the Board recruited quite actively, mothers did not respond to the apprenticeship program for girls an enthusiastically as they did to the boys' program.[62]

The leaders of the Jewish community knew that girls required expanded opportunities.[63] By 1903, the JBG consciously began the search for new apprenticeships specifically for East End girls. Young women were able to find employment in thirteen different trades by 1904; among them, flower arranging, wig-making, and hairdressing. Resistance to change, though, remained a problem. The Apprenticing Committee faced "great difficulty" in persuading "girls to go to new occupations, especially in the West End, or to any employment which they or their friends have not tried."[64]

Each year the apprenticeship program grew, but not without resistance.[65] Some girls who worked outside the East End, did not like the fact that they had to bring an "inadequate and dry" lunch to work. The Chairman of the Girls' Apprenticing Sub-Committee, Nettie Adler, encouraged women living in these areas to invite the young workers to have lunch at their homes several times per week.[66] Other complications, of a religious nature, arose. In 1904, for example, the Committee had to end apprenticeships in artificial flower-making because the industry would no longer excuse apprentices from work on the Sabbath and other holy days.[67] Four years later, however, the Committee located a flower-maker who would meet their requirements, and also added button-making, a new trade, to the list of apprenticeships.[68]

Movement out of industrial and manufacturing positions occurred quite slowly. In 1909 two girls began training for positions as civil service clerks, and two as telegraph operators. The same year the Sub-Committee introduced summer holidays for apprentices, though those able to were expected to pay. Just prior to World War I, the JBG's Industrial Committee noted they were having increasing difficulty placing all who had trained to be secretaries. Tailoring, however, had a scale of wages that once again made it a satisfactory trade.

The number of those seeking apprenticeships declined during the war. Well-paying jobs that required little training attacted many young women. During the war, work was plentiful and thus created new opportunities for Jewish women. They were soon entering a "bewildering number" of new occupations.[69] Many organizations, the UJW among them, helped women train for these new jobs.[70]

Postwar economic conditions, including the many returning soldiers, forced many women out of the job market. When economic depression set in, employers generally preferred to hire ex-soldiers and "breadwinners."[71] Women however, having enjoyed the widest range of employment in their history, had set a pattern that could not be completely reversed. By 1925, the JAPGW could report that unemployment had abated and girls with training from a trade school could find work "in good dressmaking establishments."[72]

Beyond seeking to improve the working and living conditions of the immigrants, community women sought to anglicize the workers, emphasizing self-help and the acquisition of English. While mothers could not stem their daughters' anglicization, they did not seek out career opportunities that would encourage it.[73] Employers, and even the government, moreover, continued to view women's wages as supplemental for the family, thus justifying paying women less than they required for self-support.[74] The JBG did not criticize this practice, nor the unwillingness of employers to hire women for highly skilled, and thus better-paying jobs.

Jewish women continued to remain in a very narrow range of occupations throughout the peak periods of immigration. Even though establishment Jews made every effort to promote other occupations, most immigrant women continued to find employment doing finishing work on garments. As late as 1928, for example, most of the members of the Stepney Jewish Girls' Club entered the needle trades.[75] The growing demand for ready-made clothes fueled the expansion of the garment industry, and made such work abundant. Family and neighborhood connections to bosses, the need for some to work for Yiddish-speaking employers, the proximity of workshops, the comfort of working with other Jews who shared one's belief that home and family should be a woman's first priority, all continued to attract women to the industry.

For all the reasons discussed, it is not surprising to find a slow pace of change in women's occupational patterns evident in the census returns.[76] After the early years of the twentieth century, however, changing conditions brought occupational diversification. No longer hampered by language barriers, having seen their mothers' endless toil, and encouraged by school care committees, apprenticeship programs, and settlement workers, second-generation women did begin to enter more lucrative and less crowded professions.[77]

RECREATIONAL SUPPLEMENTS

Reflecting the Victorian ethos of voluntarism, self-help, and physical fitness, middle-class, volunteer workers tried to expose daughters, and often their mothers, to their own anglicized life-style. Immigrant women and children entered into a matrix of services—educational, social, and medical—that sought to acculturate them and strip them of their foreign ways.

In essence, the now familiar exhortations of communal mothering were extended to the educational, recreational, and medical services.

World War I and the end of mass immigration did not eliminate Anglo-Jewry's concern over the East End's young Jewish women. In 1913, the *Jewish Chronicle* estimated that nearly three thousand fourteen-year-old girls and boys left school each year. This period in a child's life was a difficult one. Typically, these young workers failed to earn enough money to support themselves, and their continuing needs caused conflict with their hard-pressed parents. Club leaders welcomed school-leavers, but the numbers of potential members surpassed available space, leaving many new working girls unaffiliated. Anglo-Jewish leaders feared that these children would respond to the temptations of the street or even drift into crime. The clubs offered "discipline and mild restraint during the most impressionable year of their [children's] lives."[78] The Jewish Working Girls' Club also maintained a "Comforts Fund" that supplied extra care for girls ill at home or in the hospital, and they provided holidays for the needy girls.[79]

Club leaders did not confine their efforts to the club building. Workers from the Beatrice [girls'] Club, for example, engaged in home visits, and tried to befriend whole families.[80] Club leaders matched members participating in Jewish Board of Guardians apprenticeships with guardians who were from the girl's club. Such relationships proved to be effective because the girls got to know their guardians in a congenial atmosphere.[81] The St. George's Jewish Settlement sought to reinforce middle-class values by starting a Mothers' Club to offer social and recreational facilities to members' mothers.[82]

Basil Henriques, founder of the St. George's Jewish Settlement saw the settlement house as a place that would help actualize the expectations England had for its young people.[83] Prior to World War II, four hundred fifty working boys and three hundred fifty working girls belonged to clubs at Bernhard Baron St. George's, and one hundred girls a night attended the Stepney B'nai B'rith Club. The girls not only enjoyed the activities, but often developed lifelong friendships with managers, who often came from middle-class neighborhoods in North London to assist with Club programs.

Club leaders took their role seriously. Growing concern over lax religious observance after World War I led to renewed promotion of religious education and observance. The Jewish Working Girls' Club encouraged the girls to be "Jewesses of the right sort, who knew and understood, and therefore were proud of their religion." The Club tried "to surround the girls with uplifting and refined influences, and make them see life from a different angle, which would ultimately result in them being better as well as happier for being members."[84] The Clubs depended on the Jewish community for financial support and staff. Perhaps Anglo-Jewry's leaders overrated their achievements, but Henriques believed that "through the Settlement the Jewish slum child may become the glory of England."[85]

Clubs did not attract or serve all of the Jewish East End's female adolescents. Girls who chose not to join clubs were a cause for concern.

> There is very little for a girl to do once she has finished work. The cinema, the public dancing hall, or mild flirtations down the Commercial Road are the only forms of recreation if your house is . . . crowded. . . . When you see a girl of 16 with her face painted and powdered, and in a manner to draw your notice . . . , and you recognise her as a girl who, two years before, had refused to belong to the Club . . . and was as modest . . . as you could ever wish to see, it feels like a dagger thrust.[86]

Those whose behavior did not meet the standards of the girls' clubs often received attention from the JAPGW. Primarily a "rescue" organization, the agency branched out into preventive care. During the years following World War I, the JAPGW worked with other agencies dedicated to discouraging young girls from loitering on the streets of London. Club leaders viewed their programs as offering a formative alternative. Over time, Jewish girls' and young women's recreational interests had come to resemble other working-class patterns more closely.

CONCLUSION

Biological mothers' goals did differ from communal mothers' in tone and approach. Most mothers wanted, first and foremost, for their daughters to have the best marriage prospects possible given their economic status, and they taught them creative means of supporting, clothing, and feeding their families. Mothers certainly provided an example that included hard work, devotion, and, when necessary, money from either home or outside work.

Communal mothers, on the other hand, worried about morality, pauperization, occupational dispersal, and opportunity adequate enough for girls while they remained single. Established Jews wanted above all to keep girls busy, probably from excessive fears as to the precariousness of the girls' morals. Jewish female criminals or prostitutes were few in number, and the rate for out-of-marriage childbirth was very low.[87] But such genuine concern, mixed with fears as to behavior that might stimulate anti-Semitism, stand out as the motivating factors behind communal mothering.

Despite the importance of employment that took young Jewish women outside the home, evidence indicates that most immigrant women and their daughters worked outside only while single. Married women generally participated in homework industries, and made frequent, if irregular, contributions to the family economy for much of their married lives. For some women, however, especially those who found employment outside home workshops, even low-paying and low-status work became liberating. While parents, communal workers, and club leaders exerted significant control over the behavior of single girls, the workplace offered greater freedom than school or home. Most made new friends; some left the confines of the East End. For young single girls, the factory provided a social life beyond watchful parental eyes, and even a chance for some rebellion.[88]

The programs of the JAPGW after 1918 indicate the new concerns over the welfare of young Jewish women. The need for neighborhood patrols and the opening of a "drop-in center" suggest a decline in the effectiveness of social control mechanisms developed for Jewish working-class girls. Increased criminal activity, even of a petty nature, indicates behavioral changes among the East End's Jewish women.[89] The JAPGW had to concern itself with only a small minority of the girls and women; its efforts reflect a grim determination to prevent the numbers from increasing. Most Jewish women responded to their new freedom without slipping into immoral or criminal activity. They remained in school longer, entered a wider range of occupations, and tended to move out of the East End upon marriage. Stripped of their alien ways, second- and third-generation Jews extended the movement of Jews north, northwest, and south. They brought with them the lessons learned in school, clubs, and from contact with native Anglo-Jewry.

Despite the enormous adjustment required of immigrants and their children, most, in time, were able to support themselves, and to climb up the socioeconomic ladder and out of the East End. By the interwar years, mothers had equipped their daughters with a range of skills. Along with their communal counterparts, these mothers taught a generation of daughters about their domestic duties, about the values of education (even if largely for boys), about devotion to family, and about appropriate behavior for newcomers to England. Immigrants learned their lessons well; by the 1930s their success at assimilation, however, led to new concerns about declining religious observance, and the dangers of the weakening of religious ties. The specter of Hitler, and virulent anti-Semitism looming on the horizon at that time remind us of one of the central paradoxes of communal mothering: in essence, that anglicization could become too successful.

Notes

I would like to express my gratitude to Grace Chang, Ruth Schwartz Cowan, Todd Endelman, Linda Rennie Forcey, J. Matthew Gallman, Evelyn Nakano Glenn, Martha May, and Martha Vicinus for encouragement and helpful suggestions. I am pleased to acknowledge support from the Sachar Fellowship Program and Tauber Institute at Brandeis University, the Memorial Foundation for Jewish Culture, the Faculty Research Committee at Bowdoin College, and the National Endowment for the Humanities.

1. Census of England and Wales, 911, *Birthplaces* Vol. IX, Cd. 7017, Table 4, "Country of Birth, Condition as to Marriage, and Ages of Males and Females of Foreign Nationality," pp. 176–177.

2. Nearly eighty percent of all Russian and Russian-Polish women (approximately eighty percent of whom were Jewish) over the age of fifteen were married. Among other foreign-born women (excluding Russians and Russian-Poles), this figure was only fifty-two percent. Among Russian and Russian-Polish men over the age of twenty, approximately eighty percent were married, as compared with nearly fifty-five percent of other foreign-born men. See Census of England and Wales, 1911, pp. 176–177.

3. Bernard Kops, *The World is A Wedding* (London: Vallentine, Mitchell, 1963), pp. 11, 25.

4. I am grateful to Ruth Schwartz Cowan for highlighting these points in her comments, prepared for the conference on "Contested Terrains: Constructions of Mothering," SUNY Binghamton, October 12–12, 1990, pp. 1–2.

5. A. M. Hyamson, "The Ten Lost Tribes and the Return of the Jews to England," *Transactions of the Jewish Historical Society of England TJHSE* 5 (1902–1905), pp. 115–147; David Katz, *Philo-Semitism and the Readmission of the Jews to England 1603-1655* (Oxford: Clarendon Press, 1982); Nathan Osterman, "The Controversy over the Proposed Readmission of Jews to England, (1655)," *Jewish Social Studies JSS* 3 (1941), 301–328; Don Patinkin, "Mercantilism and the Readmission of the Jews to England," *JSS* 8 (1946), pp. 161–178; M. Wilensky, "The Royalist Position Concerning the Readmission of Jews to England," *Jewish Quarterly Review* 42 (1950–1951), pp. 397–409; Lucien Wolf, *Menasseh ben Israel's Mission to Oliver Cromwell* (London: Macmillan & Co., Ltd, 1901).

6. The tradition apparently continued in some form into the 1930s when several girls from the Norwood Orphanage received twenty-five pounds from the Isaac Davis Dowry Fund or Palmer Trust Fund upon their marriage. See The Jewish Orphanage, *Report for the Year 1933*, p. 26; *Report for the Year 1934*, p. 24; *Report for the Year 1935*, p. 20.

7, David Schloss, "The Jew as Workman," *Nineteenth Century* 29 (1891), p. 108.

8. As early as 1890, Chief Rabbi Adler offered financial support to an East End *Talmud Torah* (a school for religious education) only if they would eliminate Yiddish as the language of instruction. This stance not only attacked the traditional places and methods of Jewish education, it was "also an attempt to Anglicize parents through children and thereby eliminate the language of Eastern European Jewish civilization and perhaps the culture itself." See Suzanne Greenberg, "Compromise and Conflict: The Education of Jewish Immigrant Children in London in the Aftermath of Emancipation, 1881-1905," PhD Dissertation, Stanford University, 1985, p. 91.

9. For a description of such problems for a mother and her children travelling to America, see, for example, Mary Antin, *From Plotzk to Boston,* 1899, (reissued by Markus Weiner Publishing, New York, 1986), pp. vii, 13.

10. Ruth Adler, *A Family of Shopkeepers* (Hodder and Stoughton: Coronet Edition, 1984) pp. 16–29. While a novel in form, *A Family of Shopkeepers* offers many insights into the lives of immigrants, and is one of the few written from the point of view of a woman. A note from the author speaks to this point: "The characters in this novel are all, in appearance and mannerism, drawn from life."

11. JAPGW, *Annual Report,* 1898, p. 27.

12. See Carol Dyhouse, *Girls Growing Up in Late Victorian and Edwardian England* (London: Routledge and Kegan Paul, 1981); and by the same author: "Good Wives and

Little Mothers: Social Anxieties and the Schoolgirl's Curriculum," *Oxford Review of Education* 3, No. 1 (1977), pp. 21–35; and "Social Darwinistic Ideas and the Development of Women's Education in England, 1880–1920," *History of Education* 5, No. 1 (1976), pp. 41–58.

13. Adler, *A Family of Shopkeepers*, pp. 31–2, 38.

14. Ena Abrahams, "I had this Other Life," in Jewish Women in London Group, eds., *Generations of Memories—Voices of Jewish Women* (London: The Women's Press, 1989), pp. 94–95.

15. Jewish Women in London Group, Oral History Interviews with F.V. and E.H.

16. JBG, *Annual Report,* 1884, p. 3. The work of middle-class, Jewish women suggests an interesting comparison with efforts to acculturate Mexican immigrants in the US between 1915 and 1929. In the case of Chicanos, social workers consciously focused their efforts on women. While Congress debated restricting Mexican immigration, others established Americanization programs specifically directed at women. See George Sanchez, " 'Go After the Women': Americanization and the Mexican Immigrant Woman, 1915–1929," in Ellen Carol Dubois and Vicki L. Ruiz, eds., *Unequal Sisters: A Multicultural Reader in U.S. Women's History* (New York: Routledge, 1990), pp. 250–263.

17. Continued anxiety over the reception of poor Jews, and the potential that they would arouse feelings of anti=-Semitism toward all Jews living in England is evident throughout the period of this study. In discussing their approach to charitable assistance, the Jewish Board of Guardians noted, in their published annual report for 1932, that they did not assist any young, able-bodied, unemployed persons, and directed such cases to the Public Assistance Department of the London County Council. The community formerly sought "to keep its poor off the rates." With the cessation of immigration, the Board concluded that "the Jew is as much entitled as his Gentile brother to the statutory assistance afforded by the State and the Municipality, and it is unreasonable to suggest that the authorities should be relieved of their obligation towards one portion of their citizens rather than another." Nonetheless, in a characteristic mode, they also contended that "it is perhaps politic to avoid sending to the Public Assistance committee those of foreign birth and pronouncedly foreign appearance, but even this is a matter of opinion." JBG *Annual Report,* 1932, p. 13.

18. Rev. S. Singer, "The Russo-Jewish Immigrant II," *English Illustrated Magazine* (1890–91), p. 846.

19. "Sermon at the West London Synagogue of British Jews—December 13, 1924," *Jewish Guardian* (December 26, 1924).

20. Ibid.

21. C. Baum, P. Hyman, and S. Michel, *The Jewish Woman in America* (New York: New American Library, 1975), pp. 55–71. Susan Glenn notes that, while this reality gave women "the rights and responsibilities of breadwinners," it also "limited their activities to work and domestic cares, privileging higher pursuits, such as education, for men." Susan A. Glenn, *Daughters of the Shtetl: Life and Labor in the Immigrant Generation* (Ithaca: Cornell University Press, 1990), p. 8ff.

22. Baum, Hyman, and Michel, *The Jewish Woman in America*, p. 55.

23. John Dyche, "The Jewish Workman," *Contemporary Review* 76 (September, 1899), p. 431.

24. Interdepartmental Committee on Physical Deterioration, *Parliamentary Papers,* 1904, XXXII, Minutes of Evidence, Cd. 2210, q. 1165–1166, p. 54.

25. Ena Abraham's grandmother, for example, cooked a midday meal for her daughter and two coworkers, who paid her "a couple of coppers [pennies] a day." Abrahams, "I Had this Other Life . . . ," p. 78.

26. Rickie Burman, "The Jewish Woman as Breadwinner: The Changing Value of Women's Work in a Manchester Immigrant Community," *Oral History Journal* 10 (1982), pp. 28, 30.

27. Jewish Colonization Association, *Recueil de Materiaux* I, pp. 251, 255, 285, and passim; 2: table 53 as quoted in Glenn, *Daughters of the Shtetl,* p. 19.

28. Board of Trade (Alien Immigration), Report on the Volume and Effects of Recent Immigration from Eastern Europe into the United Kingdom, *PP,* 1894, LXVIII, C. 7406, p. 105.

29. Board of Trade (Alien Immigration), Report on the Volume and Effects of Recent Immigration, pp. 101–102.

30. Board of Trade (Alien Immigration), Report on the Volume and Effects of Recent Immigration, p. 135.

31. Michele Barrett and Mary Mcintosh, "The 'Family Wage', Some Problems for Socialists and Feminists" *Capital and Class* (1980): pp. 56–7.

32. The Jewish Board of Guardians, established in 1859, offered a wide range of social services. The premiere charitable organization in the Jewish community, the JBG prided itself on its scientific methods, its ability to remain current with changing needs, and the widespread support and accolades it received. The JBG created programs and offered charitable assistance that raised health standards while attempting to improve the popular image of East End Jewry. For a fuller description of the work of the Jewish Board of Guardians, see, Laurie Magnus, *The Jewish Board of Guardians and the Men Who Made It* (London: The Jewish Board of Guardians, 1909); V. D. Lipman *A Century of Social Service, 1859–1959: The History of the Jewish Board of Guardians* (London: Routledge and Kegan Paul, 1959).

33. Union of Jewish Women, "Report of the Conference of Jewish Woman, 1902," Reprint, London: *Jewish Chronicle Office,* 1902, p. 36.

34. Union of Jewish Women, "Report of the Conference of Jewish Women, 1902," p. 36.

35. Board of Guardians for the Relief of the Jewish Poor, "A Short Account of the Work of the Jewish Board of Guardians and Trustees for the Relief of the Jewish Poor," London, N.D. [approx. 1924–5], p. 8.

36. Jewish Women in London Group, Oral History Interviews, Pearl Osen and Helen Goldstein.

37. Jewish Women in London Group, Oral History Interviews, Sara Oppenheim (pseudonym).

38. Tawney corroborates this view of women's labor, noting that the seasonal nature of male labor and low wages in London meant women had to work. He argues that more married women worked in London than in the North, where men earned higher wages. See R. H. Tawney, "The Establishment of Minimum Rates in the Tailoring Industry under the Trades Boards Act of 1909," *Studies in the Minimum Wage* No. 2, The Ratan Tata Foundation, University of London (London: G. Bell and Sons, Ltd., 1915), p. 113.

39. Barrett and McIntosh, "The 'Family Wage'," p. 57.

40. Census of England Wales, 1911, pp. 176–177.

41. Jewish Women in London Group, Oral History Interview, Sara Mashluck.

42. See James Schmiechen, *Sweated Industries and Sweated Labor—The London Clothing Trades, 1860–1914* (Urbana, IL: University of Illinois, 1984).

43. "*The Lancet* Special Sanitary Sommission on 'Sweating' among Tailors at Liverpool and Manchester," *The Lancet* (April 14, 1888), p. 740.

44. S. P. Dobbs, *The Clothing Workers of Great Britain* (London: George Routledge & Sons, Ltd., 1928), p. 178.

45. Schmiechen, *Sweated Industries and Sweated Labor,* p. 26.

46. JBG, *Annual Report,* 1885, p. 3; JAPGW, *Annual Report,* 1925, p. 3. Jewish Welfare Board Archives, JAPGW, May, 1918. JAPGW, *Annual Report,* 1926, p. 6.

47. Rudimentary calculations based on an average annual wage of twenty-seven pounds for domestics between 1883 and 1892, and a weekly wage of twelve to fourteen shillings for an average textile worker between 1886 and 1887, suggest that even with significant "slack" periods, those employed in the garment industry earned more than domestics. See

Edward Higgs, "Domestic Service and Household Production," in Angela V. John, ed., *Unequal Opportunities—Women's Employment in England 1880–1918* (Oxford: Basil Blackwell, 1986), pp. 138, 148. House of Lords, Select Committee on the Sweating System, Second Report, *PP* 1889, pp. 584–588.

48. The Jewish Welfare Board Archives, the Jewish Association for the Protection of Girls and Women, "Minutes of the General Purposes Committee," Letter to Lady Battersea, Hon. Secretary JAPGW, May 24, 1918.

49. UJW, *Annual Report*, 1903, pp. 7, 8; 1904, pp. 13, 14; 1906, pp. 11–12.

50. UJW, *Annual Report*, 1904, p. 13.

51. UJW, *Annual Report*, 1903, p. 13.

52. Union of Jewish Women, "Report of the Conference of Jewish Women," 1902, p. 66.

53. For an exception to this pattern see Anzia Yezierska's novel *Bread Givers* (Doubleday, 1925, reissued by Persea Books, New York 1975).

54. JBF, *Annual Report*, 1882, pp. 1, 2; JBG, *Annual Report*, 1886, p. 4; Union of Jewish Women, "Report on the Conference of Jewish Women," 1902, p. 66.

55. JBG, *Annual Report*, 1881, pp. 15, 48; *Annual Report*, 1882, p. 22; *Annual Report*, 1886, p. 23.

56. JBG, *Annual Report*, 1882, p. 22.

57. JBG, *Annual Report*, 1897, p. 57.

58. JBG, *Annual Report*, 1881, p. 48.

59. JBG, *Annual Report*, 1881, p. 48.

60. JBG, *Annual Report*, 1883, p. 61.

61. JBG, *Annual Report*, 1896, p. 64.

62. Archives of Jewish Care, University of Southhampton, MS 173, Minute Book, Industrial Committee, Oct. 27, 1904.

63. Barry Kosmin, "Traditions of Work Amongst British Jews," in Sandra Wallman, ed., *Ethnicity at Work* (London: Macmillan Press, 1979), p. 46.

64. JBG, *Annual Report*, 1904, p. 67.

65. JBG, *Annual Report*, 1904, p. 67.

66. JBG, *Annual Report*, 1905, p. 73.

67. JBG, *Annual Report*, 1904, pp. 73, 74.

68. JBG, *Annual Report*, 1908, p. 80.

69. *Daily Telegraph* (January 27, 1915, and February 1, 1916).

70. *Daily Telegraph* (February 1, 1916).

71. See Gail Braybon, *Women Workers in the First World War* (London: Croom Helm, 1981).

72. JAPGW, *Annual Report*, 1925, p. 49 and 1935–6, p. 49.

73. Revd Levy (term used for Jewish clergy) offered an explanation for the limited parental resistance to the anglicization program. Anglicization, which "is the act or process by which persons learn to conform to English modes or usages, in speech, in matter, in mental attitude and in principles" did not make demands on the conscience, and therefore parents "willingly submit their children in thousands to its beneficent influence." Reverend S. Levy, "Problems of Anglicization (1911)," Reprinted in the *Jewish Annual* VI London (1943), p. 76.

74. "A daughter," noted Ada Heather-Bigg, "receiving subsistence and a certain amount of pocket money, 'helps' her father; a wife, receiving subsistence and no pocket money, 'helps' her husband. It is not till the wife as a widow, and the daughter as an orphan, do precisely similar work at fixed rates for a tailor not related to them, that the world realizes that what is called 'helping' father or husband is really 'maintaining' herself." See Ada Heather-Bigg, "The Wife's Contribution to the Family Income," *Economic Journal* IV (1894), p. 53.

75. Phyllis Gerson, Gerson Papers, (privately held), London, p. 4.

76. A rough comparison of the occupational censuses for 1891 and 1911 shows remarkable consistency in the pattern of employment for Jewish women over a twenty-year period. Both the 1891 and 1911 census record sixty-nine percent of Russian and Russian-Polish immigrant women's work as "unspecified," and about twenty-three percent in the garment industry. In 1891 about two percent of the women worked as domestic servants, this figure rising to three percent by 1911. The tobacco industry saw a small growth in female employees, increasing from about 1.5 percent in 1891 to 2.1 percent in 1911. See Census of England and Wales, 1921, Vol. 7, *General Tables*, p. 134.

77. The 1921 census illustrates these shifts. Nearly eighteen percent of Russian-born women now entered commercial and financial occupations. Another eight percent worked as clerks, draughtsmen, and typists; yet fifty percent still found their employment in some branch of the textile industry. While some of these Russian women were non-Jewish emigres who left Russia after the revolution, this shift undoubtedly also reflects the changing work opportunities for women in the years following World War I. Census of England and Wales, 1921, p. 134.

78. *Jewish Chronicle* (Jan. 31, 1913).

79. Jewish Working Girls' Club, *Annual Report*, 1932, p. 8, 9.

80. The Beatrice Club, *Annual Report*, 1938, p. 8.

81. JBG, "A Short Account of the Jewish Board of Guardians," p. 12.

82. Bernhard Baron Oxford and St. George's Jewish Settlement, *Annual Report*, 1930–31, p. 10.

83. *Jewish Graphic* (February 11, 1927).

84. *Jewish Graphic* (December 17, 1926).

85. St. George's Jewish Settlement, *Annual Report*, 1926–1927, p. 8.

86. St. George's Jewish Settlement, *Annual Report*, 1919–1920, pp. 9–10.

87. Charcroft House, the Jewish Association for the Protection of Girls and Women's Rescue Home, assisted "poor Jewish fallen girls, and child mothers." For the year 1888–1889 there were only fifteen inmates. The House had beds that went unused, and the organizers regretted that some "poor outcasts" avoided their home because they believed it to have a prisonlike routine. Nonetheless, the House generally housed fewer than thirty young women, an indication of the relative rarity of illegitimacy among Jewish girls and women. See *Report of the Jewish Ladies Association for Preventive and Rescue Work*, 1888–9, p. 15. In 1912, Charcroft had sixteen inmates, twenty-nine mothers in 1923–4, and eighteen mothers between April, 1937 and March, 1938. JAPGW, *Annual Report*, 1912, p. 62; *Annual Report*, 1923–4, p. 54; *Annual Report*, 1938, p. 60.

88. David Schloss, "The Jew as Workman," *Nineteenth Century* 29 (1891), p. 108. The anxiety over boys focused on their employment training and prospects, and less on controlling their behavior.

89. JAPGW, *Annual Report*, 1926, pp. 43–44; *Annual Report*, 1927, p. 24.

Chapter 15

NEGOTIATING LESBIAN MOTHERHOOD: THE DIALECTICS OF RESISTANCE AND ACCOMMODATION[1]

Ellen Lewin

When I first began to assemble resources for a study of lesbian mothers in 1976, very few people were aware of the existence of such a category, and if they were, they usually saw it as an oxymoron. Lesbian mothers occasionally gained the attention of the general public when they were involved in custody cases that received publicity, but such notoriety was infrequent and typically fleeting. In fact, aside from those who had lesbian mothers in their social circles, even the wider lesbian population was aware of lesbian mothers mainly in connection with custody cases. In the early collections of articles on lesbian issues that emerged from the lesbian feminist movement, lesbian mothers were almost never mentioned except in connection with their vulnerability to custody litigation.[2] Mothers in these cases either lost custody of their children, or won custody only under highly compromised conditions, sometimes with the stipulation that the child have no contact with the mother's partner.[3]

Well-known custody cases in the 1970s demonstrated the likelihood that lesbian mothers would face considerable discrimination in court. The Mary Jo Risher case, in which a mother lost custody of her younger son after her teenaged son testified against her, was perhaps the best documented of these, particularly after the story was dramatized as a made-for-TV movie.[4] And the case of Sandy and Madeleine, two mothers who became lovers and subsequently had custody challenged by both ex-husbands, was extensively publicized in the lesbian community with the circulation of a film called "Sandy and Madeleine's Family." The case demonstrated that lesbian mothers' custody could be challenged repeatedly, even after a favorable ruling in court, at least until the children achieved majority. The film, originally produced for use in court, emphasized the strong religious values of the mothers, their involvement in wholesome activities with both sets of children, and the warmth and nurturance of the family environment they provided.[5]

All these images of lesbian mothers were defensive. When lesbian mothers found themselves in court, they necessarily had to convince the judge (and in the Risher case, the jury) that they were as good at being mothers as any other women, that they were, in fact, *good* in the sense of possessing the moral attributes of altruism and nurturance that are culturally demanded of mothers in North American cultures. In these formulations, mothers are assumed to be *naturally* equipped to place their children's interests ahead of their own, to be selfless in a way that precludes or overshadows their own sexuality;[6] such assumptions are at the heart of twentieth-century presumptions of maternal suitability for custody.[7] When mothers are lesbians, however, the courts, reflecting popular views of homosexuality as "unnatural," tend to view them as morally flawed, and thus as unfit parents. Their task in dealing with the legal system, therefore, is to demonstrate that they possess the "natural" attributes expected of mothers, and are thus worthy of receiving custody of their children. Maternal virtue, therefore, shifts from being a quality inherent to women to being a behavior one must actively demonstrate in order to pursue a claim to custody.[8]

While many lesbian mothers understood that the way to keep custody of their children was to show that they were "as good as" heterosexual mothers, they firmly believed that they would eventually be shown to be superior parents who were bringing new, nonsexist families into being. They viewed the two-parent, heterosexual, nuclear family as the arena in which the patriarchy inscribed gender expectations onto both women and men. If the power dynamics of that family form were largely responsible for the continuing devalued status of women, and for a variety of abusive practices, then a domestic arrangement based on presumably nongendered relations between two "equal" women partners would constitute a first step toward the better sort of world feminists dreamed of. Jeanne Vaughn, the coeditor of *Politics of the Heart: A Lesbian Parenting Anthology,* put it this way:

> We have an opportunity for radical social change beginning in our homes, change that requires rethinking our views of family, of kinship, of work, of social organization. We need to develop some specifically lesbian-feminist theories of family. How would/did/could we mother our children without the institution of compulsory heterosexuality?[9]

The image many lesbian mothers conjured up was utopian, resembling the broad outlines of Charlotte Perkins Gilman's *Herland,* a fictional society of women in which motherhood and caring were elevated to the center of the inhabitants' lives. Without the need to serve and please powerful males, without the degradations of daily experience in a patriarchal society, Gilman's image suggests, women might be free to express their true, nurturant natures. They would reveal abilities unlikely to emerge in male-dominated society, and would focus on creative, constructive projects rather than on frivolities such as fancy dress and (hetero)sexuality.[10]

The popular images of mothers and families that dominated the lesbian community in the 1970s, then, focused on the ways in which being a mother and having a family could constitute a form of resistance to traditional, and thereby patriarchal, family forms. In particular, success at motherhood (as measured by how well one's child turned out) would demonstrate that children did not need the structure of a heterosexual family, and, most significantly, the regular contribution of a father, to develop normally. The achievement of lesbian mothers would both counteract the notion that lesbianism and motherhood are inherently contradictory and, in fact, redefine and desexualize what it means to be a lesbian.

At the same time, however, the complexities of living as a mother required lesbian mothers to reinstate the dichotomy of natural/unnatural and mother/nonmother that their redefinition of lesbianism sought to subvert. Negotiating the daily issues of being a mother and meeting obligations to one's children brought them into conflict both with the dominant heterosexist society and with lesbians who had not chosen motherhood.

FEMINIST VIEWS OF RESISTANCE

When many of us took up a feminist agenda in our scholarship, directing our attention to documenting the experience of women from their point of view, it seemed that we had no choice but to concentrate on describing a depressing history of victimization and oppression. As we examined the social and cultural lives of women, not only in familiar terrain, but also outside Western traditions, we found over and over again that women were confined to secondary social status, relegated to devalued cultural roles, and often brutalized and demeaned in their daily lives. The evidence of despair poured in, bolstered at every turn by the grim discoveries we continued to make about our own society and our own lives.[11]

In many instances, the best it seemed that we could offer to help remedy this situation was to produce astute, woman-centered descriptions of the conditions under which women's lives were lived, paired with analyses geared toward change. In many instances, feminist scholars directed their energies toward the documentation of women's point of view, focusing on ways to dissolve the hegemony of male-centered assumptions about the organization of social life and women's place in it. In anthropology, such work often proposed alternative views of traditionally patriarchal institutions.[12] But in other instances, feminist interpretations came to center on resistance, looking at how even clearly oppressed women might take action on their own behalf, either by directly sabotaging the instruments of male dominance, or by constituting their consciousness in a way that undermined their subordination.[13]

Feminist scholars have most commonly applied the concept of resistance to studies of women in the work force. Bonnie Thornton Dill's research on Black women household workers, for example, focuses on the way they manage their relationships with employers to enhance their own self-respect. She documents how these workers organized "strategies for gaining mastery over work that was socially defined as demeaning and . . . actively resisted the depersonalization of household work."[14]

Along similar lines, Aihwa Ong, writing about women factory workers in Malaysia, shows how labor practices introduced by capitalism lead to the reconstruction of meanings of gender and sexuality. In response to proletarianization, Malay women organize cultural responses to their changing status, most markedly in the form of episodes of spirit possession. "Spirit attacks," Ong tells us, "were indirect retaliations against coercion and demands for justice in personal terms within the industrial milieu."[15]

Notions of resistance have also informed studies of women outside the workplace. Emily Martin, for example, has contrasted women's ideas about their bodies and the ideology of mainstream medicine, describing instances in which women resist medical assumptions at variance with their own experience. She sees working-class women as most able to reject scientific metaphors of women's bodies, particularly those that focus on production and failed production, perhaps because "they have less to gain from productive labor in the society."[16] Self-consciousness and verbal protest are taken as evidence of resistance in Martin's analysis, as are instances of sabotage or outright refusal to cooperate with medical instructions.

Louise Lamphere's study of immigrant factory workers in New England also looks carefully at resistance, but frames it as one of several strategies women can mount to cope with employers' efforts to control their lives. She views women "as active strategists, weighing possibilities and devising means to realize goals, and not as passive acceptors of their situations."[17] Lamphere cautions, however, against viewing all of women's actions on their own behalf as resistance. Rather, she emphasizes the importance of distinguishing between "strategies of resistance" and "strategies of accommodation," pointing out that some strategies may best be seen as adjustments that allow women to cope with their place in the labor market by diffusing employers' control of the workplace. Such strategies ought not to be viewed, Lamphere says, as resistance only, since they may not be based in purposeful opposition to the employer, and since they may only result in continuing exploitation of the workers, and, as such, constitute a kind of consent to existing relations of domination.[18]

Taking a different approach, Judith Butler has proposed that scholars reconsider their dependence on the concept of gender, arguing that gender, as a dualistic formulation, rests on the same asymmetry that feminists seek to overturn. She urges the adoption of strategies that would "disrupt the oppositional binary itself,"[19] and suggests that calling into question the "continuity and coherence" of gender identities, sabotaging the "intelligibility" of gender, would undermine the "regulatory aims" of gender as a cultural system.[20] Butler's claim seems to be that lesbianism, or other sexual stances at odds with normative heterosexuality, could constitute a kind of resistance to the very existence of gender. She locates gender continuities within the domain of sexuality, viewing "intelligible" genders ... as those which in some sense institute and maintain relations of coherence and continuity among sex, gender, sexual practice, and desire."[21] The decisions one takes with regard to one's identity, then, and in particular, the extent to which they may be said to destabilize conventional expectations and representations, may constitute resistance not only to specific forms of oppression, but to the oppressive effects of gender as an ideological straitjacket.

All of these approaches to resistance reveal a commitment to render women as active subjects. While these scholars are reluctant to blame women for their subordination, neither are they willing to cast them as hapless victims of actions wholly beyond their control. Women are thus seen as capable of framing strategies for enhancing their situations, whether the battleground be material—as when women's resistance improves their working conditions—or symbolic—as when refusal to conform to common conventions of gender may be interpreted as constituting sabotage of the larger system.

This concern with subjectivity and agency raises significant questions for the study of women who seem to defy gender limitations in any aspect of their lives. Just as Butler has suggested that incongruent sexuality might be viewed as resistance, one might ask whether other "disorders" of sexuality and gender could also be viewed in this light. The question becomes particularly pressing when women themselves explain their behavior as subversive. We must then ask whether apparently conscious refusals by lesbian mothers, or any other group of women, to accept the strictures of gender are best understood as instances of resistance.

LESBIAN MOTHERS AND RESISTANCE TO HETEROSEXISM

By the time I was well into my research, at the end of the 1970s, the custody problems that had concerned me at the outset were no longer the only issues facing lesbian mothers. Pregnant women were starting to appear at lesbian social gatherings, at political meetings and concerts, sometimes alone and sometimes in the company of their lovers. These women were not, for the most part, new to lesbian life; most had never been married, and child custody fears did not figure prominently for them. They certainly had not become pregnant by accident. While some of the mothers and mothers-to-be had had romantic interludes with men, more explained how they had "made themselves pregnant" by arranging a sexual situation with a man, or by using some form of "insemination."[22]

The emphasis in these women's accounts of their experiences was on how they had to overcome their earlier fears that being lesbian would preclude motherhood. Lesbians reported that they had often thought of themselves as not being suitable mothers, having internalized images of homosexuals as self-serving, immature, or otherwise not capable of the kind of altruism basic to maternal performance.

Sarah Klein,[23] a lesbian who lives with her one-year-old daughter and her lover, explained the conflict as she perceived it:

> I've always wanted to have a child. In terms of being real tied up with being gay, it was one of the reasons that for a long time I was hesitant to call myself a lesbian. I thought that automatically assumed you had nothing to do with children. . . . I felt, well, if you don't *say* you're a lesbian, you can still work with children, you can still have a kid, you can have relationships with men. But once I put this label on myself, [it would] all [be] over.

By having a child, Sarah repudiated the boundaries she had once associated with being a lesbian; she has claimed what she sees as her right to be a mother.

But other lesbians' accounts indicate that not all perceive themselves as having had a lifelong desire for motherhood. Among those who claim not to remember wanting children when they were younger was Kathy Lindstrom. She had a child by insemination when she was in her early 30s, but says that she never considered the possibility until a few years earlier. She could only explain her behavior as arising from some sort of "hormonal change."

> It just kind of came over me. It wasn't really conscious at first. It was just a need.

Kathy's understanding of her desire to be a mother as something "hormonal," that is, natural, suggests an implicit assertion that this is something so deep and so essentially part of her that nothing, including her lesbianism, can undermine it. Her account indicates that she refuses to allow the associations others have with her status as a lesbian to interfere with her own perception of herself and her needs.

Other lesbian mothers view their urge to have a child as stemming from a desire to settle down, to achieve adulthood, and to counteract forces toward instability in their lives. Ruth Zimmerman, who had a five-year-old son from a relationship with a man she selected as a "good" father, had ended the relationship soon after she became pregnant.

> I definitely felt like I was marking time, waiting for something. I wasn't raised to be a career woman. I was raised to feel like I was grown up and finished growing up and living a regular normal life when I was married and had kids. And I knew that the married part wasn't going to happen. I feel like I've known that for a long time.

Like Kathy, Ruth defined her progress as a human being, and as a woman, in terms that are strikingly conventional and recall traditional feminine socialization. While clearly accepting motherhood as a marker of adulthood and "living a normal life," Ruth tried to overcome the equally conventional limits placed on lesbians in order to have her child.

The notion that having a child signifies adulthood, the acceptance of social responsibility, and demonstrates that one has "settled down" appears in the accounts of many lesbian mothers. Most often, lesbian mothers speak of their lives before motherhood as empty and aimless, and see the birth of their children as having centered them emotionally. They frequently cite new interests in education, nutrition, and health, and reconciliations with family members with whom they had not been on good terms, as evidence of their new maturity. As Louise Green, a young lesbian mother who describes herself as a former hippie, explains: "I think [having my daughter] has turned my life into this really good thing."

Louise describes herself as living a marginal, disorganized existence until she finally decided that she would have a child. She did not consider using mainstream medicine to get pregnant, assuming that such resources would never be available to her, both for financial reasons and because she would be viewed with hostility by medical professionals. Instead, she went about asking men she met whether they would like to be sperm donors; she finally located a willing prospect and obtained a sperm sample from him. Louise never told this man her real name, and once she had conceived she left the area, concerned that he could somehow pose a threat to her relationship with her child.

Louise's account focuses on conception and birth as spiritual transitions to a higher and better existence. She became pregnant on her first attempt, which she explained as evidence that mystical forces "meant" for this to happen. She wanted very much to have a home delivery, but after a protracted and complicated labor, she was transferred to a hospital, where she finally gave birth with the aid of multiple technological interventions. Despite this interference with the kind of spiritual environment she had hoped to give birth in, Louise describes the entire experience in mystical terms.

> It was about the best thing I ever experienced. I was totally amazed. The labor was like I had died. . . . I had just died. The minute she came out, I was born again. It was like we'd just been born together.

Louise did not allow either her counterculture life-style or her status as a lesbian to interfere with the spiritual agenda she felt destined to complete. She says the mystical process she underwent in becoming a mother has permitted her to become more fully herself, to explore aspects of her being that would have remained hidden if she allowed lesbianism alone to define who she is.

> [After] I had [my daughter] I felt it was okay to do these things I've been wanting to do real bad. One of them is to paint my toenails red. I haven't done it yet, but I'm going to do it. I felt really okay about wearing perfume and I just got a permanent in my hair. . . . I feel like I'm robbing myself of some of the things I want to do by trying to fit this lesbian code. I feel like by my having this child, it has already thrown me out in the sidelines.

Louise has used the process of becoming a mother to construct her identity in a way that includes being a lesbian but also draws from other sources. She sees her need to do this as essential and intended, and has moved along her path with the assurance that she is realizing her destiny.

Not all lesbians become mothers as easily as Louise. On a purely practical level, of course, the obstacles to a lesbian becoming pregnant can be formidable. Even if she knows a man who is interested in such a venture, she might not contemplate a heterosexual liaison with enthusiasm and might be equally reluctant to ask him to donate sperm. Mainstream medicine may not seem like an option either, because of financial considerations, or because of fears that doctors will be unwilling to inseminate a lesbian or even a single woman—a realistic concern, of course.

Once one has defined oneself as a lesbian, the barriers to becoming a mother are so significant, in fact, that many of the formerly married lesbian mothers I interviewed explained that they had gone through with marriages (sometimes of long duration) because this seemed the only way to realize their dream of being mothers and being normal in the eyes of their families and communities.

Harriet Newman, an artist who lives with her two daughters in a rural area north of San Francisco, fell in love with another woman during her first year in college. Her parents discovered the affair and forced her to leave school and to see a psychiatrist. The experience convinced her that it would be safer "to be a regular person in the world." When she met a gay man who also wanted to live more conventionally, they married, and almost immediately had their two children.

> The main thing that made us decide to get married was that we very much wanted to part of the mainstream of life, instead of on the edges. We wanted to be substantial . . . part of the common experience.

For lesbians who become mothers through insemination or some other method,[24] then, conscious resistance to rigid formulations of "the lesbian" seems to be central to their intentions. Unwilling to deny their identity as lesbians, they also demand the right to define what that identity constitutes. The intrinsic benefits of motherhood—the opportunity to experience birth and child development—are experiences they do not want to forego. In particular, once the relatively simple technology of donor insemination became widely known, and given the haphazard controls exerted over access to sperm donations, lesbians have come to understand that they can, indeed, be mothers. Access to motherhood thus comes to be viewed as a "civil right" not dissimilar to equal opportunity in the job market, or other rights lesbians and gay men now demand with increasing insistence.

In some instances, women explained that their age made having a child imperative. Laura Bergeron, who had two sons from a relationship prior to coming out, decided to find a donor for a third child when she entered her late 30s.

> I really did want to have a girl, and I was getting older. . . . I was feeling that I didn't really want to have children past the appropriate childbearing age. I had been doing too much reading about retardation and mongoloids and everything else . . . so I put some ads [for donors] in the paper.

Annabel Jessop voices similar concerns, explaining that she decided to use artificial insemination to become pregnant even though she would have preferred being settled in a long-term relationship before embarking on motherhood.

> I decided that I wanted to have a kid, and that because I'm in my 30s my time was limited. I look at it as a life choice. There's only so many things you can do in your life, and this is one of the things I wanted to do, and it was time to do it. Waiting wasn't going to do any good. Professionally,

I was together, I was as stable as I was every going to be financially, I had a little put away, and there was just no reason not to do it now.

Becoming a mother is central to being able to claim to an identity as a "good" woman, drawn from one's association with children. Mothers describe childhood as a time of innocence and discovery, and a mother can gain spiritual benefits through her contribution to a child's development. One lesbian mother explained:

> You get to have a lot of input in another human being's very formative years. That's real special to have that privilege of doing that, and you get to see them growing and developing and it's sort of like you put in the fertile soil and . . . hopefully what will happen is that they grow and blossom and become wonderful. . . . I think it's definitely the most important thing that people do . . . to build the next generation.

As Louise Green's narrative indicated, lesbians often characterize their transformation into mothers as a spiritual journey, an experience that gives them access to special knowledge and that makes them worthier than they otherwise could have been. Regina Carter, whose daughter is six, put it this way:

> My kid has given me more knowledge than any other experience in my life. She's taught me more than all the teachings I've ever learned as far as education, and I mean that as far as academic education, spiritual education. Taught me things that no other person, place or thing could possibly teach me. And those are, you know, those things are without words.

Similarly, Bonnie Peters echoed these views when she told me that being a mother connected her with sources of honesty and worthiness.

> I've become more at peace with me [since having my daughter]. She's given me added strength; she's made me—it's like looking in the mirror in many ways; she's made me see myself for who I am. She's definitely given me self-worth. I've become, I think, a more honest person.

Motherhood, then, can draw a woman closer to basic truths, sensitizing her to the feelings of others and discovering a degree of altruism they had not perceived in themselves prior to having a child. It may provide the opportunity for a woman to make clear her involvement with a kind of authenticity, a naturalness, that brings her closer to profound, but ineffable, truths.

MANAGING LESBIAN MOTHERHOOD

While the accounts given by some lesbian mothers suggest that they have resisted the cultural opposition between "mother" and "lesbian" and demanded the right to be both, the ongoing management of being a lesbian mother may depend on separating these two statuses, thus intensifying their dichotomization. Lesbian mothers frequently speak of these two dimensions of their identities as competing or interfering with each other; conflicts with lesbians who are not mothers sometimes further solidify these divisions.

Tanya Petroff, who lives with her seven-year-old daughter in an East Bay city, speaks evocatively of how being a mother overshadows her identity as a lesbian.

> The mothering thing, the thing about being a mother seems to be more important to me than my sexual orientation. . . . I've had [lesbians] tell me that I had chosen a privileged position in having a child and if it was going to be difficult for me then it was too goddam bad.

For Tanya, the conflict is most acute when she is developing a new relationship with another woman. She must then make clear that she views herself and her daughter as an indivisible social unit that takes precedence over other attachments.

> I'm definitely part of a package deal. I come with my daughter and people who can't relate to both of us are not people I want to relate to for very long.

What this means in terms of other relationships is that Tanya sees other mothers, regardless of whether they are gay or straight, as the people with whom she has the most in common. Since relocating to the Bay Area from a town in the Midwest, Tanya has tended to minimize her contact with what she calls the "lesbian community" in favor of socializing with other mothers. She feels that she is better able to resist pressures to raise her daughter to be a "little amazon," an expectation she believes common to lesbians who are not mothers. Beyond this, Tanya feels that there are simply too many practical obstacles to meaningful friendships with women who are not mothers. Living alone and having a demanding job mean that Tanya has to plan ahead to arrange child care. People who don't have children are no help with this; she accounts for this by explaining that they are "single," meaning that they have no children. There is such a deep gulf between mothers and nonmothers, in her view, that there is simply no meaningful basis for understanding or trust.

There is a difference between people who have children and people who don't have children. People who don't have children, to my way of thinking, are very selfish. . . . They needn't consider anyone other than themselves. They can do exactly what they want to do at any given time. And though I admire that, it's not possible for me to do that and I guess for that reason most of my friends are single mothers, because it's hard for me to coordinate my needs and my time with someone who's in a completely different head set. "Why can't you get a sitter for the kid?"—that kind of thing. . . . I just prefer being with people who have some sense of what it's like to be me, and I understand where they are too.

Tanya's belief that she can only find truly supportive friends among those whose situations closely mirror her own with respect to single motherhood grows not only out of her very real need for material assistance, but also from the importance she places on having friends who affirm or validate her identity. The most essential aspect of her identity, by this account, is that of being a mother. It supersedes her sexual orientation, her ethnicity, her job.

For some lesbian mothers, difficult experiences with lovers parallel disappointments with the wider lesbian community. Leslie Addison, who lives alone with her twelve-year-old daughter, describes a long series of conflicts with lesbian community groups over support for mothers. While she can easily explain the failure of these women to be conscious about mothers as stemming from their being "single," she has had a harder time dealing with lovers and prospective lovers who do not understand or are unwilling to accommodate her needs as a mother. Shortly after her divorce, she began her first relationship with a woman with the expectation that a woman lover would naturally help her with her child, and be eager to participate in their family activities. Leslie found instead that her lover was reluctant to spend more than minimal amounts of time with her daughter, never offering to help with child care or domestic responsibilities. Ironically, when she was straight, she says that she could always get a boyfriend to baby-sit for her; as a lesbian, she finds that women usually refuse to do child care.

That wasn't quite what I expected. I expected there would be more sharing between women of the child. But I found it's really not, because another woman has a role identity crisis. She can't be the mother, because you're already the mother. She can't be the father, because she's not the father, whereas the men sort of played that role. It was easier for them to fall into it. They could just play daddy, I could play momma, and everybody'd be happy.

The stark separation between "mother" and "lesbian" as elements of identity may be even more sharply drawn for women concerned with maintaining secrecy about their sexual orientation. In these instances, daily life is segregated into time when they are "mothers" and time when they are "lesbians," creating constant concern about information management and boundary maintenance. While some mothers who voice these concerns are motivated by fears about custody, others seem to be more worried by what they understand to be broad community standards. Segregation may seem the best way to protect children from being stigmatized, but in addition, lesbian mothers know that motherhood itself tends to preclude their being suspected of homosexuality. As one mother explained, "Of course, I have the mask. I have a child. I'm accepted [as heterosexual] because I have a child and that kind of protection."

Laura Bergeron, who had three children outside of marriage, is not only secretive about her lesbianism in her relations with the wider community, but she has not allowed her children to find out that she is a lesbian. Her lover, a married woman, is unwilling to do anything that might disrupt current arrangements, and Laura explains that her lover's situation is the major reason for her secrecy. But she is also concerned that the father of her two sons might try to get custody if he know about her sexual orientation, despite the fact that he only agreed to help her get pregnant with the stipulation that he would never have any formal obligations to their children. And she fears that her civil service job would somehow be compromised as well were her sexual orientation known.

> There's just no way that we could ever be anything but heavily closeted. We have a lot of women's activities that go on here, but we don't mix the worlds. . . . That's why my children can't know. . . . I've set up my life so that it doesn't include my children.

Laura has made complicated arrangements for supervising her children before and after school and, in order to spend more time with her lover, has installed an intercom between the two houses that enables her to monitor her kids' activities. Meeting both her children's and her lover's needs means that she has little time for herself, and she sees most of her time with her children as mechanical. While she describes motherhood as separate from her "life," it is clear that managing the division between the two worlds creates a problem in organizing her identity.

For some women who maintain strict separation between their identities as mothers and as lesbians, the threat of custody litigation is more than an abstract fear. Theresa Baldocchi, whose son is nine years old, survived a protracted custody trial at the time she divorced her former husband, John. Her legal expenses and liability for debts incurred by John during their marriage left her virtually bankrupt, and it has taken years for her to solidify her financial situation. Theresa was not a lesbian at the time of the divorce, but John made allegations that she was. Now that she has come out, she is convinced that she must carefully separate her life as a mother and as a lesbian, lest her former husband decide to institute another custody case against her. Despite the fact that John has an extensive history of psychiatric hospitalization, and that she is a successful professional, she is sure that her chances of winning in such a trial would be slim.

> Now that I'm gay, I'd lose. There's just no way in the world I would win, after having had my fitness questioned when I was Lady Madonna, let alone now.

Theresa has decided that living in a middle-class suburban area and arranging her home in an impeccably conventional fashion help shield her from suspicion of being anything other than a typical "mom." The Bay Bridge, which she must cross each day between her home and San Francisco, where she works and socializes with her lesbian friends, symbolizes her strategy. She feels that each trip involves a palpable transition, as she prepares herself to meet the requirements of her destination—home or San Francisco. Most crucial for her strategy is not telling her son that she is a lesbian, since she feels it would be inappropriate to expect him to maintain her secret.

If Theresa was concerned only with managing information about her homosexuality, she would probably avoid seeing her former husband, and thus be able to relax, at least, at home. But Theresa firmly believes that being a good mother demands that she take every opportunity to maximize her son's contact with John, a model father in her eyes. Because John is not regularly employed, he has offered to take care of their son each day while Theresa is at work. This arrangement has meant both that Theresa does not have to obtain paid child care during these hours, and that her son has daily contact with his father. It also means that she has virtually no privacy. She must control the kinds of friends who visit her, and must make sure that nothing that might reveal her sexual orientation can be found in her home. Most poignantly, she must limit her lover's access to her home for fear that her presence would somehow make the situation transparent. She consigns her most reliable potential source of support to the background, leaving herself isolated and anxious much of the time.

In other instances, lesbian mothers may separate the two aspects of their lives in order to maintain fragile relationships with their families. Rita García, who lives in San Francisco with her eight-year-old son and her lover, Jill Hacker, has made arrangements with her family that she believes can be sustained only if she avoids mention of her partner and their relationship. She comes from a large and close Mexican-American family. When they first learned that she was a lesbian, shortly after her divorce, they were so angry, and so convinced that she was no longer a fit parent, that they briefly considered supporting her husband's claim for custody. Once the case finally came to trial, however, Rita's husband abandoned his interest in custody. The family learned, during these proceedings, that he had abused her on numerous occasions, once beating her so severely that she had to go to the hospital. They withdrew their support from her husband, but also refused to communicate with Rita.

Rita did not see her parents at all for over a year. When Rita's grandmother had surgery and demanded to see her favorite granddaughter, the family relented, and Rita became a central figure in the grandmother's nursing care. The crisis allowed her to be reintegrated into the family, and she began once again to be her mother's closest confidante. This rapprochement, however, was founded on an unspoken agreement that Rita not mention her lover or anything about her home life.

The situation had stabilized, with Rita spending a great deal of time with her parents. Her sons attends a Catholic school in her parents' neighborhood, so she drops him off there each day on her way to work. Rita's mother makes him breakfast every morning, and after school he returns to his grandparents' house to play and do his homework. Before Rita picks him up in the evening, he usually eats dinner as well, which allows Rita to work overtime at her job. Whenever Rita and Jill have plans in the evening, he spends the night with his grandparents. Besides this kind of practical support, Rita depends on her father for help with her car and for advice about financial matters. She is close to her sister, and often exchanges overnight baby-sitting with her.

But Rita never mentions her lover to her family, and her parents have established a strict policy of never visiting her home. Jill is never invited to family events, spending Christmas and Thanksgiving with her own family. While her parents know that she is a lesbian, Rita has decided not to tell her son, reasoning that it might be difficult for him to manage his relations with his grandparents if he had to be secretive about this topic. Separating her identity as a lesbian from her identity as a mother is consistent with her notion of being a good mother. Her son's welfare is enhanced by his ties to his grandparents, and Rita is able to provide better for him with the assistance they provide. Anything that might undermine that relationship would have the effect of harming her child, and that would make her a bad mother, undeserving, should the issue come up again, of being the custodial parent.

Other mothers explain the separation of motherhood from other dimensions of their lives, and the centrality of being a mother, to framing their identities more practically, citing the weighty and unrelenting obligations faced by parents. Peggy Lawrence, who lives with her lover, Sue Alexander, her ten-year-old daughter, and Sue's two sons, spoke at length about the effects of being a mother on her personal freedom. Being a mother means that she must be concerned about continuity and stability in ways that constrain her spontaneity, and earning money must be a priority no matter how oppressive her work. Peggy and Sue live in a neighborhood close to their children's school, and have chosen to live in San Francisco because they think their children will encounter less discrimination here as the children of lesbians than in the Midwest, where they would prefer to live. Peggy explains what being a mother means to her:

> Being a mother, to me—being a mother is more consuming than any other way that I could possibly imagine identifying myself . . . any other way that I identify myself is an identification of some part of my being a mother. I am a lesbian mother, I am a working mother—"mother" hardly ever modifies any other thing. Mother is always the primary—it's always some kind of mother, but it's never a mother-anything. Mother is—mother, for mothers, is always the thing that is more consuming.

But others understand motherhood to mean the uniquely intense feelings that exist between mother and child. Lisa Stark, who describes the weightiness of single parenthood as almost unbearable, has come to see her children as the reason she can continue to struggle with her obligations, paradoxically the explanation for both her suffering and her very survival.

> I've . . . never had to live for myself. The only reason I get up in the morning is to get them off to school. For me to trot off to work in order to earn the money to support them. I don't know what I'd do if I didn't have them. They're everything I've got. . . . I love them so much that it really is painful.

Having a child or being a mother may be said to create and reinforce meaningful ties with the world, and to make struggle worthwhile. While being a lesbian mother can be difficult, and may make a woman's life complicated and stressful, children offer significant intrinsic rewards—most importantly, a way to experience feelings of special intimacy, and to be connected to higher-order, spiritual values. Motherhood allows lesbians to be more like other women, at least with respect to the most defining feminine role expectation, but segregating these two dimensions of the self becomes the most efficient way to manage practical obligations, and intensifies the dichotomization of "lesbian" and "mother."

LESBIAN MOTHERHOOD: RESISTANCE OR ACCOMMODATION?

The goals motherhood allows lesbians to enhance are, of course, no different from those heterosexual women describe for themselves. Being a mother, in particular, becoming a mother, is perceived as a transformative experience, an accomplishment that puts other achievements in their proper perspective. It is also construed as an individual achievement, something a woman can "do" to make herself a mother, that is, to transform herself into an altruistic, spiritually-aware human being. In a culture that elevates what has been characterized as "mythic individualism" as a central value, individuals idealize autonomy, self-reliance, and the notion that one must "find oneself" and "make something" of oneself.[25]

> Clearly, the meaning of one's life for most Americans is to become one's own person, almost to give birth to oneself.[26]

Women in America have particular difficulty living up to this cultural ideal. Individualistic and assertive behaviors valued in men are discouraged in women. Dependency, particularly through marriage, is represented as a specifically feminine sort of success. I have discussed elsewhere the remarkable congruences I observed in accounts both lesbian and heterosexual women offered of their divorces, and the similarities between these stories and lesbians' coming-out narratives.[27] These narratives are constructed around themes of agency, independence, and individuality, and celebrate women's ability to define their own lives, to decide how to represent their identities, and to achieve adulthood and autonomy. Despite the fact that both divorce and coming out as a lesbian are popularly understood to be problematic, and, indeed, have historically been defined as stigmatized statuses, women represent them as odysseys of self-discovery leading to more authentic formulations of the self.

Accounts of becoming a mother, in similar fashion, focus on the power of the individual to construct herself as a mother, to negotiate the formation of her self and to bring something good into her life. For lesbians, particularly for lesbians who decided to become mothers once their identification as lesbians was firm, the process of becoming a mother demands agency. At the same time, to the extent that wanting to be a mother is perceived as a *natural* desire, one unmediated by culture or politics, then becoming a mother permits a lesbian to move into a more natural or normal status than she would otherwise achieve. In this sense, becoming a mother represents a sort of conformity with conventional gender expectations. At the same time, to the extent that becoming a mother means overcoming the equation of homosexuality with *unnaturalness,* then this transformation allows the lesbian mother to resist gendered constructions of sexuality. This act of resistance is paradoxically achieved through compliance with conventional expectations for women, so it may also be construed as a gesture of accommodation.

Placing motherhood at the center of one's identity often involves, as we have seen, simultaneously placing other aspects of the self, most notably lesbianism, at the margins. Demanding the right to be a mother suggests a repudiation of gender conventions that define "mother" and "lesbian" as inherently incompatible identities, the former natural and intrinsic to women, organized around altruism, the latter unnatural, and organized around self-indulgence. But living as a mother means making other choices, and these choices reinscribe the opposition between "mother" and "lesbian." Subversion of orderly gender expectations is hypothetical, at best, in the lives of many lesbian mothers, at the same time that knowledge of their existence can only be imagined by the wider public as a rebellion of the most fundamental sort.

The model I would suggest based on the accounts presented here is that lesbian mothers are neither resisters nor accommodators—or perhaps that they are both. A more accurate way of framing their narratives is that they are strategists, using the cultural resources offered by motherhood to achieve a particular set of goals. That these are the goals framed by past experience in a heterosexist and perhaps patriarchal society, and that these resources are culturally constrained and shaped by the exigencies of gender, does not simplify the analysis. While such women are often conscious resisters, others gladly organize their experience as a reconciliation with what they view as traditional values. At the same time that some outsiders may see their behavior as transgressive (and thereby label them resisters or subversives), others perceive lesbian motherhood (along with other indications of compliance with conventional behaviors, such as gay/lesbian marriage) as evidence that lesbians (and other "deviants") can be domesticated and tamed.[28]

The search for cultures of resistance continues to be a vital dimension of the feminist academic enterprise. At the same time that we cannot limit our analyses of women's lives to accounts of victimization, we cannot be complacent when we discover evidence of resistance and subversion. Either interpretation may fail to reveal the complex ways in which resistance and accommodation, subversion and compliance, are interwoven and interdependent, not distinct orientations, but mutually reinforcing aspects of a single strategy. Lesbian mothers are, in some sense, both lesbians and mothers, but they shape identity and renegotiate its meanings at every turn, reinventing themselves as they make their way in a difficult world.

Notes

1. This paper draws on research conducted with the support of National Institute of Mental Health Grant MH–30890 and a grant from the Rockefeller Foundation Gender Roles Program. A more extensive treatment of this material appears in Ellen Lewin, *Lesbian Mothers: Accounts of Gender in American Culture* (Ithaca, N.Y.: Cornell University Press, 1993).

2. See, for example, Ginny Vida, ed., *Our Right to Love: A Lesbian Resource Book* (Englewood Cliffs, N.J.: Prentice-Hall, 1978).

3. Donna Hitchens, "Social Attitudes, Legal Standards, and Personal Trauma in Child Custody Cases," *Journal of Homosexuality,* vol. 5, (1979), pp. 89–95; Ellen Lewin, "Lesbianism and Motherhood: Implications for Child Custody," *Human Organization,* vol. 40, No. 1, (1981), pp. 6–14; Rhonda R. Rivera, "Our Strait-Laced Judges: The Legal Position of Homosexual Persons in the United States," *Hastings Law Journal* 30, (1979), p. 799.

4. Clifford Guy Gibson, *By Her Own Admission: A Lesbian Mother's Fight to Keep Her Son* (Garden City, N.Y.: Doubleday, 1977).

5. Sherrie Farrell, John Gordon Hill, and Peter M. Bruce, "Sandy and Madeleine's Family" (film) (San Francisco: Multi Media Resource Center, 1973).

6. Not only lesbians, but heterosexual mothers whose sexual activity comes to the attention of the authorities, may be vulnerable in cases where their custody is challenged. See Nancy D. Polikoff, "Gender and Child Custody Determinations: Exploding the Myths," in Irene Diamond, ed., *Families, Politics, and Public Policy: A Feminist Dialogue on Women and the State* (New York: Longman, 1983), pp. 183–202.

7. Nan Hunter and Nancy D. Polikoff, "Custody Rights of Lesbian Mothers: Legal Theory and Litigation Strategy," *Buffalo Law Review* 25, (1976), p. 691; Lewin, "Lesbianism and Motherhood."

8. Ellen Lewin, "Claims to Motherhood: Custody Disputes and Maternal Strategies," in Faye Ginsburg and Anna Lowenhaupt Tsing, eds., *Uncertain Terms: Negotiating Gender in American Culture* (Boston: Beacon Press, 1990), pp. 199–214.

9. Jeanne Vaughn, "A Question of Survival," in Sandra J. Pollack and Jeanne Vaughn, eds., *Politics of the Heart: A Lesbian Parenting Anthology* (Ithaca, N.Y.: Firebrand Books, 1987), p. 26.

10. Charlotte Perkins Gilman, *Herland* (1915, New York: Pantheon Books, 1979).

11. A number of works that have chronicled the second wave of feminism in the United States have noted that the treatment of agency and victimization has been a central issue in the framing of feminist theory. See, for example, Alice Echols, *Daring to be Bad: Radical Feminism in America, 1967–1975* (Minneapolis: University of Minnesota Press, 1989); Hester Eisenstein, *Contemporary Feminist Thought* (Boston: G. K. Hall, 1983); Alison M. Jaggar, *Feminist Politics and Human Nature* (Totowa, N.J.: Rowman & Allanheld, 1983). Central issues giving rise to these theories, particularly the essentialist stances taken by adherents of cultural feminism, were those of violence and abuse—rape, incest, battering, and the like.

12. See, for example, Jane Goodale, *Tiwi Wives: A Study of the Women of Melville Island, North Australia* (Seattle: University of Washington Press, 1971); Annette B. Weiner, *Women of Value, Men of Renown: New Perspectives in Trobriand Exchange* (Austin: University of Texas Press, 1976); Margery Wolf, *Women and the Family in Rural Taiwan* (Stanford: Stanford University Press, 1972).

13. Lila Abu-Lughod has reviewed the diverse forms an emphasis on resistance has taken in anthropology and in other disciplines in "The Romance of Resistance: Tracing Transformations of Power Through Bedouin Women," *American Ethnologist,* vol. 17, No. 1 (February 1990), pp. 41–55. Abu-Lughod urges us not to romanticize resistance, but to use its appearance "to teach us about the complex interworkings of historically changing structures of power."

Some scholars, notably James Scott, have suggested that interest in resistance has blossomed as scholars on the left have been forced to confront the failure of socialist revolutions. See *Weapons of the Weak: Everyday Forms of Peasant Resistance* (New Haven: Yale University Press, 1985).

14. Bonnie Thornton Dill, "Domestic Service and the Construction of Personal Dignity," in Ann Bookman and Sandra Morgen, eds., *Women and the Politics of Empowerment* (Philadelphia: Temple University Press, 1988), p. 33.

15. Aihwa Ong, *Spirits of Resistance and Capitalist Discipline: Factory Women in Malaysia* (Albany: State University of New York Press, 1987), p. 220.

16. Emily Martin, *The Woman in the Body: A Cultural Analysis of Reproduction* (Boston: Beacon Press, 1987), p. 110.

17. Louise Lamphere, *From Working Daughters to Working Mothers: Immigrant Women in a New England Industrial Community* (Ithaca, N.Y.: Cornell University Press, 1987), pp. 29–30.

18. Lamphere, *From Working Daughters to Working Mothers,* p. 30.

19. Judith Butler, *Gender Trouble: Feminism and the Subversion of Identity* (New York: Routledge, 1990), p. 27.

20. Butler, *Gender Trouble,* p. 17.

21. Ibid.

22. Although artificial insemination is often included among the "new" reproductive technologies such as *in vitro* fertilization, embryo transfer, and sex predetermination, there is actually nothing particularly new about the procedure. Originally developed for use in animal husbandry, artificial insemination by donor (AID) conceptions are estimated as accounting for thousands of births in the United States each year. See Martin Curie-Cohen, Lesleigh Luttrell, and Sander Shapiro, "Current Practice of Artificial Insemination by Donor in the United States," *New England Journal of Medicine* 300 (11) (1979), pp. 585–590.

The procedure itself introduces sperm into the vagina with a needle-less syringe at a time calculated to coincide with the woman's ovulation. Once methods for freezing sperm were perfected in 1949, the possibility of expanded use presented itself (both for animals and for humans), as sperm banks and various sorts of matching services came into existence; Gena Corea, *The Mother Machine: Reproductive Technologies from Artificial Insemination to Artificial Wombs* (New York: Harper and Row, 1985), p. 36. At present, there is only minimal government regulation of artificial insemination or of sperm banks. Sperm banks and access to medically supervised insemination are controlled almost exclusively by physicians, who act as gatekeepers in terms of who may have access to frozen sperm. This means both that medical screening of donors is far from consistent or reliable, and that physicians tend to use their personal values to determine who should have access to these services; Judith N. Lasker and Susan Borg, *In Search of Parenthood: Coping with Infertility and High-Tech Conception* (Boston: Beacon Press, 1987). Since frozen sperm can be expensive, unmarried women, as well as low-income patients may not have the same access to insemination as affluent couples; Curie-Cohen, Luttrell, and Shapiro, "Current Practice of Artificial Insemination"; Maureen McGuire and Nancy Alexander, "Artificial Insemination of Single Women," *Fertility and Sterility* 43 (1985), pp. 182–184; Carson Strong and Jay Schinfeld, "The Single Woman and Artificial Insemination by Donor," *Journal of Reproductive Medicine* 29 (1984), pp. 293–299.

Despite these obstacles, the low-tech nature of artificial insemination and the possibility of mobilizing alternatives to physician-controlled sperm banks have meant that women, in fact, can easily retain control of the procedure. Women whose physicians may be unwilling to inseminate—whether they be single, low-income, or lesbian—can use their informal networks to carry out insemination outside conventional medical settings; Rona Achilles, "Donor insemination: The Future of a Public Secret," in Christine Overall, ed., *The Future of Human Reproduction* (Toronto: The Women's Press, 1989), pp. 105–119; Francie Hornstein, "Children by Donor Insemination: A New Choice for Lesbians," in Rita Arditti, Renate Duelli Klein, and Shelley Minden, eds., *Test-Tube Women: What Future for Motherhood?* (London: Pandora Press, 1984), pp. 373–381; Ellen Lewin, "By Design: Reproductive Strategies and the Meaning of Motherhood," in Hilary Homans, ed., *The Sexual Politics of Reproduction* (London: Gower, 1985), pp. 123–138.

In the late 1970s, this process was generally called "artificial insemination." Within a few years, however, mothers began to use alternate language, labelling the procedure either "donor insemination" or simply "insemination" in an effort to downplay the implication that there was anything intrinsically "unnatural" about getting pregnant in this way.

23.   Names and some other details have been changed to preserve the anonymity of women whom I interviewed. For a detailed account of the methods used in this research, see Lewin, *Lesbian Mothers.*

24.   Adoption, though difficult, was another approach used by lesbians who wished to become mothers. Because of the large number of two-parent families who wish to adopt, and the small number of healthy newborn babies available for adoption, single women (and men) are rarely considered prime candidates as adoptive parents. Their chances are, of course, even slighter if they are known to be lesbian or gay. Adoption is more in reach of these prospective parents if they can arrange a private adoption or if they are willing to adopt an older, disabled, abused, or minority/mixed-race child—those considered less desirable. See Editors of the Harvard Law Review, *Sexual Orientation and the Law* (Cambridge, MA: Harvard University Press, 1989).

25.   Robert Bellah, et al., *Habits of the Heart: Individualism and Commitment in American Life* (Berkeley: University of California Press, 1985), p. 65.

26.   Bellah, *Habits of the Heart,* p. 82.

27.   Lewin, *Lesbian Mothers.*

28.   See Ellen Lewin, *Lesbian Mothers,* and "On the Outside Looking In: The Politics of Lesbian Motherhood," in Faye Ginsburg and Rayna Rapp, eds., *Conceiving the New World Order: Local/Global Intersections in the Politics of Reproduction* (Berkeley: University of California Press, forthcoming, for a discussion of how the popular media has accommodated images of lesbian families and poses them in opposition to still-abnormal childless lesbians.

Chapter 16

FEMINIST PERSPECTIVES ON
MOTHERING AND PEACE[1]

Linda Rennie Forcey

INTRODUCTION

In the past decade we have witnessed numerous regional wars and low-intensity conflicts throughout the world, unparalleled "peacetime" military expenditures, and an extraordinary concentration of wealth in many countries, including the United States. As for the latter, we are told there has been "no parallel upsurge of riches . . . since the late nineteenth century."[2] The gap between rich and poor has widened virtually everywhere, placing mothers and children in increasingly precarious economic positions, and allowing tens of thousands of children each day to die of preventable causes throughout the world.

What is going on? Where are the voices of mothers, the caretakers of the world, the hands that rock the cradle? As we all know, the connection between women and peace is ancient; peace is often symbolized as the mother, the preserver of life, the angel in the house. Appeals to peace have often been made in the name of women and children, and there is a long history of women as peace activists. After all, don't mothers have certain essential qualities derived from their roles as nurturers that can be universalized? Aren't they really nicer, kinder, gentler? Isn't it women as mothers who might possess the special peacemaking skills required for a new, more peaceful, and more just world order?

Or could it be that the very asking of such questions is part of the age-old trap of oversimplifying the notion of "woman," denying her differences with other women, exaggerating her differences with men, and thereby lessening her power? It is these kinds of questions that are placing peace researchers squarely in the center of the contemporary feminist debate about the nature and power of women, and the social construction of mothering. For those of us concerned with the search for theories and strategies that can best mobilize for peace and justice all people—mothers, fathers, women, and men alike—these are extremely important questions.

After defining some key terms, this paper begins with a brief outline of the feminist theoretical debate among three groups: (1) those arguing that women's differences from men are minimal and should be minimized in the fight for equality in education, employment, and the law (the equality position); (2) those holding that women, for any number of reasons related to their nurturing qualities and mothering responsibilities, are *essentially different* from men—essentially nicer, kinder, gentler, and this fundamental difference should be honored (the essentialist position); and (3) those arguing that because language itself is socially constructed, no categories of women are natural or inevitable, and attempts to categorize must be resisted (the social constructionist and poststructuralist positions). I then show how, when we integrate feminist theoretical perspectives with feminist peace research in the emerging interdisciplinary field of peace studies, we find, not surprisingly, that this theoretical debate is replicated in feminist peace research; with peace scholars generally taking the second position, the essentialist standpoint emphasizing the caring, relational, mothering qualities of women.

Because of the nature of the field of peace studies (as defined in the section to follow), there is a special urgency, poignancy, if you will, to the debate. First, who among us would want to imply that there could ever be too much *caring* in this violent world? To argue that women are *essentially* different because they are more nurturing, more caring, is to valorize many women's experiences as peacemakers in the home. Second, as is true with all oppressed groups, this feeling of difference is a powerful consciousness-raising tool to promote solidarity for collective action. Humanist aspirations for a more peaceful world, where peace by definition must include an ethic of caring and a valuing of caring labor, are at the heart of the peace studies endeavor. The central question for peace studies, as Ann Snitow phrases it, is: "*How* can the caring that belongs to mother travel out to become the responsibility of everyone?"[3]

Furthermore, peace studies can be seen as a critique of one of the most male-dominated of the social sciences fields, international relations. Feminist peace research, in this sense, can be said to be at an earlier stage than feminist thought emerging from the fields of literature, philosophy, history, sociology, psychology, and anthropology. For peace researchers, a feminist standpoint that focuses on caring, nurturing, feeling, intuiting, empathizing, relating, remains an important new catalyst to challenge militarism. This contribution of essentialist thinking to the field of international relations and the peace endeavor can be wonderfully refreshing, comforting, energizing, and affirming for women. It poses a very different set of questions from those traditionally asked by practitioners (mostly male) in both international relations and peace studies.

It is thus with more than a little ambiguity and hesitation that I myself have come to see its limitations and weaknesses, and the need to move on. I must note at the outset, too, that while most feminist peace researchers generally take an essentialist position, many are not comfortable with this label. They clearly acknowledge the dangers and pitfalls of this essentially polarized thinking too. This chapter calls first for feminist appreciation of the contribution of an essentialist standpoint to peace research, activism, and pedagogy; second, for feminist appreciation of the importance of the poststructuralist critique of essentialism; and, third, for the need to move beyond the debate with a finely tuned appreciation of a variety of approaches, a tolerance for ambiguity, and more than a little theoretical untidiness.

DEFINING THE TERMS

For readers unfamiliar with the fields of either women's or peace studies, definitions of mothering, feminism, and peace studies as used in this discussion are in order.

Mothering is a socially constructed set of activities and relationships involved in nurturing and caring for people.[4] It is also the main vehicle through which people first form their identities and learn their place in society. As Sara Ruddick points out, mothering is the procedure by which children learn "mother-tongue," a special language in which they assimilate "a sense of what can be named and what must remain secret; what is unavoidably given and what can be changed; who is to be feared and whose authority is only a sham."[5] At the heart of mothering as it is commonly understood in contemporary Western society is an ethic of caring—of knowing, feeling, and acting in the interests of others. Although mothering usually refers to the thoughts and activities of women who have willingly assumed the responsibility for the caring, nurturing, and socialization of their biological, adopted, or stepchildren, the process of defining mothering is not this simple or clear-cut. I have all "caring labor" in mind when I speak of mothering—from birthing labor, to all kinds of teaching, to care of the disabled and of the frail elderly.[6] This is because all women, and some men too, have in one way or another internalized the socially constructed mandates of mothering in their given societies at any given point in time.

As for feminism, the general working definition with which I am comfortable can be stated quite simply. It takes as proven the historical oppression of women and stresses the interrelationship of theory and practice to eliminate it. Virginia Sapiro describes this sense of feminism more fully as:

> ... both a way of thinking about the world, and a way of acting in it. ... [It] is a perspective that views gender as one of the most important bases of the structure and organization of the social world. Feminists argue that in most known societies this structure has granted women lower status and value, more limited access to valuable resources, and less autonomy and opportunity to make choices over their lives than it has granted men. Feminists further believe that although this gender-based world may be organized around biological facts such as the exclusive capacity of men to create sperm and the exclusive capacity of women to bear children, gender inequality is due to the social construction of human experience, which means that it should be possible to eradicate it.[7]

Feminism, as I view it, then, is both a way of viewing the world, and an evolving social movement. As noted, feminism does not embrace one theoretical approach, but rather several. This chapter will focus on the contributions of (1) the essentialist standpoint that holds that women are essentially different from men (nicer, kinder, gentler), and should be so regarded in analyses of peace, power, and gender; and (2) its feminist critics (poststructuralists and others), who argue that essentialists have been oblivious to the social construction of language itself, leaving women resistant to change and insensitive to the diverse experiences among women.

Peace studies, as defined by one widely accepted guide, is a relatively new, interdisciplinary, academic field that "analyzes the causes of war, violence, and systemic oppression, and explores processes by which conflict and change can be managed so as to maximize justice while minimizing violence." It includes "the study of economic, political and social systems at the local, national and global levels, and of ideology, culture, and technology as they relate to conflict and change."[8] One of its primary and most controversial assumptions centers on the interrelationship of peace research, education, and action.[9]

There are within the field, of course, widely divergent views as to definitions of peace, much controversy over issues of an "implicit ideological bias," and even more worry about the "activist orientation" of peace studies curricula. My definition focuses on the values, norms, and institutions of peace. It incorporates such concepts as structural violence, racism, sexism, class, religious and ethical perspectives, international law, and global cooperation. It leans toward the proactive and methodologically qualitative bent of many, if not most, of the over three hundred university peace studies programs.[10]

As a feminist, I would have to say that peace studies so broadly and positively defined can have no meaning unless it is in the context of feminist thought, particularly that of the social construction of gender and mothering. Militarism has shaped our economic priorities for the past forty years; its use of the resources and capital of this country has depleted medical, educational, and social programs, thus creating a new, primarily mother and child poverty class. When the concept of peace implies that every human being regardless of sex has the right to a life that includes fulfillment of basic human needs, then much of feminist research can also be considered peace research. And much of peace research *must* focus on the intrinsic value of caring, of mothering as we have come to understand it.

WOMEN AS PEACEMAKERS AND FEMINIST THEORY

The gentle, caring, peacekeeping qualities attributed to women have not always been celebrated by feminists. Virginia Woolf, the harbinger of much in contemporary feminist thought, described her relationship with Coventry Patmore's *Angel in the House* like this:[11]

> It was she who used to come between me and my paper when I was writing reviews. It was she who bothered me and wasted my time and so tormented me that at last I killed her. You who come of a younger and happier generation may not have heard of her—you may not know what I mean by The Angel in the House. ... She was intensely sympathetic. She was immensely charming. She was utterly unselfish. She excelled in the difficult art of family life. She sacrificed daily. If there was chicken, she took the leg; if there was a draught, she sat in it—in short she was so constituted that she never had a mind or wish of her own, but preferred to sympathize always with the minds and wishes of others. Above all ... she was pure.[12]

In what has been referred to as "liberal feminism," the "equality position," or Stage One of the contemporary feminist movement, the angel in the house was, if not squashed, at least repressed. That is to say, the caring, peacekeeping aspects of women's activities were not the focus. Mothers certainly were not the focus. Building on the work of Simone de Beauvoir in the late forties, and Betty Friedan in the early sixties, feminists saw the glorification of mothering as an instrument of women's oppression.[13] Feminists called for the right not to mother, documented the darker side of the mothering experience, and advocated a more equitable sharing of the responsibilities for child rearing in the struggle for job equity. They argued that the institution of motherhood as currently defined was harmful to children, and to mothers themselves. In fact, up until the early 1970s, feminists tended to deny any important differences between women and men, thereby playing down the central role of nurturing in gender identity.

Many feminist theorists outside the liberal camp, rather than focusing on the joys of mothering, began to analyze the inequities of home labor. Radical, Marxist, and socialist feminists showed how capitalism combined with patriarchy made both home labor and market labor gender specific, with women's status both economically and psychologically disadvantageous. They argued that most women's work as presently carried on in home and market, including child care, helped to perpetuate male domination and the capitalist form of production.[14]

Although there was only a most tenuous relationship between feminist and peace research until the mid-1970s, portrayals of women as peace activists generally reflected this feminist theoretical position. Most peace researchers were neither women nor feminists, and many femininists considered peace studies a diversion from the main task of liberating women. It was left primarily to a few feminist scholars (most of whom would not have called themselves "peace researchers") to acknowledge the role of earlier pioneers such as Bertha von Suttner, Jane Adams, Emily Greene Balch, and members of the Women's Peace Party and the Women's International League for Peace and Freedom (WILPF). The major objective of these early peace researchers was to show that some women did play a role in social and political history, and could be counted among men for equal citizenship.

By the mid-1970s, however, a number of scholars had begun to argue that the first wave of feminist theorizing had invalidated ways of knowing that seemed characteristically womanly. This second wave of feminist theorizing takes a posture that seeks to discover and validate women's lives in the concrete labors of their daily experiences. The standpoint (later to be labeled "essentialist") assumes a separate female world, one in which women are essentially different from men—more caring, more cooperative, more peaceful.

With a psychoanalytic lens, sociologist Nancy Chodorow, for example, argued that women, because of the ways in which they were mothered, are more caring, more nurturing, less differentiated, more preoccupied with relationships than men. In fact, they spend their lives nurturing in one way or another, and reproduce daughters who do the same.[15] Carol Gilligan, while acknowledging her intellectual debt to Chodorow, takes the celebration of traditional female virtues a step further. Challenging developmental theorists like Freud, Piaget, Erikson, and Kohlberg, she regards the nurturing traits so frequently associated with mothers as strengths rather than weakness. In fact, women with their mothering/caring labor are, in a certain sense, more moral than men. Women know that:

in a world that extends through an elaborate network of relationships, the fact that someone is hurt affects everyone who is involved, complicating the morality of any decision and removing the possibility of a clear or simple solution. Thus, morality, rather than being opposed to integrity or tied to an ideal of agreement, is aligned with the "kind of integrity" that comes from "making decisions after working through everything you think is involved and important in the situation," and taking responsibility for choice. In the end, morality is a matter of care.[16]

Many feminists enthusiastically agreed with Gilligan that because of maternal practices, women have developed an ethic of care quite different from men. They, along with Gilligan, believed this ethic amounted to a certain way of thinking characterized by such descriptive words as receptivity, relatedness, responsiveness, connectedness, intuitiveness, ambiguity, ambivalence, feelings, empathy, and caring.[17] It is a way of thinking that, actually and not just theoretically, should socialize each new generation to nonviolent behavior and to a peaceful world order.

Male violence, according to Gilligan, stems from problems in communication and men's lack of knowledge about human relationships.

> If aggression is tied, as women perceive, to the fracture of human connection, then the activities of care . . . are the activities that make the social world safe, by avoiding isolation and preventing aggression rather than by seeking rules to limit its extent.

In this light, she contends,

> aggression appears no longer as an unruly impulse that must be contained but rather as a signal of a fracture of connection, the sign of a failure of relationship.[18]

Among feminists concerned with peace studies and peace education, strongly influenced by Nancy Chodorow and Carol Gilligan, were Betty Reardon, Birgit Brock-Utne, Nell Noddings, and Sara Ruddick.[19] With the Nuclear Freeze movement, and increased peace activism globally in the early eighties, they and others began to turn to issues involving peace, but their research was of a very different kind from that being done by the World Policy Institute, and male-dominated established journals such as *The Journal of Peace Research* and *The Journal of Conflict Resolution*. Their perspective grew out of the realization that the earlier peace researchers' processes of conducting corrective and compensatory research in order to fit women into the historical picture had shown that the scientific method itself was tightly structured around such conventions mirroring ideal traits of Western, white males as objectivity, freedom from values, abstract reasoning.

Betty Reardon's influential monograph, *Sexism and the War System,* growing out of her experiences with the World Policy Institute and the World Order Models Program in the 1970s and early eighties, is representative of this second stage of feminist thinking.[20] Contending that within the field of peace studies most researchers have viewed women's issues as secondary or collateral to the central concerns of peace, she calls for an integration of feminist scholarship with peace research, whereby the need for inner psychic transformation on a personal level is appreciated as much as the need for global political and economic change. She develops a feminist peace paradigm focused on the yin and yang aspects of being, contrasting such characteristics as gentleness and strength, receptivity and dominance, caring and competing.

One of Reardon's central metaphors is mothering: conception, labor, birth, and nurture. She writes of humane and fulfilling human relationships, personal change, vulnerability, and pastoral images of peace:

> The lion can lie down with the lamb in a nurturing rather than devouring relationship, only if each is able to transform its reality by transforming itself. These transformations are what peace studies should be about.[21]

Reardon and other feminist peace researchers see an unhealthy imbalance toward male principles in modern society, leading to war, aggression, greed, and other embodiments of "manly" aspects, rather than the more conciliatory and constructive "womanly" aptitudes. "If the world itself seems under siege, and if that siege holds any community and all children hostage, the effort of world protection may come to seem a 'natural' extension of maternal work," writes philosopher Sara Ruddick.[22] The logical extension of the argument is that the world would be a safer place if the female element was stressed. Clearly, according to this standpoint, mothers should find war a contradiction and global peace an integral part of their maternal work.

But, as Reardon, Brock-Utne, Noddings, Ruddick and most essentialist thinkers readily acknowledge, women often support wars enthusiastically and vigorously. Noddings points out that "Women . . . too want to belong. . . . An important virtue of the good woman . . . is her generous support of her man's conception of honor."[23] Ruddick, however, calls this maternal trait "inauthenticity," and she laments that mothers all too often believe that their children's interests depend on their country's military strength, even though they may hate wars in general. She finds that very few mothers "take the world as an object of extended maternal care,"[24] and she, too, fears the temptation to celebrate the caretakers while forgetting their failures. She also fears an emergent self-righteousness that, while condemning violence, forgets to tend to its root causes.[25]

In the final analysis, most feminist peace researchers cautiously yet hopefully conclude that it is women and mothers with a feminist consciousness and politics who are most likely to become truly effective peacemakers. For example, Ruddick writes: "By increasing mothers' powers to know, care, and act, feminism actualizes the peacefulness latent in maternal practice." It is her belief that "feminism is already conjoined with a peace politics that is marked by its double origins in women's traditional work and feminist resistance to abuse against women."[26]

FEMINIST CRITICISM OF WOMEN AS PEACEMAKERS

Not all contemporary feminists are as sanguine about the nurturing attributes of women as the theorists discussed above. As bell hooks writes:

> The resurgence of feminist interest in motherhood has positive and negative implications for the feminist movement. On the positive side there is a continual need for study and research of female parenting which this interest promotes and encourages. ... On the negative side, [by] romanticizing motherhood, employing the same terminology that is used by sexists to suggest that women are inherently life-affirming nurturers, feminist activists reinforce central tenets of male supremacist ideology.[27]

Critics argue that essentialist theory has an exaggerated focus on the differences between men and women. British feminist Lynne Segal, striking her central theme as to the inadequacy of polarized thinking about men and women, writes:

> This has meant a minimal interest in conflicts and contradictions as they are experienced within feminine identity, a false universalizing of our own gender categories and a disregard for other social practices (outside mother-daughter bonding) as they impinge upon gender identity.[28]

We need to be asking a different set of questions, Segal and others assert. How else can we explain diverse historical and cultural forms of femininity and masculinity? How else can we explain women's behavior that does not conform to maternal thinking? How else can we explain mothers who send their sons to war? How else can we explain the angry, sad, and bitter stories of some mothers? How else can we understand the lives of women who do not wish to be mothers?

Even on the familial level, the record of women as being inherently more life-affirming appears to be mixed. For generations we have been reading from the male perspective about the pathological implications of these mothering qualities—with mothers being blamed for all "social deviations" of their children, from mental illnesses to juvenile delinquency to matters of life-styles and sexual orientation. While the essentialist standpoint has done much to modify this crazy arrangement of responsibility to women alone, it has not left mothers with a sense that they are standing on terra firma. Jane Flax, criticizing Ruddick's "maternal thinking" thesis argues that:

> important things like rage, frustration, aggression, sexuality, irrational intense love and hate, re-experiencing of one's own childhood, blurring of body boundaries, conflict between demands of a child, one's mate, other children and other work are missing.[29]

And Lynne Segal writes:

> The weight of one's own children can mean a contradiction of social vision, an envy and resentment of the welfare of others. . . . While it may be true that women are more concerned about peace and a better world . . . this does not necessarily mean that women are any less nationalistic, racist, or committed to class privilege than men.[30]

My own conclusions from a study of mothers of sons (one hundred twenty mothers with sons age fifteen and older) are that, on the familial level, women's perceptions of their roles as peacemakers are far more ambivalent, complex, and conflict-ridden than one might conclude from a reading of Chodorow, Gilligan, Reardon, Noddings, or Ruddick.[31] Although most of the women with whom I spoke identified themselves as peacemakers within the family, some expressed ambivalence and often downright anger with their roles, especially when their peacemaking was between father and son. They would say: "To be in the same room with them is to set my stomach churning. I am sick to death of it"; or "I've lied for my son so many times just to keep the peace that I hardly know how to stop!"[32] A woman describes how she feels it is time to detach herself from her adolescent son and his father, to abandon the mediator role for her own psychic health:

> You know, you get tired of being this intermediary. Being the sponge for everyone's pain, being the only shoulder there is to cry on, being the only one for whom they can utterly fail. There have been days when I have been so obsessed with what was going on between Lee [son] and his father that I hardly knew who *I* was or what *I* felt about anything. You know, you only owe your children so much.[33]

When women define peace in the family as merely the absence of conflict, as many in my study did, their communications with sons often become limited to the inconsequential or noncontroversial. They feel impelled to sweep differences under the carpet, at tremendous cost to their own self-esteem, growth, and peace of mind, as well as that of their children. For example, a mother poignantly described how her fear of confrontation made it doubly difficult for both her and her son to come to terms with his homosexuality. Two women told me they could not bear to burden their sons with the knowledge of their battles with cancer. Another described how she could not bring herself to ask her son about his experiences in Vietnam, thereby shutting herself out of a part of her son's life both he and she needed to share.[34] Researchers in the field of alcohol and drug addiction find that mothers of addicted sons tend to forgive, cover up, make excuses, and avoid communication on this subject, while feeling angry, hurt, and responsible on the inside.[35] I concluded that in what mothers of sons considered to be the line of duty, many opted for a limited honesty and openness—one that suppresses anger and hides the self.

In the public sphere, as we have seen, most feminist peace researchers themselves readily acknowledge that the record regarding women's support of national wars is problematic at best. Women as well as men are committed to what they regard as "the national interest." Jean Elshtain writes:

> The woman of republican militancy is no mere victim of events; rather, she is empowered in and through the discourse of armed civic virtue to become an *author* of deeds—deeds of sacrifice, of nobility in and through suffering, of courage in the face of adversity, of firmness in *her*, and not just her polity's "right."[36]

The old mothering myth, as expressed in the work of Simone de Beauvoir, has it that "every mother entertains the idea that her child will be a hero," and the hero is, of course, a son. "A son will be a leader of men, a soldier . . . and his mother will share his immortal fame . . ." she asserted. Woman as second sex, as other, as the inauthentic one, seeks to define herself in her son's deeds, and what better path than that of patriotism.[37]

This myth needs revision, however. In my study of mothers of sons I discovered many women who encouraged their sons to join the military, not at all for reasons of patriotism, but rather because they view the military as the only available means of shifting the mothering responsibility—be it psychological, social, or economic—from themselves alone.[38] I concluded that mothers who turn to the military in search for such things as help in making their sons more mature, more self-disciplined, less addicted to drugs and alcohol, or better trained for a job certainly were not to be castigated. Similarly, Barbara Omolade points out that African-American women have a legacy of support of war because the military represents economic opportunity and social status for Black men, and now for Black women too. "Few black women can live outside the dilemmas posed by this predicament. Which war zone does she protect her son from: the military or the street?"[39] Ironically, while many mothers like myself celebrate the recent talk of base closings and troop cutbacks, many other mothers lament the prospect of a demilitarized society, because they have nowhere else to turn but to Uncle Sam.

And what about ordinary women outside the United States who, by no choice of their own, are participants in national political conflicts? An emerging literature is providing portraits of women who have sacrificed bravely and fought fiercely for principles beyond the familial.[40] For example, Marjorie Agosin tells a moving story of the *arpilleristas,* women in Chile who make the small appliqued and embroidered wall hangings that portray the suffering of women and their families under the repressive military dictatorship of Pinochet. It was the upheaval in their personal lives (the arrests, "disappearances," exiles, and deaths of their sons and loved ones), that obliged them to take political action, and to learn to speak as a collective voice. As one woman put it, "Because of all this suffering we are united. I do not ask for justice for my child alone, or the other women just for their children. We are asking for justice for all."[41]

Another example of this emerging literature are the ten essays in *Women and Political Conflict,* edited by Rosemary Ridd and Helen Callaway, describing women's experiences in the war in Cyprus, the Islamic revolution in Iran, the national struggle in Northern Ireland, the ideological conflict within an Israeli kibbutz, the Breton separatist movement in France, and the struggle by Turkish migrants in West Berlin to maintain their ethnic identity. It needs to be pointed out, however, that while rich with portraits of courageous women, this book, like others, concludes that these women see themselves as powerless beyond their genius to survive, and, the editors argue, "in terms of the wider political systems, must be seen as relatively so."[42]

As I have written elsewhere, these books give voice to women whose lives have been turned upside down by political conflict.[43] The stories serve to remind those of us who care about women's and peace issues that the terrible cost of war and political conflict is paid by women as well as men; that women have used their informal powers to express their political will, bravely and even heroically. The books also remind us how cautious we must be about embracing a theoretical perspective that celebrates "mothering" values and virtues, while minimizing the fact that this gender construct falters before broader power structures. The experiences of many women involved in conflict throughout the world illustrate the fact that the force of what women as nurturers do on the interpersonal level—whether in the family or the work place—is painfully problematic in the global arena.

In addition, what about the women who *choose* to be part of their country's political and military conflicts? What about the growing numbers of women, including mothers, serving in the United States military since 1973, for example? The National Organization for Women (NOW) supports the move for women to be eligible for combat on the perfectly rational ground of professional opportunity equity. Congresswoman Pat Schroeder has written a bill to adopt a Pentagon group's suggestions that the Army test women in combat roles. Also, syndicated columnist Ellen Goodman has come down on the side of women in combat, arguing that "any war that isn't worth a woman's life isn't worth a man's life." And what about the voices of the eager, young, American women who served in the Persian Gulf War, pleading for the privilege of combat duty.

POSTSTRUCTURALISM

With this growing literature on women's relationship to issues of peace and war, it has become clearer than ever that men throughout the world continue to have greater access to power, wealth, and privilege than women. However, it also has become clearer that feminists are having increasing difficulty coming to agreement on the theories and strategies needed to explain and challenge these inequities. Feminist peace theorizing now fluctuates ambivalently between a standpoint (one increasingly supported by men in the field) that focuses on the identification of essential psychological and sociological differences between men and women, and one that acknowledges the distortion and disadvantages of this stance. It grapples with this difference versus equality debate both on theoretical and strategic levels. The tension, writes Anne Phillips, is:

> built into the feminist project. Men and women are different; they are also unequal; feminists will continue to debate and disagree over how far the inequality stems from the difference, and how far the difference can or should be eliminated.[44]

That it is time, however, to move beyond the difference-versus-equality debate is the emerging consensus, at least outside the peace studies field. As long as women find themselves in the political context of these present times, comments historian Ruth Milkman:

> feminist scholars must be aware of the real danger that arguments about "difference" or "women's culture" will be put to uses other than those for which they were originally developed. That does not mean we must abandon these arguments or the intellectual terrain they have opened up; it does

mean that we must be self-conscious in our formulations, keeping firmly in view the ways in which our work can be exploited politically.[45]

Joan Scott, taking Milkman's point further, argues that the equality-difference debate can be an intellectual trap, one out of which feminists must move.

> When equality and difference are paired dichotomously, they structure an impossible choice. If one opts for equality, one is forced to accept the notion that difference is antithetical to it. If one opts for difference, one admits that equality is unattainable.

How then, Scott asks, "do we recognize and use notions of sexual difference and yet make arguments for equality?" The only response, she answers, is a double one:

> the unmasking of the power relationship constructed by posing equality as the antithesis of difference, and the refusal of its consequent dichotomous construction of political choices.[46]

In other words, feminists need to recognize that the antithesis of difference is not equality but rather sameness; and the antithesis of equality is not difference, but rather inequality.

The analytic perspective Scott and many contemporary feminist social scientists find most valuable for moving beyond the difference-versus-equality debate is poststructuralism. This approach, based on borrowings from the humanities, with its attack upon the methodological assumptions of modern science, on the one hand, and its questioning of the status of all knowledge, on the other, is providing a major challenge to the essentialist standpoint in the fields of international relations and peace studies.[47] In this context, it is referred to as "the third debate"—a loosely defined and evolving cluster of attitudes toward theory and practice that takes into account a whole range of analytical approaches and "for all its heterogeneity has a number of thematic connections that help to identify it and explain its overarching critical purpose."[48]

Poststructuralism does not have one fixed meaning; rather, it is applied to a wide range of theoretical positions derived from the work of Derrida, Lacan, Kristeva, Althusser, and Foucault.[49] It can be defined as a broadly interdisciplinary approach that disputes the underlying assumptions of most social sciences—epistemological foundations, the Enlightenment heritage (faith in the idea of progress and rationality), and a social science methodology modeled after the hard sciences, with its search for generalizations, simplifications, and verifications. Rather than focusing on personality, behavior, attitudes, goals, and choices, it turns attention to language, symbols, alternative discourses, and meaning. It holds that knowledge is grounded in language, and that language does not reflect "reality." And it is language itself that creates and reproduces a world that is never definitive but always in transition.[50] In some senses, it is really easier to say what poststructuralism is not than what it is. This is partly because it resists definition on empirical grounds, and partly because it is still in its infancy. Poststructuralism's positive identity has yet to be formed. Its proponents, however, do agree that it aims "to destabilize and render open to question all claims to an absolute foundation."[51]

In her discussion of the contribution poststructuralism can offer contemporary feminism, linguist Chris Weedon articulates a specific version that is able to address the questions of how social power is exercised and how social relations of gender, class, and race might be transformed. This is not to say that the differences among forms of poststructuralism are not important; but rather, that they are not equally productive for feminism.[52] Poststructuralists, according to Weedon, deny the assumption that women and men have essential natures. They refuse to "fall back on general theories of the feminine psyche or biologically based definitions of femininity which locate its essence in processes such as motherhood or female sexuality." This does not, however,

> rule out the specificity of women's experiences and their difference from those of men, since, under patriarchy, women have differential access to the discursive field which constitutes gender, gendered experience and gender relations of power in society.[53]

Clearly influenced by poststructuralism, Carol Cohn's widely discussed essay, "Sex and Death in the World of the Defense Intellectuals," is another example of new directions toward which feminist peace research may be turning. Cohn considers how the language of the defense intellectuals who plot the Pentagon's strategy is a reflection of the ideas that express and construct men's power in relation to women. It is a language tenaciously rooted in and around us, reinforcing sexism and militarism.[54] Cohn describes her own transformative process, that of learning the language while participating in a Harvard-MIT summer program on nuclear weapons designed for college teachers, followed by a year as a participant observer at the Center on Defense Technology and Arms Control.

The language (she calls it technostrategic) is clearly masculine, one based on a uniquely male, rational, conceptual system that excludes human beings and connections. Her own transformation went through several stages: Stage 1: learning to listen to white men in ties discussing clean bombs and clean language, missile size, fathers, sons and virgins, domestic bliss, male birth and creation, God and nuclear priesthood; Stage 2: learning to speak the language (noting the allure of power and white male privilege) and feelings of control, escape from thinking of oneself as victim; Stage 3: learning to dialogue and finding that it could not be done in English (she notes, for example, that the word "peace" is not part of the vocabulary; one must use "strategic stability" instead); and Stage 4: feeling the Terror as she realized that she herself was being transformed, that not only was she speaking in this language—she was thinking in it.

The transformative process Cohn describes is truly a dilemma for feminist peace researchers—one for which Cohn offers no simple answers. The dilemma is this: women will not be listened to by those in power if they cannot speak the language—yet the very process of learning the language leaves them unable to speak their concerns, that is, to stay connected to human lives, to be caring, nurturing, mothering. Cohn suggests that the language itself may not really articulate the "rational strategies" upon which nuclear weapons development and deployment decisions are in fact made. Rather, technostrategic discourse might be functioning more as a gloss, an ideological curtain behind which the actual reasons for these decisions are made. Nevertheless, she believes women have two tasks: one is a deconstructive project that involves first learning, and then deconstructing the language ("beating the boys at their game"); the other is a reconstructing project to create "alternative visions of possible futures"—with "diverse voices whose conversations with each other will invent those futures."[55]

Preferring the term postmodernism to poststructuralism, political scientist Christine Sylvester defines the project as:

> a form of critical theory which questions secure knowledges and practices and seeks to open up policy processes to those who have been spoken for and "protected" by purveyors of certitude and security. It is a community— of radical doubters, tolerant dissenters, neo-anarchists, seekers of knowledge at the hyphens of lived experience. Unabashedly pro-women, it also is alert to other groups historically silenced within the master discourses of androcentric modernity.[56]

From this position, Sylvester challenges the theses of essentialists like Brock-Utne, Reardon, Chodorow, and Ruddick, arguing that women are not naturally opposed to war and for peace, and that peace and war are all of a piece, rather than negations of each other. At this time, she argues, that piece is patriarchal. It is patriarchy itself that damages and distorts women's perspectives, as well as those of men: women may be embracing (and calling our own) peacemaker images that reflect and serve the prevailing gender order, leading to a denial that liberation brings pain, confusion, and loss. She questions the value of what she calls "establishment-supporting gender expectations" for the end of patriarchal society as we now know it. "It is inappropriate," concludes Sylvester,

> to draw sharp conclusions about interrelationships of women, peace-lovingness, women warriors, and strategies for tipping patriarchal war-peace pieces in more feminist directions. This thinking is very much in process and is also healthfully incoherent. Suffice it to say we should carefully examine claims that war and peace are negations of each other, and that women are unified in a natural or conditioned opposition to war and embrace of peace.[57]

THE FEMINIST CHALLENGE FOR PEACE STUDIES

The challenge for feminist peace researchers, as I see it, is to recognize such dilemmas as those highlighted by Cohn and Sylvester. It is to acknowledge the tension between needing to act as women who value mothering/caring labor, and needing an identity not overdetermined by our gender. The challenge is about difference and equality; it dramatizes women's differences from men and from each other—and it sees the necessity of sometimes making common cause. It is about resisting claims that some categories (like mothering) are natural and inevitable. It is to remember that, as literary critic Ann Snitow points out:

> in a cruel irony that is one mark of women's oppression, when women speak *as women* they run a special risk of not being heard because the female voice is by our culture's definition that-voice-you-can-ignore.

And it is to remember that, again as Snitow puts it, "the alternative is to pretend that public men speak for women or that women who speak inside male-female forums are heard and heeded as much as similarly placed men."[58]

This is not to argue that poststructuralism offers the *only* acceptable theoretical approach to feminist peace research. On the contrary, I fear there is a danger that rigidly self-defined poststructuralist advocates, particularly those on the extremely skeptical side, can lessen the critical and constructive voices of women for peace. As Marx put it, "The philosophers have only *interpreted* the world . . . the point, however, is to *change* it." If we can do nothing more than acknowledge the multidimensionality of all reality, than where does this leave us? It is difficult, to say the very least, to be part of this community of radical doubters, and also to be part of the feminist peace activist community.

After having considered feminist analyses of women's diverse experiences as peacemakers and nonpeacemakers on many levels, from the familial to the international, I conclude that the argument that women, because of their nurturing capacities, are essentially different from, and perhaps on some levels better at peacemaking than, men should be neither dismissed out of hand nor embraced as the *truth*. Rather, I argue for a more complex picture, one that sees the essentialists and their poststructural critics as part of the whole picture—part of the changing social construction of gender. I argue that both positions are politically vital catalysts for developing strategies for change—a "don't throw the baby out with the bathwater" position.[59] As Sara Lennox has recently pointed out, this means:

> acknowledging both similarity with men and difference from them; seeking solutions to women's problems in (or from) both the public and the private sector, the public and the private sphere; understanding women's embodiment as both natural and cultural; and both making universalist claims to women's common humanity and insisting on differences among them.[60]

Feminist peace researchers, then, must be both radical doubters *and* believers. Lynne Segal puts it this way: "What guarantees we have ... come from women's and men's engagement in a whole variety of political campaigns against militarism and arms production, and more."[61] The challenge for a feminist peace studies is to honor the special, mothering, peacemaking skills of many women (and men) while questioning impulses to universalize them. The challenge, to put it another way, is to be ever vigilant of the age-old trap of oversimplifying the notion of "mother," denying her differences with other mothers and other women, exaggerating her differences with men, and thereby lessening her power. And, most importantly for me as a feminist peace researcher, peace educator, and peace activist, the challenge is to continue to reflect upon, value, and question the feminist assumptions, theories, and strategies that can best mobilize mothers and fathers, women and men for a more peaceful and just world.

Notes

1. Portions of this paper appeared in Linda Rennie Forcey, "Women as Peacemakers: Contested Terrain for Feminist Peace Studies," in *Peace & Change* vol. 16, No. 4 (October 1991), pp. 331–354.

2. See conservative political analyst Kevin Phillips' description of wealth in the Reagan aftermath in *The Politics of Rich and Poor* (New York: Random House, 1990).

3. Ann Snitow, "A Gender Diary," in Adrienne Harris and Ynestra King, eds., *Rocking the Ship of State: Toward a Feminist Peace Politics* (Boulder, CO: Westview, 1989), p. 52.

4. This is the definition agreed upon by Evelyn Nakano Glenn, Elsa Barkley Brown, and myself as organizers of a conference entitled "Contested Terrains: Constructions of Mothering," held at the State University of New York at Binghamton, October 12–13, 1990.

The approach is closely linked to feminist theoretical work on the concept of gender as a central organizing feature of political, cultural, and social life developed over the past fifteen years. We agree with Belenky, et al., (Mary Belenky, Blythe Clichy, Nancy Goldberger, and Jill Tarule, *Women's Ways of Knowing* [New York: Basic Books, 1986], pp. 137–138) that "all knowledge is constructed . . . that answers to all questions vary depending on the context in which they are asked and on the frame of reference of the person doing the asking."

5. Sara Ruddick, *Maternal Thinking: Toward a Politics of Peace* (New York: Ballentine Books, 1989), p. 35.

6. I agree with Sara Ruddick's position, in *Maternal Thinking,* that mothering is hard to define precisely. She takes the position, however, that while maternal work is central to caring work, it is not the whole and should not be made to stand for it. I find the lines between "caring labor" of most women and mothering to be fuzzier. See also Nancy Hartsock, *Money, Sex, and Power* (New York: Longman, 1983); and Nel Noddings, *Caring* (Berkeley: University of California Press, 1984).

7. Virginia Sapiro, *Women in American Society* (Palo Alto, CA: Mayfield, 1986), pp. 440–441.

8. Daniel C. Thomas, ed., *Guide to Careers and Graduate Education in Peace Studies* (Amherst, MA: The Five College Program in Peace and World Security Studies, 1987), p. 5.

9. COPRED (the Consortium on Peace Research, Education and Development) by its very title illustrates this point.

10. It should be emphasized that this is my sense of the field based on my work with COPRED and the Peace Studies Association (PSA). Others may disagree, particularly in the greyer area of conflict resolution. George A. Lopez has developed a useful conceptual map of peace studies for those beginning or developing peace studies programs. It includes three areas of substantive foci: (1) causes and consequences of violence; (2) methods for reducing or resolving violent conflict; and (3) the values, norms, and institutions of peace. "Strategies for Curriculum Development," in Thomas, Daniel, and Michael Klare, *Peace and World Order Studies* (Boulder, CO: Westview Press, 1989), p. 76.

11. Coventry Patmore, *The Angel in the House* (New York: E.P. Dutton, 1876).

12. Virginia Woolf, "Professions for Women," in *Collected Essays* (London: Hogarth Press, 1966) 2, p. 285, as quoted in Nel Noddings, *Caring* (Berkeley: University of California Press), 1984, p. 59.

13. Simone de Beauvoir, *The Second Sex* (New York: Random House, 1974); Betty Friedan, *The Feminine Mystique* (New York: Dell, 1963). I discuss their contributions to mothering more fully in *Mothers of Sons: Toward an Understanding of Responsibility* (New York: Praeger, 1987).

14. See for example, Margaret Benson, "The Political Economy of Women's Liberation," *Monthly Review* 21, No. 4 (September 1969); Lise Vogel, "The Earthly Family," *Radical America* 7, Nos. 4 and 5 (July-October 1973); Maxine Molyneux, "Beyond the Housework Debate," *New Left Review* 116 (July-August 1979); Martha E. Gimenez, "Structuralist Marxism on 'The Woman Question,'" *Science and Society* 42, No. 3 (Fall 1978). For a history of the contributions of early radical feminists, see Alice Echols, *Daring to Be Bad: Radical Feminism in America, 1967–1975* (Minneapolis, MN: University of Minnesota Press, 1989).

15. Nancy Chodorow, *The Reproduction of Mothering* (Berkeley: University of California Press, 1978).

16. Carol Gilligan, *In a Different Voice* (Cambridge: Harvard University Press, 1982), p. 147.

17. Belenky et al., *Women's Ways of Knowing.*

18. Gilligan, *In a Different Voice,* p. 43.

19. See for example, Birgit Brock-Utne, *Education for Peace: A Feminist Perspective* (New York: Pergamon, 1985, and *Feminist Perspectives on Peace and Peace Education*

(New York: Pergamon, 1989); Nel Noddings, *Caring: A Feminine Approach to Ethics and Moral Education* (Berkeley, CA: University of California Press, 1984); Ruddick, *Maternal Thinking.*

20. Betty A. Reardon, *Sexism and the War System* (New York: Teachers College Press, 1985).

21. Betty A. Reardon, "Toward a Paradigm of Peace," in Linda Rennie Forcey, ed., *Peace: Meanings, Politics, Strategies* (New York: Praeger, 1989), p. 25.

22. Ruddick, *Maternal Thinking,* p. 81.

23. Noddings, *Caring,* p. 203.

24. Ruddick, *Maternal Thinking,* pp. 81, 113.

25. Ruddick, *Maternal Thinking,* p. 135.

26. Ruddick, *Maternal Thinking,* p. 242.

27. bell hooks, *Feminist Theory from Margin to Center* (Boston: South End Press, 1985), p. 135.

28. Lynne Segal, *Is the Future Female?* (London: Virago Press, 1987), p. 148.

29. Jane Flax, "Theorizing Motherhood," *Women's Review of Books,* vol. 1, No. 9 (1984), p. 13.

30. Segal, *Is the Future Female?* p. 6.

31. Forcey, *Mothers of Sons.*

32. Forcey, *Mothers of Sons,* p. 86.

33. Forcey, *Mothers of Sons,* p. 87.

34. Forcey, *Mothers of Sons,* p. 91.

35. Forcey, *Mothers of Sons,* p. 94.

36. Elshtain, Jean Bethke. *Women and War* (New York: Basic Books, 1987), p. 93.

37. Simone de Beauvoir, *The Second Sex* (New York: Random House, 1974), pp. 55, 576.

38. Forcey, *Mothers of Sons,* pp. 117–135.

39. Barbara Omolade, "We Speak for the Planet," in Harris and King, eds., *Rocking the Ship of State: Toward a Feminist Peace Politics,* p. 184.

40. See, for example, Rosemary Ridd and Helen Callaway, eds., *Women and Political Conflict: Portraits of Struggle in Times of Crisis* (New York: New York University Press, 1987); Marjorie Agosin, *Scraps of Life: Chilean Arpilleras* (Toronto: Williams-Wallace, 1987); Eleni Fourtouni, *Greek Women in Resistance* (Chicago: Lake View Press, 1986); and Daniela Gioseffi, *Women on War* (New York: Simon & Schuster, 1988).

41. Agosin, *Scraps of Life.*

42. Ridd and Callaway, *Women and Political Conflict.*

43. Linda Rennie Forcey, "When Women Fight?" *The Women's Review of Books,* vol. V, No. 8 (May 1988), pp. 8–9.

44. Anne Phillips, ed., *Feminism and Equality* (New York: New York University Press, 1987), p. 22.

45. Ruth Milkman, "Women's History and the Sears Case," *Feminist Studies,* vol. 12 (1986), pp. 394–395.

46. Joan Wallach Scott, *Gender and the Politics of History* (New York: Columbia University Press, 1988), p. 172.

47. See Pauline Rosenau, "Once Again Into the Fray: International Relations Confronts the Humanities," *Millennium: Journal of International Studies,* vol. 19, No. 1 (Spring 1990), pp. 83–105, for a skeptical overview of poststructuralists' challenge to international relations.

48. Jim George, "International Relations and the Search for Thinking Space," *International Studies Quarterly,* vol. 33, No. 3 (September 1989), p. 270. See, also, Yosef Lapid, "The Third Debate: On the Prospects of International Theory in a Post-Positivist Era," *International Studies Quarterly,* vol. 33, No. 3 (September 1989), pp. 235–254; and Pauline Rosenau, "Once Again Into the Fray."

49. Jacques Derrida, *Of Grammatology* (Baltimore: Johns Hopkins University Press, 1976); Julia Kristeva, *The Kristeva Reader* (Oxford: Blackwell, 1986); Louis Althusser, *Lenin and Philosophy and Other Essays* (London: New Left Books, 1971); and Michel Foucault, *Les Mots et les Choses* (Paris: Gallimard, 1966); *The Birth of a Clinic* (London: Tavistock, 1973); *Discipline and Punishment* (Harmondsworth: Penguin, 1979).

50. Rosenau, "Once Again Into the Fray," p. 86.

51. Rosenau, "Once Again Into the Fray," p. 102.

52. This is the position taken by Chris Weedon, *Feminist Practice & Poststructuralist Theory* (New York: Basil Blackwell, 1987), p. 20. In this article I have chosen to use the term "poststructuralism" rather than "postmodernism" for convenience, and because there is considerable overlap, with some even finding the terms synonymous. See, for example, R.B.J. Walker, "Genealogy, Geopolitics and Political Community: Richard K. Ashley and the Critical Social Theory of International Politics," *Alternatives,* vol. 13 (1988), p. 86.

53. Weedon, *Feminist Practice,* p. 167. I choose to focus on poststructuralism's more moderate, feminist adaptation from an international relations perspective as a useful framework for understanding power and for developing strategies for peace and change.

54. Carol Cohn, "Sex and Death in the Rational World of Defense Intellectuals," in Forcey, ed., *Peace: Meanings, Politics, Strategies,* pp. 39–72.

55. Cohn, "Sex and Death in the Rational World of Defense Intellectuals," 64.

56. Christine Sylvester, "Feminist Postmodernism, Nuclear Strategy, and International Violence," paper delivered at the International Studies Association Conference, London, March 1989, 1.

57. Christine Sylvester, "Patriarchy, Peace & Women," in Forcey, ed., *Peace: Meanings, Politics, Strategies,* pp. 97–112.

58. Ann Snitow, "A Gender Diary," in Harris and King, ed., *Rocking the Ship of State,* p. 40.

59. Most of the essays in Marianne Hirsch and Evelyn Fox Keller's *Conflicts in Feminism* (New York: Routledge, 1990) also argue that feminists must take a "both/and" position on this difference debate.

60. Sara Lennox, Book Review of *Conflicts in Feminism,* Marianne Hirsch and Evelyn Fox Keller, eds., (New York: Routledge, 1990), in *Signs* (Spring 1992), p. 652.

61. Segal, *Is the Future Female?* p. 201.

INDEX

CONTRIBUTORS

Eileen Boris, Associate Professor of History at Howard University, is a mother as well as the author of *Art and Labor* and *Sweated Motherhood.* Her new project, tentatively entitled *Desperate Equality: Race, Gender and Federal Employment Policy from World War II to the Present,* will place the 1991 Civil Rights Act in historical context.

Linda M. Burton is Associate Professor of Human Development in the Department of Human Development and Family Studies, Pennsylvania State University.

Grace Chang is pursuing her Ph.D. in Ethnic Studies at the University of California at Berkeley while mothering her two children. Her research interests include women of color's relationship to the welfare state and third world women's resistance to western development. She has taught history in public and private secondary schools.

Barbara T. Christian is Full Professor of African American Studies and an active professor in the Ethnic Studies Ph.D. program at the University of California at Berkeley. She is the author of *Black Women Novelists* and *Black Feminist Criticism, Perspectives on Black Women Writers.* Recently she has published essays on the state of black feminist criticism.

Patricia Hill Collins is an Associate Professor of African-American Studies and Sociology at the University of Cincinnati. She is the author of *Black Feminist Thought: Knowledge, Consciousness and the Politics of Empowerment* and is the co-editor with Margaret Andersen of *Race, Class and Gender: An Anthology.*

Linda Rennie Forcey is a Professor in the School of Education and Human Development at SUNY/Binghamton. She is the author of *Mothers of Sons* and editor or co-editor of *Disarmament, Economic Conversion, and the Management of Peace; Learning to Breathe Free: Liberation Theologies in the U.S.* and *Peace: Meanings, Politics, Strategies.* She is currently working on a project on "Women Thinking about Peace."

Evelyn Nakano Glenn is Professor of Ethnic Studies and Women's Studies at the University of California at Berkeley. She is the author of *Issei, Nisei, Warbride* and has written extensively about women, work and technology. Her current research is a comparative study of African American, Mexican American and Asian American women's involvement in paid reproductive labor.

E. Ann Kaplan is Director of the Humanities Institute and Professor of English and Comparative Studies at the State University of New York at Stony Brook. Her many publications include *Women and Film, Rocking Around the Clock,* and, most recently, *Motherhood and Representation.* She is currently working on a book about race, psychoanalysis and cinema.

Ellen Lewin has taught anthropology and women's studies at several universities, including the University of California, Berkeley and is 1993–1994 Visiting Professor of Women's Studies at the University of Cincinnati. She is the author of *Lesbian Mothers: Accounts of Gender in American Culture* and is currently doing research on gay and lesbian weddings and commitment rituals.

Margaret K. Nelson is Professor of Sociology at Middlebury College. She is author of *Negotiated Care: The Experience of Family Day Care Providers.* She has also written *Circles of Care: Work and Identity in Women's Lives* with Emily K. Abel.

Barbara Katz Rothman is Professor of Sociology at Baruch College and the Graduate Center of the City University of New York. Her books include *In Labor: Women and Power in the Birthplace, The Tentative Pregnancy, Recreating Motherhood,* and, with Wendy Simonds, *Centuries of Solace.* She is editor of *The Encyclopedia of Childbearing: Critical Perspectives.*

Denise A. Segura is Associate Professor of Sociology at the University of California, Santa Barbara. She has published articles on Chicanas and Mexicanas in the labor force, and Chicana feminism and political consciousness. Currently she is working on a book titled *Beyond Ambivalence and Antipathy: Chicana Political Consciousness and Feminist Discourse* with Dr. Beatriz M. Pasquera, University of California, Davis.

Stephanie J. Shaw is an Assistant Professor of History and Women's Studies at Ohio State University. Her research and teaching focus on women and work and on African American women's history. She has a book forthcoming from the University of Chicago Press entitled *"What a woman ought to be and to do": Work, Family, and Community in the Lives of Black Professional Women, 1870–1954.*

Rickie Solinger is author of *Wake Up Little Susie: Single Pregnancy and Race Before Roe v. Wade, The Abortionist* (forthcoming), and other works on the history of the politics of female fertility. She is a visiting scholar in Women's Studies at the University of Colorado at Boulder.

Carol B. Stack, Professor of Women's Studies and Education at University of California, Berkeley, is author of *All Our Kin* and *Holding on to the Land of the Lord,* edited with Robert L. Hall. She is currently completing *The Call to Home: African Americans Reclaim the Rural Self,* a book on the migration of urban black families of rural homeplaces.

Susan L. Tananbaum is Assistant Professor of History at Bowdoin College, Brunswick, Maine. She is currently preparing a manuscript on the acculturation of Jewish immigrant women in London at the turn of the century. Her research interests include the history of public health, philanthropy, and multiculturalism in Britain.

Sau-ling C. Wong is Associate Professor in the Asian American Studies Program, Department of Ethnic Studies, University of California, Berkeley. She is author of *Reading Asian American Literature: From Necessity to Extravagance,* and has published in the areas of gender and ethnicity, Chinese immigrant literature, and diasporic studies.